Introduction to Hospitality

John R. Walker, D.B.A.,

Professor and Director
Hotel, Restaurant, and Tourism Management
United States International University
San Diego, California

Prentice Hall
Upper Saddle River, New Jersey 07458

Library of Congress Cataloging-in-Publication Data
Walker, John R., 1944–
    Introduction to hospitality/John R. Walker.
        p. cm.
    Includes bibliographical references and index
    ISBN 0-13-199514-6
    1. Hospitality industry—Management. I.Title
TX911.3.M27W35 1996
647.94' 068—dc20   95-36604
                                                         CIP

Production Editor: Eileen M. O'Sullivan
Acquisitions Editor: Robin Baliszewski
Director of Manufacturing & Production: Bruce Johnson
Managing Editor: Mary Carnis
Designer: Laura Ierardi
Marketing Manager: Frank Mortimer, Jr.
Cover Design: Susan Newman
Cover Illustration: Barbara Masien
Copyeditor: Susan Geraghty
Art Director: Marianne Frasco
Manufacturing Manager: Ed O'Dougherty
Editorial Assistant: Rose Mary Florio
Formatting/page make-up: Laura Ierardi
Formatting Assistance: Kathryn Kasturas/Stephen Hartner
Printer/Binder: R.R. Donnelley-Willard

©1996 by Prentice-Hall, Inc.
A Simon & Schuster Company
Upper Saddle River, New Jersey 07458

Printed in the United States of America

10 9 8 7 6 5 4 3 2 1

ISBN 0-13-199514-6

Prentice-Hall International (UK) Limited, *London*
Prentice-Hall of Australia Pty. Limited, *Sydney*
Prentice-Hall Canada Inc., *Toronto*
Prentice-Hall Hispanoamericana, S.A., *Mexico*
Prentice-Hall of India Private Limited, *New Delhi*
Prentice-Hall of Japan, Inc., *Tokyo*
Simon & Schuster Asia Pte. Ltd., *Singapore*
Editoria Prentice-Hall do Brasil, Ltda., *Rio de Janeiro*

Contents

Chapter 1

Hospitality: A Historical Perspective   2-3

Chapter 2

Tourism   22–23

Chapter 3

The Hotel Business: Development and Classification 54–55

Chapter 4

Hotel and Rooms Division Operation   88-89

Chapter 5

Hotel Operations: Food and Beverage Division 126-27

Chapter 6

The Restaurant Business: Development and Classification 154–55

Chapter 7

Restaurant Operations   180-81

Chapter 8

Noncommercial Food Service Management   210–11

Chapter 9

Beverages   234–35

Chapter 10

Recreation and Leisure   256-57

Chapter 11

Meetings, Conventions, and Expositions 278-79

Chapter 12

Marketing, Human Resources, and Culture 302-303

Chapter 13

Leadership   330-31

Chapter 14

Management Service and Professionalism   354-55

Preface

Hospitality management is an exciting professional discipline. *Introduction to Hospitality* is a comprehensive tour through the fascinating and challenging related fields in the hospitality industry: travel and tourism, lodging, food service, meetings, conventions and expositions, leisure and recreation. The book also discusses marketing, human resources, leadership and management and how they apply to hospitality management.

This text is designed for hospitality management professionals of tomorrow. By dynamically involving the readers in each step of this exciting journey, *Introduction to Hospitality* invites students to share the unique enthusiasm surrounding the field of hospitality.

The increase in globalization is reflected in the hospitality industry. Through the stories and examples presented in the text, readers are encouraged to share the deep appreciation for, and gain exposure to, the diversity of existing traditions and cultures.

Other features unique to this book include:

➤ The thorough identification and analysis of trends, issues, and challenges that will have a significant impact on hospitality into the twenty-first century

➤ The scope of coverage and the international perspective on present and future industry issues

➤ The presentation and description of numerous career opportunities in hospitality

➤ Numerous suggestions for educational and professional development

This wide variety of learning tools provides a fundamental aid to students and encourages their active participation in the course.

Features of the Chapters

Chapter 1

"Hospitality: A Historical Perspective" introduces and presents a brief historical overview of the hospitality industry, describing the evolution of hospitality from Greek and Roman times to the present day.

Chapter 2

"Tourism" outlines the scope of tourism and identifies the major influences on the increase of tourism, the various travel modes, and the key organizations and the role they play from a global to a local perspective.

Chapter 3

"The Hotel Business: Development and Classification" illustrates the various forms of hotel development, the different types of hotels, their classification, and describes ways hotels cater to the business and leisure travel markets.

Chapter 4

"Hotel and Rooms Division Operation" provides a hands-on perspective that details the rooms division department functions and activities. A complete overview of the guest cycle from reservations to check out is included. The chapter also outlines the duties and responsibilities of key executives and department heads.

Chapter 5

"Hotel Operations: Food and Beverage Division" details the food and beverage departments and illustrates the duties and responsibilities of the key food and beverage executives.

Chapter 6

"The Restaurant Business: Development and Classification" traces the history and development of the restaurant business. Restaurant development from operating philosophy and mission statements to market, concepts, location, ambiance, menu planning, and classification of restaurants is discussed.

Chapter 7

"Restaurant Operations" focuses on the operations of a restaurant. The chapter discusses forecasting, purchasing, receiving, storage/issuing, food production, and service. Budgeting, controllable expenses, restaurant accounting, operating ratios, and controls are also discussed.

Chapter 8

"Noncommercial Food Service Management" outlines the different noncommercial food service segments, and describes the factors that distinguish noncommercial food service operations from commercial ones. Characteristics and trends in airline, military, elementary and secondary schools, colleges and universities, healthcare, business, and industry food service are illustrated.

Chapter 9

"Beverages" presents the various types of wines and wine making, beer and the brewing process, spirits, nonalcoholic beverages, bars, beverage management, and liquor liability and the law.

Chapter 10

"Recreation and Leisure" introduces recreation, leisure, and wellness as essential to our cultural, moral, and spiritual well-being. Government-sponsored recreation, national parks, and public recreation agencies are illustrated together with commercial recreation/theme parks and clubs. Noncommercial recreation in the form of voluntary organizations, campus, armed forces, employee recreation, and recreation for special populations are discussed.

Chapter 11

"Meetings, Conventions, and Expositions" introduces readers to the different types of meetings, conventions, and expositions. Meeting planners, convention and visitors bureaus, event management, and specialized services are also covered in detail.

Chapter 12

"Marketing, Human Resources, and Culture" presents the elements of marketing, sales, human resources, and culture that are common to all segments of the hospitality industry.

Chapter 13

"Leadership" provides the reader with an overview of the characteristics and attributes of leaders, and offers a comparison of the different styles of leadership.

Hospitality leaders such as Wayne Calloway, CEO of PepsiCo.; Herb Kelleher, president and CEO of Southwest Airlines; Ray Krock, founder of McDonald's; Bill Fisher, executive director, National Restaurant Association; Isadore Sharp, president and CEO of Four Seasons Hotels and Resorts; John Martin, president and CEO of Taco Bell Corporations; and Van E. Eure, president of The Angus Barn Restaurant, offer their insights into successful leadership. Ethical, moral, and social responsibilities in business are also discussed.

Chapter 14

"Management Service and Professionalism" focuses on corporate philosophy, culture, mission, goals, and objectives. Emphasis is placed on the key management functions, service, total quality management, and professionalism. The chapter also invites the reader to look at the future, and helps the reader prepare for a rewarding career by suggesting methods for career pathing, resumé writing, and interview preparation.

Learning Tools

Each chapter contains a number of tools designed to assist in the learning process.

- ➤ *Learning objectives,* which help the reader focus on the main points discussed in the chapter
- ➤ *Benchmarking,* with individuals and corporate examples of excellence
- ➤ *Personal profiles,* focusing on the achievements and contributions to the industry by individuals who represent success models, such as Auguste Escoffier, Patti Roscoe, Steve Wynn, Jim Gemignani, Herman Cain, Richard Melman, Robert Mondavi, Walt Disney, Carol Wallace, Carroll Armstrong, and Herb Kelleher
- ➤ *Industry profiles,* which provide extensive input from industry professionals, such as the Hospice de Beaune, Club Med, Carlson Companies, Hyatt Hotels, Sheraton Hotels, TGI Friday's, Joseph E. Seagram and Sons, The Disney Corporation, Las Vegas Convention and Visitor Authority, Marriott Corporation, The Ritz-Carlton Hotel Corporation
- ➤ *A day in the life,* which selects key hospitality individuals and real-life accounts that provide exposure to the issues and challenges one might have on the job
- ➤ *Summaries,* which correspond to the chapter learning objectives
- ➤ *Key words and concepts,* provided to help the reader internalize the various topics presented in the chapter

➤ SCANS (Secretary's Commission on Achieving Necessary Skills)–related critical thinking *Exercises,* which help readers master the material presented and apply what they have learned

➤ A Glossary which explains the meaning of special words used throughout the text.

The extensive supplement package includes the following:

➤ *An instructor's manual,* which contains teaching notes and interactive class exercises

➤ *Color overheads* of selected charts and graphs from the text

➤ *A computerized test bank,* which consists of multiple choice, matching, fill-in-the-blank, and short essay questions

➤ *A video,* highlighting hospitality organizations which is keyed specifically to the text. The video provides insight into the hospitality industry, and offers students a glimpse of the opportunities, issues, and challenges that lie ahead.

All of these features were designed to stimulate and promote student involvement, participation, and interaction with the course. I hope you will derive as much pleasure from reading the text as I did in writing it.

John R. Walker

San Diego, California
April 1995

Chapter opening Photo Credits

1. Hospice de Beaune, French Tourist Office; 2. A Cote d'Azure beach, French Tourist Office; 3. Hotel del Coronado, Hotel del Coronado, San Diego, CA.; 4. Banff Springs Hotel, Banff Springs Hotel, Alberta, Canada; 5. A Marriott Hotel dinner table setting, Marriott Hotels; 6. Remi Restaurant, New York, Adam D. Tihany. Photo credit, Peter Paige; 7. A TGI Friday's Restaurant, TGI Friday's; 8. A non-commercial foodservice operation, ARAMARK; 9. A Napa Valley winery, Robert Mondavi; 10. Yellowstone National Park, Yellowstone National Park; 11. San Diego Convention Center, San Diego Convention Center; 12. A Human Resources Director, Sheraton Grande Torrey Pines; 13. Wayne Calloway, Pepsico; 14. Executive Committee Meeting, La Jolla Marriott, La Jolla, CA.

Additional Photo Credits

Chapter 1 Escoffier (Courtesy of UPI/The Bettmann Archive)
Chapter 2 Model T-Ford (Courtesy of The Bettmann Archive)
Chapter 3 Conrad Hilton (Courtesy of Hilton Hotels Corporation)
U.S. Grant Hotel, San Diego, CA (Courtesy of U.S. Grant Hotel, San Diego, CA)
Banff Springs Hotel (Courtesy of Banff Springs Hotel)
Morena Valley Travelodge (Courtesy of Forte Hotels)
The Mirage Hotel and Casino (Courtesy of Mirage Resorts Incorporated)
MGM (Courtesy of MGM Grand Casino and Theme Park)
Fairfield Inn and Residence Inn (Courtesy of Marriott)
Cesar Ritz (Courtesy of The Bettmann Archive)
Chapter 4 Ritz-Carlton Interior (Courtesy of Ritz-Carlton Hotel Company)
Hyatt Hotels (Courtesy of Hyatt Hotels and Resorts)
Clarion Hotel Bayview (Courtesy of Clarion Hotel Bayview)
Chapter 5 Old King Cole Bar (Courtesy of St. Regis Hotel)
Chapter 6 The Eccentric and Papagus (Courtesy of Steinkamp/Ballogg, Chicago)
Tavern on The Green (Photo Credit: ©Gayle Gleason, 1990. Courtesy of Tavern on The Green)
Chapter 7 T.G.I. Friday's (Courtesy of T.G.I. Friday's)
Chapter 9 Napa Valley (Courtesy of The Napa Valley Wineries Association)
Robert Mondavi (Courtesy of Robert Mondavi Winery)
Bernini's (Courtesy of Bernini's)
Chapter 10 New York Marathon (Courtesy of Reuters/Bettmann)
Banff Springs Hotel and Park (Courtesy of Banff Springs Hotel)
Chapter 11 Jacob K. Javits Convention Center (Courtesy of Jacob K. Javits Convention Center)
Chapter 12 Marriott International, Inc. (Courtesy of Marriott International)
Chapter 13 Martin Luther King, Jr. (Courtesy of UPI/Bettmann)

Acknowledgments

This book is dedicated to you—the students, instructors, and professors—and to the industry professionals, many of whom contributed to this text.

To your success.

Thanks also goes to all my CHRIE colleagues, who encouraged me to undertake this project. In particular, I would like to thank Professor Jennifer Aldrich of Johnson & Wales University who has done a great job on the instructor's manual. She has created an invaluable guide for instructors teaching this course.

This book would not have been possible without the extraordinary help of my team, especially Michael Thorpe, Elena Cormio, and Jana Sczersputowski, who worked so diligently on numerous key aspects of this project. Also invaluable was the assistance from Marian Prokop, Nicole Daane, and Yiannis Lampousakis. I am very grateful to the following reviewers, whose comments and suggestions considerably improved the text:

Jennifer Aldrich
  Johnson & Wales University
  Providence, Rhode Island
Maureen Blesson
  Morris County Community College
  Randolph, New Jersey
Carl Boger
  University of Wisconsin–Stout
Carl Braunlich
  Purdue University
  West Lafayette, Indiana

Melissa Dallas
  Seattle Central Community College
Evan Enowitz
  Grossmont College
  San Diego, California
Tom Jones
  University of Nevada–Las Vegas
Carol Kizer
  Columbus State Community College
  Columbus, Ohio
Daniel J. Mount
  Pennsylvania State University
  University Park, Pennsylvania
Jay Schrock
  San Francisco State University
Andrew Schwarz
  Sullivan County Community College
  Loch Sheldrake, New York

Finally, special thanks to Robin Baliszewski, whose vision and encouragement were an inspiration, to Eileen O'Sullivan, production editor, whose attention to detail and expertise added much to this project, and to the rest of the Prentice Hall staff, who were a pleasure to work with.

About the Author

Dr. John R. Walker is professor and director of the Hotel, Restaurant and Tourism Management Program at the United States International University in San Diego, California. John's fifteen years industry experience includes management training at the Savoy Hotel London. This was followed by terms as food and beverage manager, assistant rooms division manager, catering manager, and general manager with Grand Metropolitan Hotels, Selsdon Park Hotel, Rank Hotels, Inter-Continental Hotels and the Coral Reef Resort Barbados, West Indies.

For the past seventeen years he has taught at two- and four-year schools in Canada and the United States. In addition to being a hospitality management consultant, he has been published in *The Cornell Hotel Restaurant Administration Quarterly* and *The Hospitality Educators Journal.* He is co-author of *The Restaurant: from Concept to Operation,* with Dr. Donald Lundberg, published by John Wiley & Sons in 1993. Dr. Walker is an editorial advisory board member for Progress in Tourism and Hospitality Research, published by John Wiley & Sons. John is a past president of the Pacific chapter of the Council on Hotel, Restaurant, and Institutional Education (CHRIE). He is a certified hotel administrator and a certified food service management professional.

Hospitality: An Historical Perspective

After reading and studying this chapter you should be able to do the following:

- ➤ Describe the evolution of the hospitality industry
- ➤ Relate the evolution of the lodging and foodservice industry to world events
- ➤ Describe the history of restaurants

The concept of hospitality is as old as civilization itself. Its development from the ancient custom of breaking bread with a passing stranger to the operations of today's multifaceted hospitality conglomerates makes fascinating reading.

The word *hospitality* comes from *hospice,* an old French word meaning "to provide care/shelter for travelers." The most famous hospice is the Hospice de Beaune in the Burgundy region of France, also called the Hotel Dieu or the House of God. It was founded as a charity hospital in 1443 by Nicolas Rolin, the chancellor of Burgundy, as a refuge for the poor. During the time of his power, he was regarded as an extremely efficient tax collector, one of the most assiduous Burgundy had ever had. King Louis XI sarcastically remarked that it was very right that Rolin was the one to have constructed a house for the poor, since he had made so many of them!

The Hospice de Beaune is located in one of the most beautiful regions in France, the Côte de Beaune, located in northeastern France near Dijon. The Côte de Beaune owes its name to the town it embraces, Beaune, a center of about sixteen thousand people. A thriving community during the Roman ages, Beaune became an important city in Burgundy during the Middle Ages. Today Beaune is rightly considered the capital of the Burgundian wineland. The wines of the Côte de Beaune are among the finest of their type. The delicacy of the reds compensates for the slight lack of fullness, thus making them particularly appropriate to accompany dishes of subtle flavor. The whites are commonly regarded as the finest in the world.

Something about the fine wines also appears to inspire the muses: Where good wines are made, literature, music, poetry, cuisine, and architecture flourish. The extravagance of the architecture of the Hospice de Beaune is staggering, with ornate fretwork, gabled courtyards, and a dazzling polychrome tile roof. The medieval structure of the outside is mirrored in the inside; however, the building hides modern, twentieth-century medical devices, such as X-ray machines and operating rooms. The Hospice is enriched by a remarkable art collection, which displays distinguished pieces such as Roier van der Weyden's "Last Judgment."

The hospital is still functioning, partly because of its role in the wine world. Throughout the centuries, several Burgundian landowners have donated vineyards to the Hospice to help pay for maintaining its costs. Every autumn the wines from these vineyards—about a hundred acres of vines—are sold at a characteristic and colorful wine auction on the third Thursday in November, which determines the prices for the next year's Burgundy wines.

Ancient Times

Greece and Rome

Mention of hospitality—in the form of taverns—is found in writings dating back to ancient Greece and Rome, beginning with the Code of Hammurabi (circa 1700 B.C.). It is evident from these references that these taverns were also houses of pleasure. The reputation of these establishments was far from savory. The Code required owners to report any customers who planned crimes in their taverns. The penalty for not doing so was death, making tavern-keeping in those times a hazardous occupation. The death penalty could be imposed merely for watering the beer!

Increased travel and trade made some form of overnight accommodations an absolute necessity. Because travel was slow and journeys long and arduous, many travelers depended solely on the hospitality of private citizens.[1]

In the Greek and Roman empires, inns and taverns sprang up everywhere. The Romans constructed elaborate and well-appointed inns on all the main roads. Marco Polo later proclaimed these inns as "fit for a king." They were located about 25 miles apart to provide fresh houses for officials and couriers of the Roman government and could only be used with special government documents granting permission. These documents became revered status symbols and were subject to numerous thefts and forgeries. By the time Marco Polo traveled to the Far East, there were ten thousand inns.

Some wealthy landowners built their own inns on the edges of their estates. These inns were often run by household slaves. Nearer the cities, inns and taverns frequented by less affluent citizens were run by freemen or by retired gladiators who would invest their savings in the "restaurant business" in the same way that so many of today's retired athletes open restaurants.

The first "businessman's lunch" is reputed to have been the idea of Seqius Locates, a Roman innkeeper, in 40 B.C. Locates devised this idea for ships' brokers who often were too busy to go home for their midday meals.

Innkeepers, as a whole, were hardly the Conrad Hiltons of their day. They were not admitted to military service, could not usually bring a legal action in court, could not take an oath, nor could they act as guardians for children. The morals of anyone who worked at an inn were automatically suspect.

However, Roman cooks considered themselves superior beings and gave themselves splendid titles. During the reign of Hadrian (A.D. 117–138), cooks and chefs even established their own elite academy on the Palatine Hill in Rome.

Inns for the common folk were regarded as dens of vice, where degenerate aristocrats might go slumming. Generally, the upper classes sought their thrills in the public baths. By the time Caligula came to power in A.D. 37, these baths were open around the clock, mixed bathing was common, and wine flowed freely. Attached to the baths were sumptuous dining rooms available for parties. Banquets, both public and private, eventually became so elaborate and wasteful that Sumptuary Laws were passed to restrict the amounts Romans spent on food and drink.

In ancient Persia, traveling was done in large caravans, which carried elaborate tents for use along the caravan routes. Occasionally, these caravans stopped at *Khans*—combinations of stables, sleeping accommodations, and fortresses—which provided shelter from the elements—such as sandstorms—and also against enemies who found it easy to attack caravans. During this period, accommodations in Asia far surpassed those of the Western World. Trade was brisk, and so was travel. The Chinese posting system was superior to that of the Romans, although mainly confined to those travelers of means.

As the Roman Empire flourished, travelers included merchants, scholars, and actors who stayed at inns and taverns. Often people slept on straw with the animals to keep warm.

After the fall of the Roman Empire, public hospitality for the ordinary traveler became the province of religious orders. In Britain, for instance, inns catered more to the drinker than to the traveler, and traveling was discouraged. Those who did travel were mainly connected with the Royal Court or the Church and were hardly interested in the primitive accommodations provided by wayside inns. In these times, many travelers were missionaries, priests, and pilgrims, traveling to holy places such as temples. Consequently, inns were located close to these religious sites. The accommodations were very basic and were operated by slaves of the priests and holy men of the temples.

Medieval Times

On the European Continent, Charlemagne established rest houses for pilgrims in the eighth century; the sole purpose of several orders of knighthood was to protect pilgrims and provide hospitality on their routes. One such rest house, an abbey at Roncesvalles, advertised services such as a warm welcome at the door, free bread, a barber and cobbler, cellars full of fruit and almonds, two hospices for the sick with beds, and even a consecrated burial ground.

Monasteries were plain but often of a quality superior to that found elsewhere along the road. Monks usually raised their own provisions on the monastery grounds; kitchens were cleaner, better organized, and less chaotic than those in private households; and the brothers even devised a crude system of accounting to determine feeding costs. As a result, pilgrims and vagrants often fared better than the nobility.

Medieval guilds also held open houses to receive pilgrims. Accommodations in medieval guilds were much like those of the monasteries. In fact, the famous Hanseatic League operated a residence in London called *The Steelyard*; the rules for league members were as strict as those for any monk—except that these highly ambitious merchants were not required to take a vow of poverty.

In 1282, the innkeepers of Florence, Italy, incorporated a guild or association for the purpose of business. The inns belonged to the city, which sold three-year leases at auction. They must have been profitable, because by 1290, there were eighty-six innkeepers as members of the guild.

In England, the stagecoach became the favored method of transportation. A journey from London to a city like Bath took three days, with several stopovers at inns or taverns that were also called *post houses.* Today, the journey from London to Bath takes two and one-half hours by car.

As travel and travelers increased during the Middle Ages, so did the number of wayside inns in Europe; yet, they were primitive affairs by today's standards. Guests often slept on mattresses strewn in what today would be the lobby. Each person either ate what they had brought with them or what they could purchase from the house. The fare was usually bread, meat, and beer, varied occasionally with fish or capon.

As the quality of the inns improved, more people began to travel. Many of the travelers were wealthy people, accustomed to the good life; their expectations demanded that inns be upgraded. Some of these inns, however, were inclined to be rowdy, and patrons frequenting taverns in a port area were likely to wake up at sea—"Shanghaied" (a practice of forceably obtaining a crew for ships headed toward Asia).

Chaucer's fourteenth-century Canterbury pilgrims gathered in the famed Tabard Inn in London to dine and revel before and after visiting the shrine of St. Thomas á Becket. The best teller of tales during the pilgrimage was rewarded with a free meal and feted by the host, Harry Bailey. He went along on the pilgrimage to judge the best raconteur himself.

One of the first European hotels, the Hotel de Henry IV, was built in Nantes in 1788, at a cost of $17,500. At that time, this was considered a vast sum of money for the sixty beds, considered the finest in Europe.

No discussion of medieval hospitality would be complete, however, without mention of the royal and noble households themselves, which often served hundreds of guests at each meal. Although á la carte dining was practically unknown until the nineteenth century, these households practiced what might be called discriminatory feeding, where different meals were served to persons of different rank. Nobles got the best, of course; an early household book records no less than ten grades of breakfast being served at a single morning meal.

Sanitary standards in these kitchens were appalling, with food supplies poorly stored and overflowing onto the floor, refrigeration unheard of, dogs and children playing freely among the provisions, and dozens of kitchen helpers milling about. To add to the confusion, the food handlers themselves frequently had questionable sanitary habits, so communicable diseases spread freely, to rich and poor alike.

Often, dozens of dishes were prepared for a single meal, elaborately served, but eaten with less than proper ceremony. Forks were unknown. Catherine de Medici allegedly introduced forks to the French court in the sixteenth century, but their use did not become commonplace for another two hundred years. Fingers dipped and slipped and splashed in sauces and among tidbits. Knives doubled as both cutting and feeding utensils. Food was eaten from trenchers, which could be made either of wood or pieces of four-day-old bread pared smooth and cut into thick squares.

Despite this, medieval hosts, who naturally knew nothing of germs and sanitation, forks or fingerbowls, set forth their own rules for public suppers, few of which would seem out of place today.

1. Meals should be served in due time: not too early, not too late.
2. Meals should be served in a conveyable place: large, pleasant, and secure.
3. He who maketh the feast should be of the heart and glad cheer.
4. Meals should consist of many diverse messes so that who like not of one may taste another.
5. There should be diverse wines and drinks.
6. Servants should be courteous and honest.
7. There should be natural friendship and company among the diners.
8. There should be mirth of song and instruments of music.
9. There should be plenty of light.
10. The deliciousness of all that is set on the board should be guaranteed.
11. Men should eat by leisure and not too hastily.
12. Without harm and damage every man should be prayed to the dinner.
13. Each diner should rest after supper.[2]

Who could argue with rules such as these?

In the late sixteenth century, a type of eating place for commoners called an *ordinary* began to appear in England. These places were taverns serving a fixed-price, fixed-menu meal at a long common table. Ordinary diners could not be choosy, nor did they often question what they were eating. Frequently, the main dish served was a long-cooked, highly seasoned meat-and-vegetable stew. Culinary expertise was limited by the availability and cost of certain ingredients. Few diners had sound teeth, and many had no teeth at all, so the meal had to be gummable as well as edible. Fresh meat was not always available; spoiled meat was often the rule rather than the exception. Spices helped not only to preserve meat but to disguise the flavor of gamey or "high" meat.

Coffee Houses

During the sixteenth century, two "exotic" imports began to influence the culinary habits of Western Europe: coffee and tea. These beverages, so integrated into the twentieth-century way of life, were once mere taste curiosities. Tea developed much more slowly than coffee as a common beverage and attained widespread use most notably in England—and there not even until the mid-nineteenth century.

Travelers to Constantinople (now known as Istanbul, Turkey) enjoyed coffee there and brought it back to Europe. By the end of the sixteenth century, coffee had become noticed enough to bring about the censure of the Roman Catholic Church, which called it the wine of Islam, an infidel drink. When Pope Clement VIII tasted the drink, he is reputed to have remarked that the Satan's drink was too delicious to leave to the heathens so he made a Christian beverage of it.

During the next century, coffee houses sprang up all over Europe. By 1675, Venice had dozens of coffee houses, including the famous Café Florian on the piazza San Marco, still filled to capacity today. The first English coffee house was opened by an Armenian refugee in St. Michael's Alley, London, in 1652.

When the siege of Vienna by the Turks was lifted in 1683, a gentleman (named Kolschitski, by some accounts) who was credited with saving the city from destruction received permission to open Central Europe's first coffee house. It was here that the first cup of coffee sweetened with honey and lightened with milk was served.

Café Florian (Courtesy Café Florian.)

Coffee houses, the social and literary centers of their day and the forerunners of today's cafes and coffee shops, served another even more useful (though less obvious) purpose: They helped to sober up an entire continent.

In a day when water was vile, milk dangerous, and carbonated beverages centuries in the future, alcoholic drinks were the rule rather than the exception. Children were weaned on small amounts of beer and wine mixed with water (a custom occasionally observed in France). Adults drank amounts measured in gallons. Queen Elizabeth I's ladies-in-waiting, for instance, were allowed a breakfast ration of two gallons of ale. Drunkenness was rampant.

As sobering as coffee houses were, they nevertheless had their detractors. Women abhorred them because, like most public ventures, they were strictly male affairs. Women circulated petitions, to no avail, attacking coffee as a cause of illness, even death; yet coffee houses flourished.

Coffee was generally served in a dish or small bowl, a little larger than today's coffee cup, without a handle. Coffee houses were famous for their convivial atmosphere; one could sit at a table near a warm fire, meet friends, have a hot aromatic drink, and discuss the affairs of the day, a tradition that has not changed much through the years.

Hospitality on the Road

At about the time coffee houses began blossoming in cities and towns all over Europe, the advent of stagecoach travel was revolutionizing hospitality on the road. The longer and colder the trip, the greater the bouncing and jouncing, the more welcoming the passengers found the wayside inn, and the great tradition of the British stagecoach inn was born. In the cities, the more well-to-do traveler, who went on horseback or in his or her own carriage, did not stay in the same inns frequented by the coaches and their passengers. Poorer travelers who journeyed on foot had difficulty finding any kind of accommodations at all.

In rural sections, one inn served all travelers, although sharp distinctions were apparent in the treatments meted out. Travelers of means were served in the dining room or in their chambers. Poorer travelers invariably had to eat with the landlord and his family in the kitchen, and they were served the ordinary fare (what the French call *table d'hote* or *table of the host*) at a nominal cost. Wealthier guests could order special dishes a la carte and visit the kitchen to see that they were properly prepared. The fare varied with the region, each having its own specialties to tempt visitors' palates.

Inns on the European continent in no way approached the supremacy of the British variety. Even in an age where travelers got little in the way of comfort, most continental travelers were appalled at what they found, especially compared with British accommodations. Even in France, a country with high culinary standards even then, les auberges du pays were known for the poor quality of their food and the high quantity of their vermin.

Eighteenth Century

The New World

Colonial inns and taverns were based on the British type, and the British at this time maintained the highest standards of public accommodations in the Western world. Although there is some evidence that a tavern was built in Jamestown, Virginia, during the early days of the settlement, it was the Dutch who built the first known tavern—the Stadt Huys—in Nieuw Amsterdam (New York) in 1642.

Early colonial inns and taverns in America are steeped as much in history as they are in hospitality. The year after the Dutch East India Company opened the Stadt Huys, Kreiger's Tavern opened on Bowling Green. During the American Revolution, this tavern, then called the King's Arms, became the headquarters of British General Gage.

The even more famous Fraunces Tavern was the Revolutionary headquarters of General George Washington, and was the place in which he made his famous Farewell Address. It is still operating.

As the colonies grew from scattered settlements to towns and cities, more and more travelers appeared, along with more accommodations to serve them.

Fraunces Tavern (Courtesy Fraunces Tavern.)

In New York and New England, these accommodations were also usually called *taverns.* In Pennsylvania, they were called *inns* and, in the South, *ordinaries.* There were regional differences among these accommodations as well.

The local inn/tavern/ordinary in the Colonies soon became a gathering place for residents, a place where they could catch up on the latest gossip, keep up with current events, hold meetings, and conduct business. The innkeeper, unlike the landlord of Roman times, was often the most respected member of the community, and was always one of its more substantial citizens. The innkeeper usually held some local elected office and sometimes rose much higher than that. John Adams, the second president of the United States, owned and managed his own tavern between 1783 and 1789.

Little wonder that colonial inns and taverns, in addition to their social functions, became ammunition storage depots, meeting places for the Revolutionary underground, and occasionally recruiting offices for pirates, who especially liked to frequent ordinaries along the Southeastern coastline. Many a cutthroat began his career in a public house in Charleston or Savannah.

The Revolutionary War did little to change the character of these public places. They maintained their position as social centers, political gathering places, newsrooms, watering holes, and travelers' rests; now, however, these same places were going by different names: hotels, names that reflected a growing French influence in the new nation.

The French Revolution

The French Revolution took place at approximately the same time the American colonies were fighting for independence. Among many other effects, the French Revolution helped to change the course of culinary history.

France is now a nation that awaits with bated breath the Michelin's annual selection of three-star restaurants. Thus, it is hard to believe that only slightly more than two hundred years ago, only one restaurant worthy of that rating existed in all of Paris—indeed, in all of France. The Tour d'Argent opened in 1533, and for over two centuries it was unique. Inns served meals, of course, but they were not primarily eating places, as was the Tour d'Argent. Only the traiteurs, or caterers, were allowed by law to sell cooked meat to the public, and they were limited to cooking for banquets.[3]

M. Boulanger, "the father of the modern restaurant," sold soups at his all-night tavern on the Rue Bailleul. He called these soups *restorantes* (*restoratives*), which is the origin of the word *restaurant*. However, Boulanger was hardly content to let his culinary repertoire rest there. In 1767, he challenged the traiteurs' monopoly by creating a "soup" of sheep's feet in a white sauce. The traiteurs guild sued, and the case went to the French Parliament. Boulanger won, and soon his restaurant, Le Champ d'Oiseau, was restoring hundreds of patrons from the ravages of hunger with its succulent, well-prepared dishes.[4]

One of these dishes, boulangere potatoes, was a dish of sliced potatoes in stock that was baked in the bread bakers' oven. Boulanger allowed people from the neighborhood to use the heat of his oven to cook their potatoes after the bread was done.

In 1782 the Grande Taverne de Londres, a true restaurant, opened on the Rue de Richilieu; three years later, Aux Trois Freres Provencaux opened near the Palais-Royal. By 1794, when heads were literally rolling in Paris, there were five hundred restaurants. Although it really cannot be said the French Revolution was responsible for the invention of the restaurant, it was responsible for the propagation of the concept. Except for a few faithful retainers, the chefs of the noble houses of France were scattered by the Revolution. Some stayed in France; some went to other parts of Europe; many crossed the Atlantic to America, especially to New Orleans, the one truly French corner of the New World. They almost all went into the restaurant business.

The chefs brought their culinary traditions with them. Soon the plain, hearty fare of the British and the primitive cooking of the Americans were laced with sauces piquantes and pots au feu. Other countries, too, felt the effects of French culinary artistry, and most absorbed some of the principles of French cooking into their own. Exceptions were the Italians, who had developed their own very strong culinary traditions and felt, with a great deal of justification, that French cooking was itself derived from the Italian.

French cuisine was not immediately embraced even by the two nations who stood to benefit most by it—Great Britain and the United States. French cooking was point-blank better than the British, and British cooks felt naturally threatened and became extremely chauvinistic and protective toward their culinary traditions. The United States, however, had no such traditions to uphold; the Puritans simply considered French cooking sinful. The plain cooking heritage had stuck, and travelers from abroad felt that Americans did not treat their abundant raw materials properly when they prepared them.

In 1784, during a five-year period as an envoy to France, Thomas Jefferson acquired a taste for French cuisine. He later enticed a French chef to the White

House and paid handomely for his expertise. This act stimulated interest in French cuisine and enticed U.S. tavern owners to offer better quality and more interesting food.

During this time, several French chefs emigrated to the United States. Many found their way to New Orleans, which was a French enclave. In fact, New Orleans is named after a French city and, over the years, was occupied by Britain, Spain, France, and America. One famous restaurant in New Orleans is the Court of the Two Sisters. It has the names of prisoners from the various wars inscribed on the walls of the entrance way.

Court of the Two Sisters (Courtesy Court of the Two Sisters.)

Nineteenth Century

By the early 1800s, the English had begun to borrow the concept of the restaurant from their French neighbors. The English restaurant was a lofty place, brimming with haute cuisine, haute decor, haughty service, and affordable by only a few.

Restaurants in Europe continued to flourish. In 1856, Antonin Careme published *La Cuisine Classique* and other volumes detailing numerous dishes and their sauces. The grande cuisine offered a carte (or list) of suggestions available from the kitchen. This was the beginning of the á la carte menu.

In 1898 the Savoy Hotel opened in London. The general manager was the renowned Cesar Ritz (today, the Ritz-Carlton hotels bear his name) and the Chef des Cuisines was Auguste Escoffier. Between them they revolutionized hotel restaurants. Escoffier was one of the greatest chefs of all time. He is best known for his classic book *Le Guide Culinaire,* which simplified the extraordinary works of Careme. He also installed the kitchen Brigade System.

The Americans used their special brand of ingenuity to create something for everyone. By 1848, a hierarchy of eating places existed in New York City. At the bottom was Sweeney's "sixpenny eating house" on Ann Street, whose proprietor, Daniel Sweeney, achieved questionable fame as the father of the greasy spoon. Sweeney's less-than-appetizing fare ("small plate sixpence, large plate shilling") was literally thrown or slid down a well-greased path to his hungry customers, who cared little for the social amenities of dining.

The next step up was Brown's, an establishment of little more gentility than Sweeney's, but boasting a bill of fare, with all the extras honestly marked off and priced in the margin, and waiters who would occasionally pass within hearing range to attend a customer's wants.

The famous Delmonico's was at the top of the list of American restaurants for a long time. Delmonico's was known as the only expensive and aristocratic restaurant in the United States. From the day the Delmonico family opened its first

Personal Profile: Auguste Escoffier (1846–1935)

Auguste Escoffier is considered the patron saint of the professional cook. Called the "emperor of the world's kitchens," he is considered as a reference point and a role model for all chefs. His exceptional culinary career began at the age of thirteen, when he apprenticed in his uncle's restaurant. He worked until 1920, and retired to die quietly at home in Monaco in 1935. Uneducated, but a patient educator and diligent writer, he was an innovator who remained deeply loyal to the regional and bourgeois roots of French cookery. He exhibited his culinary skills in the dining rooms of the finest hotels in Europe, including the Place Vendome in Paris and the Savoy and Carlton Hotels in London.

When the Prince of Wales requested something light but delicious as late dinner after a night in the Casino in Monte Carlo, Auguste Escoffier responded with *poularde Derby*, a stuffed chicken served with truffles cooked in champagne, alternating with slices of butter-fried *foie gras*, its sauce basted with the juices from the chicken and truffles. Another interesting anecdote regarding the chef's originality in making sauces tells of a special dinner for the Prince of Wales and Kaiser Wilhelm. Escoffier was asked to create a special dish to honor such an occasion. Struggling with an apparent loss of creativity until the night before the event, the chef finally noticed a sack of overripe mangos, from which he created a sauce that he personally came out from the kitchen to serve. As he placed the plate on the table, he looked at the Kaiser and with a wicked smile said, "zum

Escoffier

Teufel"—to the devil. Then was born sauce diabla, today a favorite classic sauce. Escoffier's insistence on sauces derived from the cooking of main ingredients was revolutionary at the time and in keeping with his famous instruction: faites simple—keep it simple.

In fact, in his search for simplicity, Escoffier reduced the complexity of the work of Careme, the "cook of kings and king of cooks," and aimed at the perfect balance of a few superb ingredients. In *Le Livre des Menus* (1912), Escoffier makes the analogy of a great dinner as a symphony with contrasting movements that should be appropriate to the occasion, the guests, and the season. He was meticulous in his kitchen, yet wildly imaginative in the creation of exquisite dishes. In 1903, Escoffier published *Le Guide Culinaire,* an astounding collection of more than five thousand classic cuisine recipes and garnishes. Throughout the book, Escoffier emphasizes technique, the importance of a complete understanding of basic cookery principles, and ingredients he considers to be essential to the creation of great dishes.

Escoffier's refinement of Careme's *grand cuisine* has been so radical as to credit him with the development of a new cuisine referred to as *cuisine classique*. His principles have been reinstated by successive generations, most emphatically by the *novelle cuisine* brigade. Francois Fusero, *chef de cuisine* at the Hotel Hermitage, Monte Carlo, regards Escoffier as his role model, and he schools his chefs in Escoffier's style: No detail is left to chance.

coffee and pastry shop at 23 William Street in 1827 until the farewell meal was served in Delmonico's Restaurant at 5th Avenue and 44th Street in 1923 (due to Prohibition), the name was synonymous with fine food, exquisitely prepared and impeccably served—the criteria by which all like establishments were judged.

Delmonico's served Swiss-French cuisine and became the focus of American gastronomy (the art of good eating). Delmonico's is also credited with the innovation of the bilingual menu, Baked Alaska, Chicken á la King, and Lobster Newberg. The Delmonico steak is named after the restaurant. Realizing that his customers would have difficulty ordering from a menu printed entirely in French, John Delmonico paid a linguist, Robert Greenhow, $100 to translate the French menu into an English bill-of-fare, with the menu and its translation printed side by side. This custom has survived and even expanded with the years. Delmonico's changed the way Americans ate.

More and more, eating places in the United States and abroad catered to residents of a town or city and less to travelers forced to make do with wayside fare. The custom of eating out for its own sake had arrived.

Other American cities had their own hotel-palaces: Chicago had the Palmer House; New Orleans had the St. Charles and St. Louis hotels; St. Louis had the Planter's Hotel. The Hotel del Coronado in San Diego is a historic landmark. The "Hotel del's" unique architectural style has contributed to its worldwide fame. Philadelphia, Baltimore, Washington, D.C., and Buffalo all have their fashionable hostelries, each one the last word in-gilt-edge opulence. Sometimes they are filled with "antiques" of questionable origin and decorations of questionable taste. The one thing that could not be called questionable was the food. By 1852, any first-class hotel worth its guest register had a French chef. Americans were reputed not to be too fond of "fussy" French meals, with their souffles and sauces, but those who frequented these hotels would have been loathe to admit it. Although the modern hotel was admittedly an American invention, the Europeans had made some contributions of their own. For instance, there was the European plan, which meant a guest need not pay for both room and meals in one lump sum, but could pay for only his room and order his meals separately from an á la carte menu, or eat elsewhere, if preferred.

Although big cities of the nineteenth century had their marble palaces, small towns had their serviceable imitations. Resort areas like Saratoga Springs, New York, and White Sulphur Springs, West Virginia, offered a whole new world of social and sensual pleasures. Yet, west of St. Louis, there was still no such thing as a decent night's lodging or a square meal. It's said, however, that the cafeteria concept originated in the California Gold Rush, when prospectors, eager to return to their claims, stood in line to be served from big communal bowls and pots rather than wait their turn at table.

Hotel del Coronado (Courtesy Hotel del Coronado, San Diego, California.)

By the 1870s, general conditions in the West had begun to civilize; unfortunately, the quality of the hospitality had not improved correspondingly. Rail travelers were warned to bring along nonperishable viands (foods) that could last several days. There were no dining cars or vendors. Meals were served in grimy lunchrooms, whose greedy proprietors often split their profits with train workers to ensure that the "all aboard" would sound before passengers had a chance to eat. The exact same reheated food was often served to three or four trainloads.

In 1876, Fred Harvey opened a small railway restaurant on the second floor of the Santa Fe railway depot in Topeka, Kansas. The restaurant was different from others of its kind in that it featured good, well-cooked food, spotless facilities, and courteous service. Business boomed.

Later that same year, Harvey opened his first hotel in Florence, Kansas, on the Santa Fe railway. During the 1880s and 1890s, Harvey Houses opened every 100 miles along the Santa Fe. They were renowned not only for genteel accommodations, incomparable seven-entree meals, and superb service, but also for their famous "Harvey Girls." These attractive, well-trained servers were recruited from good homes in the East, and eventually contributed more than their share to taming the untamed West. Thousands found husbands and settled from Kansas to California. "Grandma was a Harvey Girl" is today proclaimed proudly by many of the West's first families.

One could say that the nineteenth century saw more innovations in hospitality than in all previous recorded history. Women began to dine out in most of the Western world's distinguished restaurants. The famed Cesar Ritz, whose last name has entered the vocabulary as a synonym for the ultimate in luxury, made restaurant dining at London's Savoy almost a must for the fashionable aristocracy of both sexes. For those not so formally disposed, the "grill room," another English concept, made informal dining possible in a congenial, well-appointed atmosphere.

In the nineteenth century, better methods of preserving food through canning and vacuum packing made out-of-season culinary delights commonplace on tables everywhere. Many contributed to this development, primarily Napoleon I, who in 1809 awarded a prize of 12,000 francs (nearly a quarter of a million dollars in modern currency) to a man named Nicholas Appert for inventing a process to keep foodstuffs edible when preserved in glass jars. Napoleon's motivations were military rather than altruistic, as his armies were depleted as much by deficiency diseases and starvation as from wounds.

There was also an enormous growth in mass feeding. In schools, until the nineteenth century, no one had ever considered lunches for schoolchildren, because there were so few children who went to school. For those few who were fortunate enough to attend college, there had been a tradition of student hostels both in England and on the European Continent since sometime in the twelfth century. Through the centuries these hostels—sometimes run by the students themselves, sometimes through endowments, sometimes by the school—had provided some sort of living quarters and sustenance for the student population. Eventually, many of them evolved into the houses, clubs, fraternities, and sororities of today.

It was not until the Industrial Revolution freed great numbers of children from child labor that the school-age population increased to where feeding children of an elementary school age became a problem. Canteens for schoolchildren started in France in 1849. In 1865, Victor Hugo, the famous French author, started school feeding in England by providing hot lunches at his home in Guernsey for the children of a nearby school. In 1853, the Children's Aid Society in New York opened an industrial school and offered food to all consumers. Some decades later, men and women concerned with nutrition for children sponsored the development of school lunchroom programs in several urban centers; state extension services, PTAs, and other organizations saw to it that these services were available in rural schools as well.

P.J. Clarke's (Courtesy P.J. Clarke's.)

The nineteenth century also saw the development of hospital feeding that did not kill as many patients as it helped cure. For this the world owes another great debt of gratitude to Florence Nightingale, who was the founder of dietetics as well as modern nursing. In the diet kitchen she set up at the hospital at Scutari (now part of Istanbul) during the Crimean War, she replaced the ill-cooked, ill-served fare with punctual and more appetizing meals.

The nineteenth century also saw the birth of the ice cream soda, and marble-topped soda fountains began to make their appearances in so-called ice cream parlors.

This century brought about enormous changes in our traveling and eating habits. Tastes have been refined and expanded in the twentieth century, but it is interesting to note how many restaurants have stood the test of time.

Thirty-five restaurants in New York City have stood the test of time and celebrated their one-hundredth birthdays. One of them, P.J. Clarke's, established in 1890, is a "real" restaurant-bar that has changed little in its hundred years of operation. On entering, one sees a large mahogany bar, its mirror tarnished by time, the original tin ceiling, and the tile mosaic floor. Memorabilia ranges from celebrity pictures to Jessie, the house fox terrier that customers had stuffed when she died and who now stands guard over the ladies' room door. Guests still write their own checks at lunch time, on pads with their table numbers on them (this goes back to the days when one of the servers could not read or write and was struggling to memorize orders).[5]

Twentieth Century

In 1921, Walter Anderson and Billy Ingraham began the White Castle hamburger chains. The name White Castle was selected because white stood for purity and castle for strength. The eye-catching restaurants were nothing more than stucco building shells, a griddle, and a few chairs. People came in droves, and within ten years White Castle had expanded to 115 units.[6]

Marriott's Hot Shoppe and root beer stands opened in 1927. About this time, the drive-in roadside and fast food restaurants also began springing up across America. The expression *car hop* was coined because as an order taker approached an automobile, he or she would hop onto the auto's running board. The drive-in became an established part of Americana and a gathering place of the times.

In 1925, another symbol of American eateries, Howard Johnson's original restaurant, opened in Wollaston, Massachusetts.

After the stock market crash of 1929 and the Depression, America rebounded with the elegance and deluxe dining of the 1930s á la Fred Astaire. The Rainbow Room opened in 1934. This art deco restaurant championed the reemergence of New York as a center of power and glamour.

Trader Vic's opened in 1937. Although the idea was borrowed from another restaurant known as the Beachcomber, Trader Vic's became successful by drawing the social elite to the Polynesian theme restaurant where Vic concocted exotic cocktails including the Mai-tai, which he invented.[7]

At the World's Fair in 1939, a restaurant called Le Pavillion de France was so successful that it later opened in New York. By the end of the 1930s, every city had a deluxe supper club or night club.

The Four Seasons opened in 1959. The Four Seasons was the first elegant American restaurant that was not French in style. It expressed the total experience of dining, and everything from the scale of the space to the tabletop accessories was in harmony.[8]

The Four Seasons was the first restaurant to offer seasonal menus (summer, fall, winter, spring) (see Figure 1–1), its modern architecture, and art as a theme. Joe Baum, the developer of this restaurant, understood why people go to restaurants—to be together and to connect with one another. It is very important that the restaurant reinforce why customers chose it in the first place. Restaurants exist to create pleasure, and how well a restaurant meets this expectation of pleasure is a measure of its success.[9]

The Four Seasons Restaurant (Courtesy Four Seasons Restaurant.)

DINNER

WINTER 1994   We Suggest That You Order The Dessert Soufflé
At The Beginning Of The Meal

COLD APPETIZERS

Parma PROSCIUTTO with Poached Pears	17.00	A Service of SHRIMP	19.00
Breast of QUAIL Salad with Chestnuts	15.50	LITTLENECKS, A Platter	13.00
Smoked Scottish SALMON Roulade with Caviar	25.00	Cherrystone CLAMS	13.00
Roasted PEPPERS, Mozzarella and Basil	15.00	CRAB Lump Cocktail	19.00
TUNA Carpaccio with Ginger and Coriander	17.00	A Selection of OYSTERS	15.00
		Smoked Scottish SALMON	25.00
		Beluga CAVIAR	90.00

HOT APPETIZERS

LOBSTER Ravioli	20.00
RISOTTO Cake with Wild Mushrooms	15.00
Sautéed Fresh FOIE GRAS	25.00
Crisp SHRIMP with Mustard Fruits	19.50

SOUPS

SEAFOOD Gumbo with Okra	10.50
PHEASANT Consommé	9.50
Pumpkin BISQUE with Pepitas	9.50

THIS EVENING'S ENTREES

Grilled Curried SWORDFISH with Pickled Vegetables 37.50
Seared SALMON with Braised Belgium Endive, Saffron Vinaigrette 38.50
CRABMEAT Cakes with Mustard Sauce 37.50
Maine LOBSTER: Broiled, Poached or Steamed 42.00
DOVER SOLE Meunière or Broiled 45.00
Breast of PHEASANT Braised in Port with Mashed Potatoes 35.00
Médaillon of VENISON with Stuffed Savoy Cabbage and Cranberries 40.00
Grilled LAMB CHOPS with String Beans 37.00
Sautéed CALF'S LIVER with Olives and Avocado 34.00
VEAL Four Seasons with Crabmeat and Artichokes 42.00
Black Angus Skillet STEAK with Smothered Onions 40.00
Grilled FILET MIGNON, Béarnaise and Snow Peas 40.00
A Skewer of Grilled VEGETABLES and WILD MUSHROOMS, Bulgur and Avocado 30.00

FOR TWO (PER PERSON)

Roast Darn of SALMON with Herb Sauce 39.50
Crisp Farmhouse DUCK: au Poivre or with Apple and Cinnamon Compote 39.50
Roast Rack of LAMB with Zucchini and Pepper Timbale 42.00
CHATEAUBRIAND with Béarnaise, Snow Peas and Wild Mushrooms 45.00

SPA CUISINE ®

APPETIZERS:	BAY SCALLOPS Seviche 14.00
MAIN COURSES:	Grilled Filet of LAMB with Corona Beans and Broccoli 33.00
DESSERT:	APRICOT Semifreddo 8.50

SALADS, VEGETABLES AND POTATOES

Caesar SALAD	11.50	WILD RICE with Pine Nuts	9.00
Wilted SPINACH and Bacon	9.50	SNOW PEA Pods with Shoyu	8.00
Winter GREENS	9.00	Creamed SPINACH	7.00
Stuffed Savoy CABBAGE	9.00	Mashed POTATOES	6.50
Sautéed WILD MUSHROOMS	9.50	Baked POTATO	6.00
		ROESTI	6.50

DESSERTS

A Selection from the DESSERT WAGON	8.50
SHERBETS and ICE CREAMS	6.50
Choice of APPLE CINNAMON, CRANBERRY	
ORANGE or CHOCOLATE and KAHLUA Soufflé	8.50

BEVERAGES

A Variety of TEAS	3.50
COLOMBIAN COFFEE	3.50
CAFE Cognac Chantilly	8.50
IRISH COFFEE	8.50
ESPRESSO	3.50

THE FOUR SEASONS

Figure 1–1 *Four Seasons Menu*

The savvy restaurateur is adaptable. Being quick to respond to changing market conditions has always been the key to success in the restaurant business. An interesting example of this was demonstrated in the early 1900s by the operator of Delmonico's. As business declined during a recession in the 1930s, Delmonico's opened for breakfast, then began delivering breakfast, lunch, dinner, and other fare to Wall Street firms for late-evening meetings. Next, he turned his attention to the weekends when Wall Street was quiet. He built up a weekend catering business and developed a specialty of weddings. Later, he connected with tour groups going to Ellis Island and encouraged them to stop off for meals.[10]

Conclusion

The exclusive restaurant of yesterday may still be the exclusive restaurant of today, but the less affluent citizen can choose from a staggering array of eating places ranging from the almost-exclusive to the almost-greasy spoon.

What people have today is choice; it is truly a world in which the automobile and airplane have made almost any place in the world accessible to the average citizen. It is a world with more people who expect to have better accommodations, food, entertainment, recreation, and leisure.

Summary

1. The first references to hospitality can be traced back to ancient Greece and Rome, when increased travel and trade made some form of overnight accommodation a necessity.

2. The Romans developed a well-appointed postal system. The ancient Persians created a combination of stables and sleeping accommodations called Khans, which served traveling caravans.

3. During the middle ages, hospitality started to become more organized with the creation of a restaurant guild. In England, the stagecoach became the favorite method of transportation.

4. Many values established for hospitality during medieval times can still be applied today, such as friendly service, nice atmosphere and plenty of food. Compared with today, sanitary standards were rather poor and accommodations primitive.

5. The sixteenth century introduced two exotic imports, coffee and tea, to Europe. Coffee houses not only became social gathering places but also helped to sober up an entire continent.

6. During the Middle Ages, most inns distinguished themselves in their treatment of common and noble travelers. This led to the creation of the ordinary, a tavern that served a fixed menu at a fixed price to the common folk.

7. As colonies developed into towns, traveling increased. Taverns became a social and political gathering place reflecting a growing French influence.

8. The French Revolution influenced the culinary development by establishing the first restaurant in the new world and bringing French cuisine to America.

9. The nineteenth century created concepts such as á la carte dining, mass feeding, better preservation, ice-cream parlors, and established the custom of eating out.

10. Advanced technology and transportation in the twentieth century has opened up the world to almost everyone. People expect a wide range of dining choices, excellent service, food, accommodations, and entertainment. This fast-paced century also created the fast food industry.

Review Exercises

1. Explain the origin of the term *hospitality*.
2. Give a brief overview of the development of hospitality from ancient Rome to the New World.
3. What values of hospitality that existed during the Middle Ages are still valued today? Name one concept that originated during that time and still exists today.
4. Explain how the respectability of innkeepers changed from ancient Rome until modern times and how this related to the evolution of the lodging industry.
5. Explain the importance of the French Revolution in the history of restaurants.
6. What is the concept of modern hospitality?

Key Words and Concepts

Á la carte
Boulanger
Coffee houses
Delmonico's
European plan

French Revolution
Guild
Hospice
Hospitality

Khans
Marco Polo
Monasteries
Ordinary

Rest houses
Cesar Ritz
Table d'hote
Taverns

Notes

[1] This section draws on William S. Gray and Salvatore C. Liquori, *Hotel and Motel Management and Operations*. Englewood Cliffs, N.J.: Prentice Hall, 1980, pp. 4–5.

[2] *Hospitality Through the Ages*. Corning Glass Works Foodservice Products, Corning, N.Y. 14830.

[3] In those days a number of guilds existed as societies of merchants or tradespeople whose purpose was to promote and protect their common interests.

[4] Linda Glick Conway (ed.), *The Professional Chef*, 5th ed. Hyde Park, N.Y.: The Culinary Institute of America, 1991, p. 5.

[5] Ibid.

[6] John Mariani, *America Eats Out*. New York: William Morrow, 1991, pp. 122–124.

[7] Ibid.

[8] Martin E. Dorf, *Restaurants That Work*. New York: Whitney Library of Design, 1992, p. 9.

[9] Ibid.

[10] Ibid.

Tourism

After reading and studying this chapter you should be able to do the following:

➤ Define tourism
➤ Trace the five epochs (or periods) of tourism
➤ Describe the evolution of the major travel modes
➤ Outline the important international and domestic tourism organizations
➤ Describe the economic impact of tourism
➤ Identify promoters of tourism
➤ List reasons why people travel
➤ Describe the sociocultural impact of tourism
➤ Describe ecotourism

What Is Tourism?

Tourism is a dynamic, evolving, consumer-driven force. Tourism is the world's largest industry. This viewpoint may be correct if all the interrelated components are placed under one umbrella, as shown in Figure 2–1.

The World Travel and Tourism Council declares the travel and tourism industry to have the following characteristics:

The world's largest industry, with approximately $3.5 trillion in gross output

The world's leading industrial contribution, producing 6.1 percent of the world's Gross National Product (GNP)

A leading producer of tax revenues

Employer of 127 million people, or one in every fifteen workers

Expected to grow faster than any other sector of world employment[1]

The fact that tourism is expected to grow so rapidly presents both tremendous opportunities and challenges. The good news is the variety of exciting career prospects for today's hospitality and tourism graduates. Tourism,

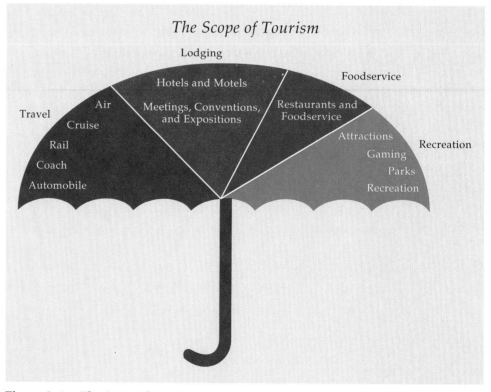

Figure 2–1   *The Scope of Tourism*

although a mature industry, is a young profession. Careful management of tourism and travel will be necessary to avoid repercussions and negativism toward the "pesky" tourist—which is already happening to some extent in Europe, where the sheer number of tourists overwhelms attractions and facilities.

Definition of Tourism

The word *tourism* did not appear in the English language until the early nineteenth century. The word *tour* was more closely associated with the idea of a voyage or perhaps a theatrical tour than with the idea of an individual "traveling for pleasure purposes, which is the accepted use of the word today."[2] *Webster's Ninth New Collegiate Dictionary* defines a tourist as "one who makes a tour for pleasure or culture."

Tourism can be defined as the science, art, and business of attracting and transporting visitors, accommodating them, and graciously catering to their needs and wants.[3]

For many developing nations, tourism represents a relatively high percentage of gross national product and an easy way of gaining a balance of trade with other nations.

A tourist, by United Nations (U.N.) definition, is a person who stays for more than one night and less than a year. Business and convention travel is included in this definition.

Tourism means different things to different people. For example, a hotelier might say that tourism is wonderful because it brings guests who fill rooms and restaurants. However, a government official might define it as the economic benefit of more money coming into the country, state, or city. In order to simplify tourism, it is sometimes categorized in terms of the following factors:

Geography:	International, regional, national, state, provincial, country, city
Ownership:	Government, quasi-government, private
Function:	Regulators, suppliers, marketers, developers, consultants, researchers, educators, publishers, professional associations, trade organizations, consumer organizations
Industry:	Transportation (air, bus, rail, auto, cruise), travel agents, tour wholesalers, lodging, attractions, recreation
Motive:	Profit or non-profit[4]

Industry practitioners use these categories to identify and interact with the various industry sectors and organizations involved with tourism.

The Five Epochs of Tourism

The historical development of tourism has been divided up into five distinct epochs (or periods),[5] four of which parallel the advent of new means of transportation.

Preindustrial revolution (prior to 1840)
The railway age
The automobile age
The jet aircraft age
The cruise ship age

Preindustrial Revolution

As early as 300 B.C., ancient Egyptians sailed up and down the river Nile, carrying huge rocks with which to build pyramids as tombs for their leaders.[6] The Phoenicians were among the first real travelers in any modern sense. In both the Mediterranean basin and the Orient, travel was motivated by trade. However, trade was not the only motivation for travel in these times; commerce and the search for more plentiful food supplies also stimulated travel.[7]

The Roman Empire provided safe passage for travelers via a vast road system that stretched from Egypt to Britain. Wealthy Romans traveled to Egypt and Greece, to baths, shrines, and seaside resorts.[8] The Romans were as curious as modern-day tourists. They visited the attractions of their time, trekking to Greek temples and to places where Alexander the Great slept, Socrates lived, Ajax committed suicide, and Achilles was buried. The Romans also traveled to Egypt to visit the Pyramids, the Sphinx, and the Valley of the Kings—just as today's tourists do.[9] The excavated ruins of the Roman town Pompeii, which was buried by an eruption of Mt. Vesuvius, yielded several restaurants, taverns, and inns that tourists visit even today.

Medieval travel was mostly confined to religious travel, particularly pilgrimages to various shrines: Moslems to Mecca and Christians to Jerusalem and Rome. The Crusades began in 1095 and lasted for the next two hundred years, stimulating a cultural exchange that was, in part, responsible for the Renaissance.

Across Europe, travel and trade flourished. With the increase in living standards came a heightened awareness of cultural pursuits. Later, aristocrats undertook Grand Tours of Europe, stopping at major cities for weeks or months at a time. It was considered a necessary part of "rounding out" a young lady's or gentleman's education. Fortunately, travel now has become possible for almost everyone.

The Railway Age

Railroads played a major role in the development of the United States, Canada, and several other countries. The pioneering spirit carried by the railroads opened up the great American West. Prior to the advent of rail travel, tourists had to journey by horse and carriage. By comparison, the railway was more efficient, less costly, and more comfortable. Resort communities came within the reach of a larger segment of the population in North America and Europe. The railroads brought changes in the lodging industry, as taverns along the turnpikes gave way to hotels near the railway stations.

AMTRAK Train (Courtesy AMTRAK.)

The first railroad was built in the United States in 1830, but only 23 miles of rail were laid by the end of that year. In contrast, by 1860, there were 30,626 miles of track. In 1869, rail journey across America was made possible by the transcontinental connection, which enabled the journey to be completed in six days.[10] Before that, such a journey took several months by wagon or several weeks by clipper ships rounding Cape Horn, South America.

To ensure passenger comfort, railroads had excellent dining cars and sleeping berths. Railroads continued to extend their lines into the twentieth century until the great Depression of the 1930s and World War II. These events began a decline in railroad usage that was accelerated by the invention of the automobile. The freedom of the open road gave automobile travel a competitive advantage over train travel.

In order to prevent a complete collapse of the passenger rail system, the United States government created AMTRAK in 1971. AMTRAK is a semipublic organization; eight of the fifteen members of its board are selected by the President of the United States, three by the railroads, and four by preferred private stockholders.[11] AMTRAK is subsidized by the United States Congress, in amounts ranging from $500 million to $800 million per year; this subsidy represents between 35 and 50 percent of its total revenue.[12] AMTRAK has eliminated many unprofitable lines and improved overall efficiency and service quality. About half of AMTRAK's trains and passengers are in the heavily populated northeastern United States.

Despite these efforts, many passengers opt for the speed and sometimes price advantages of the airlines. To counter this, AMTRAK offers special prices on regional or transcontinental travel. Tour packages are also popular, particularly with retired people who prefer relaxing and watching the ever-changing scenery to driving.

Although rail travel has declined in the United States, railroads in Europe and Asia play far more important roles in passenger and freight transportation. Railroads are more cost-effective and more efficient means of transportation in densely populated areas. Europeans have developed trains that can travel up to 250 miles per hour. The French Trés Grande Vitesse (TGV, very high speed) runs between Paris and Marseilles in three hours. The channel tunnel (Chunnel) links England with France and enables both trains and automobiles to travel the 23 miles of the English Channel.

Bullet Train (Courtesy Japan Tourist Bureau.)

In Japan, the bullet train can go up to 250 miles per hour. Not all trains go quite that fast, but the ride is remarkably smooth—a beverage glass can rest on a table and not spill. As with the United States, the Japanese and European rail systems are heavily subsidized by their respective governments. However, without such subsidies, the roads and the air would be more congested.

Many Americans visiting Europe take advantage of the Eurailpass. The Eurailpass, which must be purchased from travel agents outside of Europe, allows visitors to travel throughout Europe, with the exception of the United Kingdom. Visitors can get on and off the train at hundreds of cities and enjoy the local attractions.

Automobile Travel

Automobiles evolved from steam engines in the late 1800s, when Karl Benz and Gottlieb Daimler built a factory for internal combustion engines, which is now Mercedes Benz.[13]

In 1891, the production of automobiles began in large numbers. Before long, Henry Ford produced his first vehicle and invented the techniques for making automobiles on an assembly line. By 1914, Henry Ford was producing one Model T Ford every twenty-four seconds.[14] The assembly-line production continues today with the additional help of robots.

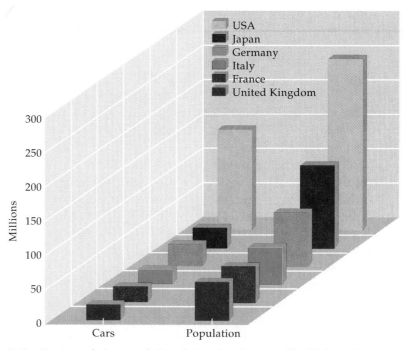

Figure 2–2   *Registered Cars and Population by Country* (R. Walters Somerset, *Travel Industry World Yearbook. The Big Picture—1993.* New York: Child and Waters, 1993.)

The United States has about 150 million autos registered. The country with the next largest amount is Japan, which has about 33 million registered. Figure 2–2 shows the number of motor vehicles registered in various countries in 1993.

The call of the great open road and the increased financial ability of more families to purchase automobiles led to a tremendous growth in travel and tourism. Motels and restaurants sprang up along the highways. The automobile made more places accessible to more people.

Model-T Ford

Air Travel

The Wright brothers, who enjoyed the hobby of gliding, decided to fit an engine to one of their gliders with movable fins and wingtip controls. To find an engine light enough, they had to build their own. In 1903, they tested their 13-horsepower engine. On the first run it lifted the craft in the air for twelve seconds and covered a distance of 120 feet.[15]

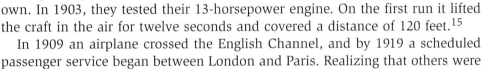

In 1909 an airplane crossed the English Channel, and by 1919 a scheduled passenger service began between London and Paris. Realizing that others were about to attempt to cross the Atlantic, Charles Lindbergh persuaded a group of investors in St. Louis to fund construction of a new airplane in San Diego. The "Spirit of St. Louis" was built in sixty days. With 450 gallons of gasoline on board (the tanks even blocked forward visibility), Lindbergh made the first solo crossing of the Atlantic Ocean in 1927. This history-making twenty-eight-hour flight was a major turning point in aviation history. This monumental achievement was a catalyst for massive investment in the airline industry.

The first scheduled air service in the United States began in 1915 between San Diego and Los Angeles. Later, in 1930, the Douglas Company in California introduced the DC-2, which could carry fourteen passengers and fly at a speed of 213 miles per hour. The most famous airplane, the DC-3, came into service in 1936. To this day, well over two thousand of them are still flying.[16]

In 1944, an international conference was held in Chicago to establish international air routes and services. American and European delegates disagreed about how much to restrict competition—the Americans pushed for unrestricted competition.

However, seventy airlines from forty nations ratified an important agreement of transportation rates and created the International Air Transportation Association (IATA). The IATA is the major trade association of the world's airlines. Through

Spirit of St. Louis

Boeing 707, 727, 737 (Courtesy Boeing Corporation.)

international agreements on financial, legal, technical, and traffic matters, the worldwide system of air travel became possible.[17]

American and European representatives met again in Bermuda in 1946 to work out a compromise. The Bermuda agreement, by which countries exchanged benefits, was to later become a model for bilateral negotiations. The "six freedoms of the air" agreed upon in Bermuda were as follows:

The right to fly across another nation's territory

The right to land in another country for noncommercial purposes

The right to disembark passengers and cargo from the carrier's home country in a foreign country

The right to pick up passengers and cargo destined for the carrier's home country from a foreign country

The right to transport passengers and cargo from one foreign country to another foreign country

The right of an airplane to carry traffic from a foreign country to the home nation of that airline and beyond to another foreign country

In 1954, the first Boeing 707 came into service. By 1958, Pan American Airways inaugurated transatlantic flights from New York to Paris. A Boeing 707 could carry 111 passengers over a range of about 6,000 miles at a cruising speed of 600 miles per hour. Also in 1958, McDonnell-Douglas introduced the DC-8, which boasted a similarly impressive performance.

Other aircraft were introduced to handle the medium- and short-range routes. The Boeing 727 was introduced in 1964. It became the workhorse of the U.S. domestic market, carrying 145 passengers at a cruising speed of 600 miles per hour. In 1968, the Boeing 737 established itself as the short-range challenger to the McDonnell-Douglas DC-9. The Boeing 747, introduced in 1970, was the first of the wide-body aircraft. It could transport four to five hundred passengers at a cruising speed of 600 miles per hour over distances of about 7,000 miles.

A consortium of European countries developed the Airbus. The Airbus A 340 is designed for the long-distance market, and the Airbus A 320 is for the short-distance market.

The Concorde was the first supersonic aircraft, developed at a cost of $3 billion by the British and French governments. However, it has been a financial

Boeing 747 (Courtesy Boeing Corporation.)   *Concorde* (Courtesy British Airways.)

white elephant. The Concorde has a cruising speed of 1,450 miles per hour, vastly reducing time needed to fly from London to New York. A 747 flight leaving at 11 a.m. London time will land at 1:40 p.m. New York time. On a Concorde, a flight leaving at 11:00 a.m. London time will land at 9:50 a.m., New York time. Air France operates the Concorde from Paris, Dakar, and Rio de Janeiro. British Airways (BA) operates Concordes between London and Bahrain and from London to Washington, D.C., or New York.

Air transportation has further reduced the cost per mile of travel, enabling millions of people to become tourists. As a result, hotels, restaurants, and attractions have grown to keep pace with demand. The speed of air transportation enables vacationers to take intercontinental trips. Europe and Asia are only hours away as are all the cities of North and Latin America.

The Airline Deregulation Act of 1978

Air transportation changed dramatically in 1978. Deregulation transferred the responsibility for airline activity to the Federal Aviation Administration (FAA) and the Department of Transportation (DOT). The purpose of the Deregulation Act was to allow a free market of competition whereby airlines could decide their own fare structures and rates. Deregulation resulted in retrenchment of major air carriers, new airlines, lower airfares, and "megacarriers."[18]

The effects of deregulation were to force several noncompetitive airlines out of business. Pan Am, once the flag bearer of international aviation, lost money and went out of business because it became bloated with too many layers of bureaucracy and too large a payroll. Simply because they had been in business longer, many of the pilots and cabin crew at Pan Am were more highly paid than their competitors. Over the years, costs such as fuel also escalated.

Not only did airlines go out of business but some were also absorbed by other airlines. For example, Texas Air bought Eastern Airlines, Continental, People's Express, Frontier, and New York Air. They are operated under Continental Airlines.

In the late 1980s, most of the major airlines were in an expansion mode. They incurred heavy debt, spending money on new planes and terminals. This debt service made major airlines vulnerable to price wars, with resultant operational losses.

Over the past few years, major U.S. airlines have lost billions of dollars. One reason is competition from international airlines, several of which are subsidized by their national governments. Although British Airways is the world's largest airline, Air France is central Europe's largest and arguably its steadiest airline. However, Air France lags behind rivals in key areas: controlling costs, starting a frequent-flier plan, and forging meaningful alliances with foreign carriers.[19]

Competition for market share within and to Europe from the United States has intensified. Since 1985, the number of U.S. carriers flying to France has increased from two to eight. This competition has cut Air France's transatlantic market share from 50 percent to 35 percent.[20]

USAir's strategic partnership with British Airways is an example of internationalism that benefits airlines that must compete in a global marketplace. For an airline like USAir to expand into the global market, such a strategic alliance makes sense. Thomas Lagow, USAir's executive vice president of marketing, says that the issue is simple: USAir answers to shareholders, employees, and passengers—if they're happy, that's all that matters.[21]

Alliances of this nature will allow airlines access to each other's feeder markets and to resources that will enable them to flourish in what will ultimately be a worldwide deregulation. A feeder market is a market that provides the source—in this case, passengers for the particular destination.

The complexities of the international business community are illustrated by the fact that Air Canada now owns 28 percent of Continental Airlines. It is possible that these airlines will cooperate if the proposed open skies accord between Canada and the United States takes place.

Ultimately, any major European airline without a strategic alliance in the United States will only limit its own horizons and lose market share.

Major U.S. carriers like TWA and Northwest have been close to bankruptcy for some time. However, they have negotiated salary cuts of up to 15 percent in return for employee representation on the board and 3.5 percent of the company's stock. American Airlines has also worked out a similar cost-reduction package with its employees.[22] At United Airlines, labor proposes to give $3.4 billion in concessions over five years for up to 60 percent of the company's stock, plus significant control over major decisions.[23]

Southwest, a regional carrier, operates more efficiently than the competition despite the fact that its workforce is unionized. Southwest gets more flight time from its pilots than American—672 hours a year versus 371, and racks up 60 percent more passenger miles per flight attendant. These efficiencies have helped Southwest to turn a profit in 1993 while the rest of the industry lost $4 billion.[24]

Regional carriers, such as Southwest, with lower operating costs and consequently lower fares, have forced larger companies to retreat. This has a growing impact on the airline industry.

In order to reduce losses brought about by deregulation, major carriers eliminated unprofitable routes, often those serving smaller cities. New airlines began operating shuttle services between the smaller cities and nearest larger or hub city. This created the hub-and-spoke system (see Figure 2–3).

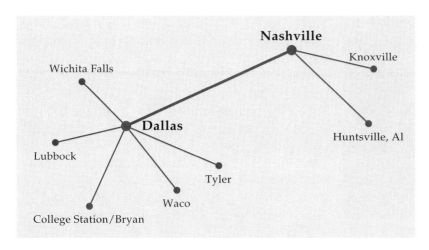

Figure 2–3　*The Hub-and-Spoke System*

The Hub-and-Spoke System

In order to remain efficient and cost effective, major U.S. airlines have adopted a hub-and-spoke system. The hub-and-spoke system enables passengers to travel from one smaller city to another smaller city via a hub or even two hubs. Similarly, passengers may originate their travel from a small city and use the hub to reach connecting flights to destinations throughout the world.

The hub-and-spoke system has two main benefits: (1) airlines can service more cities at a lower cost and (2) airlines can maximize passenger loads from small cities, thereby saving fuel.

Cruise Ships

More than two hundred cruise lines offer a variety of wonderful vacations, from the "Love Boat" to freighters that carry only a few passengers. Travelers associate a certain romance to cruising to exotic locations and being pampered all day.

Being on a cruise ship is like being on a floating resort. Accommodations range from luxurious suites to cabins that are even smaller than most hotel rooms. Attractions and distractions range from early morning work-outs to fabulous meals, with night life consisting of dancing, cabarets, and possibly gambling. Day life might involve relaxation, visits to the beauty parlor, organized games, or simply reclining in a deck chair by the pool reading a novel. Nonstop entertainment includes language lessons, charm classes, port-of-call briefings, cooking, dances, bridge, table tennis, shuffleboard, and more.

For example, the new Crown Princess is a "super Love Boat" weighing in at 70,000 tons and costing

Love Boat (Courtesy Princess Cruise Lines.)

Radisson Diamond (Courtesy Carlson Corporation.)

$200 million. This ship is longer than two football fields and capable of carrying up to 1,596 passengers. The Crown Princess was designed by Italian architect Reizo Piano. Its exterior resembles a head of a dolphin, and it features the "Dome," a 13,000-square-foot entertainment complex forward on the top deck. The Dome boasts a casino with black-jack, craps, roulette tables, and masses of slot machines as well as a dance floor, bar, and lounge with wrap-around windows.

Radisson Hotels International has entered the $4.6 billion cruise business with a dramatic catamaran—a twin-hulled ship designed to prevent most of the pitching and rolling that causes seasickness. The new ship, the Radisson Diamond, can carry up to 354 passengers. Completed in 1992 for about $125 million, its cost was about 10 to 15 percent higher than a comparable single-hull ship. With rates at about $600 per day, this ship has joined the top end of the cruise market.

The cruise market increased more than 500 percent between 1970 and 1990. However, only about 6 percent of Americans have been on a cruise. Rates vary from a starting point of $195 per person per day on Carnival Cruise Lines to $600 on the Radisson Diamond. Rates typically are quoted per diem (per day) and are cruise-only figures, based on double occupancy.

No two ships are alike. Each has its own personality and character. The nationality of the ship's officers and staff contributes greatly to the ship's ambiance. For example, the ships under the Holland America flag have Dutch officers and Indonesian/Filipino crew, and those belonging to the Epirotiki flag have Greek officers and crew.

Casual ships cater to young couples, singles, and families with children. At the other end of the spectrum, ships that appeal to the upscale crowd draw a mature clientele that prefers a more sedate atmosphere, low-key entertainment, and dressing for dinner.

About four million people took cruises in 1993. Many passengers are remarkably loyal to their particular vessel; as many as half of the passengers on a cruise may be repeat guests.

See Figure 2–4 for examples of cruise lingo.

Most cruise ships sail under foreign flags because they were built abroad for the following reasons:[25]

1. U.S. labor costs for ships, officers, and crew, in addition to maritime unions, are too high to compete in the world market.
2. U.S. ships are not permitted to operate casino-type gambling.
3. Many foreign shipyards are government subsidized to keep workers employed, thereby lowering construction costs.

Most cruise ships sail under foreign flags (called "flags of convenience") for the added reason that registering these ships in countries such as Panama, the

Aft:	Toward the rear or stern of the ship
Beam:	Ships's width at the widest point
Bridge:	Part of the ship where the navigation is done
Bulkhead:	Shipboard name for wall or partition
Cabin:	Name given to a passenger's room
Captain:	Master of the ship; the captain is the final authority and has total responsibility for every aspect of the ship's safety and operations.
Companion way:	Flight of stairs
Cruise director:	Individual who plans and directs all shipboard entertainment, including passenger activities, shows, shore excursions
Forward:	Toward the bow or front of ship
Galley:	Seagoing word for kitchen
Gangway:	Ship's boarding ramp
Knot:	Nautical speed (about 1-1/16 of a land mile per hour)
Port side:	Left-hand side of the ship as you face forward
Starboard side:	Right-hand side of the ship as you face forward
Stern:	Aft or rear of the ship
Tonnage:	A customary measure of a ship's size
Wake:	Waves behind a ship

Figure 2-4   *Cruise Lingo*

Bahamas, and Liberia means fewer and more lax regulations and little or no taxation.

Employment opportunities for Americans are mainly confined to sales, marketing, and other U.S. shore-based activities, such as reservations and supplies. On board, certain positions such as cruise director and purser, are sometimes occupied by Americans.

Anecdote

The maître d' on the Love Boat was explaining the dining room staff's duties beginning with breakfast at 6 a.m., followed by lunch and dinner. A student asked, "When does the second shift come on?" The maître d' laughed and said, "There is no second shift." Needless to say, that student's interest declined, especially when he realized the crew would be at sea for months at a time.

Table 2–1 shows the number of passengers taking a cruise lasting more than two days according to the Cruise Lines Association (CLA).

Table 2-1
Passengers Taking a Cruise Longer Than Two Days

Year	Passengers
1970	500,000
1980	1.4 million
1990	3.6 million
1992	4.4 million (est.)

Perry Hobson, "Analysis of the US Cruise Line Industry," *Tourism Management,* December 1993, p. 454.

Segmenting the Cruise Market

Mass Market: Generally people with incomes in the $20,000 to $39,000 range, interested in an average cost per person of between $125 and $200 per day, depending on the location and size of the cabin

Middle Market: Generally people with incomes in the $40,000 to $59,000 range, interested in an average cost per person of $200 to $350 per day. This is the largest part of the market. These ships are capable of accommodating 750 to 1,000 passengers.

Luxury Market: Generally people with incomes higher than $60,000, interested in an average cost per person of more than $350 per day. In this market the ships tend to be smaller, averaging about seven hundred passengers, with superior appointments and service.

Tourism Organizations

Governments are involved in tourism decisions because tourism involves travel across international boundaries. Governments regulate the entrance and exit of foreign nationals. They become involved in the decisions surrounding national parks, heritage, preservation, and environmental protection, as well as cultural and social aspects of tourism. Tourism is to some extent an international ambassador, fostering goodwill and closer intercultural understanding among the peoples of the world.

International Organizations

Looking first at the macro picture, the World Tourism Organization (WTO) is the most widely recognized organization in tourism today.[26] The WTO is the only organization that represents all national and official tourism interests among its allied members.

The International Air Transportation Association (IATA) is the global organization that regulates almost all international airlines. The purpose of IATA is to facilitate the movement of people and goods via a network of routes. In addition to tickets, IATA regulations standardize waybills and baggage checks and coordinate and unify handling and accounting procedures to permit rapid interline bookings and connections. The IATA also maintains stability of fares and rates.

International Civil Aviation Organization (ICAO) is comprised of more than eighty governments. ICAO coordinates the development of all aspects of civil aviation, specifically with regard to the formulation of international standards and practices.

Each of several international development organizations shares a common purpose that includes tourism development. The better known organizations include the following:

The World Bank (WB), which lends substantial sums of money for tourism development. Most of this money is awarded in the form of low-interest loans to developing countries.

The International Bank for Reconstruction and Development, which is similar to the World Bank

United Nations Development Program (UNDP), which assists countries with a variety of development projects, including tourism

Organization for Economic Cooperation and Development (OECD), which was established by an international convention signed in Paris in 1960. The purpose of the OECD is to do the following:

1. Achieve the highest sustainable economic growth and employment and a rising standard of living in member countries while maintaining financial stability—thus contributing to the development of the world economy
2. Contribute to sound economic expansion in member as well as nonmember countries, through economic development
3. Contribute to the expansion of world trade on a multilateral, nondiscriminating basis, in accordance with international obligations

The OCED's tourism committee studies various aspects of tourism, including tourism problems, and makes recommendations to governments. The committee also works on standard definitions and methods of data collection, which are published in an annual report entitled "Tourism Policy and International Tourism in OECD Member Countries."

Other banks and organizations with similar interests include the Asian Development Bank, Overseas Private Investment Corporation, Inter-American Development Bank, and Agency for International Development.

The Pacific Area Travel Association (PATA) represents thirty-four countries in the Pacific and Asia that have united behind a common goal: excellence in travel and tourism growth. PATA's accomplishments include shaping the future of travel in the Asia/Pacific region; it has had a remarkable record of success with research, development, education, and marketing.

Domestic Organizations

The United States Travel and Tourism Administration (USTTA) is the main government agency in the United States that is responsible for the promotion of tourism. USTTA was established in 1981 by the National Tourism Policy Act. The mission of USTTA is to develop travel to the United States from other countries, expand growth of the U.S. travel industry, and encourage foreign exchange earnings. USTTA is responsible to the Secretary of Commerce, whose job it is to coordinate the various governmental policies, issues, and programs that affect tourism development.

The Travel Industry of America (TIA) is the national association that speaks for the common interests and concerns of all components of the U.S. travel industry. Its mission is to benefit the whole U.S. travel industry by unifying its goals, coordinating private sector efforts to encourage and promote travel to and within the United States, monitoring government policies that affect travel and tourism, and supporting research and analysis in areas vital to the industry. Established in 1941, TIA's membership represents more than two thousand travel-related businesses, associations, and local, regional, and state travel promotion agencies of the nation's 6.02-million-employee travel industry.

State Offices of Tourism

The next level of organizations concerned with tourism is the state office of tourism. State offices of tourism are charged by their legislative bodies with the orderly growth and development of tourism within the state. They promote information programs, advertising, publicity, and research in terms of their relationship to the recreation and tourism attractions in the state.

City-Level Offices of Tourism

Cities have also realized the importance of the "new money" that tourism brings. Many cities have established convention and visitors bureaus (CVBs) whose main function is to attract and retain visitors to the city. The convention and visitors bureaus comprise representatives of the city's attractions, restaurants, hotels and motels, and transportation. These bureaus are largely funded by the transient occupancy tax (TOT) that is charged to hotel guests. In most cities, the TOT ranges from 8 percent to 18 percent. The balance of funding comes from membership dues and promotional activities.

The Economic Impact of Tourism

The World Travel and Tourism council, a Brussels-based organization, commissioned a study from the Wharton Economic Forecasting Association. Their report put the total gross output for travel and tourism in 1993 at close to $3.2 trillion, or 6 percent of the World's gross national product (GNP). Tourism, says the study, grows about twice as fast as world GNP. Of the industry's total world spending, about 31 percent takes place in the European Community and 30 percent on the North American Continent.

International travel, according to the WTO, is expected to reach 935 million people by the year 2010—more than double the 475 million people who traveled abroad in 1992.

In 1994, an estimated 46 million overseas residents visited the United States. Nearly every state publishes its own tourism economic impact study. New York, for example, estimates its tourism revenue to be $36.7 billion; Florida, about $49.3 billion; Texas, $31 billion; and California, just over $50 billion. Tourism is Hawaii's biggest industry with revenues of $21.9 billion.

The National Travel and Tourism Awareness Council's 1993 Annual edition "The Tourism Work for America Report" indicates that travel and tourism is one of the nations's leading industry sectors:

Domestic and international travelers spent $361.8 billion on travel-related expenses (e.g., lodging, food, and entertainment) in the United States during 1992, a 5 percent increase from 1991.

Six million people were directly employed in the industry during 1992, making travel and tourism the nation's second largest employer (after health services).

Travel generated $51.6 billion in tax receipts during 1992.

During 1992, spending by international visitors within the United States was $20.4 billion higher than travel-related spending by Americans outside the United States.

During 1992, nearly 45 million international travelers visited the United States.[27]

Travel and tourism supported 183 million jobs worldwide in 1991. This represents 10.2 percent of the global workforce, according to World Travel and Tourism Council (WTTC). By employing one out of every ten workers, travel and tourism is the "world's largest employer and largest industry." The industry accounts for approximately 10.6 percent of the total employment (204 million jobs), or nearly one in every nine jobs. The report also estimates that by 1994 these jobs will account for $1.7 trillion, or 10.3 percent of all employee wages and sales worldwide.[28]

The Multiplier Effect

Tourists produce secondary impacts beyond their original expenditures. When a tourist spends money to travel, to stay in a hotel, or to eat in a restaurant, that money is recycled by those businesses to purchase more goods, thereby generating further use of the money. In addition, employees of businesses who serve tourists spend a higher proportion of their money locally on various goods and services. This chain reaction continues until there is a *leakage*, meaning that money is used to purchase something from outside the area. Figure 2–5 (next page) illustrates the multiplier effect.

"Most developed economies have a multiplier effect between 1.7 and 2.0."[29] This means that the original money spent is used again in the community between 1.7 and 2.0 times.

Tour Operators

The National Tour Association estimates that nearly five hundred thousand tours were conducted by 1,636 U.S. tour operators during 1992. These tours carried 16.5 million passengers, who spent an average of $118.38 per passenger per day on both one-day and multi-day tours.

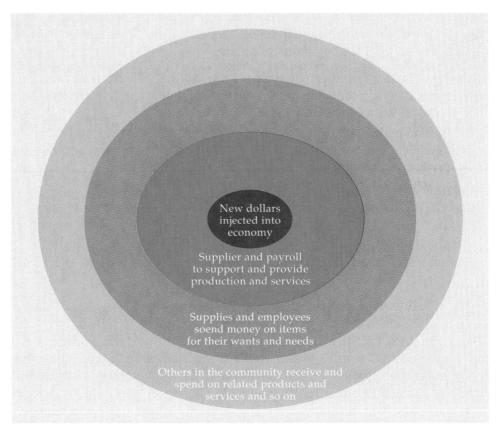

Figure 2–5   *The Multiplier Effect*

Promoters of Tourism

Travel Agencies

A travel agent is a middle-person who acts as a travel counselor and sells on behalf of airlines, cruise lines, rail and bus transportation, hotels, and auto rental companies. Agents may sell individual parts of the overall system or several elements, such as air and cruise tickets. The agent acts a broker, bringing together the client (buyer) and the supplier (seller). An agent has quick access to schedules, fares, and advice for clients about various destinations.

The first U.S. travel agents emerged in the 1880s, selling steamship and rail tickets and some arranged tours. "Ask Mr. Foster," the oldest U.S. travel agency got its name because a Mr. Foster opened a travel information office in St. Augustine, Florida. Anyone in the area who had any travel questions was told to "Ask Mr. Foster." As business grew, more offices opened and Mr. Foster decided to adopt the phrase as a business slogan. Eventually, offices opened in various parts of Florida and spread to New York and other major U.S. cities.

The American Society of Travel Agents (ASTA) has twenty thousand members in 125 countries who include both travel agencies and travel suppliers. Total airline sales processed by travel agencies reached $51 billion in 1992. The Airlines Reporting Corporation (ARC) reports that travel agencies had 32,147 retail locations in 1992. The average travel agency's yearly sales are about $3 million. According to *Travel Weekly Magazine,* the top fifty travel agencies in terms of sales generated (approximately $25 billion in revenue) represent 30 percent of total agency sales.

Agents use computer reservation systems (CRS) to access availability and make bookings. In the United States, the main vendors are as follows:

1. Sabre, which is owned by American Airlines and has over one hundred thousand terminals and a 37.4 percent market share
2. Apollo, which is owned primarily by United Airlines and has a similar market share by location but fewer terminals
3. Worldspan, which is shared by four companies (Delta, Northwest, TWA, and Abacus) and has a 19.3 percent market share with 8,500 sites in the United States
4. System One, which is owned by Continental Airlines and has a 14.9 percent marketshare and 6,800 locations.[30]

According to the American Society of Travel Agents (ASTA), a travel agent is more than a ticket seller. Agents serve their clients in the following ways:

➤ Arranging transportation by air, sea, rail, bus, car rental, etc.
➤ Preparing individual itineraries, personally escorted tours, group tours, and prepared package tours
➤ Arranging for hotel, motel, resort accommodations, meals, sightseeing tours, transfers of passengers and luggage between terminals and hotels, and special features such as tickets for music festivals, the theater, etc.
➤ Handling and advising on many details involved with travel, such as insurance, travelers checks, foreign currency exchange, documentary requirements, and immunizations and other inoculations
➤ Using professional know-how and experience (e.g., schedules of air, train, and bus connection, rates of hotels, quality of accommodations, etc.)
➤ Arranging reservations for special-interest activities, such as group tours, conventions, business travel, gourmet tours, sporting trips, etc.[31]

Approximately forty-three thousand travel agencies are currently operating in the United States, up from 29,548 in 1987. The average agency has between four and seven full-time employees. The average starting salaries are $12,428. The average salary for an agent with three to five years service is $17,975. Agents with ten plus years average $25,007. Managers make an average of $20,573. Twenty-one percent of agents receive commissions ranging between 6 to 11 percent of their sales. The average sales volume per agency is as follows:[32]

➤ 33 percent of agencies have sales less than $1 million
➤ 26 percent of agencies have sales between $1 and $3 million

➤ 27 percent of agencies have sales between $2 and $5 million

➤ 14 percent of agencies have sales more than $5 million

Agencies make their money on commissions. They usually make 10 percent on air travel within the United States and about 11 percent on international travel. Commission on hotel accommodations ranges from 10 to 15 percent and commission on cruise packages ranges from 11 to 14 percent.

Corporate Travel Manager

A corporate travel manager is a type of entrepreneur working within the framework of a large corporation. For example, Mitsubishi Electronics, in Cypress, California, was spending about $4 million in travel and entertainment. In addition, twenty-nine field offices operated independently across the United States, Canada, and Mexico. The total expenditure for travel and entertainment was $11 million. Enter John Fazio, recruited by Mitsubishi to improve efficiency and reduce costs. Fazio invited interested agencies to submit proposals based on Mitsubishi's travel needs. The fifteen initial proposals were narrowed to eight; finally two were asked to submit their best and last offers. These offers were evaluated based on Mitsubishi's criteria: technological capabilities, locations, and ability to give personal service.[33]

An interesting trend in corporate travel is agentless booking via electronic mail (E-mail). Travel is initiated at the keyboard, not at the switchboard. Increasingly, technologically savvy corporations are making travel bookings via E-mail. A forerunner in this process is Wal-Mart Stores. Seeking to increase booking efficiency and trim costs, Wal-Mart requested that World Wide develop a system, now known as Quality Agent, to meet their goals. Quality Agent is a Windows-based front end to the reservation system that processes reservations without human intervention. Currently, larger travel agencies are developing similar E-mail programs for their clients.[34]

Travel and Tour Wholesalers

Tour wholesalers consolidate the services of airline and other transportation carriers and ground service suppliers into a tour that is sold through a sales channel to the public.[35] Tour wholesaling came into prominence in the 1960s because airlines had vacant seats—which, like hotel rooms, are perishable. Airlines naturally wanted to sell as many seats as possible, and found that they could sell blocks of seats to wholesalers close to departure dates. These tickets were for specific destinations around which tour wholesalers built a tour. Wholesalers then sold their tours directly through retail agents.

The tour wholesale business is concentrated with about one hundred independent tour wholesalers; however, ten major companies account for about 30 percent of the industry's business. Tour wholesalers offer a wide range of tours at various prices to many destinations. This segment of the industry is characterized by three key types of wholesalers:

1. An independent tour wholesaler
2. An airline working in close cooperation with a tour wholesaler
3. A retail travel agent who packages tours for his or her clients

In addition, incentive travel houses and various travel clubs round out the tour wholesale business.[36]

Certified Travel Counselor (CTC)

Leading experts in travel industry worked together to form an Institute of Certified Travel Agents (ICTA). The ICTA offers specialized professional studies for those seeking higher proficiency in the travel industry. The professional designation of CTC is awarded to individuals who have successfully passed examinations and who have five years full-time experience in a travel agency or in the marketing and promotion of travel.[37]

National Offices of Tourism (NOT)

National offices of tourism seek to improve the economy of the country they represent by increasing the number of visitors and consequently their spending in the country. Connected to this function is the responsibility to oversee and ensure that hotels, transport systems, tour operators, and tour guides maintain high standards in the care and consideration of the tourist.[38] The main activities of NOTs are as follows:

➤ Publicizing the country
➤ Assisting and advising certain types of travelers
➤ Creating demand for certain destinations
➤ Supplying information
➤ Ensuring that the destination is up to expectations
➤ Advertising[39]

Destination Management Companies (DMCs)

A destination management company is a service organization within the visitor industry that offers a host of programs and services to meet clients' needs. Initially, a destination management sales manager concentrates on selling the destination to meeting planners and performance improvement companies (incentive houses).

The needs of such groups may be as simple as an airport pick-up or as involved as an international sales convention with theme parties. DMCs work closely with hotels; sometimes DMCs book rooms, and other times hotels request the DMC's know-how on organizing theme parties.

Patricia Roscoe, Chairperson of Patti Roscoe and Associates (PRA), says that meeting planners often have a choice of several destinations and might ask, "Why should I pick your destination?" The answer is that a DMC does every-

Personal Profile: Patti Roscoe

Patricia L. Roscoe, Chairman of Patti Roscoe and Associates (PRA) and Roscoe/Coltrell Inc. (RCI), landed in California in 1966, charmed by the beautiful San Diego sun compared to the cold winters in Buffalo, New York, her hometown. She was a young, brilliant middle manager who was to face the challenges of a time period when women were expected to become either nurses or teachers. She became involved with the hotel industry, working for a large private resort hotel, the Vacation Village. Those were the years to be remembered. She gained a very thorough knowledge of Southern California tourism, as well as of the inherent mechanisms of the industry. With the unforgettable help and guidance of her manager, she began to lay the foundations of her future career as a very successful leader in the field. The outstanding skills that she learned are, in fact, the very basis of her many accomplishments.

The list of her awards and honors is astounding: She earned the prestigious CITE distinction (Certified Incentive Travel Executive), she was named San Diego Woman of Accomplishment in 1983, and in February, 1990, Ms. Roscoe was honored as San Diego's 1989 Allied Member of the Year during the tourism industry Gold Key Awards. In 1990, she was given the Wonder Woman Award by the U.S. Small Business Administration for her outstanding achievements in the field. In 1993, the San Diego Convention and Visitors Bureau conferred her with the prestigious RCA Lubach Award for her contributions to the industry.

She is also extremely involved in civic and tourism organizations, including the Rotary Club, the American Lung Association of San Diego and Imperial Counties, and the San Diego Convention and Visitors Bureau.

Patti Roscoe

The key to her success perhaps lies in her remarkable skills of interacting with people. It is the human resources, in fact, that represent the major strength of PRA. Its employees are experienced, dedicated, and service oriented. But what makes them so efficient is their dedication to working together as a team. Patti Roscoe guides, inspires, and motivates these teams. She is a self-admitted "softy," a creative and emotional leader who enjoys training her employees and following their growth step by step, to eventually give them the power of initiative they deserve, as a tool to encourage their creativity and originality. She constantly seeks to balance the concept of teamwork with the individual goals and private lives of her employees. It is through the achievement of such a balance that a profitable, healthy community is preserved. PRA is a bit more than a community, however: It is a family, and just like a mother, Patti's formula is discipline and love. At the same time, Patti's leading efforts are aimed at training her employees to "think outside of the box," and "keep one's view as broad as possible," which is the only way to rise above the commonplace, the rhetorical, and the trivial, to escape provincialism, and thus become unique individuals.

That's how the magic is done. PRA excels in creating "something that becomes exclusively yours—that has never been done before." PRA is decentralized into service teams to foster an entrepreneurial environment in which initiative and creativity can be boosted at the fullest. Therefore, PRA staff design personalized, unique events to give their customers an unforgettable time.

Since its opening in 1981, PRA has become one of the most successful destination management companies in the country, providing personal, caring service characterized by flexibility and creativity.

thing from airport greetings, transportation to the hotel, VIP check-in, theme parties, sponsor programs, organizing competitive sports events, and so on, depending on budget.

Sales managers associated with DMCs obtain leads, which are potential clients, from the following sources:

➤ Hotels
➤ Trade shows
➤ Convention and visitors bureaus

➤ Cold calls
➤ Incentive houses
➤ Meeting planners

Each sales manager has a staff or team that would include the following:

Special events manager, who will have expertise in sound, lighting, staging, and so on

Accounts manager, who is an assistant to the sales manager

Operations manager, who coordinates everything, especially on-site arrangements, to ensure that what is sold actually happens

For example, Patti Roscoe's destination management company recently organized meetings, accommodations, meals, beverages, and theme parties for two thousand Ford Motor Company dealers in nine groups over three days.

Roscoe also works closely with incentive houses, such as Carlson Marketing or Meritz Travel. These incentive houses approach a company and offer to evaluate and set up incentive plans for the sales team, including whatever it takes to motivate them. Once approved, Carlson contacts a destination management company and asks for a program.

In conclusion, thousands of companies and associations hold meetings and conventions all over the country. Many of these organizations use the services of professional meeting planners, who in turn seek out suitable destinations for the meetings and conventions.

Why People Travel

Meetings and Conventions

According to the Convention Liaison Council, meetings and conventions generated $75.6 billion. Of this amount, $49.9 billion was from conventions and expositions, $23.1 billion came from meetings, and $2.7 billion from incentive travel.[40]

Pleasure Travel

Most domestic travel (69 percent) is for pleasure purposes. Approximately 636.4 million person-trips were taken for pleasure during 1992, according to the United States Travel Data Center's (USTDC) national travel survey. Nearly half of all the pleasure travelers visited friends and relatives.

Why do people travel? The answers depend on the individual and his or her cultural conditioning. The answers also have psychological and sociological aspects.[41] Lundberg suggests the reasons that travelers give for traveling may not be totally accurate; there may be deeper motives that even they themselves do not understand, are not aware of, or do not wish to articulate.[42]

The motivation for pleasure travel can be compared to Maslow's hierarchy of human needs. Maslow suggests that people have five sets of basic need:[43]

1. Physiological needs: food, water, oxygen, sex, etc.
2. Safety needs: security, stability, order, protection
3. Love needs: affection, identification, belonging (family and friends)
4. Esteem needs: self-respect, prestige, success, achievement
5. Self-actualization needs: self-fulfillment

Some people in their late teens and early twenties may be the sun, sand, and sea travelers—the spring break variety. Others may be more interested in the cultural and sporting activities associated with travel—or even the educational aspects.

McIntosh suggests that basic travel motivations can be divided into four categories:[44]

1. Physical motivator: Physical rest, sporting and beach activities, healthful and relaxing entertainment
2. Cultural motivator: The desire for knowledge of other countries—music, art, folklore, dances, paintings, and religion
3. Interpersonal motivator: The desire to meet new people; to visit friends or relatives; to escape from the routine, family, or neighbors; or to make new friends
4. Status and prestige motivator: The desire for recognition, attention, appreciation, and a good reputation

When surveyed, people tend to list the following reasons for travel:

To experience new and different surroundings
To experience other cultures
To rest and relax
To visit friends and family
To view or participate in sporting/recreational activities

Travel is likely to increase in the coming years, which will have a significant impact on tourism. Some of the reasons for the anticipated increases are as follows:

Longer Life Span.   The average person in the United States now has a life expectation of about seventy-five years. In fact, in just a few years, some baby-boomers will be taking early retirement.

Flexible Working Hours.   Today, many people work four ten-hour days and have longer weekends. Of course, many others—especially in the hospitality and tourism industries—work on weekends and have leisure time during the week.

Early Retirement.   Increasingly, people are being given the opportunity to retire at fifty-five. This early retirement is generally granted to employees with thirty years of service to their company or government agency.

Greater Ease of Travel.   Today, it is easier to travel on holidays and weekends, for both business and leisure purposes. Each mode of travel affords increasing opportunities to take advantage of the additional leisure time.

Tendency to Take Shorter, More Frequent Trips.   People now tend to take shorter but more frequent minivacations, rather than taking all of their vacation time at once. Europeans generally take much longer vacations than North Americans. For them, four weeks is the normal vacation benefit of new employees, and six weeks is typical after a few years service.

Increase in the Standard of Living.   More people in many developing countries have increased their income and wish to travel. China, with its new-found enterprise zones is producing hundreds of thousands of entrepreneurs who will soon be traveling to foreign countries. Millions of East European residents of the former Soviet Block countries now have the capability and the right to travel. In total, an additional three hundred million people will soon have passports.

Stanley Plog, a respected social scientist has suggested that travelers may be separated into two extremes: (1) psychocentrics, who prefer familiar travel destinations and (2) allocentrics, who prefer new and different destinations.

Most travelers fall into a large bell-shaped curve between these two extremes. Figure 2–6 illustrates the types of destinations that psychocentrics and allocentrics are likely to visit. Psychocentrics, as the figure illustrates, prefer to travel to well-known destinations that have been visited by millions before. These destinations tend to be constant and predictable. Allocentric personalities tend to be more adventurous, curious, energetic, and outgoing; they will usually be attracted to novel destinations like the South Pacific, Asia, and Africa. Generally, twice as many people are inclined to be allocentric. This has an effect on small-scale tourist areas. First visited by allocentrics, the area (be

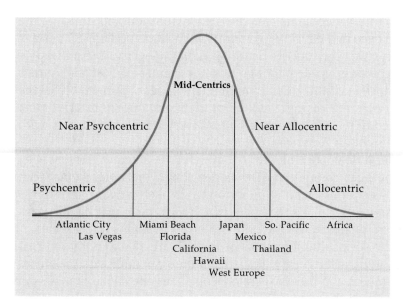

Figure 2–6 *Psychocentric and Allocentric Types of Destinations* (Adapted from Stanley Plog, "Why Destination Areas Rise and Fall in Popularity," a paper presented to the Southern California Chapter of the Travel Research Association, October 10, 1972, as cited in Edward Mayo and Lance Jarvis, *The Psychology of Leisure Travel,* Boston: CBI Publishing Company, 1981, p. 118.)

it a village, town, or resort) then becomes more popular and is forced into becoming more commercialized. Waikiki Beach on Oahu is an example of this—as few as thirty years ago there were no high-rise hotels there.

Social and Cultural Impact of Tourism

From a social and cultural perspective, tourism can leave both positive and negative impacts on communities. Undoubtedly, tourism has made significant contributions to international understanding. World tourism organizations recognize that tourism is a means of enhancing international understanding, peace, prosperity, and universal respect for, and observance of, human rights and fundamental freedom for all without distinction as to race, sex, language or religion. Tourism can be a very interesting sociocultural phenomenon. Seeing how others live is an interest of many tourists, and the exchange of sociocultural values and activities is rewarding.

Providing that the number of tourists is manageable and that they respect the host community's sociocultural norms and values, tourism provides an opportunity for a number of social interactions. A London pub or a New York café are examples of good places for social interaction. Similarly, depending on the reason for the tourist visit, myriad opportunities are available to interact both socially and culturally. Even a visit to another part of the United States would be both socially and culturally stimulating. For example, New Orleans has a very diverse social and cultural heritage. Over the years, the city has been occupied by Spanish, French, British, and Americans. The food, music, dance, and social norms are unique to the area.

However, sociocultural problems can also result from tourism. Imagine the feelings of an employee in a developing country who earns perhaps $5 per day when he or she sees wealthy tourists flaunting money, jewelry, and a life-style not obtainable. Another example might be nude or scantly clad female tourists sun bathing in a Moslem country. Critics argue that, at best, tourism dilutes the culture of a country by imposing the culture of the mass tourism market. Most of the food prepared in the Western-style hotels is American or European, with perhaps the addition of an Americanized local dish.

Most resorts offer little opportunity for meaningful social interaction between the tourist and the host community. Developers build the hotel (which can cause disruptions as well as creating opportunities); likely as not, an international hotel company will manage the hotel, which may mean that the top positions are filled by non-natives, leaving only the lower positions to the locals.

Proponents of the sociocultural benefits of tourism are able to point out that tourism is a clean and green industry, that some hotels are built with great concern for the environment and use local crafts people, designers, and materials in order to harmonize with the locals. Tourism brings new revenue to the area; it also creates and maintains higher levels of employment than if there were no tourism. In some countries, a hotel may be restricted as to the number of foreign employees and the length of their contract. This allows for the promotion of the local employees to higher positions. Tourism may act as a catalyst for the development of the community because taxes help the government provide other services such as schools, hospitals, and so on. In addition, tourists often enjoy the cultural exchanges they have at all levels in the community. The excursions, shopping, dancing, and so on serve to embellish the tourists' experiences.

Tourism is not likely to have a significant sociocultural impact in developed countries, where the economy is active and well diversified.[45] The most noticeable change in established value patterns and behavior occurs when tourism is a major contributor to the gross national product.

In some developing countries tourism is a major contributor to the GNP. However, tourism may contribute to the generation gap between the young, who are quick to adapt to the ways of the tourists, and the older people, who hold more traditional values.

Efforts to preserve the cultural heritage of a community may be further eroded when tourist "junk" is imported and offered for sale to tourists. In every society, people have opposing points of view about tourism development and cultural heritage preservation. The important thing to remember is to strike a balance between what is appropriate for a destination in terms of the number of tourists and the type of tourists that the community is capable of sustaining.

An example of how tourism can have a negative impact is shown in the center of Paris, in the once-beautiful park known as the Bois de Bologna, which now looks more like a refugee camp. Tourists have been allowed to take over with a massive campsite that includes dilapidated trailers, laundry hanging on make-shift clothes lines, and pets along for the vacation. This is a real shanty town in the heart of one of the world's most beautiful cities.

Further examples of tourism pollution include the famous beaches in the south of France. The Cote d'Azure for years has been a popular haunt of the

Beach Scenes Cote d'Azure (Used with permission of the French Government Tourist Office.)

Corporate Profile: Club Med

In 1950, a Belgian diamond cutter and water polo champion conceived the first Club Med village, funded with army surplus tax money, on the little Spanish island of Majorca. The goal of that first resort was to unite people from diverse backgrounds, encourage them to share a good time, and offer them a unique escape from the stress and the tension of the everyday events of post–World War II Europe. The first adventurous vacationers to experience that new environment were mostly young couples or singles, living together in a beautiful natural setting, enjoying the atmosphere of camaraderie and no worries, playing sports, or just simply relaxing on a warm soft beach.

The following decade was a particularly profitable one, because of the overall social climate that characterized the 1960s. The young generation, generally speaking, was wrapped up in a whirl of ideals, such as peace, communion, and the sharing of feelings and experiences, all in the framework of a return to nature. The so-called flowerchild phenomenon saw the young long for a return to primitive purity, innocence, and freedom of expression. It is not surprising, then, that Club Med's clientele rose by 500 percent in that decade. In fact, the features that characterized the resorts made them just the right environment to meet the needs of this target market. Club Med began its expansion throughout the Mediterranean coastlines and islands, including Greece and Italy. Centers began to spring up on the coasts of Africa and the Middle East. Today Club Med–short for Mediterranean–has more than one hundred resorts and vacation villages around the world, hosted by twenty-eight countries in the Mediterranean as well as in the Caribbean, Africa, Mexico, the Bahamas, South Pacific, South America, Asia, and the United States. The little village in Majorca blossomed into a colorful, joyful, sunny, colossal empire: Club Med is the world's largest vacation village organization and the ninth largest hotel chain, with ninty-three thousand beds and twenty thousand employees. More than 9 million guests have come to the villages since 1950.

Today's philosophy doesn't differ much from the original one. Club Med intends to provide a spectacular natural setting in which its guests can enjoy life and its amenities, away from the troubles and the worries of the everyday frantic rat race. The theme on the printed advertisements points straight to this: "Club Med: Life as it should be." Sports, various entertaining activities, good food, real concern for guests' needs, and a carefree life-style worked wonders. Imagine all of these amenities in the context of white sand beaches and a clear blue sea that seems to stretch out indefinitely to meet a virtually cloudless sky at the horizon.

Club Med's original formula was copied by several other organizations in the travel and tourism industry. The increased competition caused Club Med to revise its management strategies and develop a different product in order to gain and hold market share. Changes in the industry were accompanied by social changes. As the years went by, the baby-boomers of the 1960s and 1970s grew up, got married, and began to travel with their families. The target market thus changed again, and the necessity to change along with the market was promptly acknowledged.

The policy Club Med's managers embraced was one of differentiation and flexibility. Through assiduous market research, studies, and surveys, Club Med identified the continuously changing needs and characteristics of both the market and the clientele. On the basis of their results, they were able to take effective action to keep up with such evolution. Marketing strategies therefore were re-elaborated, and the product Club Med offers was repackaged accordingly to the demands of the industry, while still remaining faithful to the original philosophy. The image of Club Med was also reconsidered in order to determine the most appropriate one at all times.

Other significant changes included an entrance in the cruise business—Club Med I is a luxurious cruise ship that offers the excitement of yachting (thanks to a retractable platform that allows activities such as waterskiing, diving, etc.) together with the comforts of the cruise. Activities within the village were also improved and upgraded, following the guests' requests for more in-depth sports teaching, more amenities in the rooms, specialized restaurants, more security, and communication tools.

The clientele target was also widened: Club Med now attempts to attract customers other than the original youth/couples. As a consequence, the individual villages were updated by specializing in a particular area. Although all clubs offer the same basic services, some focus mainly on sports, some on tours and excursions, some on convention and meeting facilities, some on entertainment, and so on. Customers now range from sports enthusiasts to families (mini-clubs and baby-clubs were recently established), honeymooners, and corporate clients. The new trend at the moment is that of finding ways to attract the older clientele.

Club Med also has had another innovative idea: Wild Card, which offers a bargain rate to vacationers who don't mind gambling on which village they visit. Wild Card confirms participants on a one-week vacation at one of Club Med's Villages in the Bahamas, Caribbean, or Mexico for $999 per person, double occupancy; this is a savings up to $500 over the weekly standard rate. Included is the price of the airfare from specified gateway cities.

Wild Card presents a win-win situation. Club Med wins because it can utilize vacant space on air charters and accommodations; guests win because they get a great vacation at a bargain price. As a result, about 75 percent of wild card bookings are from first-time guests. This means a great deal of new business is being generated in addition to Club Med's 50 percent repeat business rates—one of the highest in the resort industry.[1]

To cope with the changes and implementations in the global structure of the villages, human resources staff (GOs—gentle organizers, etc.) also have been selected and trained more thoroughly. GOs come from all over the world; they must have some foreign language proficiency (to keep up with an extremely cosmopolitan clientele), skills in sports or entertainment, and, most of all, be extremely enthusiastic and very people oriented. In fact, the spirit of the village depends almost entirely on the creative ideas and contact generated by the staff.

Overall, Club Med has shown a very remarkable ability to reinvent itself according to the continuous evolution of the market and society. The genuine commitment to excellence that has been demonstrated should help Club Med retain its status as the ultimate destination resort organization.

[1] Joel Sleed, "Club Med Tells Its Customers Where to Go," *San Diego Union-Tribune,* February 4, 1993, p. D4.

rich and famous. Cities like Nice, St. Tropez, and Juez le Pain became celebrity hangouts once they were discovered in the 1950s and 1960s. Now at the height of the season, public beaches are wall-to-wall people. Private beaches will rent a parasol and a 6' x 4' plot for the day for approximately $40.

The effects of too many tourists have necessitated that the famous Cathedral of Notre Dame restrict the number of visitors to four hundred per day, down from several thousand. The sheer number of visitors was causing serious problems for the building.

Similarly, the prehistoric cave paintings at Lascoux in southwest France were closed in 1964 to prevent further deterioration of the paintings. Human breath, which gives off CO_2, is harmful to paint. Now, its replica, Lascoux II, which was built to allow visitors a chance to experience the caves, is in trouble for the same reason.

Just imagine what will happen when another three hundred million people become tourists by virtue of increasing standards of living and more people obtaining passports. Currently only 10 percent of the U.S. population has a passport. The population of Eastern Europe and the nouveau riche of the Pacific Rim countries will substantially add to the potential number of tourists.

The Prehistoric Cave Paintings at Lascoux (Used with permission of the French Government Tourist Office.)

Ecotourism

Ecotourism is a buzzword attached to the growing trend in adventure tourism. Ecotourism has swept across the Americas and has taken hold in Asia and Europe during the past few years.

In practical terms, ecotourism tour operators prepare participants for encounters by educating them about local regions, culture, animals, and plants.

Ecotourism strives to minimize visitor impact on natural environments and cultures by keeping groups small and well organized. Whether it's a visit to the Brazilian rain forest, a Safari in Kenya, or bird watching on the Delaware shore, participants are able to play a valuable role in conserving the natural heritage of the area they visit.

Summary

1. Tourism can be defined as the idea of attracting, accommodating, and pleasing groups or individuals traveling for pleasure or business. It is categorized by geography, ownership, function, industry, and travel motive.
2. The development of tourism started before the Industrial Revolution and continued parallel with the improvement of means of transportation: railway, automobile, aircraft, and cruise ships.
3. Tourism involves international interaction and, therefore, government regulation. Several organizations, such as the World Tourism Organization, are responsible for environmental protection, tourism development, immigration, and cultural and social aspects of tourism.
4. Tourism is the world's largest industry and employer. It affects other industry sectors, such as public transportation, food service, lodging, entertainment, and recreation. In addition, tourism produces secondary impacts on businesses that are affected indirectly, which is known as the multiplier effect.
5. Travel agencies, tour operators, travel managers, wholesalers, national offices of tourism, and destination management companies serve as middle persons between a country and its visitors.
6. Physical needs, the desire to experience other cultures, and an interest in meeting new people are some of the motives people have when they travel. Because of flexible work hours, early retirement, and the easy accessibility of traveling, tourism is constantly growing.
7. From a social and cultural perspective, tourism can further international understanding and economically improve a poor country. However, it can also disturb a culture by confronting it with mass tourism, causing the destruction of natural sites. A trend in avoiding tourism pollution is Ecotourism.

Review Exercises

1. Give a broad definition of tourism and explain why people are motivated to travel.
2. Describe the importance of Benz, Ford, and Lindbergh in the development of tourism.
3. Explain the differences in the development of the European and U.S. railway systems.
4. What is the significance of the Airline Deregulation Act of 1978?
5. Give a brief explanation of the economic impact of tourism. Name two organizations that control or further the economic impact of tourism.
6. Choose a career in the tourism business and give a brief overview of what your responsibilities would be.
7. Discuss the positive and negative impacts that tourism can have on a country in consideration of tourism pollution and ecotourism.

Key Words and Concepts

Airline Deregulation Act of 1978	Destination-management companies	Multiplier effect	Strategic alliance
The Bermuda agreement	Economic impact of tourism	National tourism organizations	Tour operators
Business travel	Hub-and-spoke system	Pacific Area Travel Association	Tourism
Concorde	International Air Transportation Association	Pleasure travel	Tourism promotion organizations
Conventions and visitors' bureaus	International Development Organization	Segmenting the cruise market	Travel agents
Corporate travel manager			Travel and tours wholesalers
			World Tourism Organization

Notes

[1] *American Hotel and Motel Report*, 1, 7, July/August, 1993.

[2] A. J. Butkarat and S. Meddlik, *Tourism: Past, Present and Future.* London: Heinemann, 1974, p. 3.

[3] Ibid., p. vii.

[4] Robert McIntosh and Charles R. Goeldner, *Tourism Principles, Practices, Philosophies*, 6th ed. New York: John Wiley and Sons, 1990., pp. 11–13.

[5] Ibid.

[6] Edward J. Mayo and Lance P. Jarvis, *The Psychology of Leisure Travel: Effective Marketing and Selling of Travel Services.* Boston: CBI Publishing Company, 1981, p. 5.

[7] Donald E. Lundberg, *The Tourist Business*, 6th ed. New York: Van Nostrand Reinhold, 1990, p. 16.

[8] Ibid., p. 16.

[9] Lundberg, op. cit., p. 16.

[10] Jan Van Harssel, *Tourism: An Exploration*, 3d ed. Englewood Cliffs, N.J.: Prentice Hall, 1994.

[11] Paul R. Dittmer and Gerald G. Griffen, *The Dimensions of the Hospitality Industry: An Introduction.* New York: Van Nostrand Reinhold, 1993, p. 359.

[12] Lundberg, op. cit., p. 93.

[13] Dittmer and Griffen, op. cit., p. 352.

[14] Ibid.

[15] Van Harssel, op. cit., p. 27.

[16] Ibid.

[17] Ibid.

[18] Dittmer and Griffen, op. cit., p. 365.

[19] Stewart Toy and Andrea Rothman, "Air France: Is This the Right Flight Plan?" *Business Week*, August 2, 1993, p. 48.

[20] Ibid.

[21] Michele McDonald, "USAir's Lagow: BA Link's Strategic Partnership," *Travel Weekly*, August 30, 1993, p. 10.

[22] Kevin Kelly and Aaron Bernstein, "Labor Deals That Offer a Break from Us vs. Them," *Business Week*, August 2, 1993, p. 30.

[23] Ibid.

[24] Marc Levinson, "Something Novel in the Air," *Newsweek*, August 2, 1993, p. 34.

[25] Lundberg, op. cit., p. 102.

[26] McIntosh and Goeldner, op. cit, p. 43.

[27] National Travel and Tourism Awareness Councils, *The Tourism Work for America Report.* Washington, D.C., 1993, p. 3.

[28] CHRIE Communique, *Travel and Tourism: World's Largest Industry*, May 15, 1994, p. 1.

[29] Robert Christie Mill and Alastair M. Morrison, *The Tourism System: An Introductory Text.* Englewood Cliffs, N.J.: Prentice Hall, 1985, p. 228.

[30] Rik Fairlie, "Dividing the Pies," *Travel Weekly*, November 8, 1993, p. 1.

[31] Courtesy of the American Society of Travel Agents.

[32] Rick Fairlie, "It's in the Mail," *Travel Weekly*, May 31, 1993, p. 32.

[33] Based on Stephen Arrendell, "Getting It Together," *Travel Weekly*, May 31, 1993.

[34] Rick Fairlie, "It's in the Mail," op cit.

[35] Tour Wholesaler Industry Study, Touche Ross & Co., 1976, p. 68, as cited in Mill and Morrison, op. cit., p. 400.

[36] This section draws on McIntosh and Goeldner, op cit., pp. 100–103.

[37] This section draws on Gregory, Aryear, *The Travel Agent: Dealer in Dreams*, 3d ed. Englewood Cliffs, N.J.: Prentice Hall, 1989, p. 21.

[38] Ibid., p. 276.

[39] Ibid.

[40] Incentive travel is a technique used to motivate employees by offering travel and vacation accommodation rewards for achieving specific goals.

[41] Donald E. Lundberg, *The Tourist Business*, 2d ed. Boston: CBI Publishing, 1974, p. 118.

[42] Mayo and Jarvis, op. cit., p. 146.

[43] Abraham Maslow, "A Theory of Human Motivations," *Psychological Review*, 50, 1943, pp. 370–396.

[44] Robert W. McIntosh and Charles R. Goeldner, op cit., p. 131.

[45] Van Harssel, op. cit., p. 190.

The Hotel Business: Development and Classification

3

After reading and studying this chapter you should be able to do the following:

- ➤ Describe briefly the development of the U.S. lodging industry
- ➤ Define the following terms: *hotel franchising, partnerships, leasing, syndicates,* and *management contracts*
- ➤ Discuss financial aspects of hotel development
- ➤ Classify hotels by type, location, and price
- ➤ Explain vertical and horizontal integration
- ➤ List ways hotels cater to the business and leisure travel markets
- ➤ Describe the effects of a global economy on the hotel industry

Hotel Development in the United States

Hotels in North America began as inns or taverns, which were vastly different from today's full-service hotels. It is interesting to trace this development over the years, especially from a financial viewpoint.

The industry, as we know it today with a number of high-profile companies, is vastly different from even a generation ago. The taverns in Boston were called "the candles of liberty" by Patrick Henry. In fact, the Green Dragon and the Bunch of Grapes were meeting places for the Sons of Liberty during the American Revolution. The Boston Tea Party was planned in the Green Dragon.[1]

Taverns soon sprang up in all the colonies and became a focal point of the community. They flourished, not only in the major cities, but also along the communication routes known as turnpikes. Later, canals also became a part of the growing transportation system. Naturally, then as now, people on the move required food, beverages, and accommodations.

The first hotel to open in the United States was the seventy-room City Hotel on Broadway, New York City, in 1794. This was followed by others, notably the 170-room Tremont House, which opened in Boston in 1829. The Tremont was the first hotel to have bellpersons, front desk employees, locks on guestroom doors, and free soap for guests.

Perhaps because there was no royalty in the New World, hotels emerged as people palaces. Each new hotel featured a new architectural design, displayed grand lobbies, ballrooms, superior plumbing, or some other guest convenience—such as elevators, which were first installed in New York's Fifth Avenue Hotel in 1859. Electricity was first used by the Hotel Everett on Park Row in New York.[2]

Transportation changed the nature of the hotel industry. First it was rail travel that prompted hotels to develop as the popular resorts and frontiers opened. From the Hotel del Coronado, near San Diego, California, to the five-star Breakers Resort in Palm Beach, Florida, and the famous Greenbriar Resort in West Virginia, railroads and hotels complemented one another in providing the traveling public with remarkable experiences. In Canada, the Canadian Pacific (CP) railroad enabled passengers to view the spectacular Rocky Mountains. To this day, CP operates the largest chain of Canadian hotels.

The first motel was opened by California architect Arthur Hineman in 1925, in San Luis Obispo, California. This location is about 200 miles north of Los Angeles—a long day's drive in those days. Hineman designed the motel so guests could drive right up to the doors of their rooms or to an adjacent garage. The forty one-story bungalows were grouped around a courtyard. It cost $80,000 to build in its ornate Spanish-mission style, with a three-tiered tower, white pillars, and tree-fringed courtyard—unusually luxurious for the 1920s.

During the Depression of the 1930s, many hotel owners defaulted on their mortgages. As a result, banks and institutions soured on the idea of mortgage

The Motel Inn, San Luis Obispo, California

loans for hotels. For this reason, few downtown hotels were built after World War II, even in the 1950s and early 1960s. Hilton, the preeminent emerging chain at the time, acquired and rebuilt older hotels, like the Stevens in Chicago (now the Chicago Hilton and Towers) and the Plaza in New York.[3]

The automobile created a wave of hotel and motel construction in the 1940s, 1950s, and 1960s. As Americans began to explore the open road, hotels and motels developed to cater to their accommodation needs. Likewise, air transportation was another catalyst for the development and redevelopment of city hotels and destination resorts. In 1958, the Boeing 707 enabled faster transcontinental and trans-Atlantic flights. Business and leisure travel took off on what was to become the largest worldwide industry.

The vibrant economy of the 1950s meant that there was more disposable income for travel and tourism. With the advent of rail, automobile (car and bus), and air transportation, society became more mobile. This mobility began to transform the industry from small, wholly owned, and independently operated properties to the concepts of development by franchising, partnership, leasing, and management contracts.

Franchising

Franchising in the hospitality industry is a concept that allows for a company to expand more rapidly by using other people's money than if it had to acquire its own financing. The company or franchisor grants certain rights, for example, to use its trademark, signs, proven operating systems, operating procedures and possibly reservations system, marketing know-how, purchasing discounts, and so on for a fee. In return, the franchisee agrees by signing the franchise contract to operate the restaurant, hotel, and so on in accordance with the guidelines set by the franchisor. Franchising is a way of doing business that benefits both the franchisor—who wants to expand the business rapidly—and the franchisee—who has financial backing but lacks specific expertise and recognition. Some corporations franchise by individual outlets and others franchise by territory.

Franchising began in the hotel industry in 1907, when the Ritz Development Company franchised the Ritz-Carlton name in New York City.[4]

Howard Johnson began franchising his hotels in 1927. This allowed for a rapid expansion, at first on the East Coast and later in the Midwest and finally in the mid-1960s into California. Today, there are more than nine hundred restaurants in the chain.

Holiday Inns (now Holiday Corporation, the largest lodging enterprise in the world) also grew by the strategy of franchising. In 1952, Kemons Wilson, a developer, had a disappointing experience while on a family vacation when he had to pay for an extra room for his children. Therefore, Wilson decided to build a moderately priced family-style hotel. Each room was comfortably sized and had two double beds; this enabled children to stay for free in their parents' rooms. In the 1950s and early 1960s, the economy and Holiday Inn grew in size and popularity. Holiday Inns added restaurants, meeting rooms, and recreational facilities. They upgraded the furnishings and fixtures in the bedrooms and almost completely abandoned the original concept of being a moderately priced lodging operation.

One of the key factors in the successful development of Holiday Corporation was that they were the first company to enter the mid-price range of the market. These inns or motor hotels were often located away from the expensive downtown sites, near important freeway intersections and the more reasonably priced suburbs. Another reason for their success was the value they offered: comfort at a reasonable price, avoiding the expensive trimmings of luxury hotels.

About this time, a new group of budget motels emerged. Motel 6 (so named because the original cost of a room was $6 a night) in California slowly spread across the country, as did Days Inn and others. Day was in the construction business and found Holiday Inns too expensive when traveling on vacation with his family. He bought cheap land and constructed buildings no more than two stories to keep the costs down. These hotels and motels were primarily for the commercial travelers and vacationing families, were located close to major highways, and were built to provide low-cost lodging without frills. Some of these buildings were of a modular construction: Entire rooms were built elsewhere, transported to the site, and placed side-by-side.

It was not until the 1960s that Hilton and Sheraton began to franchise their names. Franchising was the primary growth and development strategy of hotels and motels during the 1960s, 1970s, and 1980s. However, franchising presents two major challenges for the franchisor: maintenance of quality standards and avoidance of financial failure on the part of franchisee.

It is difficult for the franchise company to state in writing all of the contingencies that will ensure that quality standards are met. Recent franchise agreements are more specific in terms of the exterior maintenance and guest service levels. Franchise fees vary according to the agreements worked out between the franchisor and the franchisee; however, an average agreement is based on 3 or 4 percent of room revenue.

The world's largest franchisor of hotels, with 3,413 hotels, is Hospitality Franchise System (HFS) of Parsippany, New Jersey. Choice Hotels International, ranked second with 2,487 franchised hotels, is a subsidiary of the Blackstone Group, New York. Holiday Inn Worldwide is now the third largest franchisor. Table 3–1 (page 60) shows the top twenty-five largest franchise chains.

Franchising provides both benefits and drawbacks to the franchisee and franchisor. The benefits to the franchisee are as follows:

➤ A set of plans and specifications from which to build
➤ National advertising
➤ Centralized reservation system
➤ Participation in volume discounts for purchasing furnishings, fixtures, and equipment
➤ Listing in the franchisor's directory
➤ Low fee percentage charged by credit card companies

The drawbacks to the franchisee are as follows:

➤ High fees—both to join and ongoing
➤ Central reservations generally producing between 17 and 26 percent of reservations
➤ Franchisees must conform to the franchisor's agreement.
➤ Franchisees must maintain all standards set by the franchisor.

The benefits to the franchise company are as follows:

➤ Increased market share/recognition
➤ Up-front fees

The drawbacks to the franchise company are as follows:

➤ The need to be very careful in the selection of franchisees
➤ Difficulty in maintaining control of standards

Partnership

Another interesting mode of developmental financing was used by Travelodge: a partnership. Under this plan a husband and wife who wanted to enter the motel business invested one-half the cost of the motel. The couple received a salary for managing the property, and profits from the operations were divided 50-50 between the company and the couple.[5] Travelodge, now a part of Forte Hotels and Motels, began and expanded utilizing the partnership arrangement.

Table 3–1
Top Twenty-five Franchise Chains

Chain	Headquarters	Total franchised properties/rooms	Additional properties/rooms (by year-end)	Total sales (US$) (1992)
1. Hospitality Franchise Systems	Parsippany, N.J.	3,646/376,730	378/26,927	
•Howard Johnson		565/62,208	69/4,450	113 franchises
•Ramada		649/103,359	88/10,795	139 franchises
•Park Inn International		35/7,282	7/1,400	$150 million plus
•Days Inns of America		1,397/142,671	181/8,500	237 franchises
•Super 8 Motels		1,000/61,210	33/1,782	n/a
2. Holiday Inn Worldwide	Atlanta	1,751/336,212	43/5,046	$5.7 billion
3. Best Western International*	Phoenix	3,349/273,851	92/10,000	$6.8 billion
4. Choice Hotels International**	Silver Springs, Md.	2,661/239,696	219/28,088	$2 billion
•Comfort		1,081/89,403	49/5,220	
•Quality		531/66,999	42/8,820	
•Clarion		80/15,071	15/2,468	
•Sleep		24/1,932	12/1,540	
•Rodeway		105/10,615	27/3,220	
•Econo Lodge		703/49,068	54/5,320	
•Friendship Inns		137/6,608	20/1,500	
5. Carlson Hospitality Group	Minneapolis	347/77,643	38/10,577	$1.9 billion
•Radisson Hotels International		268/66,976		
•Colony Hotels & Resorts		42/7,570		
•Country Lodging by Carlson		37/3,097		
6. ITT Sheraton Corp.	Boston	242/56,094	2/441	$1.8 billion
7. Promus Cos.	Memphis	402/53,547	31/2,773	n/a
•Hampton Inns		339/40,486	26/2,162	
•Homewood Suites		16/1,794	2/228	
•Embassy Suites		47/11,267	3/383	

8. **Forte Hotels Inc.**	El Cajon, Calif.	600/50,000	75/6,000	$650 million
9. **Hilton Inns Inc.**	Beverly Hills, Calif.	178/44,722	8/2,000	n/a
10. **Marriott Corp.** •Marriott Hotels, Resorts, & Suites •Residence Inn by Marriott	Bethesda, Md.	209/39,487 82/25,328 68/8,159	29/2,777 1/245 2/132	n/a
•Courtyard by Marriott		15/2,000	9/900	
•Fairfield Inn by Marriott		44/4,000	17/1,500	
11. **Accor**	Evry, France	344/31,854***	14/1,673	n/a
12. **Hospitality International Inc.** (Scottish Inns, Red Carpet Inns Passport Inn, Downtowner Inns, Master Host Inns)	Tucker, Ga.	375/24,675	70/5,130	n/a
13. **Economy Lodging Systems** (Knights Lodging)	Beachwood, Ohio	185/20,000	8/800	$148 milion
14. **Omni Hotels**	Hampton, N.H.	19/9,026	3/825	n/a
15. **National 9 Motels Inc.**	Salt Lake City, Utah	169/8,160	8/400	n/a
16. **ShoLodge Inc.** (Shoney's Inns)	Gallatin, Tenn.	60/7,500	21/1,800	n/a
17. **Budget Host International***	Arlington, Texas	163/6,535	20/900	n/a
18. **Nendels Corp.**	Seattle, Wash.	65/5,000	15/1,275	$32 million
19. **Budgetel Franchises International**	Milwaukee	21/2,200	4/500	n/a
20. **Clubhouse Inns**	Overland Park, Kan.	15/2,177	1/100	$27.5 million
21. **Admiral Benbow Inns**	Marietta, Ga.	20/2,049	6/450	n/a
22. **Americinn International**	Deephaven, Minn.	35/1,426	5/250	n/a
23. **Best Inns/Suites of America**	Marion, Ill.	15/1,409	4/262	n/a
24. **Microtel**	Rochester, N.Y.	13/1,356	5/500	n/a
25. **Inn Suites Hotels**	Phoenix	8/1,044	2/310	n/a

Reprinted with permission from *Hotel and Motel Management*, 208, 14, August 16, 1993.

Leasing

Leasing became popular in the 1950s and 1960s; it still exists, but to a lesser extent. The leasing arrangement allows both the individual and the chain to enter the market or expand within it. A hotel is leased for a percentage of gross sales, generally 20 to 50 percent.[6] For example, U.S. international hotel expansion began with the lease of the Hotel Caribe Hilton in San Juan, Puerto Rico. The government of Puerto Rico wanted to encourage tourism by having a brand name hotel with management expertise. The government leased the hotel to Hilton in return for two thirds of the gross operating profit plus marketing expenses.[7]

Several developing countries have adopted the lease concept. In Cuba, all went well until Castro took over after the Cuban Revolution. The Havana Hilton's occupancy dropped to 14 percent, which resulted in a loss. The lessons learned from this led to the management contract, which involved less risk for hotel corporations. Profit-sharing lease agreements became management contracts. A base fee of 5 percent of gross revenues was introduced, plus an incentive fee of 10 percent of the gross operating profit.

In some locations, like Western Europe, the lease was to the hotel corporation's advantage. In London, the Hilton had a twenty-five-year lease, and rent was fixed at 8 percent of the original cost with little provision for increase. As a result, Hilton took out almost 75 percent of the gross operating cost.[8]

Leasing may make a comeback with the lack of capital in the current marketplace. Hotel brokers have been looking for new ways to deal with under-financed properties. Krieger and Snyder of Scottsdale, Arizona, have developed a new type of leasing. Leasing gives the benefits of ownership without the initial capital outlay. The hotel operator or lessee manages the hotel with a lease based on gross guest room revenues. The operator is responsible for insurance, hiring and firing, food and beverage, and the marketing of the hotel. In return the operator gets a major part of every dollar of room revenue that comes into the hotel and the major part of every increase in revenue.[9]

Syndicates

Syndicates were and still are a popular form of hotel financing. A syndicate involves a group of investors who may (or may not) be friends or acquaintances of the eventual hotel operator. The group arrangement usually allows for a larger investment and a larger property, and naturally allows for the risk to be spread among the syndicate members.

Management Contracts

Management contracts have been responsible for the hotel industry's rapid boom since the 1970s. They became popular among hotel corporations because little or no up-front financing or equity was involved. Even if the hotel corporation was involved in the construction of the hotel, ownership generally reverted to a large insurance company. This was the case with the La Jolla, California, Marriott Hotel. Marriott Corporation built the hotel for about $34 million, then sold it to Paine Webber, a major investment banking firm, for about $52 million on completion. Not a bad return on investment!

The management contract usually allows for the hotel company to manage the property for a period of five, ten, or twenty years. For this, the company receives as a management fee a percentage of gross and/or net operating profit, usually about 2 to 4.5 percent of gross revenues. Lower fees in the 2 percent range are more prevalent today, with an increase in the incentive fee based on profitability. Some contracts begin at 2 percent for the first year, 2.5 the second, and 3.5 the third for the remainder of the contract.[10] Increased competition among management companies has decreased the management contract fees in the past few years. In recent years, hotel companies increasingly have opted for management contracts because considerably less capital is tied up in managing as compared with owning properties. This has allowed for a more rapid expansion of both the U.S. and international markets.

Hotel management companies often form a partnership of convenience with developers and owners who generally do not have the desire or ability to operate the hotel. The management company provides operational expertise, marketing, and sales clout, often in the form of a centralized reservation system (CRS).

Some companies manage a portfolio of properties on a cluster, regional, or national basis. The largest twenty-five management companies are listed in Table 3–2. Most of these companies manage hotels in the same classifications. This enables them to focus their efforts on managing properties of a similar nature rather than properties in different classifications.

In the early 1990s, because of plummeting real estate values, hotel-operating results and cash flows fell drastically. Recent contracts have called for an increase in the equity commitment on the part of the management company. Between 1988 and 1992, there was an increase from about 25 percent to about 42 percent in chain operators' equity contributions.[11] In addition, owners increased their operational decision-making options—something seldom done previously.

The strongest trend in contract negotiations is the expansion of the variety of contract provisions. For example, some owners may need or want equity participation. However, they may be unwilling to share control with an

Table 3–2
Top Twenty-five Management Companies

Hotel	Total Properties
1) Richfield Hotel Management	141
2) Beck Summit/ELS Managing Partners	110
3) Tharaldson Enterprises	106
4) H.I. Development Corp.	105
5) Prime Hospitality Corp.	84
6) Interstate Hotels Corp.	80
7) Motels Of America	80
8) American General Hospitality	77
9) Larken Inc.	65
10) The Continental Cos.	63
11) Windegardner & Hammons	58
12) Amerihost Properties	54
13) Hostmark Management Group	53
14) Ocean Hospitalities Inc.	50
15) Sage Development Resources	49
16) Vista Host	44
17) Servico Hotels & Resorts	40
18) John Q. Hammons Hotels Inc.	39
19) CapStar Hotels	37
20) Commonwealth Hospitality Ltd.	36
21) Universal Hotels	35
22) Atlific Hotels & Resorts	33
23) The Hotel Group	31
24) Lane Hospitality	30
25) HLC Hotels	29

Reprinted with permission from *Hotel and Motel Management*, 209, 5, March 21, 1994, p. 19.

equity partner.[12] Generally, a compromise is worked out. Hotel owners focus on management companies with the following characteristics:[13]

➤ Experience and reliability
➤ Excellence in reporting
➤ Communication and human resources
➤ Successful strategies for improved profitability
➤ Proven ability to meet rigorous operator performance standards

With international expansion, a hotel company entering the market might actively seek a local partner or owner to work with in a form of joint venture.

Financial Management and Profits

The hotel industry is characterized by a high degree of risk, which primarily is the result of two factors: the cyclical nature of demand and the high degree of capital investment.[14] A greater proportion of profit from hotels comes from the manipulation of real estate rather than from the sale of food, beverages, and lodging.

People construct hotels for a variety of reasons: pride of ownership or ego, profit from building, profit from promoting and financing, or profit from appreciation in value of the property. The great increase in value of the Hilton and Sheraton companies has not come from operating profits but from buying, selling, tax advantage, and in appreciation of value of the hotels with time. Financial management is the name of the game and the game is complex.

Perhaps the most amazing corporate development was that accomplished in just twenty-six years by Ernest Henderson. His financial skill, keen analysis, and shrewdness, combined with energy and hard work, catapulted the Sheraton Corporation from very modest beginnings to 154 hotels at his death in 1967. How was this financial success performed? It was not with Disney's magic wand! Henderson was a capitalist and an opportunist. He bought and sold hotels whenever and wherever a deal could be worked out. The incentives and depreciation won out over ego and sentiment.

Leveraged money was used whenever possible. For example, if the Sheraton Corporation was interested in buying a hotel that had a $100,000 income each year, the corporation might be willing to buy at eight times the income ($800,000). Henderson would borrow half of the $800,000 from a bank or insurance company at 6 percent interest. If the owner would agree to take a second mortgage of $500,000, Sheraton could take over the property for a cash outlay of only $100,000, or a down payment of 12½ percent.[15]

Creative Financing

The 1970s and 1980s were a difficult time for hotel expansion. Some hotels were planned for questionable markets as companies tried to stretch their abilities to manage fast growth. This situation was brought about by several factors:[16]

➤ A period of inflation-fueled expansion from 1976 to 1978, following on the heels of the recession and real estate bust of the mid-1970s
➤ A transitional period of stagnation from 1979 to mid-1981, characterized by economic stagflation and rapidly increasing inflation
➤ The recession of 1989 to 1993 was characterized by further decreases in productivity, a decreasing rate of inflation, and above-average interest rates

These factors forced lenders to be more active in the financial decision-making process regarding hotel development. Cash-flow decisions became more important, and lenders kept a watchful eye on developers who, until the early 1980s, were generally left to provide an "adequate," unaided return.

The early 1980s were years of extremely high interest rates. It was this critical factor that caused alarm bells to ring because projects were unable to meet the internal rate of return standards demanded by the lender as a condition of credit. Consequently, many projects were suspended; others were financed with short-term floating-rate loans.

Another result of the downturn in the economy and overbuilding of first-class properties in most United States cities was a softening of the real estate market. These factors led to what has now become known as *creative* or *portfolio* financing.

Portfolio financing occurs when a number of properties are cross-collateralized and cross-defaulted in a securitized format. This offers both investors and lenders a win-win situation, with greater overall protection against risk than would otherwise be possible with a single property.

By spreading the portfolio pool among more than one location or market, (e.g., resort, city center, convention, or resort properties in a variety of locations), the effect of an economic downturn on a particular property will be buffered by other properties. However, care must be exercised when setting up such an arrangement to ensure that if one property were in default of a loan payment, the lender could not automatically foreclose on all the other properties. This creative form of financing will often be able to access funds at a lower rate of interest, one of the critical factors in the success of a hotel venture.

However, in a publicly traded corporation, the chief executive officer's (CEO's) and chief financial officer's (CFO's) primary mission is to maximize the price of the organization's common stock. To do this, the CEO must constantly assess the two key determinants of share price: risk and return. All major hotel financial decisions must be viewed in terms of expected risk, expected return, and their combined impact on share price. These expected values are often difficult to measure; the process requires considerable judgment as well as factual knowledge. In some states, public funds have been used to finance hotel developments. The Westin Hotel, Providence, Rhode Island, is a good example. It was built with state funds as part of the convention center project.

Personal Profile: Conrad Hilton and Hilton Hotels Corporation

Conrad Hilton "King of Innkeepers" and Master of Hotel Finance

Hilton's success was attributed to two main strategies: (1) hiring the best managers and letting them have total autonomy, and (2) being a cautious bargainer who, in later years, was careful not to overfinance. Conrad Hilton had begun a successful career in the banking business before he embarked on what was to become one of the most successful hotel careers ever.

In 1919, while on bank business in Cisco, Texas, he bought the Mobley Hotel with an investment of $5,000. Hilton rented rooms to oil industry prospectors and construction workers. Because of high demand for accommodations and very little supply, Hilton often rented a room to three or four strangers. On some occasions, he even rented out his own room and slept in a lobby chair.

Conrad Hilton

Because Hilton knew the banking business well and had maintained contacts who would lend him money for down payments on properties, he quickly expanded to seven area hotels. Hilton's strategy was to borrow as much money as possible in order to expand as rapidly as possible. This worked well until the Great Depression of the early 1930s. Hilton was unable to meet the payments on his properties and lost several in bankruptcy proceedings.[1]

Hilton, like many great leaders, had the determination to bounce back. In order to reduce costs, he borrowed money against his life insurance and even worked on the side for another hotel company.

Hilton's business and financial acumen is legendary. *The New York Times* described Conrad Hilton as "a master of finance and a cautious bargainer who was careful not to over finance" and had "a flawless sense of timing."[2]

Hilton was the first person to notice vast lobbies with people sitting in comfortable chairs not spending any money. So he added the lobby bar as a convenient meeting place and leased out space for gift shops and news-stands. Most of the additional revenue from these operations went directly to the bottom line. The following shows a chronology of Conrad Hilton's and Hilton Corporation's highlights:

1919—Hilton bought the Mobley Hotel.
1925–The first Hilton hotel was built in Dallas, Texas.
1938—Hilton purchased the lease on the Sir Francis Drake Hotel in San Francisco, California. This was the first Hilton outside Texas.
1942—The Town House in Los Angeles became Hilton's headquarters. The Roosevelt and the Plaza in New York became Hilton's first East coast ventures.
1949—Conrad Hilton bought the lease of Waldorf Astoria in New York and made it successful because he and his organization knew how to run it. Hilton opened the first Hilton International in San Juan Puerto Rico.
1954—The Statler hotel company was bought for $111 million. At this time, this was the largest transaction in the history of the hotel industry.
1960—Conrad Hilton was made chairman of the board of Hilton Hotels Corporation.
1967—Hilton International was acquired by Trans World Airlines.
1971—The Las Vegas Hilton and the Flamingo Hilton marked Hilton's entry into the gaming market.
1977—Ownership of the building and land for the Waldorf-Astoria in New York was purchased for a mere $35 million.
1979—Conrad Hilton died at the age of 92. Baron Hilton, Conrad's son, became chairman of the board of directors.
1982—With the addition of 391 rooms, the Las Vegas Hilton became the largest hotel in the world, with 3,174 guest rooms and an extensive gaming area.
1983—Construction began on the Conrad International Hotel and Jupiters Casino on the Gold Coast of Queensland, Australia, the company's first property under Conrad International.
1984—The sixteen-hundred-room Anaheim Hilton and Towers opened adjacent to the Anaheim Convention Center in California.

[1] Paul R. Dittmer and Gerald G. Griffen, *The Dimensions of the Hospitality Industry: An Introduction.* New York: Van Nostrand Reinhold, 1993, pp. 91–92.
[2] Joan Cook, "Conrad Hilton, Founder of Hotel Chain, Dies at 92," *The New York Times,* January 5, 1979, sec. 11, p. 5.

1988—Completion of the renovations at the Hilton Hawaiian Village and the San Francisco Hilton and Towers marked the culmination of Hilton's $1.2 billion restoration and expansion program of its American hotels from coast to coast.

1989—The first Hilton suites property opened in Anaheim, California. The first Crest Hill by Hilton opened in Illinois.

1991—Hilton purchased and announced a massive nine-month renovation of the O'Hare Hilton in Chicago. Hilton established Hilton Grand Vacation Company, a nationwide system of vacation ownership resorts.

1992—Hilton assumed management of the Pointe Resorts in Phoenix, Arizona. Hilton acquired the two-thousand-room Bally's Casino Resort in Reno, Nevada.

Financing Package

The process of determining the required return involves the calculation of the appropriate level of return to compensate the firm for the risk undertaken. Financing for a hotel that is conducive to success requires that the needs and objectives of the developer, operator, and lender or investor be understood and dealt with realistically. The arrangements made depend on the state of the money market; the results of feasibility and market studies; and the strength, credit rating, and reputation of the corporations involved. Generally speaking, about 60 to 80 percent of the total budget required to bring a hotel into being can be raised by debt financing.

It must be recognized that the financing of a hotel is only a part of the total package, albeit an important part. The extent to which the property will be successful will be dependent on the quality of management. The following points may help lay the groundwork for favorable financing:

➤ Affiliation with a quality franchisor or referral group
➤ Identification with a national chain through a management contract
➤ A lease arrangement with a strong, well-recognized hotel operator
➤ Identification with a national chain by way of a joint-venture agreement
➤ Conventional first mortgage loans—the most common real estate financing, even for hotels
➤ Lenders, including insurance companies, commercial banks, investment banks, savings banks, institutional investors, pension funds, syndicates, partnerships, and families

In recent years, hotel financing in North America has experienced an influx of overseas capital; that has been both a blessing and a blight—depending on which type of financial package is agreed to.

One of the dangers of a foreign currency loan is that currency fluctuations may cause an increase or decrease in the amount of the loan repayment. Fortunately, there are safeguards, including having the loan negotiated in U.S. dollars and repaid in U.S. dollars, thereby avoiding any currency fluctuations on the part of the borrower.

Current financing conditions are the most difficult in the industry's history. Viable hotel development opportunities do exist, but developers and franchisors must be creative in locating funding. Having been caught short in the 1980s, lenders are now basing loans on more conservative occupancy and rate projections.[17]

How Some Hotels Become Overvalued

In the mid-1970s, the United States experienced 12 percent inflation and a shortage of good hotel room inventory. Approximately twenty thousand new rooms a year were constructed. This meant that there was too much money (demand) chasing too few rooms (supply). Then inflation crept up to 12 percent, with money market accounts yielding 8 to 9 percent. This meant that savings and loan institutions began to become involved in lending for domestic and commercial mortgages; they could lend at 12 to 14 percent while their clients would receive 8 to 9 percent interest on their deposits.

The insurance and pension funds industry, which at the time was cash rich, began to invest heavily in new hotels. Many of these were massive, mixed-use commercial projects consisting of hotels, office blocks, and shopping malls. In some cities, these complexes were not built for the right reasons. America's inner cities had declined in the 1960s and 1970s. However, because hotels are a catalyst for other businesses, every city mayor offered significant benefits to major hotel investments. These benefits included being given land, superstructure, construction, and tax breaks.

The hotel industry is not known as a leading industry; rather, it generally reacts to circumstances. Frequently, the hotel industry is caught by outside forces and swept along. An example of this is the fact that hotels in the 1970s and 1980s were assets managed. This was because the value of the assets—the hotel—increased in value.

In 1981, President Ronald Reagan initiated the Income Recovery Act, which was intended to rebuild America's capital structure. The depreciation period of hotels went from forty to nineteen years, and there was a 10 percent tax credit for capital improvement. Thus, as other tax loopholes closed, hotels became a hot investment item. Brokers began syndicating hotels to doctors, lawyers, and other professionals.

The so-called tax laws of 1986 significantly reduced the tax deductions corporations could take on depreciation of property. The Accelerated Cost Recovery System was modified causing the term of depreciation to go from 19 to 31½ years. This legislation had an immediate impact on the bottom lines of hotel corporations. This is still being felt today in the form of increased taxation (or more accurately a decrease in deductions). The recession that began in 1990 indicated that many hotel properties were overvalued. However, the bankers who had lent money did not want to admit that they had overvalued assets; therefore, they denied any problems. Hotel properties became highly leveraged. In fact, many could not service their debt (pay their mortgages). So the savings and loan industry and banks began to experience serious problems as federal regulators became more aware of the situation.

Another interesting example of how a hotel's fortunes go up and down is the U.S. Grant Hotel in San Diego, named after the infamous Civil War general who later became a U.S. president. The hotel opened about a hundred years ago and was successful for a number of years but eventually required an $80 million renovation program in 1986. The hotel then had a succession of owners and management companies—none of whom could pay the debt service. Ultimately, in 1994 the owners declared bankruptcy and the hotel was sold at auction for approximately $10 million. This price was considered a bargain for a 285-room property in a prime downtown location. The hotel is now being successfully managed by Joe Dunclafe and Grand Heritage Hotels.

Changes in ownership and management are not uncommon in the hotel business. In light of this, hotel operators, no matter how talented they are, must be cognizant of external factors, such as property values, interest rates, and debt service, that impact the property's operation and profitability.

Other factors fall within the domain of hotel developer; these activities include the overly creative financing that burdened many hotels with unrealistic levels of debt service. Owners, developers, operators, and lenders have each made their own peculiar contribu-

U.S. Grant Hotel, San Diego, Ca.

tion to today's hospitality industry problems. Some predictions for the lodging industry include a return to basics, global hospitality involvement, and equity/debt restructuring.[18]

Classification of Hotels

According to the American Hotel and Motel Association, the United States lodging industry consists of 44,700 hotels and motels, with a total of 3.1 million rooms. The gross volume of business generated from these rooms is $62.9 billion.

Unlike many other countries, the United States has no formal government classification of hotels. However, the American Automobile Association (AAA) classifies hotels by Diamond Award, and the Mobile Travel Guide offers a five-star Award. Of the more than twenty-one thousand star-rated establishments, fewer than 2 percent have been awarded five-star status. The guide currently bestows the five-star award to thirty-five lodging properties.

The AAA has been inspecting and rating the nation's hotels since 1977. Less than 2 percent of the 19,500 properties inspected annually throughout the United States, Canada, and Mexico earned the five-diamond award, which is the association's highest award for excellence. In 1995, the five-diamond award was bestowed on forty-six U.S. hotels and resorts in twenty states. Twelve of the properties received both the five-diamond and the five-star awards.

Hotels may be classified according to location, price, and type of services offered. This allows guests to make a selection on these as well as personal criteria. A list of hotel classifications follows:

City Center—luxury, first class, mid-scale, economy, suites
Resort—luxury, mid-scale, economy suites, condominium, time-share, convention
Airport—luxury, mid-scale, economy, suites
Freeway—mid-scale, economy suites
Casino—luxury, mid-scale, economy

Alternatively, the hotel industry may be segmented according to price. Figure 3–1 gives an example of a national or major regional brand-name hotel chain in each segment.

Budget $25–$35	Economy $35–$55	Mid-Price $55–$95	Up Scale $95–$195	Luxury $125–$425	All Suites $65–$125
	Holiday Inn Express	Holiday Inn		Crown Plaza	
Residence Inns	Fairfield Inn	Courtyard Inn	Marriott	Marriott Marquis	Marriott Suites
Motel 6		Days Inn	Omni		
		Radisson Inn	Radisson		Radisson Suites
	Ramada Limited	Ramada Inn	Ramada	Ramada Renissance	Ramada Suites
	Sheraton Inn		Sheraton	Sheraton Grande	Sheraton Suites
			Hyatt	Hyatt Regency Park Hyatt	Hyatt Suites
Sleep Inns	Comfort Inn	Quality Inn	Clarion Hotels		Quality Suites Comfort Suites
		Hilton Inn	Hilton	Hilton Towers	Hilton Suites
		Doubletree Club	Doubletree		Doubletree Suites
Thrift Lodge	Travelodge Hotels		Forte Hotels		
			Westin		
Sixpence Inn	La Quinta				
E-Z-8	Red Roof Inn				
	Best Western				
	Hampton Inn				Embassy Suites

Figure 3–1   *Hotels by Price Segment*

City Center Hotels

City center hotels, by virtue of their location, meet the needs of the traveling public for business or leisure reasons. These hotels could be luxury, mid-scale, business, suites, economy, or residential. They offer a range of accommodations and services. Luxury hotels might offer the ultimate in decor, butler service, concierge and special concierge floors, secretarial services, computers, fax machines, beauty salons, health spas, twenty-four-hour room service, swimming pools, tennis courts, valet service, ticket office, airline office, car rental, and doctor/nurse on duty or on call. Generally, they offer a signature restaurant, coffee shop, or an equivalent name restaurant, a lounge, a name bar, meeting and convention rooms, a ballroom, and possibly a fancy night spot.

City center hotels were constructed in waves; stimulated by government regulations, investors developed hotels when the climate was right. For example, tax incentives for urban renewal projects created favorable economic conditions in the 1960s. This led to the construction of new downtown hotels in many cities. Another boom time for hotel development was the 1980s. Together with convention centers and office buildings, hotels have been one of the catalysts in inner-city revitalization. The Copley Center in Boston and the Peachtree Plaza in Atlanta are examples of this.

The St. Regis Hotel in New York is another good example of a city center luxury hotel. An example of a mid-scale hotel in New York is the Ramada Hotel; an economy hotel is the Days Inn; and a suites property is the Embassy Suites.

Resort Hotels

Resort hotels came of age with the advent of rail travel. Increasingly, city dwellers and others had the urge to vacation in locations they found appealing. Traveling to these often more-exotic locations became a part of the pleasure experience. In the late 1800s, luxury resort hotels were developed to accommodate the clientele that the railways brought.

Such hotels include the famous Greenbrier at White Sulphur Springs, West Virginia, The Hotel del Coronado in Coronado (near San Diego), California, and the Homestead at Hot Springs, Virginia. In Canada, the Banff Springs Hotel and Chateau Lake Louise drew the rich and famous of the day to their picturesque locations in the Canadian Rocky Mountains.

The leisure and pleasure travelers of those days were drawn by resorts, beaches, or spectacular mountain scenery. At first, many of these grand resorts were seasonal. However, as automobile and air travel made even the remote resorts more accessible and an increasing number of people could afford to visit, many resorts became year-round properties.

Banff Springs Hotel

Resort communities sprang up in the sunshine belt from Palm Springs to Palm Beach. Some resorts focused on major sporting activities such as skiing, golf, or fishing; others offered family vacations. Further improvements in both air and automobile travel brought exotic locations within the reach of the population. Europe, the Caribbean, and Mexico became more accessible. As the years passed, some of the resorts suffered because the public's vacation plans changed.

The traditional family month-long resort vacation gave way to shorter, more frequent get-aways of four to seven days. The regular resort visitors became older; in general, the younger guests preferred the mobility of the automobile and the more informal atmosphere provided by the newer and more informal resorts.

In order to survive, the resort hotels became more astute in marketing to different types of guests. For example, some resorts allow no children in the high season because they would interfere with the quiet ambiance for guests who do not want the noise of children. Other resort hotels go out of their way to encourage families; Camp Hyatt is a prominent example. Hyatt hotels have organized a program consisting of a variety of activities for children, thereby giving the parents an opportunity of either enjoying some free time on their own or joining their children in some fun activities. Many resort hotels began to attract conventions, conferences, and meetings. This enabled them to maintain or increase occupancy, particularly during the low and shoulder seasons.

Airport Hotels

Many airport hotels enjoy a high occupancy because of the large number of travelers arriving and departing from major airports. The guest mix in airport hotels consists of business, group, and leisure travelers. Passengers with early or late flights may stay over at the airport hotel, while others rest while waiting for connecting flights.

Airport hotels are generally in the two-hundred- to six-hundred-room size and are full service. In order to care for the needs of guests who may still feel as if they are in different time zones, room service and restaurant hours may be extended, even offered twenty-four hours. More moderately priced hotels have vending machines.

As competition at airport hotels intensified, some have added meeting space to cater for business people who want to fly in, meet, and fly out. Here, the airport hotel has the advantage of saving the guests from having to go downtown.

Freeway Hotels and Motels

Freeway hotels and motels came into prominence in the 1950s and 1960s. As Americans took to the open road, they needed a convenient place to stay that was reasonably priced with few frills. Guests could simply drive up, park outside the office, register, and rent a room outside of which they could park. Over the years more facilities were added: lounges, restaurants, pools, soft drink machines, game rooms, and satellite TV.

Motels are often clustered near freeway off-ramps on the outskirts of towns and cities. Today, some are made of modular construction and have as few as eleven employees per hundred rooms. These savings in land, construction, and operating costs are passed on to the guest in the form of lower rates.

Morena Valley Travelodge #982

Casino Hotels

The casino industry is now coming into the financial mainstream, to the point that, as a significant segment of the entertainment industry, it is reshaping the U.S. economy. The entertainment sector has become a very important engine for U.S. economic growth. As a matter of fact, since the recovery of the economy in 1991, entertainment and recreation have provided the biggest boost to consumer spending, thus creating tremendous prosperity in the industry. The fastest-growing sector of the entertainment field is gambling: Casinos took in about $13 million in 1993, a figure gambling experts say will double by the year 2000. Furthermore, legalized gambling has spread from being introduced in two states in 1989 to sixteen in 1993, and by the end of the decade, thirty states are expected to sanction casinos within their borders. Casinos, which until very recently were confined to the main centers of Las Vegas and Reno, Nevada, and Atlantic City, New Jersey, now are expanding to Native American reservations, mining towns, and riverboats, especially along the Mississippi. A further trend, legalized gambling, is being gradually brought into major metropolitan areas, such as New Orleans and Chicago.

Among the factors that introduced and continuously boosted this development are the need for sources of revenue, jobs, economic development, and the stimulation of tourism. A look at some figures underlines the instant wealth that casinos can bring in: Atlantic City casinos showed $3.4 billion net revenues in 1991, with $570 million in taxes paid and forty-nine thousand jobs provided. Las Vegas, in 1992, hosted 21.8 million visitors, with an average stay of 3.3 nights—city-wide occupancy was 83.9 percent.

As compared with conventional hotels, casinos can develop a very rapid cash flow and yield higher profit levels. In addition, because of the peculiar entertaining features of this type of hotel, they generally run at high occupancy.

The traditional casinos of the legendary West, flush with profits, entered the hospitality business and became a destination unto themselves. The development includes the very structure of the casino: restaurants, entertainment centers, even golf courses now are added to the thousand-room hotels.

Casinos today attract guests with low rates, subsidized food and beverages, and incredible star entertainment. For example, consider Atlantic City, "where as long as you gamble, everything is complimentary."[19] If it isn't exactly free, it is extravagantly cheap, which attracts the great majority of guests to a casino. In fact, "Gamblers are not the typical 'upper-hand' restaurant patron," says Timothy Ryan, an economist at the University of New Orleans.

> They want to spend time in the casino. They tend to be middle or lower income. We get this image of James Bond in his tuxedo playing baccarat, but that's not the profile of the gambler. It's more the little old lady in stretchpants who plays the slot machine. Most of these visitors, then, will tend to decline good restaurants and instead take advantage of the cheap, subsidized foodservice in the casino.[20]

Richard Melman has said that he is actually interested in adding casinos to his Lettuce Entertain You Enterprises restaurant group.

The main hotel-casino companies are the Promus Group and Hilton Hotels. Promus Companies, Inc., of Memphis, Tennessee, was formed after the sale of Holiday Inn. Heavily involved in owning and operating casino hotels, they mainly concentrate in Nevada and Atlantic City, although they are actively pursuing options in riverboats and Native American Reservations. Promus is a diversified company that also operates and franchises Embassy Suites, Hampton Inns, and Homewood Suites. The Promus companies operate Harrah's Casinos in Las Vegas, Reno, Lake Tahoe, and Atlantic City, and are among the largest casino hotel operators. Both Hilton and the Promus corporation derive a substantial portion of their operating profits from casino operations.

In 1970, Conrad Hilton realized that casinos were bound to be a profitable aspect of hotel operations. He led Hilton Hotels into casino ownership by acquiring a controlling interest in the Flamingo and International Hotel—now the Las Vegas Hilton. At that time, it was the largest hotel in the world, with 40,000 square feet of gambling area. Hilton Hotels, now one of the leading hotel-casino companies, attributes two thirds of its earnings to its casino group, which includes the Flamingo Hilton and the Las Vegas Hilton in Las Vegas, the Flamingo Hotel in Laughlin, and two hotels in Reno. Through its Conrad International division, it also operates a casino in Queensland, Australia, and now has hotels in twelve countries such as Turkey, Indonesia, Egypt, Hong Kong, Greece, Belgium, the United Kingdom, Malaysia, Uruguay, and two Midwest (U.S.) riverboats.[21]

To counteract any potential dilution of market share, Las Vegas has positioned itself as a family entertainment destination. The Las Vegas hotels are, because of gambling revenues, able to offer their guests greater perceived value in attractive room rates, entertainment, and food than can resort hotels in competing cities like Orlando. As a matter of fact, the MGM casino in Las Vegas is characterized by a grand slogan that boasts: "There's no place like home." The trend, therefore, is to enhance the casino environment by adding a wider variety of recreational activities than the mere gambling. Instances of these new features are the introduction of theme parks, extravagant shows by popular entertainers, children's recreation centers, and so on.

Circus Circus is another prominent Las Vegas casino-hotel that caters to the mid-market in Las Vegas, Reno, and Laughlin. The four-thousand-room Excalibur runs at close to 100 percent occupancy by offering modest room and food rates. The Circus Circus company has another mega-operation, Luxor, with 2,526 rooms, next to the Excalibur. This, the world's first pyramid-shaped hotel, has a Nile River ride, a replica of King Tut's tomb, and a civilization ride that travels through time from ancient Egypt to the present day and into the future. Cutting-edge technology makes possible the transformation of visualization into virtual reality.

Theming has now been used in a number of new Las Vegas hotels to create a distinctive ambiance. Some themes have been inspired by or borrowed from the popularity of theme parks. The Mirage has been an innovator; this three-thousand-room megaresort has white tigers in the lobby, a gigantic aquarium with sharks behind the front

The Mirage Hotel and Casino

desk, and a dolphin pool next to the guest swimming pool. In November 1993, a sister hotel resort to the Mirage opened in Las Vegas—Treasure Island, another twenty-nine-hundred-room megaresort that caters to a mid-market clientele.

The MGM Hotel Casino and Theme Park opened in December 1993, with 5,005 rooms, including 744 suites, 175,000 square feet of gaming on one level, eight theme restaurants, an entertainment complex (including a grand production theater with seventeen hundred seats), a casino lounge, and MGM Grand Adventures—a 15,475-square-foot theme attraction at the entrance to the Las Vegas Strip. In addition, MGM offers special-events seating for 14,050 for concerts, sporting events, exhibitions, and meetings.

Caesar's operates upscale hotel-casinos in Las Vegas and Atlantic City and is considering expansion in Chicago and New Orleans. Caesar's also operates a limited-games casino on Native American land in Palm Springs, California.

To cope with accelerated growth and change in the casino industry, we are seeing a successful, new trend: joint-ventures and strategic partnerships. For

MGM

instance, MGM Grand and Primadonna Resorts will merge to create a new casino, the New York–New York, which will feature New York-theme attractions. It is scheduled to be completed in 1996. Furthermore, Mirage Resorts, Inc., and Gold Strike Resorts will unify their strength to erect a hotel casino, the Beau Rivage, on part of the Dunes hotel site. Casino hotels are big business and the winner takes all!

Gambling is a $30 billion industry that is increasing at an annual rate of 11 percent.[22] Even Donald Trump, who is no newcomer to the gaming industry, is getting in on the act by constructing two river boat casinos.

Full-Service Hotels

Another way to classify hotels is by the degree of service offered: full-service, economy, extended-stay, and all-suite hotels. Full-service hotels offer a wide range of facilities, services, and amenities, including many that were mentioned under the luxury hotel category: multiple food and beverage outlets including bars, lounges, and restaurants; both formal and casual dining; and meeting, convention, and catering services. Business features might include a business center, secretarial services, fax, in-room computer hook ups, and so on.

Most of the major U.S. cities have hotel chain representation such as Doubletree, Four Seasons, Hilton, Holiday Inn, Hyatt, Marriott, Omni, Ramada, Radisson, Ritz Carlton, Loew's, Le Meridian, Sheraton, and Westin. Some of these chains are positioning themselves as basic full-service properties. An example of this strategy is Marriott's Courtyard hotels, which have small lobbies and very limited food and beverage offerings. The resulting savings are passed on to the guests in the form of more competitive rates. Thus, the full-service market may also be subdivided into upscale and mid-priced hotels.

Economy/Budget Hotels

An economy or budget hotel offers clean, reasonably sized and furnished rooms without the frills of full-service hotels. Chains like Travelodge, Motel 6, Days Inn, and La Quinta became popular by focusing on selling beds, but not meals or meetings. This enabled them to offer rates at about 30 percent lower than the mid-priced hotels. The average rate for an economy hotel is about $30 to $50 per night.

More recent entrants to this market sector are Promus's Hampton Inns, Marriott's Fairfield, and Choice's Comfort Inns. These properties do not have restaurants or offer substantial food and beverages, but they do offer guests a continental breakfast in the lobby.

Another example of a relatively new budget concept is Microtel. In 1989, despite a credit crunch and a weak economy, a group of entrepreneurs developed a new budget concept called Microtel. Success criteria were developed: The group wanted an economy hotel product, the downside risk had to be limited, and the product would have to demonstrate a competitive advantage over other national budget chains. The result of several months of careful planning and construction was the ninety-nine-room Microtel in Rochester, New York, at a total cost of $2,798,000 or $28,263 per room. The land cost $266,000; construction, interest, taxes, furniture, and equipment cost $2,164,000. The room rates began at $29, and the occupancy was 89.4 percent in the first year. The franchise was sold a year later for a 117 percent return on investment (ROI).[23] This is a remarkable success story that illustrates that entrepreneurs can thrive even in a weak economy.

Fairfield Inn

Extended-Stay Hotels

Other hotels cater to guests who stay for an extended period. They will, of course, take guests for a shorter time when space is available. However, the majority of guests are long term. Guests take advantage of a reduction in the rates based on length of their stay. The mix of guests is mainly business and professional/technical, or relocating families.

Residence Inn

Residence Inns and Homewood Suites are market leaders in this segment of the lodging industry. These properties offer full kitchen facilities and shopping services or a convenience store on the premises. Complimentary continental breakfast and evening cocktails are served in the lobby. Some properties offer a business center and recreational facilities.

All-Suite, Extended-Stay Hotels

All-suite hotels typically offer approximately 25 percent more space for the same amount of money as the regular hotel in the same price range. The additional space is usually in the form of a lounge and possibly kitchenette area.

Embassy Suites, owned and operated by the Promus Corporation, and Residence Inn by Marriott are the market leaders in the all-suites, extended-stay segment of the lodging industry. Several of the major hotel chains have all-suite, extended-stay subsidiaries, including Radisson, Choice hotels (which dominates the economy all-suite segment with Comfort and Quality Suites), ITT Sheraton Suites, and Hilton Suites, Inc. These properties provide a closer to home feeling for guests who may be relocating, attending training seminars, or are on work-related projects.

Hotel Integration

Vertical Integration

Vertical integration is a trend that began a few years ago. Lodging companies realized that guests' accommodation needs were not just at one level; rather, they seemed to vary by price and facilities/amenities. Almost all major lodging companies now have properties in each segment of the market. An example to illustrate this point is given in Figure 3–2.

Luxury—Clarion
Midscale—Quality Inn, Quality Suites
Budget—Comfort Inn, Friendship Inns, Rodeway Inn
Economy—Sleep Inn

Figure 3–2   *Vertical Integration of Choice Hotels*

Horizontal Integration

Since Pan American opened the first of its Inter-Continental hotels back in the late 1940s, several airlines have opened or managed hotels as a form of horizontal integration. It is a natural progression for an airline, which is transporting passengers, often over great distances, to own and operate hotels for its passengers to stay in. Airlines differ in their strategies toward hotel ownership. For example, Nikko hotels are owned by Japan Airlines. However, American and United Airlines have sold their hotel interests, most likely as a result of financial difficulties they have experienced in recent years.

Business and Leisure Travel

The hotel market mix is sometimes referred to as business and leisure travel. Fifty-six percent of travelers are leisure or personal travelers, and 44 percent are on business. Business travelers tend to stay longer than leisure travelers and they account for more than half of the room nights in the United States.

Female business travelers represent 22 percent of the market, and this percentage is likely to grow.[24] Juergen Bartels, president of Carlson Hospitality, which includes Radisson hotels, estimates that there are two thirds as many women traveling alone as men and that 52 percent of all managers under the age of thirty-five are women.[25]

Hotels that meet the needs of women travelers are likely to be more prosperous. Women prefer separate floors; additional security; wide, well-lit corridors; good room service; make-up mirrors; irons/ironing boards; and hair dryers. They are also likely to pay slightly more for these features and amenities.

In recent years, there has been an increase in the leisure and personal travel market. The aging baby-boomers are boosting the middle-aged market.

However, as their children move into their late teens and become more independent, they will likely make separate vacation plans. It is unclear as to what effect this will have on hotels.

The senior market will continue to grow and be a useful way to fill the off-peak gaps when business travel is down. These off-peak gaps occur either side of major vacations and in the fall and spring when children are in school.

Airlines have had a major impact on hotel occupancy by offering flights at a reduced rate if they include a Saturday night stopover. This allows many business, convention, and trade show attendees to fly back home on a Sunday, which would otherwise be a quiet day.

Best, Biggest, and Most Unusual Hotels and Chains

So which is the best hotel in the world? The answer may depend on whether you watch the "Lifestyles of the Rich and Famous" or read polls taken by a business investment or travel magazine. According to the article "The World's Best Hotels," written for the *Institutional Investor,* the Oriental Hotel in Bangkok, Thailand, was for several years rated number one in the world by a poll of one hundred bankers from around the world. The Oriental was followed by the Regent of Hong Kong, Vier Jahrenzeiten of Hamburg, The Mandarin Oriental of Hong Kong, and the Connaught of London. By 1992, that list had changed, with the Regent Hong Kong and the Bel-Air of Los Angeles being number one and two respectively. Singapore's Shangri-La was third, bringing the total of Asian hotels in the top ten to six.[26]

The Biggest

The largest hotel in the world is the 5,505-room MGM Grand in Las Vegas. Table 3–3 (page 80) shows the twenty-five largest hotel chains in the world.[27]

The Best Hotel Chains

The Ritz-Carlton and the Canadian-owned and -operated Four Seasons are generally rated the highest quality chain hotels. In 1993, Ritz-Carlton hotels were awarded the Malcolm Baldrige National Quality Award. Congress created this award in 1987 to promote and recognize quality achievements in U.S. businesses. Named after the late Secretary of Commerce Malcolm Baldrige, an early proponent of total quality management (TQM), the award is regarded as the ultimate prize among those U.S. companies that pride themselves on the quality of their products and services.[28] Ritz-Carlton has long been recognized as one of the best luxury hotel chains in the industry; however, president and chief operating officer (COO) Horst Schulze wanted more. "We

Table 3–3
Twenty-five Largest Hotel Chains as of June 30, 1994

Top 25 Largest Hotels in the world

NAME OF COMPANY	NUMBER OF GUESTROOMS	NUMBER OF PROPERTIES	NUMBER OF COUNTRIES REPRESENTED
1. Hospitality Franchise Systems—*Parsippany, N.J.*	407,245	4,041	5
2. Holiday Inn Worldwide—*Atlanta*	354,817	1,891	61
3. Choice Hotels International—*Silver Springs, Md*	284,509	3,219	32
4. Best Western International—*Phoenix*	277,467	3,363	54
5. Accor—*Paris*	252,887	2,205	73
6. Marriott International—*Bethesda, Md*	175,181	806	45
7. ITT Sheraton—*Boston*	127,762	396	61
8. Hilton Hotels Corp.—*Beverly Hills, Calif.*	94,092	230	9
9. Carlson Hospitality Group—*Minneapolis*	79,435	335	39
10. Forte plc—*London*	76,450	801	39
11. Promus Cos.—*Memphis*	75,801	540	3
12. Club Méditerranée—*Paris*	65,000	262	36
13. Hyatt Hotels Corp.—*Chicago*	54,111	103	4
14. Hilton International—*Watford, England*	52,872	164	49
15. Inter-Continental Hotels—*London*	50,000	134	55
16. Renaissance Hotels & Resorts—*Coral Gables, Fla.*	49,438	134	39
17. Golden Tulip International—*Hilersum, Netherlands*	44,000	220	50
18. Sol Group—*Mallorca, Spain*	43,178	165	20
19. Westin Hotels & Resorts—*Seattle*	35,293	73	18
20. Minotels Europe—*Lausann, Switzerland*	30,050	700	27
21. La Quinta Inns—*San Antonio, Texas*	28,951	224	2
22. Richfield Hotel Management—*Denver*	26,796	182	4
23. Doubletree Hotel Corp.—*Phoenix*	25,584	99	1
24. Interstate Hotels Corp.—*Pittsburgh*	24,859	102	5
25. Red Roof Inns—*Hilliard, Ohio*	23,574	211	1

Reprinted with permission from *Hotel and Motel Management, 209,* 16, September 19, 1994

asked ourselves how we could become even better than we were," says Schulze. "The hardest thing for me to do was overcome my ego and admit that I really didn't know how to take the company beyond where it was. Once we did that, the job became easier."

The Ritz-Carlton approach to quality centers on a number of basic but complex principles, many drawn from traditional TQM theory, and is discussed in Chapter 14.

The Most Unusual Hotels

Among the world's most unusual hotels are ones like The Treetops Hotel in one of Kenya's wild animal parks—literally in the treetops. It was at this hotel in 1952 that Queen Elizabeth II learned that she had become queen of England. The uniqueness of the hotel is that it is built on the tops of trees overlooking a wild animal watering hole in the park.

Australia boasts an underwater hotel at the Great Barrier Reef, where guests have wonderful subterranean views from their rooms.

Japan has several unusual hotels. One is a cocoonlike hotel, called Capsule Hotel, in which guests do not have a room as such. Instead, they have a space of about 7 feet by 4 feet. In this space is a bed and a television—which you almost have to operate with your toes! Such hotels are popular with people who get caught up in the obligatory late night drinking with the boss and visiting professors who find them the only affordable place to stay in expensive Tokyo.

Japan also has love hotels, which are hotels used by couples for a few hours because they have insufficient privacy at home.

Capsule Hotel

The highest hotel in the world, in terms of altitude, is nestled in the Himalayan mountain range at an altitude of 13,000 feet. Weather permitting, there is a marvelous view of Mount Everest. As many 80 as percent of the guests suffer from nausea, headaches, or sleeplessness caused by the altitude. No wonder the hottest-selling item on the room-service menu is oxygen—at $1 a minute.[29]

International Perspective

We are all part of a huge global economy that is splintered into massive trading blocks, such as the European Economic Community (EEC) and the recently formed North American Free Trade Agreement (NAFTA) among Canada, the United States, and Mexico, and comprising a total population of 350 million consumers.

The EEC, with a population 320 million people in twelve nations, is an economic union that has removed national restrictions not only on trade but also on the movement of capital and labor. The synergy developed between these twelve member nations is beneficial to all and is a form of self-perpetuating development.[30] As travel, tourism, commerce, and industry have increased within the EEC and beyond, so has the need for hotel accommodations.

NAFTA will likely be a similar catalyst for hotel development in response to increased trade and tourism among the three countries involved. But Argentina, Brazil, Chile, and Venezuela may also join an expanded NAFTA, which would become known as the Americas trading block.

It is easy to understand the international development of hotels given the increase in international tourism trade and commerce. The growth in tourism in Pacific Rim countries is expected to continue at the same rate as in recent years. Several resorts are planned in Indonesia, Malaysia, Thailand, Mexico, and Vietnam. Further international hotel development opportunities exist in Eastern Europe, Russia, and the other republics of the former Soviet Union, where some companies have changed their growth strategy from building new hotels to acquiring existing properties.

In Asia, Hong Kong's growth has been encouraged by booming economies throughout Asia and the kind of tax system for which supply-siders hunger. Hong Kong levies a flat 16.5 percent corporate tax, a 15 percent individual income tax, and no tax on capital gains or dividends. Several hotel corporations have their headquarters in Hong Kong. Among them are Mandarin Oriental, Peninsula, and Shangri-La, all world-renowned for their five-star status. They are based in Hong Kong because of low corporate taxation and the ability to bring in senior expatriate executives with minimum bureaucratic difficulty.[31]

Seeking to diversify its hotel portfolio globally, New World Hotel (Holdings) Ltd. of Hong Kong bought Ramada, Inc., in 1989. Quickly it sold all but 108 Ramada International properties and fourteen Renaissance hotels in the United States. Ramada International is now expanding primarily in Europe, Asia, and North America. The European market is considered to be the one with the greatest potential because of the common market linkage to other European countries.[32]

In developing countries, once political stability has been sustained, hotel development quickly follows as part of an overall economic and social progression. An example of this would be the former Eastern European countries and former Soviet republics, who for the past few years have offered development opportunities for hotel corporations.

U.S.–International Hotel Development

The future of the lodging industry involves globalization. Companies can not grow unless they venture beyond the United States. International hotel development took off with the advent of the Boeing 707 in the late 1950s and the 747 in the early 1970s. With the boom in international business and tourism came the need for larger international hotel chains. American hotel chains and their management techniques were in demand by many developing countries who wanted premium-name hotels. Several hotel chains were owned by or in partnership

Corporate Profile:

Robert Hazard, Gerald Petitt, and the Building of the Choice Hotels International[1]

This awesome story began in 1968 when Gerald Petitt, a Dartmouth engineering and business student was seeking summer employment with IBM. He blew the roof off the company's pre-employment test scores. The test scores were brought to the attention of Robert C. Hazard, Jr., who at that time was in charge of the Coors Brewery account. This had an appeal for the ski-bum in Petitt, who was originally from Denver. Robert Hazard says that Jerry Petitt did more in one summer for IBM's efforts to design a production system for the brewery than a team of five engineers did in two years.

Robert Hazard decided then, over twenty-five years ago, to keep this talented person. They progressed in their careers with spells at American Express, Best Western, and eventually went on to Silver Spring, Maryland, where they would take a sleepy, stagnating lodging company called Quality Inns from three hundred properties to 3,058-property Choice brand. Because they had been so successful at Best Western, they were enticed to join Quality in 1980 for equity plus half-million dollar salaries.

Bob and Jerry brought to Quality a combination of engineer-builders and entrepreneur-marketers. They

quickly set about changing the mausoleum management style—"where you don't get creative thinking, where you try to pit good minds against each other." Instead, you get, "What will the chairman think?" and "We can all go along with it—or look for another job."[2]

To illustrate the change of management style, Bob Hazard draws the upside-down management organization, where the bosses are the 92 million guests, three thousand franchisees, and thirty-seven thousand prospective franchises. He and Jerry Petitt, of course, are on the bottom.

The strategy of changing the corporate culture, of taking advantage of emerging technological and management trends with emphasis on marketing-driven management over operations has worked for Choice hotels. The development of brand segmentation was perhaps their best move. Choice Hotels International is now an international hotel franchisor comprising seven brands: Sleep, Comfort, Quality, Clarion, Friendship, Econo Lodge, and Rodeway.

[1] This draws on Philip Hazard, *The Bob and Jerry Show Lodging*, 19, 4, December 1993, pp. 37–41.
[2] Ibid, p. 58.

with airlines; some still are. In 1948, the U.S. government, casting about for ways of improving the economy of Latin American countries, asked several hotel companies if they would be willing to build properties in these countries. By the late 1950s, only Pan American Airways agreed to do so.[33] As a Pan Am subsidiary, InterContinental had properties in Venezuela, Brazil, Uruguay, Chile, Colombia, Mexico, Curacao, Cuba, and the Dominican Republic. By 1981, InterContinental had eighty-one hotels in about fifty countries. Subsequently, Pan Am sold the InterContinental hotel chain to the Saison Japanese Corporation, who later sold it to Grand Metropolitan. Pan Am, after a long decline from its peak, declared bankruptcy and ceased operations in 1992.

Conrad Hilton was another pioneer in U.S. international hotel development. In 1948, he secured the contract to operate the Caribe Hilton in San Juan,

Puerto Rico. Hilton won this contract over other U.S. hotel chains primarily because he was the only one to respond with a letter written in Spanish. By 1974, Hilton International was operating sixty-one hotels (23,263 rooms) in thirty-nine countries outside the continental United States.[34] In 1964, Hilton International Company became a separate company from Hilton U.S.; in 1967, it was bought by TWA. Hilton International is now owned by Britain's Ladbroke Group Plc.

Sheraton Hotel Corporation, a subsidiary of ITT, now has 131,007 rooms and 422 hotels in sixty-two countries. It is second only to Group Accor of France, which operates in sixty-six countries under its brands of Novotel, Sofitel, Pullman, Motel 6, and Formule 1.

International Investment in U.S. Hotels

Foreign investors have bought and sold not just individual U.S. hotels but also hotel chains. Bass Plc (UK) bought Holiday Corporation; Grand Metropolitan (UK) bought InterContinental Hotels; Group Accor (France) bought Motel 6.

During the late 1980s and very early 1990s, Japanese investors bought several U.S. hotels. According to Christopher Mead, principal of Mead Ventures, as of 1991, Japanese interests owned all or part of 296 U.S. hotel properties. Mead predicts that the Japanese will continue to invest; the number of U.S. properties in which they have an investment may surpass four hundred by the end of the decade.[35]

One interesting statistic to note is the price paid per room. Every $1,000 paid for the purchase or construction of the room equates to $1 in room rate that must be charged to make a reasonable return on investment. By these calculations, the room rate at the hotel Bel Air should be about $1,200 per night. Clearly, the hotel was overvalued and was not purchased to make a profit; more likely prestige and ego were the motivating factors in the purchase decision.

During the second half of the 1980s, Japanese investors were cash rich and in a position to purchase U.S. real estate. This situation was aided by a sharp rise in the value of the yen against the dollar. U.S. land and property was valued far below what it would have been valued in Japan and was perceived to be offered at discount prices. Eventually, however, property, including hotels, became overpriced. An example of this is the La Costa Resort and Spa in La Costa, California. This 470-room property with a golf course was purchased by Sports Shinko in 1986 for $250 million—$531,914 per room. Two interesting things happened with regard to the purchase of this hotel. First, during the few months that elapsed between the signing of the sale documents and the time when the amount was to be paid (the escrow period), the purchaser saved $43 million because of the increase in the value of the Japanese yen compared to the dollar. The second was that the hotel lost $26 million in the first year of operation under the new owner. This was partly because of a lack of "due diligence." An extensive survey of the condition of the hotel would have shown that substantial amounts of money would be necessary to maintain the hotel's condition. The investors were obviously thinking long-term by anticipating that the value of land in Southern California would undoubtedly increase in the next few years. Meanwhile, they built and sold a number of high priced condos along the edge of the golf course.

About 1990, Japanese investment in U.S. hotels peaked; others, notably Hong Kong, Taiwan, and Korea, took their place. The Cheng family of Hong Kong recently purchased the forty-property Stouffer hotel chain from Nestle S.A. based in Switzerland. Cheng Yu-Tung also owns controlling interest in New World Development Co. Ltd. New World is the parent company of the 124-unit Ramada International chain and of New World Hotels, which has eleven properties in Asia. The Chengs also own the Regent and Grand Hyatt hotels in Hong Kong.[36] Needless to say Mr. Cheng is a billionaire.

Hotel Industry Pioneers

The hotel industry has a number of outstanding individuals who have made a significant contribution to the growth and development of the profession. Among the better known hotel pioneers of the late nineteenth and early twentieth century are Ellsworth Statler, Conrad Hilton, Ernest Henderson, Howard Johnson, and J. Willard (Bill) Marriott. Cesar Ritz's story is a good example of an industry pioneer.

Cesar Ritz was a legend in his own time; yet, like so many of the early industry leaders, he began at the bottom and worked his way up through the ranks. In his case it did not take long to reach the top because he quickly learned the secrets of success in the hotel business. His career began as an apprenticed hotel keeper at the age of fifteen. At nineteen he was managing a Parisian restaurant. Suddenly, he quit that position to become an assistant waiter at the famous Voisin restaurant. There he learned how to pander to the rich and famous. In fact, he became so adapt at taking care of the guests— remembering their likes and dislikes, even their idiosyncrasies—that a guest would ask for him and only be served by him.

Cesar Ritz

At twenty-two, he became manager of the Grand National Hotel in Lucerne, Switzerland, one of the most luxurious hotels in the world. It was not very successful at the time Ritz became manager, but with his ingenuity and panache he was able to attract the "in" crowd to complete a turnaround. After eleven seasons, he accepted a bigger challenge: the Savoy Hotel in London, which had only been open a few months and was not doing well. Cesar Ritz became manager of one of the most famous and luxurious hotels in the world at the age of thirty-eight.

Once again, his flair and ability to influence society quickly made a positive impression on the hotel. To begin with, he made the hotel a cultural center for the high society. Together with Escoffier as executive chef, he created a team that produced the finest cuisine in Europe in the most elegant of surroundings. He made evening dress compulsory and introduced orchestras to the restaurants. Cesar Ritz would spare no expense in order to create the lavish effect he sought.

On one occasion he converted a river-side restaurant into a Venetian waterway, complete with small gondolas and gondoliers singing Italian love songs.[37]

Ritz considered the handling of people as the most important of all qualities for a hotelier. His imagination and sensitivity to people and their wants contributed to a new standard of hotel keeping. The Ritz name remains synonymous with refined elegant hotels and service;[38] however, Ritz was a driven man, driving himself to the point of exhaustion. At fifty-two, he suffered a nervous breakdown.

Summary

1. Improved transportation has changed the nature of the hotel industry from small, independently owned inns to big hotel and motel chains, operated by using concepts such as franchising, partnership, leasing, and management contracts.
2. The cyclical nature of demand, periods of inflation and recession, and the high degree of capital investment put hotel industries at high risks and call for smart financial management.
3. The financial decisions of a hotel must be based on expected risk, expected return, and their combined impact on common stock. The success of a hotel depends on creative financing in combination with quality management.
4. Drastic changes in tax laws, deregulation of the thrift industry, and a softening of regional economics are reasons for the overvaluation of hotels.
5. The future of tourism involves international expansion and foreign investment, often in combination with airlines and with the goal of improving economic conditions in developing countries. It is further influenced by increased globalization, as evidenced by such agreements as NAFTA.
6. Hotels can be classified according to location (city center, resort, airport, freeway, casino), according to the types of services offered, and according to price (luxury, mid-scale, budget, and economy). Hotels are rated by Mobil and AAA Awards (five-star or the five-diamond rankings).
7. Every part of the world offers leisure and business travelers a choice of unusual or conservative accommodations that cater to the personal ideas of vacation or business trips.

Review Exercises

1. Describe the development of the motel. What impact did the Great Depression of the 1930s have on the development of the hotel industry?
2. What are the advantages of (a) management contracts and (b) franchising? Discuss their impacts on the development of the hotel industry.
3. Explain the concept of creative financing. What led to the overevaluation of many hotel businesses?
4. In what ways has the trend in globalization affected the hotel industry?
5. Explain how hotels cater to the needs of business and leisure travellers in reference to the following concepts: (a) resorts, (b) airport hotels, and (c) vertical integration.

Key Words and Concepts

Creative financing	First mortgage loans	Leveraged money	Portfolio financing
Currency fluctuations	Franchise	Management contracts	Recession
Debt service	Inflation	Money market	Superstructure
Economic downturn	Interest rates	Overvalued	Syndicates
Financing	Leasing	Partnership	

Notes

[1] This section draws from Donald E. Lundberg, *The Hotel and Restaurant Business,* 4th ed. New York: Van Nostrand Reinhold, 1984, p. 24.

[2] Daniel J. Boorstin, *The Americans: The National Experience.* New York: Vintage Books, 1965, p. 139

[3] Charles A. Bell, "Agreements with Chains-Hotels Companies," *The Cornell Hotel and Restaurant Administration Quarterly, 34* 1, February 1993, pp. 27–33.

[4] Lundberg, op cit., p. 121.

[5] Lundberg, op cit., p. 48.

[6] Ibid, p. 83.

[7] Ibid, p. 44.

[8] This section draws on Bell, op cit., pp. 27–33.

[9] Steve Bergsman, "Arizona Company Applies Leasing to Lodging Deals," *Hotel and Motel Management, 206,* 16, September 23, 1991, pp. 2, 29.

[10] James Eyster, "The Revolution in Domestic Hotel Management Contracts," *The Cornell Hotel and Restaurant Administration Quarterly, 34,* 1, February 1993, p. 19.

[11] Ibid.

[12] The International Hotel Association, Paris, "The Management Game: How to Keep One Step Ahead," *Hotels, 27,* 6, May 1993, p. 65.

[13] Heather A. Sanders and Leo M. Renaghan, "Southeast Asia: A New Model for Hotel Development," *The Cornell Hotel and Restaurant Administration Quarterly, 33,* 5, October 1992, pp. 16–23.

[14] Arbel Avner and Paul Grier, "The Risk Structure of the Hotel Industry," *The Cornell Hotel and Restaurant Administration Quarterly, 28,* 3, November 1987, p. 26.

[15] This section draws on Lundberg, op cit., p. 76.

[16] James J. Eyster, "Creative Financing in the Lodging Industry, Cornell University," *The Hotel and Restaurant Administration Quarterly, 23,* 4, February 1983, pp. 29–37.

[17] Donald H. Dempsey, "Financing Trends in the Hotel Industry," *Real Estate Finance, 7,* 4, Winter 1991, pp. 74–76.

[18] Michael J. Flannery and Joseph J. Flannery, "Causes of Hotel Industry Distress," *Real Estate Review, 19,* 3, Fall 1990, pp. 35–39.

[19] Joan Oleck, "Are They Gambling with Your Future?" *Restaurant Business,* November 20, 1992, p. 112.

[20] Ibid, p. 117.

[21] This section draws on Saul Leonard, "Casinos Gaming Fever Grips the United States," *Hotels, 27,* 6, June 1993, p. 45.

[22] "CNN World News," December 16, 1993.

[23] This section draws on George R. Justus, "Microtel: How 'Simple' Translates into Success," *The Cornell Hotel and Restaurant Administration Quarterly, 32,* 4, December 1991, pp. 50–54.

[24] Juergen Bartels, Address to the Carlson Travel Network Convention, Phoenix, Ariz., May 3, 1991, as noted in Tom Powers, *Introduction to Management in the Hospitality Business,* 4th ed. New York: John Wiley and Sons, 1992, p. 221.

[25] *Lodging, 17,* 8, April 1991, p. 11.

[26] Lois Madison Reamy, *Institutional Investor, 26,* 10, September 1992, pp. 106–112.

[27] Sally Wolchuk, "World's Largest Hotels," *Hotels,* August 1991.

[28] This section draws on Edward Watkins, "How Ritz-Carlton Won the Baldrige Award," *Lodging Hospitality, 48,* 11, November 1992, p. 22.

[29] Jeannie Realston, "Inn of Thin Air," *American Way,* October 15, 1992.

[30] Belgium, Denmark, France, Germany, Great Britain, Greece, Ireland, Italy, Luxembourg, Portugal, Spain, the Netherlands.

[31] Murray Baily, "Travel Business: Rooms at the Top," *Asian Business, 27,* 9, September 1991, pp. 60–62.

[32] Steve Bergsman, "Ramada International Flourishes Globally," *National Real Estate Investor, 35,* 5, May 1991, pp. 73–75.

[33] Lundberg, op cit., p. 44.

[34] Ibid.

[35] M. Chase Burritt, "Japanese Investment in U.S. Hotels and Resorts," *The Cornell Hotel and Restaurant Administration Quarterly, 32,* 3, October 1991, p. 64.

[36] Bill Eillette, "Cheng Family Acquires Stouffer," *Hotel and Motel Management, 208,* 7, April 26, 1993, p. 1.

[37] Richard A. Wentzel, "Leaders of the Hospitality Industry or Hospitality Management," *An Introduction to the Industry,* 6th ed. Dubuque, Iowa: Kendall/Hunt, 1991, p. 29.

[38] This section draws on Lundberg, op cit., pp. 33–34.

Hotel and Rooms Division Operation

After reading and studying this chapter you should be able to do the following:

- ➤ Describe the functions and departments of a hotel
- ➤ Trace the guest cycle from reservations to check out
- ➤ Outline the duties and responsibilities of key executives and department heads
- ➤ Draw an organizational chart of a hotel and identify the executive committee members
- ➤ Describe the main functions of the front desk
- ➤ Describe property management systems and discuss yield management
- ➤ Calculate occupancy percentages, average daily rates, and actual percentage of potential rooms revenue
- ➤ Outline the importance of the reservations and guest services function
- ➤ List the complexities and challenges of the housekeeping and security/loss prevention departments.

*T*his chapter describes the function of a hotel and the many departments that constitute a hotel. It also helps to explain why and how the departments are interdependent in successfully running a hotel.

The Functions and Departments of a Hotel

The primary function of a hotel is to provide lodging accommodation. A three-hundred-plus room hotel is run by a general manager and an executive committee comprised of the key executives who head major departments: rooms division director, food and beverage director, marketing and sales director, human resources director, chief accountant or controller, and chief engineer or facility manager. These executives generally have a regional or corporate counterpart with whom they have a reporting relationship, although the general manager is their immediate superior.

A hotel is made up of several businesses or revenue centers and cost centers. A few thousand products and services are sold every day. Each area of specialty requires dedication and a quality commitment for each department to get little things right all the time. Furthermore, hotels need the cooperation of a large and diverse group of people to do it. Godfrey Bler, the general manager (GM) of the elegant eight-hundred-room General Eisenhower Hotel calls it a business of details. Another wise comment is from Matthew Fox: "If you ignore the little stuff, it will become big stuff."[1]

Hotels are places of glamour that may be awe inspiring. Even the experienced hotel person is impressed by the refined dignity of a beautiful hotel like a Ritz Carlton or the artistic splendor of a Hyatt. The atmosphere of a hotel is stimulating to a hospitality student. Let us step into an imaginary hotel to feel the excitement and become a part of the rush that is similar to show business, for a hotel is live theater and the GM is the director of the cast of players.

Hotels, whether they are chain affiliated or independent properties, all exist to serve and enrich society, and at the same time make a profit for the owners. Frequently, hotels are just like pieces of property on a Monopoly board. They often make or lose more money with equity appreciation or depreciation than via operations.

Hotels have been described as people palaces. Some are certainly palatial, and others are more

Ritz Carlton Interior

functional. Hotels are meant to provide all the comforts of home to those away from home. A gracious feeling of warmth and welcome is a hotel's most valuable ambiance. Hotels have personalities; they are created by the combined chorus of effort, interest, and sincerity on the part of every member of the staff.[2]

Role of the Hotel General Manager

Hotel general managers have a lot of responsibilities. They must provide owners with a reasonable return on investment, keep guests satisfied and returning, and employees happy. This may seem easy, but because there are so many interpersonal transactions and because hotels are open every day, all day, the complexities of operating become challenges that the general manager must face and overcome.

Larger hotels can be more impersonal. Here, the general manager may only meet and greet a few VIPs (very important persons); in the smaller property, it is easier—though none the less important—for the GM to become acquainted with guests, to ensure their stay is memorable, and to secure their return. One way that experienced GMs can meet guests, even in large hotels, is to be visible in the lobby and F&B (food and beverage) outlets at peak times (check out, lunch, check in, and dinner time). Guests like to feel that the GM takes a personal interest in their well-being. Max Blouet, who was general manager of the famous George V Hotel in Paris for more than thirty years, was a master of this art. He was always present at the right moment to meet and greet guests. In fact, he often made such a spectacle that other guests would inquire who he was and then would want to meet him. Hoteliers always remember they are hosts.

Rick Segal, vice president of Sheraton's luxury hotel division, credits his success to several things, but the one quality he mentions first is paying attention to detail. As general manager of the famous St. Regis Hotel in New York City, he has plenty of opportunities to do just that.

The GM is ultimately responsible for the performance of the hotel and the employees. The GM is the leader of the hotel. As such, she or he is held accountable for the hotel's level of profitability by the corporation or owners.

General managers with a democratic, situational, and participating leadership style are more likely to be successful. There are, however, times when it is necessary to be somewhat autocratic—when crisis situations arise.

Rick Segal

To be successful, GMs need to have a broad range of personal qualities. Among those most often quoted by GMs are the following:[3]

➤ Leadership
➤ Attention to detail
➤ Follow through—getting the job done
➤ People skills
➤ Patience
➤ Ability to delegate effectively

Not surprisingly, a survey of general managers revealed that GMs were hard-working and responsible. Each had overcome difficulties and challenges and each had made sacrifices to become successful. But each was also extremely satisfied doing what he or she was doing.[4]

Another attribute of a successful GM is to hire the best people. The GM of Chicago's Four Seasons Hotel, Hans Willimann, deliberately hired division heads who knew more about what they were hired for than he did. Willimann says he sets the tone—a structure of excellence—and others try to match it. Once the structure is in place, each employee works to define the hotel commitment to excellence. People who are hired need to be accomplished at what they do, and then they have to fit into the framework of the structure and be compatible with the rest of the group.[5]

As general manager of the Stouffer Wailea Beach Resort, Maui, Hawaii, Donn Takahashi's management philosophy is that to achieve a first-class facility, workers must be viewed as being vital to the operation. He instituted programs designed to cut turnover, engender loyalty, and stave off competition for workers from competing hotels. He says a key to keeping employees happy is to make sure there is mutual respect among all levels of workers.[6]

Management functions are generally classified into forecasting, planning, organizing, communicating, and evaluating. Centralized companies such as Marriott give detailed general manager profiles, whereas Hyatt, a decentralized company, does not. Given that the primary purpose of the hotel is to sell rooms and ensure that guests have a wonderful stay, it has been suggested that GMs assume the director of sales position and spend up to 75 percent of their time directly involved with sales.[7]

General managers need to understand, empathize, and allow for the cultures of both guests and employees. For example, in the Pacific Rim, spiritual dictates are frequently believed to directly affect hoteliers' profits. At the Westin Kyoto Takaragaike Prince, hotels with floors numbered four or nine are not likely to be very popular. The pronunciation of the number four and the Japanese word for *death* sound the same, and the number nine sounds very similar to *pain* in Japanese.[8]

Often, success can be heavily influenced by the country's culture. For instance, in Southeast Asia, many hoteliers employ Fung Shui experts. Fung Shui is a centuries-old tradition that maintains that placing architectural elements in correct configurations or holding events at correct times pleases spirits. For instance, at the Hyatt Regency Singapore, doors were originally

Personal Profile: Stephen A. Wynn

Chairman and CEO of Mirage Resorts, Las Vegas

Hotels magazine selected Stephen Wynn as the ninth independent hotelier of the world for playing a major role in transforming Las Vegas from a gambling venue for adults into a multi-dimensional resort destination for the whole family and also for managing the Mirage, one of the world's best-run megahotels.

The $750-million, three-thousand-room Mirage resort casino changed the face of Las Vegas. Mirage has fine gourmet restaurants, a huge lagoonlike pool, an atrium filled with palm trees, a children's game arcade, and, of course, a first-rate casino.

Wynn also operates Treasure Island, the mid-casino hotel, which beckons tourists inside every night with a sign featuring a smiling pirate. Treasure Island has free street-side mock battles nightly, complete with cannon fire and a sinking ship. When the show is over, many in the crowd walk over the dock into the thirty-six-story hotel's casino, seven restaurants, and retail shops. The hotel has a pool, spa, game arcade, showrooms, convention center, and two wedding chapels—with built-in video cameras.

Steve also runs two other casino-hotels: the two-thousand-room Golden Nugget in downtown Vegas and the three-hundred-room Golden Nugget in Laughlin, Nevada. With close to 8,200 rooms, Mirage, Inc., is ranked number sixty-one among the world's largest hotel chains.

Steve has eighteen thousand highly motivated employees who keep guest rooms, casinos, and other attractions impeccable, according to industry analysts. The Mirage properties are exceptional, drawing a commanding share

of a demanding market with an exceptionally high company-wide occupancy.

Wynn began his career in Vegas twenty-seven years ago, as a 25-year-old with a degree in English literature from the University of Pennsylvania. In a very short time, he became an executive and part owner of the Frontier Hotel. He owned and operated a Nevada wine-importing company from 1969 to 1972. Then he turned a real estate deal into a profit, which allowed him to begin a major investment in Golden Nugget in 1972. (The Golden Nugget was renamed the Mirage in 1991.)

In 1973, Wynn acquired control of the company, which, at the time, had no rooms. In 1980, he opened the $140 million Golden Nugget/Atlantic City, which he sold to Bally Corporation for $400 million in 1987. That year, Wynn started building the Mirage. He is currently planning another Nevada casino resort complex. The following information tracks the performance of the Mirage Resort, Inc.:

Stephen A. Wynn

Revenues (in millions)	1992	1993
Casino	$534	$586
Rooms	147	181
Food and beverage	137	159
Other	102	127
Promotional allowances	(88)	(100)
Total revenues	$833	$953
Operating income	126	132 (includes $29.8
preopening expenses for Treasure Island)		

Source: Mirage Hotels

positioned at right angles to the street. A fung shui master recognized and told the general manager that the hotel, which was then having problems, would never be successful until the angle was changed. After the doors were repositioned, occupancies began to rise.[9]

About a year after the 850-room megaresort Westin Kauai opened, it became apparent that the "Share the Fantasy" a la Disney theme chosen by management did not fit. After careful consideration a management by values system was introduced. Operating synergistically with the more traditional management by objectives, management by values extracts the moral essences of the local culture and makes them goals of the hotel. Responses from a survey that asked employees to share their values were used to help create a mission statement for the hotel. Management discontinued the Disney model and its vocabulary. Employee uniforms changed from stiff corporate style to flowing Hawaiian clothes.[10]

Management Structure

Management structure differs among larger, mid-scale, and smaller properties. The mid-scale and smaller properties will be less complex in their management structures than the larger ones. However, someone must be responsible for each of the key result areas that make the operation successful. For example, a small property may not have a director of human resources, but each department head will have general day-to-day operating responsibilities for the human resources function. The manager will have the ultimate responsibility for all human resources decisions. The same scenario is possible with each of the following areas: engineering and maintenance, accounting and finance, marketing and sales, food and beverage management, and so on.

The Executive Committee

The general manager, together with input from the executive committee (Figure 4–1), makes all the major decisions affecting the hotel. These executives, who include the directors of human resources, food and beverage, rooms division, marketing and sales, engineering, and accounting, compile the hotel's occupancy forecast together with all revenues and expenses to make up the budget. They generally meet once a week for one or two hours and might typically cover some of the following topics:

Guest satisfaction
Employee satisfaction
Total quality management
Occupancy forecasts
Sales and marketing plans
Training
Major items of expenditure
Renovations
Ownership relations
Energy conservation
Recycling
New legislation
Profitability

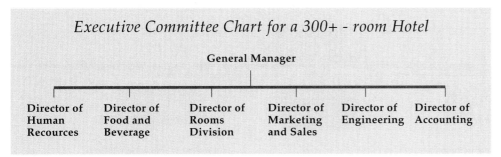

Figure 4–1   *Executive Committee Chart*

Some GMs rely on input from the executive committee more than others, depending on their leadership and management style. These senior executives determine the character of the property and decide on the missions, goals, and objectives of the hotel. For a chain hotel, this will be in harmony with the corporate mission.

In most hotels, the executive committee is involved with the decisions but the ultimate responsibility and authority rests with the GM. One of the major roles of the committee is as communicator, both up and down the line of authority. This helps build interdepartmental cooperation.

The Departments

Rooms Division

The rooms division director is responsible to the GM for the efficient and effective leadership and operation of all the rooms division departments. They include concerns such as the following:

Financial responsibility for rooms division
Employee satisfaction goals
Guest satisfaction goals
Guest relations
Security
Gift shop

The rooms division consists of the following departments: front office, reservations, housekeeping, concierge, guest services, security, and communications. Figure 4–2 shows the organizational chart for a three-hundred-plus-room hotel rooms division.

The guest cycle in Figure 4–3 shows a simplified sequence of events that take place from the moment the guest calls to make a reservation until check out.

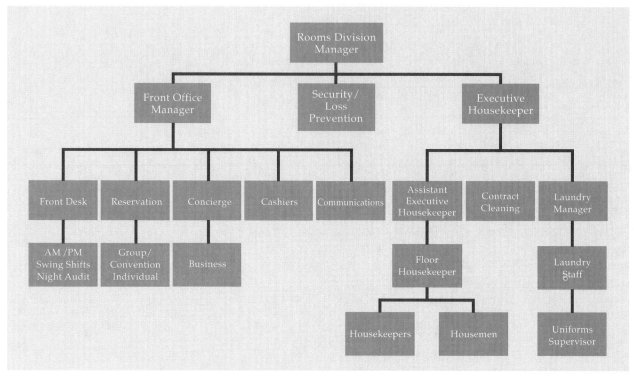

Figure 4–2 *Rooms Division Organizational Chart*

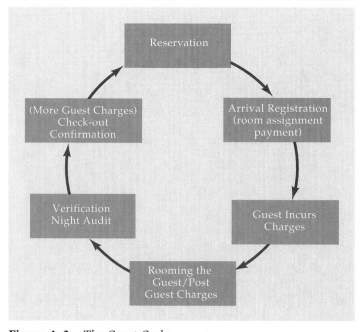

Figure 4–3 *The Guest Cycle*

Front Office

The front office manager's (FOM) main duty is to enhance guest services by constantly developing services to meet guest needs. An example of how some FOMs practice enhancing guest services is to have a guest service associate (GSA) greet guests as they arrive at the hotel, escort them to the front desk, and then personally allocate the room and take the guest and luggage to the room. This innovative way of developing guest services looks at the operation from the guest's perspective. There is no need to have separate departments for door person, bellperson, front desk, and so on. Each guest associate is cross-trained in all aspects of greeting and rooming the guest. This is now being done in smaller and mid-sized properties as well as specialty and deluxe properties. Guest service associates are responsible for the front desk, concierge, PBX, bellpersons, valet, and reservations.

Front Office Manager Reviewing the Arrivals and Departures List

During an average day in a hotel—if there is such a thing—the front office manager performs the following duties:

➤ Check night clerk report
➤ Review previous night's occupancy
➤ Review previous night's average rate
➤ Look over market mix
➤ Check complimentary rooms
➤ Verify special notes (make sure they can collect)
➤ Verify group rooms to be picked up for next thirty days
➤ Review arrivals and departures for the day
➤ Review the VIP list and prepare preregistration
➤ Arrange preregistrations for all arrivals
➤ Attend rooms divisions and operations meeting
➤ Review arrivals and departures for next day
➤ Make staffing adjustments needed for arrivals and departures
➤ Review scheduling (done weekly)
➤ Meet with lead GSAs (done daily)

In some hotels, the reservations manager and associates report to the director of sales. These positions report to the chief accountant: night auditor, night audit associates, and cashiers.

Figure 4–4 (page 98) shows an organization chart of a front office. The front office has been described as the hub or nerve center of the hotel. It is the department that makes a great impression on the guest and one that the guest relies on throughout his or her stay for information and service. Positive first impressions are critical to the successful guest experience.

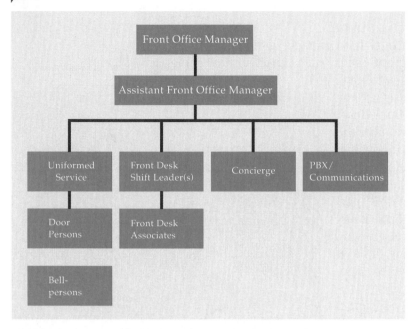

Figure 4-4   *Front Office Organization Chart*

Many guests arrive at the hotel after a long and tiring trip. They want to be greeted by someone with a warm smile and a genuine greeting. If a guest should have a negative experience in checking into a hotel, he or she will be on guard in encounters with each of the other departments. The positions description for a guest service agent details the work performed. Position description for the three main functions of the front office are as follows:

1. To sell rooms.   The hotel departments work like a team in a relay race. Sales or reservations staff make or take the room sales up until the evening before the guest's arrival. At 6 p.m, when the reservations office closes, all the expected arrivals and available rooms are then handed over to the front desk p.m. shift. Reservations calls after 6 p.m. may either be taken by the front desk staff or the 1-800 number. The front desk team will try to sell out (achieve 100 percent occupancy) by selling the remaining rooms to call-in or walk-in guests—and of course the frantic calls from preferred guests who need a favor! The front desk staff must not only aim to sell all the rooms but also achieve the optimum average daily rate (ADR) for the rooms. The ADR is calculated by adding up the rate charged for each room and then dividing by the number of rooms. A simple example would be as follows:

A group booking of	100 rooms at $140	=	$14,000
	10 suites at $250	=	2,500
Individual corporate bookings	250 rooms at $160	=	40,000
Special promotions	50 rooms at $125	=	6,250
Total	410 rooms		$62,750

Total room sales

$62,750 / 410 = $153 Average daily rate

Optimizing the ADR is achieved by "up-selling" and yield management. Up-selling is when the guest service agent/front desk clerk suggestively sells the features of a larger room, a higher floor, or perhaps a better view. Yield management originated in the airline industry where demand also fluctuates. Basically, a percentage of guests who book and send in a deposit in advance will be able to secure a room at a more reasonable price than someone book-

ing a room with just three days' notice. The price will be higher for the booking at three days' notice if demand is good.

Many other factors influence the hotels ability to sell out. Chief among these
are: *demand,* the number of people needing rooms, and *supply,* the number of
available rooms. A good example is the New York Hotel Convention and Trade
show. This event takes place in a city that has a high demand for hotel rooms
in proportion to its inventory (number of available rooms). Because there is a
fairly constant demand for rooms in New York, special events tend to increase
demand to a point that forces up room rates. Another example comes from the
airline industry, which always seems to raise prices at the peak travel times
(Thanksgiving, Christmas, Easter, and the summer vacation times). They only
give special fares when school is in session. Yield management is explained in
more detail later in this chapter.

2. To maintain balanced guest accounts.   This begins with advance deposits,
opening the guest folio (account), and posting all charges from the various
departments. Many hotels now have property management systems (PMS)[11]
(property management systems are explained in more detail later in this chapter) and point of sale terminals (POS), which are on-line to the front office.
This means that guest charges from the various outlets are directly debited to
the guest's folio, receive payment on guest check out, or transfer the account
in the case of a "city ledger" client (one whose company has established credit with the hotel). This means that the account will be sent and paid within a
specified time period. Formerly, the allotted time used to be at the end of the
month, followed by a thirty- or sixty-day grace period for payment to be made.
However, most companies now have a goal to keep accounts receivable to a
maximum of fifteen to twenty days. This helps the hotel maintain sufficient
cash flow in order to meet its obligations to the lenders for mortgage payments
and employees' salaries.

A recent innovation to the PMS is in-room check out. The system allows a
guest to check his or her account via the television screen in the room. The
guest operates the system via the remote control, verifying all charges and
authorizing payment. The total may then be charged to a credit card with a
copy sent to the guest, or (for company accounts) to his or her company.
Hotels that do not have this feature as part of their PMS sometimes leave a
copy of the guest's folio under the door on the last evening. This also allows
the guest to check all charges before departure. The guest has the option of
calling the desk to inform the cashier that the bill may be sent. Nowadays,
because cash flow is so important, payment may be required on receipt of the
invoice or a few days later. Credit cards have helped this process by speeding
up payment to hotels.

*3. To offer services such as handling mail, faxes, messages, and local and
hotel information.*   A constant flow of people approach the front desk with
questions. Front desk employees need to be knowledgeable about the various
activities in the hotel. The size, layout, and staffing of the front desk will vary
with the size of the hotel. A busy eight-hundred-room city center property will

naturally differ from a country inn. The front desk is staffed throughout the twenty-four hours by three shifts. The hours worked by front desk employees may vary. However, generally the day shift works from 7:00 a.m. until 3:00 p.m., the swing shift runs from 3 p.m. until 11:30 p.m., and the graveyard shift/night auditor works from 11:00 p.m. until 7 a.m. On a staggered schedule one person starts at 7:00 a.m. and ends at 3:30 p.m., and another one starts at 2:30 p.m. and goes to 11:00 p.m. This schedule provides time for a smooth handover between the shifts. These few minutes are vital because the shift leaders must exchange essential information such as how the house count is going (how many rooms left to sell), which room changes have been requested but have not been completed, which VIPs are still to arrive and any special arrangements (e.g., calling the manager on duty to escort the guests to their rooms/suites, knowing which guests have serious complaints, and therefore need special attention, etc.).

The main duties of the early shift are the following:

1. Check the log book and the previous night's occupancy for no shows and send information to the accounting office for billing
2. Conduct a house count and update the forecast (in some hotels this is done by reservations)
3. Decide on the number and mix of rooms to sell (in some hotels this is also done by reservations)
4. Pre-allocate VIP suites and rooms and block off group or convention rooms
5. Handle guest check outs including the following:
   a. Insure all charges are on guest's folio, especially any last-minute telephone calls and breakfast. (Most medium and large hotels now have a PMS so that the moment a guest incurs charges in the restaurant, the charge will automatically be included on the guest folio. In the old days, some guests would skip off without paying for some charges incurred before check out.)
   b. Verify the accuracy of the account by going through the various charges with the guest
   c. Accept the cash or credit as payment
   d. Tactfully handle any unexpected situation (for example, when the guest says the company is paying for my stay and the front desk has received no instructions to that effect)
   e. Send any city ledger accounts to the accounting office—generally this is done when the guest has signed the folio to approve all charges
6. Politely and efficiently attend to guest inquiries
7. Note important occurrences in the front office log
8. Organize any room changes guests may request and follow up
9. Advise housekeeping and room service of flowers/fruit for VIPs and any other amenities ordered
10. Check issuing and control of keys

Front Desk Associate

The desk clerk must be able to work under pressure. Constant interruptions to the actual work of the front desk occur and employees are always on stage; therefore, it is necessary to maintain composure even during moments of apparent panic.

The evening shift duties are the following:

1. Check the log book for special items. (The log book is kept by guest contact; associates at the front office note specific and important guest requests and occurrences such as requests for room switches or baby cribs.)
2. Check on the room status, number of expected check outs still to leave and arrivals by double-checking registration cards and the computer in order to update the forecast of the night's occupancy. This will determine the number of rooms left to sell. Nowadays, this is all part of the capability of the PMS.
3. Handle guest check ins. This means notifying the appropriate staff of any special requests guests may have made (e.g., nonsmoking room or a long bed for an extra tall guest).
4. Take reservations for that evening and future reservations after the reservations staff have left for the day

Figure 4–5 shows the types of rates offered by hotels.

Major hotel chains offer a number of different room rates, including the following:

> rack rate
> corporate
> association rate
> government
> encore
> cititravel
> entertainment cards
> AAA
> AARP (American Association of Retired Persons)
> wholesale
> group rates
> promotional special

The rack rate is the rate that is used as a benchmark quotation of a hotel's room rate. Let us assume that the Hotel California had a rack rate of $135. Any discounted rate may be offered at a percentage deduction from the rack rate. An example would be a corporate rate of $110, an association rate of $105, and AARP rate of $95—certain restrictions may apply. Group rates may range from $95 to $125 according to how much the hotel needs the business.

Throughout the world there are three main plans on which room rates are based:

> AP/American Plan—room and three meals a day
> MAP/Modified American Plan—room plus two meals
> EP/European Plan—room only, meals extra

Figure 4–5 *Types of Rates*

Night Auditor

A hotel is one of the few businesses that balances its accounts at the end of each business day. Because a hotel is open twenty-four hours every day, it is difficult to stop transactions at any given moment. The night auditor waits until the hotel quiets down at about 1:00 a.m. and then begins the task of balancing the guests' accounts receivable. The other duties include the following:

1. Post any charges that the evening shift was not able to post
2. Pass discrepancies to shift managers in the

Night Auditor Verifying and Balancing Guest Accounts

Corporate Profile: Hyatt Hotels

When Nicholas Pritzker emigrated with his family from the Ukraine to the United States, he began his career by opening a small law firm. His outstanding management skills led to the expansion of the law firm, turning it into a management company. The Pritzkers gained considerable financial support, which allowed them to pursue their goals of expansion and development. These dreams came into reality with the opening of the first Hyatt Hotel, inaugurated on September 27, 1957.

Today, Hyatt Hotel Corporation is a $2.5 billion hotel management and development company; together with Hyatt International, they are among the leading chains in the hotel industry, with 7.33 percent of the market share.[1] Hyatt has earned worldwide fame as the leader in providing luxury accommodations and high-quality service, targeting especially the business traveler, but strategically differentiating its properties and services to identify and market a very diverse clientele. This differentiation has resulted in the establishment of four basic types of hotels:

1. *The Hyatt Regency Hotels* represent the company's core product. They are usually located in business city centers and regarded as five-star hotels.
2. *Hyatt Resorts* are a vacation retreat. They are located in the world's most desirable leisure destinations, offering the "ultimate escape from everyday stresses."
3. *The Park Hyatt Hotels* are smaller, European-style, luxury hotels. They target the individual traveler who prefers the privacy, personalized service, and discreet elegance of a small European hotel.
4. *The Grand Hyatt Hotels* serve culturally rich destinations that attract leisure business as well as large-scale meetings and conventions. They reflect refinement, grandeur, and feature state-of-the-art technology and banquet and conference facilities of world-class standard.

Hyatt Hotels Corporation has been recognized by the *Wall Street Journal* as one of the sixty-six firms around the world poised to make a difference in the industries and markets of the 1990s and beyond. As a matter of fact, the effective management that characterized the company in its early years with the Pritzker family has continued through time. Hyatt Hotels Corporation is characterized by a decentralized management approach, which gives the individual general manager a great deal of decision-making power, as well as the opportunity to stimulate personal creativity and, therefore, differentiation and innovation. The development of novel concepts and products is perhaps the key to Hyatt's outstanding success. For example, the 1967 opening of the Hyatt Regency Atlanta, Georgia, gave the company instant recognition throughout the world. Customers were likely to stare in awe at the twenty-one-story atrium lobby, the glass elevators, and the revolving roof-top restaurant. The property's innovative architecture, designed by John Portman, revolutionized the common standards of design and spacing, thus changing the course of the lodging industry. The atrium concept introduced there represented a universal challenge to hotel architects to face the new trend of grand, wide-open public spaces.

A further positive aspect of the decentralized management structure is the fact that the individual manag-

[1] The company owns 173 hotels and resorts worldwide: 107 in North America, Canada, and the Caribbeans, and 66 in international locations.

morning. The room and tax charges are then posted to each folio and a new balance shown.

3. Run backup reports so if the computer system fails the hotel will have up-to-date information to operate a manual system
4. Reconcile point of sale and PMS to guest accounts. If this does not balance, then the auditor must do so by investigating errors or omissions. This is done by checking that every departmental charge shows up on guest folios.
5. Complete and distribute the daily report. This report details the previous day's activities and includes vital information about the performance of the hotel.
6. Find areas of the hotel where there may be theft or potential theft

er is able to be extremely customer-responsive by developing a thorough knowledge of the guests' needs and thereby providing personalized service—fundamental to achieve customer satisfaction. This is, in fact, the ultimate innkeeping purpose, which Hyatt attains at high levels. Perhaps the most striking result of this forecasting is, again, the introduction of innovative and diversified products and services. For business travelers, for example, Hyatt recently introduced the Hyatt Business Plan, which includes fax machines in every room, twenty-four-hour access to copiers and printers, and other features designed to address the needs of the targeted clientele. Hyatt has also been on the forefront in developing faster, more efficient check in options, including a phone number, 1-800-CHECK-IN, that allows guests to check in to their hotel rooms by telephone. In addition, the needs of families have been considered as well. The company offers Camp Hyatt, the hotel industry's most extensive children's program.

The other side of Hyatt's success is the emphasis on human resources management. Employee satisfaction, in fact, is considered to be a prerequisite to external satisfaction. Hyatt devotes enormous attention to employee training and selection. What is most significant, however, is the interaction among top managers and operating employees.

Darryl Hartley-Leonard, now chairman of the board of Hyatt Hotels Corporation, was the company's president in 1989 when he came up with the idea of "In-touch day." On this day, once a year, the company closes its headquarters' office and the senior management spreads out to a hundred Hyatt Hotels in the United States and Canada, "spending time in the trenches"—doing the daily activities of operating employees, taking their front-line positions. Such a strategy is extremely effective: Actually performing the job enables the top executives to learn, first-hand, the challenges and problems of their employees, thus understanding their daily routine and problems. The In-touch day concept provides tangible evidence to employees that the management is not locked into an ivory tower, but is concerned with the improvement of their jobs.

Darryl Hartley-Leonard's leadership is by far a successful one. He joined Hyatt in 1964 as a front desk clerk at a Los Angeles Hyatt hotel. After serving in a variety of management positions, he worked his way up to general manager of Hyatt Regency Atlanta (1974); two years later he became a regional vice president. But that was not it. His extraordinary abilities were further recognized and rewarded: Hartley-Leonard was named executive vice president for the corporation in 1978, president in 1986, and chairman in 1994. Hartley-Leonard "has the right stuff to lead hotels today." He is recognized as a spokesperson for travel and tourism, having made "lasting and outstanding contributions to the overall U.S. travel industry." He has surely made a difference, and provides the company with the optimal leadership and management styles.

The daily report contains some key operating ratios: room occupancy percentage (ROP), which is rooms occupied divided by rooms available. Thus, if a hotel has 850 rooms and 622 are occupied, the occupancy percentage is 622 : 850 = 73.17 percent. If 375 of the 622 occupied rooms are occupied by two or more persons, then the double or multiple occupancy percentage is calculated by taking the number of guests minus the number of rooms occupied: 750 − 622 = 128 ÷ 375 = 34.13. The ADR is, together with the occupancy percentage, one of the key operating ratios that indicates the hotel's performance. The average daily rate is calculated by dividing the rooms revenue by the number of rooms sold. If the rooms revenue was $75,884 and the number of rooms sold was 662 then the ADR would be $122. See Figure 4-6 for an example of a daily report.

Clarion Hotel Bayview

Daily Management Report Supplement   *Daily Report*
January 18, 1995   *January 18, 1995*

Occupancy%	Today	Avg or %	M–T–D Avg or %		Y–T–D Avg or %	
Rack Rooms	9	2.9%	189	3.37	189	3.37
Corporate Rooms	0	0.0%	103	1.83	103	1.83
Group Rooms	274	87.8%	2379	42.36	2379	42.36
Leisure Rooms	3	1.0%	395	7.03	395	7.03
Base Rooms	23	7.4%	348	6.14	345	6.14
Govt Rooms	2	0.6%	32	.57	32	.57
Wholesale Rooms	1	0.3%	121	2.15	121	2.15
No-Show Rooms		0.0%	0	.00	0	.00
Comp Rooms	0	0.0%	37	.66	37	.66
Total Occ Rooms & Occ %	312	100%	3601	64.12	3601	64.12
Rack	$1,011	$112.33	17207	91.04	17207	91.04
Corporate	$0	ERR	8478	82.31	8478	82.31
Group	$22,510	$82.15	178066	74.85	178066	74.85
Leisure	$207	$69.00	24985	63.25	24985	63.25
Base	$805	$35.00	12063	34.97	12063	34.97
Govt	$141	$70.59	2379	74.34	2379	74.34
Wholesale	$43	$43.00	5201	42.98	5201	42.98
No-Show/Comp/Allowance	$0		−914	−24.69	−914	−24.69
Total Rev & Avg Rate	$24,717	$79.22	247466	68.72	247466	68.72

Hotel Revenue

	Today		M–T–D Avg or %		Y–T–D Avg or %	
Rooms	$24,717		247466	77.46	247466	77.46
Food	$1,400		37983	11.89	37983	11.89
Beverage	$539		9679	3.03	9679	3.03
Telephone	$547		5849	1.83	5849	1.83
Parking	$854		11103	3.48	11103	3.48
Room Svc II	$70		1441	.45	1441	.45
Other Revenue	$1,437		963	1.87	963	1.87
Total Revenue	$29,563		319484	100.00	319484	100.00

Figure 4-6   *Daily Report*

Clarion Hotel Bayview

Daily Management Report Supplement
January 18, 1995

Daily Report
January 18, 1995

Cafe 6th & K	Today	Avg or %	M–T–D Avg or %		Y–T–D Avg or %	
Cafe Breakfast Covers	88	57.1%	1180	47.12	1180	47.12
Cafe Lunch Covers	43	27.9%	674	26.92	674	26.92
Cafe Dinner Covers	23	14.9%	650	25.96	650	25.96
Total Cafe Covers	154	100.0%	2504	100.00	2504	100.00
Cafe Breakfast	$608	$6.91	7854	6.66	7854	6.66
Cafe Lunch	$246	$5.72	5847	8.67	5847	8.67
Cafe Dinner	$227	$9.86	4309	6.63	4309	6.63
Gaslamp Lounge Food			2431	3.74	2431	3.74
Total Rev/Avg Check	$1,081	$7.02	20440	8.16	20440	8.16
Banquets						
Banquet Breakfast Covers	0	ERR	154	13.24	154	13.24
Banquet Lunch Covers	0	ERR	134	11.52	134	11.52
Banquet Dinner Covers	0	ERR	254	21.84	254	21.84
Banquet Coffeebreak Covers	0	ERR	621	53.40	621	53.40
Total Banquet Covers	0	ERR	1163	100.00	1163	100.00
Banquet Breakfast	$0	ERR	980	6.36	980	6.36
Banquet Lunch	$0	ERR	2997	22.36	2997	22.36
Banquet Dinner	$0	ERR	4530	17.84	4530	17.84
Banquet Coffeebreak	$0	ERR	1093	1.76	1093	1.76
Total Rev/Avg Check	$0	ERR	9600	8.25	9600	8.25
Room Service						
Room Service Breakfast Covers	13	40.6%	324	48.00	324	48.00
Room Service Lunch Covers	3	9.4%	53	7.85	53	7.85
Room Service Dinner Covers	16	50.0%	298	44.15	298	44.15
Total Covers	32	100.0%	675	100.00	675	100.00
Room Service Breakfast	$119	$9.13	2665	8.22	2665	8.22
Room Service Lunch	$29	$9.77	418	7.89	418	7.89
Room Service Dinner	$171	$10.67	2907	9.75	2907	9.75
Total Rev/Avg Check	$319	$9.96	5990	8.87	5990	8.87

Figure 4-6 *(continued)*

A more recent ratio to gauge a hotel rooms divisions performance is the percentage of potential rooms revenue, which is calculated by determining potential rooms revenue and dividing the actual revenue by the potential revenue.

Larger hotels may have more than one night auditor, but in smaller properties these duties may be combined with night manager, desk, or night watchman duties.

Property Management Systems

Property management systems have greatly enhanced a hotel's ability to accept, store, and retrieve guest reservations, guest history, requests, and billing arrangements. The reservations part of the property management system also provides the reservations associates with information on types of rooms available, features, views, and room rates. A list of expected arrivals can be easily generated. Before the advent of PMSs, it took reservation associates much longer to learn the features of each room, and the various room rates, and to make up the arrivals list.

A property management system contains a set of computer software packages capable of supporting a variety of activities in front and back office areas. The four most common front office software packages are designed to assist front office employees in performing functions related to the following tasks:

➤ Reservations management
➤ Rooms management
➤ Guest account management
➤ General management[12]

The reservations management component allows the reservations department to quickly accept reservations and generate confirmations and occupancy forecasts for reservations taken by the hotel directly and by the CRS. Most chain operated or affiliated hotels have a 1-800 number to allow guests to call, without charge, to make reservations anywhere in the United States and, in some cases, overseas. Travel agents also have direct computer access to the central reservations numbers. More than one hundred PMS vendors offer various features, hardware platforms, and operating systems. The various software packages handle some or all of the following:

➤ Reservations
➤ Front desk
➤ Group billing
➤ Guest history
➤ Report writer
➤ Travel agent billing
➤ Tour operations
➤ Housekeeping

- ➤ Yield management
- ➤ Package plans
- ➤ Wholesaler blocks
- ➤ Call accounting interface
- ➤ In-room movie interface
- ➤ Point-of-sale interface
- ➤ Environmental control
- ➤ Central reservations
- ➤ General ledger
- ➤ Accounts payable
- ➤ Condo owner accounting
- ➤ Association management
- ➤ Long-term rentals
- ➤ Timeshare rentals[13]

Medium- to large-sized hotels typically have a minicomputer with front and back office (accounting, control, purchasing) applications. In addition, other hardware platforms may exist within the property, and applications may include back office, point-of-sale, and conference or catering scheduling.[14]

Smaller hotels may use a microcomputer either as a stand-alone system or with a local area network to support the applications.[15]

Marriott hotels have based their property management system on the IBM 173 RISC system/6000. The worldwide installation includes 250 hotels. The goal was to set up a single architecture with one integrated database for sales, catering, human resources, back office, accounting, and front office operations.[16]

Holiday Inn Worldwide (sixteen hundred hotels) has invested over $60 million installing PMSs in all of its properties. The $60 million covers leasing the Encore PMS for use in all its properties, development of the Holiday Inn Reservation Optimization system, free use of hardware and software for all hotels, and training for employees. The system integrates revenue optimization and customer tracking software to maximize income for the properties and options for the guests.[17]

The advantages of the Holiday Inn Reservation Optimization (HIRO) and ENCORE are that they include a two-way interface with Holidex (the Holiday Corporation's reservation system) and will automate and simplify front desk procedures. The HIRO system, according to Holiday officials, is the first automated length-of-stay optimization system to be integrated with a central reservation system. This ability to manage length of stay and room type works like this: For example, in August 1991, some 81 percent of the multiple-night requests to Holidex were turned down due to no availability. With HIRO those denials will be turned into room nights and should recover at least $100 million for Holiday Inn.[18]

Until 1993 there were problems with both central reservation systems and property management systems. For example, the most important information about any given property has not been readily available to those in the best position to sell it. Too often, travel agents have been unable to tell if a room is available and at what price just by looking at the data on the terminal at her or his desk.[19]

The Hotel Industry Switch Company (THISCO) has created a pathway between the lodging industry's central reservation systems and those of the airlines. THISCO allows the travel agents to look into the hotel database.[20] This system, together with a software package from Anasail, has been installed in Hospitality Franchise Systems, which franchise Days Inn, Ramada, and Howard Johnson brands. Travelodge, Promus, and Choice Hotels have all customized the software for their own uses.

The ultimate goal is for hotels to have access to a global reservations network. Larry Chervenak, a well-known authority on hospitality technology, estimates that more than $3 billion has been invested by various players in the global competition to create reservation systems that will feed more business into hotels.[21]

Hotel systems generally piggyback on the airline systems. The two main airline computer systems, Sabre (American Airlines) and Apollo (jointly owned by United, USAir, Air Canada, and several European airlines), both have developed sophisticated global reservation systems designed to make it easy for the travel agent to make international hotel reservations.

Covla is an example of an international CRS system. It is a subsidiary of the Covla airline system known to U.S. travel agents as Apollo. It enables agents to book hotel reservations around the world. Companies like Ritz-Carlton, Swissotel, and Pan Pacific utilize this system. American Airlines has adopted Qik-Res, a software system developed by Qantas that runs on personal computers (PCs). These user-friendly software systems make it easier for travel agents to make hotel reservations in four easy steps: shop, look, check, and book. Curiously, a recent study suggests that business travelers, who account for almost half of current occupancy levels, are reached directly, with travel agents playing little or no role in formulating property selection. According to Smith Travel Research, U.S. hotel guest room revenue was $36 billion. Domestic bookings through travel agents account for only $6.6 billion, according to an estimate by the American Society of Travel Agents. A hotel and travel index study found that only 14 percent of guests booked hotel reservations through a travel agent.[22] The same study indicated that the percentage of trips involving agents declined to 21.5 percent. This indicates that according to this study, fewer hotel rooms are being booked by travel agents.

This conflicts with another survey conducted by *Hotel and Motel Management,* which shows that in 1991 business travelers were surveyed and respondents indicated that they generally make their own hotel reservations 65.2 percent of the time. When it came to choosing a hotel, basic criteria seemed to be important. Although location and price may be the top considerations, cleanliness was rated highest by 91.1 percent of the sample. Comfortable mattresses and pillows were second, with 89.1 percent rating these as important or very important. In terms of brand loyalty, frequent travelers were more likely to specify a particular chain than nonfrequent travelers.[23] It is important to note that business travelers make their own hotel reservations; consequently, the criteria for hotel selection is also important to hotel executives.

The oversupply of rooms has encouraged operators to use information technology to reduce costs and provide better service. The computerized hotel reservation system enables hotels to fill more efficiently the maximum number of rooms on any given day. Reservation programs enable the reservation clerk to provide a high level of personalized service for repeat visitors. Hotels can use yield management systems to maximize revenues by basing the selling price of a room on the expected demand for rooms on a given night.[24]

Yield Management

Yield management is a demand-forecasting technique used to maximize room revenue that the hotel industry borrowed from the airlines. It is based on the economics of supply and demand, which means that prices rise when demand is strong and drop when demand is weak. Thus, the purpose of yield management is to increase profitability. Naturally, management would like to sell every room at the highest rack rate. However, this is not reality, and rooms are sold at discounts on the rack rate. An example would be the corporate or group rate. In most hotels, only a small percentage of rooms are sold at rack rate. This is because of conventions and group rates and other promotional discounts that are necessary to stimulate demand. What yield management does is to allocate the right type of capacity to the right customer at the right price so as to maximize revenue or yield per available room.[25]

Generally the demand for room reservations follows the pattern of group bookings being made months or even years in advance of arrival and individual bookings, which mostly are made a few days before arrival. Figures 4–7 and 4–8 show the pattern of group and individual room reservations.

Group reservations are booked months, even years, in advance. Yield management will monitor reservations and, based on previous trends and current demand, determine the number and type of rooms to sell at what price to obtain the maximum revenue.

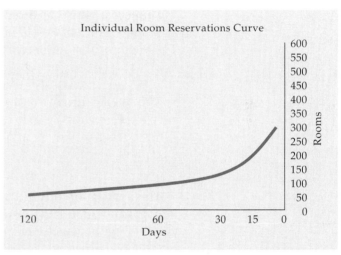

Figure 4–7   *Individual Room Reservations Curve* (Adapted from Sheryl E. Kimes, "The Basics of Yield Management," *The Cornell Hotel Restaurant Administration Quarterly,* November 1989.)

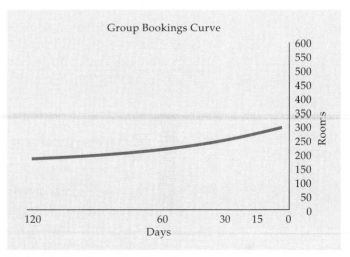

Figure 4–8   *Group Booking Curve*

The curve in Figure 4–7 indicates the pattern of few reservations being made 120 days prior to arrival. Most of the individual room bookings are made in the last few days before arrival at the hotel. The yield management program will monitor the demand and supply and recommend the number and type of rooms to sell for any given day, and the price for which to sell each room.

With yield management, not only will the time before arrival be an important consideration in the pricing of guest rooms, but also the type of room to be occupied. For example, there could be a different price for a double, queen, or king room when used for single occupancy. This rate could be above the single rack rate. Similarly, double and multiple room occupancy would yield higher room rates. It works as follows:[26]

Suppose a hotel has three hundred rooms and a rack rate of $150. The average number of rooms sold is two hundred per night at an average rate of $125. The yield for this property would be

$$\text{Occupancy percentage} = 200 \div 300 = 66.6\%$$

The rate achievement factor is

$$\$125 \div 200 = 62.5\%$$

and the yield would be

$$.666 \text{ x } .625 = 41\%$$

The application of yield management in hotels is still being refined to take into consideration factors such as multiple nights' reservations and incremental food and beverage revenue. If the guest wants to arrive on a high demand night and stay though several low demand nights, what should the charge be?

Yield management has been refined with profit analysis by segment (PABS), which uses a combination of marketing information and cost analysis. It identifies average revenues generated by different market segments and then examines the contribution margin for each of the segments considering the cost of making those sales.[27]

There are some disadvantages to yield management. For instance, if a business person attempts to make a reservation at a hotel three days before arrival and the rate quoted in order to maximize revenue is considered too high, this person may decide to select another hotel and not even consider the first hotel when making future reservations.

Reservations

The reservations department is headed by the reservations manager who, in many hotels today, is on an equal seniority with the front office manager and reports directly to the director of rooms division or the director of sales. This emphasizes the importance of the sales aspects of reservations and encompasses yield management. Reservations is the first contact for the guest or person making the reservation for the guest. Although the contact may be by telephone, a distinct impression of the hotel is registered with the guest. This calls for exceptional telephone manners and telemarketing skills. Because some guests may be shopping for the best value, it is essential to sell the hotel by emphasizing its advantages over the competition.

The reservation department generally works from 8 a.m. to 6 p.m. Depending on the size of the hotel, several people may be employed in this important department. The desired outcome of the reservations department is to exceed guest expectations when they make reservations. This is achieved by selling all of the hotel rooms for the maximum possible dollars, and avoiding possible guest resentment of being overcharged. Reservations originate from a variety of sources (in rank order with 1 being the highest source of reservations):

1. Telephone to the same property
   a. Fax
   b. Telex
   c. Letter
   d. Cable
2. Corporate/1-800 numbers
3. Travel agents
4. Hotel reservations
5. Meeting planners (may be number one in a convention hotel)
6. Tour operators (may be number one in resort areas)
7. Referral from another company property
8. Airport telephone
9. Walk in

Clearly, reservations are of tremendous importance to the hotel because of the potential and actual revenue realized. Many hotel chains have a 1-800 number that a prospective guest may call without charge to make a reservation at any of the company properties in the United States and internationally. The corporate central reservations system allows operators to access the inventory of rooms availability of each hotel in the chain. Once a reservation has been made, it is immediately deducted from the inventory of rooms for the duration of the guest stay. The central reservations system interfaces with the hotel's inventory and simultaneously allows reservations to be made by the individual hotel reservations personnel. A number of important details need to be recorded when taking reservations, as the computer screen in the photo indicates.

Central Reservations Office

Hotel Reservations Agent

Confirmed reservations are reservations made with sufficient time for a confirmation slip to be returned to the client by mail or fax. Confirmation is generated by the computer printer and indicates confirmation number, date of arrival and departure, type of room booked, number of guests, number of beds, type of bed, and any special requests. The guest may bring the confirmation slip to the hotel to verify the booking.

Guaranteed reservations are when the person making the reservation wishes to ensure that the reservation will be guaranteed. This is arranged at the time the reservation is made and generally applies in situations when the guest is expected to arrive late. The hotel takes the credit card number, which guarantees the payment of the room, of the person being billed. The hotel agrees to hold the room for late arrival. The importance of guaranteed reservations is that the guest will more likely cancel beforehand if unable to show up, which gives more accurate inventory room count and minimizes no shows.

Another form of guaranteed reservations is advance deposit/advance payment. In certain situations—for example during a holiday—in order to protect itself against having empty rooms (no shows), the hotel requires that a deposit of either one night or the whole stay be paid in advance of the guest's arrival. This is done by obtaining the guest's credit card number, which may be charged automatically for the first night's accommodation. This discourages no-shows. Corporations that use the hotel frequently may guarantee all of their bookings so as to avoid any problems in the event a guest arrives late, remembering that in cities where the demand is heavy, hotels release any nonguaranteed or nonpaid reservations at 4 p.m. or 6 p.m. on the evening of the guest's expected arrival.

Communications CBX or PBX

The communications CBX or PBX includes in-house communications; guest communications, such as pagers and radios; voice mail; faxes; messages; and emergency center. Guests often have their first contact with the hotel by telephone. This underlines the importance of prompt and courteous attention to all calls, because first impressions last.

The communications department is a vital part of the smooth running of the hotel. It is also a profit center because hotels generally add a 50 percent charge to all long distance calls placed from guest rooms. Local calls cost around $0.75 to $1.25, plus tax.

Communications operates twenty-four hours a day, in much the same way as the front office does, having three shifts. It is essential that this department be staffed with people who are trained to be calm under pressure and who follow emergency procedures.

Communications

Guest/Uniformed Service

Because first impressions are very important to the guest, the guest service or uniformed staff has a special responsibility. The guest service department or uniformed staff is headed by a guest services manager who may also happen to be the bell captain. The staff consists of door attendants and bellpersons and the concierge—although in some hotels the concierge reports directly to the front office manager.

Door attendants are the hotel's unofficial greeters. Dressed in impressive uniforms, they greet guests at the hotel front door, assist in opening/closing automobile doors, removing luggage from the trunk, hailing taxis, keeping the hotel entrance clear of vehicles, and giving guests information about the hotel and the local area in a courteous and friendly way. People in this position generally receive many gratuities (tips); in fact, years ago, the position was handed down from father to son or sold for several thousand dollars. Rumor has it that this is one of the most lucrative positions in the hotel, even more than the general manager's.

The bellperson's main function is to escort guests and transport luggage to their rooms. Bellpersons also need to be knowledgeable about the local area and all facets of the hotel and its services. Because they have so much guest contact, they need a pleasant, outgoing personality. The bellperson explains the services of the hotel and points out the features of the room (lighting, TV, air conditioning, telephone, wake-up calls, laundry and valet service, room service and restaurants, and the pool and health spa).

Concierge

The concierge is a uniformed employee of the hotel who has her or his own separate desk in the lobby or on special concierge floors. The concierge is a separate department from the front office room clerks and cashiers.

Until 1936, a concierge was not an employee of the hotel but an independent entrepreneur who purchased a position from the hotel and paid the salaries, if any, of his or her uniformed subordinates.[28]

Today's concierge, as one historically-minded concierge put it, has come to embody the core of a hotel's efforts to serve guests in a day when the inn is so large that the innkeeper can no longer personally attend to each guest.[29] Luxury hotels in most cities have concierges. New York's Plaza

Concierge

Hotel has eight hundred rooms and a battery of ten concierges who serve under the direction of Thomas P. Wolfe. The concierge assists guests with a broad range of services such as the following:

➤ Tickets to the hottest shows in town, even for the very evening on the day they are requested. Naturally, the guest pays up to about $150 per ticket.
➤ A table at a restaurant that has no reservations available
➤ Advice on local restaurants, activities, attractions, amenities, and facilities
➤ Airline tickets and reconfirmation of flights
➤ VIP's messages and special requests, such as shopping.

Less Frequent Requests
➤ Organize a wedding on two days' notice
➤ Arrange for a member of the concierge department to go to a consulate or embassy for visas to be stamped in guests' passports
➤ Handle business affairs

What will a concierge do for a guest? Almost anything, *Conde' Nast Traveler* learned from concierges at hotels around the world. Among the more unusual requests were the following:

1. Some Japanese tourists staying at the Palace Hotel in Madrid decided to bring bullfighting home. Their concierge found bulls for sale, negotiated the bulls' purchase, and had them shipped to Tokyo.
2. After watching a guest pace the lobby, the concierge of a London hotel, now operating the desk at the Dorchester, asked the pacer if he could help. The guest was to be married within the hour, but his best man had been detained. Because he was dressed up anyway, the concierge volunteered to substitute.
3. A guest at the Hotel Plaza Athenee in Paris wanted to prevent her pet from mingling with dogs from the wrong side of the boulevard while walking. Madame requested that the concierge buy a house in a decent neighborhood so that her pampered pooch might stroll in its garden unsullied. Although the dog continued to reside at the hotel, Madame's chauffeur shuttled him to the empty house for his daily constitutional.
4. A guest at London's Sheraton Park Tower needed parts for his yacht's Volvo engine for the next morning's sail. Unable to find them in England, the concierge rang the Volvo factory in Sweden and arranged for a messenger from the hotel to fly to Sweden, retrieve the parts, and deliver them late that evening.
5. Dressing for dinner, a guest at the Phoenician in Scottsdale, Arizona, suddenly realized that he had forgotten his shoes. The concierge happened to wear the same size shoe and lent the man his loafers.
6. Unable to find a room at the Palace in Madrid during bullfight season, a regular guest of the hotel contacted the concierge. There were no vacant rooms anywhere in the city. Unfazed, the concierge lent the guest a more modest but decidedly sufficient accommodation—his own apartment.

7. A guest at the Little Nell in Aspen craved lunch at Bonnie's, a star-studded restaurant high on Aspen Mountain. Alas, she could not ski. The concierge chartered a helicopter to whisk her to the summit, and a snow-mobile zoomed her off to Bonnie's.

8. In a futile attempt to be gracious, the concierge at the Bel-Air in Los Angeles sent a fruit basket to a guest with a difficult reputation. Minutes later, the guest called the concierge, fuming because the strawberries in the basket still had their stems. The contrite concierge retrieved the gift, stemmed the strawberries, returned the basket, and made a mental note: "stemless fruit only."

9. Four trained elephants from the Lincoln Park Zoo in Chicago arrived in New York City for a commercial photo shoot, but the guest who requested them had not bothered to arrange for their transportation and housing. The job fell to the resourceful concierge at the Royalton.

10. Shipping souvenirs home is a typical task for many concierges. A guest at the Windsor Court Hotel in New Orleans had clearly been to a medical convention. His shipment request: several human cadavers. (They went out parcel post.)[30]

The work of the concierge may seem glamorous, especially when seeing Michael J. Fox play a concierge in the movie *For Love or Money.* However, not all hotel concierges earn high salaries, and it does take a few years to learn the ropes. It also takes time to learn who the big spenders are and to build up a clientele who will place their confidence in a particular concierge.

The concierge needs not only a detailed knowledge of the hotel and its services, but also of the city and even international details. Many concierges speak several languages; most important of all, they need to want to help people and have a pleasant outgoing personality. At the Westin St. Francis in San Francisco, a special three-employee department has been created to refine Japanese amenities. This Japanese guest service combines the functions of concierge, front desk, and tour-briefing. Given that one third of all visitors to San Francisco are international travelers and that most Japanese visitors do not speak English, this progressive approach to guest satisfaction is receiving positive feedback.[31]

At Ritz-Carltons, concierges are responsible for providing effortless and polished service to the guests of the hotel. At the Ritz-Carlton, each concierge has completed a three-month certification program requiring extensive knowledge of the city, the hotel, and the parent company. It is consistently necessary to demonstrate patience, teamwork, resourcefulness, strong communication and organizational skills, diplomacy, discretion, and always a pleasant demeanor.[32]

The concierges' organization, which promotes high professional and ethical standards, is the U.P.P.G.H. (Union Professionelle des Portiers des Grand Hotels), more commonly called the *Clefs d'Or* because of the crossed goldkey insignia concierges usually wear on the lapels of their uniforms. The Clefs d'Or has about four thousand members in twenty-four countries, with approximately 150 U.S. members.[33]

Housekeeping

The largest department in terms of the number of people employed is housekeeping. Up to 50 percent of the hotel employees may work in this department. The person in charge is the executive housekeeper or director of services. Her or his duties and responsibilities call for exceptional leadership, organization, motivation, and commitment to maintaining high standards. The logistics of servicing large numbers of rooms on a daily basis can be challenging.

The importance of the housekeeping department is underlined by guest surveys that consistently rank cleanliness of rooms number one.

The following show the ten rules for effective housekeeping leadership:

1. Utilize people power effectively
   Spread responsibilities and tasks to get work done properly and on time
2. Devise easy methods of reporting work that has to be done
   Encourage feedback from all associates and continuous communication with the associates
3. Develop standard procedures for routine activities
   Help associates to develop consistent work habits
4. Install inventory controls
   Control costs for supplies and equipment
5. Motivate housekeeping associates
   Keep high morale, motivation, and understanding
6. Accept challenges presented by guests and management
   Remain unflappable in face of any request
7. Involve associates in planning
   Encourage associates to use imagination to make the job easier and quicker without changing standards
8. Increase educational level of staff
   Support training, encouragement, educational classes
9. Set recruitment programs to develop management trainees
   Give trainees opportunities to advance
10. Cooperate and coordinate with other departments, i.e., front office, engineering and maintenance, and laundry

The four major areas of responsibilities for the executive housekeeper are as follows:

1. Leadership of people, equipment, and supplies
2. Cleanliness and servicing the guest rooms and public areas
3. Operating the department according to financial guidelines prescribed by the general manager
4. Keeping records

An example of an executive housekeeper's day might be as follows:

7:45 Walk the lobby and property with the night cleaners and supervisors

Executive Housekeeper

Check the housekeeping log book

Check the forecast house count for numbers of check outs

Check daily activity reports, stayovers, check ins, and VIPs to ensure appropriate standards

Attend housekeepers' meeting

Meet challenges

Train new employees in the procedures

Meet with senior housekeepers/department managers

Give productivity checks

Check budget

Approve purchase orders

Check inventories

Give room inspections

Review maintenance checks

Interview potential employees

6:00 Attend to human resource activities, counseling, and employee development

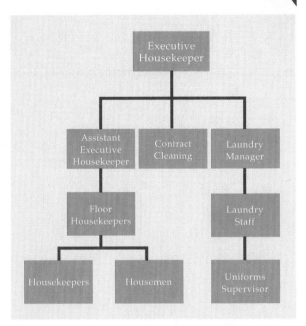

Figure 4–9   *Executive Housekeeping Personnel*

Perhaps the biggest challenge of an executive housekeeper is the leadership of all the employees in the department. Further, these employees are often of different nationalities. Depending on the size of the hotel, the executive housekeeper is assisted by an assistant executive housekeeper and one or more housekeeping supervisors, who in turn supervise a number of room attendants or housekeeping associates (see Figure 4–9). The assistant executive housekeeper manages the housekeeping office. The first important daily task of this position is to break out the hotel into sections for allocation to the room attendants' schedules.

The rooms of the hotel are listed on the floor master. If the room is vacant, nothing is written next to the room number. If the guest is expected to check out, then SC will be written next to the room number. A stayover will have SS, on hold is AH, out of order is XX, and VIPs are highlighted in colors according to the amenities required.

If 258 rooms are occupied and ten of these are suites (which count as two rooms), then the total number of rooms to be allocated to room attendants is 268 (minus any no shows). The remaining total is then divided by 17, the number of rooms that each attendant is expected to make up.

Total number of rooms occupied	258
Add 10 for the suites	10
Total number of rooms and suites occupied	268
Less any no shows	3
	265

Divide 265 by 17 (the number of rooms each attendant services) =

16 (the number of attendants required for that day)

Figure 4–10 shows a daily attendant's schedule.

Housekeepers Guest Room Self Inspection Rating

Inspection Codes:

P – POLISH	R – REPLACE	E – WORK ORDER	S – SOAP SCUM	SM – SMEAR
SA – STAIN	H – HAIR	D – DIRT	DU – DUST	M – MISSING

PART I – GUEST ROOM		S			U	COMMENTS
Entry, door, frame, threshold, latch				1		
Unusual odor OR smoke smell				3		
CLOSET, doors, loovers–containing				1		
Hangers, 8 suits, 4 skirts, 2 bags w/ invoices				2		
Two (2) Robes, with info card				2		
Extra TP & FACIAL				1		
One (1) luggage rack				1		
Current rate card				1		
VALET	Shoe Horn & Mitt			2		
DRESSER	LAMP/ SHADE/ BULB			2		
	ICE BUCKET, LID, TRAY			2		
	TWO(2) WINE GLASSES			2		
	Room Service MENU			2		
MINI BAR	TOP, FRONT, 2 Wine glasses/ price list			1		
SAFE	KEY IN SAFE, SIGN			5		
CHECK BEHIND DRESSER				2		
DRAWERS	BIBLE AND BUDDHIST BOOK			1		
	PHONE BOOKS, ATT DIRECTORY			1		
TELEVISION	ON & OFF, CH 19 BEHIND			1		
COFFEE TABLE	REMOTE CONTROL/TEST 1			2		
	T.V. LISTINGS/BOOK MARK			1		
	GLASS TOP/LA JOLLA BOOK			1		
CARPET	VACUUM, SPOTS?			2		
SOFA	UNDER CUSHION/ BEHIND			2		
3 W LAMP	BULB, SHADE & CORD			1		
WINDOWS	GLASS, DOOR, LATCH – C BAR?			2		
CURTAINS	Pull – check seams			1		
PATIO	2 CHAIRS, TABLE & DECK			3		
DESK	2 CHAIRS, TOP, BASE & LAMP/SHADE			5		
	GREEN COMPENDIUM			3		
	Waste paper can			1		
BED	Tight, Pillows, bedspread			5		
	Check Under/SHEETS, PILLOWS			3		
HVAC	Control, setting, vent			1		
SIDE TABLES	Lamps & shade			2		
	Telephone, MESSAGE LIGHT			1		
	Clock Radio CORRECT TIME?			1		
MIRRORS	LARGE MIRROR OVER DRESSER			1		
PICTURES	ROOM ART WORK			1		
WALLS	Marks, stains, etc.			3		

Figure 4–10 *Daily Attendant's Schedule*

Housekeepers Guest Room Self Inspection Rating

Inspection Codes:

P – POLISH	R – REPLACE	E – WORK ORDER	S – SOAPSCUM	SM – SMEAR
SA – STAIN	H – HAIR	D – DIRT	DU – DUST	M – MISSING

PART II – BATHROOM	S			U		COMMENTS
BATH TUBE/ SHOWER						
GROUT/TILE & EDGE			2			
ANTI SLIP GRIDS			2			
SIDE WALLS			1			
SHOWER HEAD			1			
WALL SOAP DISH			1			
CONTROL LEVER			1			
FAUCET			1			
CLOTHESLINE			1			
SHOWER ROD, HOOKS			1			
SHOWER CURTAIN/ LINER			2			
VANITY TOP, SIDE & EDGE			1			
SINK, TWO FAUCETS			3			
3 GLASSES, COASTERS			2			
WHITE SOAP DISH			1			
FACIAL TISSUE & BOX			1			
AMENITY BASKET						
1 SHAMPOO			1			
1 CONDITIONER			1			
1 MOISTURIZER			1			
2 BOXED SOAP			1			
1 SHOWER CAP			1			
MIRROR LARGE & COSMETIC			2			
WALLS CEILING & VENT			2			
TOILET TOP, SEAT, BASE & LIP			2			
OTHER TOILET PAPER, fold			1			
SCALE AND TRASH CAN			2			
FLOOR, SWEPT AND MOPPED			3			
TELEPHONE			1			
BATH LINENS, racks						
THREE (3) WASH CLOTHS			1			
THREE (3) HAND TOWELS			1			
THREE(3) BATH TOWELS			1			
ONE (1) BATH MAT			1			
ONE (1) BATH RUG			1			
LIGHT SWITCH			1			
DOOR FULL LENGTH MIRROR			1			
HANDLE/LOCK			1			
THRESHOLD			1			
PAINTED SURFACE			1			

Figure 4–10   *(continued)*

In order to reduce payroll costs and encourage room attendants to become "stars," a number of hotel corporations have empowered the best attendants to check their own rooms. This has reduced the need for supervisors. Notice how the points are weighted for various items. This is the result of focus groups of hotel guests who explained the important things to them about a room. The items with the highest points were the ones that most concerned the guests.

The assistant executive housekeeper or administrative assistant will assist the executive housekeeper with a number of the duties and will be the anchor person in the housekeeping office. This is the central headquarters for all housekeeping operations. The following are some examples from the Sheraton Grand, Torrey Pines, California:

1. All housekeeping associates report here.
2. Section assignments are given.
3. All housekeeping telephone calls are received here.
4. All check out and in order rooms are processed here.
5. All guest rooms that are not cleaned by specified time are reported.
6. All household supplies are issued.
7. Commercial laundry, counting linen, and checking linen may be handled here.
8. Table linen may be issued here.
9. All uniforms and costumes may be issued here.
10. Working records are kept.
11. All housekeeping pass keys are kept and controlled.

Guest room supplies on housekeeping associates' carts are replaced during the night shift. It is suggested that the items given away to the customer are placed on the lower shelf of the cart to discourage guests from collecting souvenirs. Taking calls and relaying information about the rooms is a vital part of the communications necessary for the smooth operation of this busy department.

The evening assistant housekeeper or housekeeper supervisor will take over the office and allocate the turndown sections to the evening. Each attendant has an allocation of sixty-three rooms to turndown and a turndown summary report to complete. The attendants also report back to the housekeeping office any discrepancies, which are in turn forwarded and communicated to the front office.

The housekeeping associates clean and service between fifteen and twenty rooms per day depending on the individual hotel characteristics. Servicing a room takes longer in some older hotels than it does in some of the newer properties. Also, service time depends on the number of check out rooms versus stayovers because servicing check outs takes longer. Housekeeping associates begin their day at 8:00 a.m., reporting to the executive or assistant executive housekeeper. They are assigned a block of rooms and given room keys, for which they must sign and return before going off duty.

Housekeeping Associate Making up a Room

The role of the executive housekeeper may vary slightly between the corporate chain and the independent hotel. An example is the purchasing of furnishings and equipment. A large independent hotel relies on the knowledge and experience of the executive housekeeper to make appropriate selections, whereas the chain hotel company has a corporate purchase agent (assisted by a designer) to make many of these decisions.

The executive housekeeper is responsible for a substantial amount of record keeping. In addition to the scheduling and evaluation of employees, an inventory of all guest rooms and public area furnishings must be accurately maintained with the record of refurbishment. Most of the hotel's maintenance work orders are initiated by the housekeepers who report the maintenance work order. Many hotels now have a computer link up between housekeeping and engineering and maintenance to speed the process. Guests expect their rooms to be fully functional, especially at today's prices. Housekeeping maintains a perpetual inventory of guest room amenities, cleaning supplies, and linens.

Productivity in the housekeeping department is measured by the person hours per occupied room. The labor costs per person hour, for a full service hotel is $1.10 or 6.6 minutes of labor for every occupied room in the hotel. Another key ratio is the labor cost, which is expected to be 5.1 percent of room sales. Controllable expenses are measured per occupied rooms. These expenses include guest supplies like soap, shampoo, hand and body lotion, sewing kits, and stationary. Although this will vary according to the type of hotel, the cost should be about $1.75 per room. Cleaning supplies should be approximately $.30 and linen costs $.75, including the purchase and laundering of all linen. These budgeted costs are sometimes hard to achieve. The executive housekeeper may be doing a great job controlling costs, but if the sales department discounts rooms, the room sales figures may come in below budget. This would have the effect of increasing the costs per occupied room.

Another concern for the executive housekeeper is accident prevention. Insurance costs have skyrocketed in recent years, and employers are struggling to increase both employee and guest safety. It is necessary for accidents to be carefully investigated. Some employees have been known to have an accident at home but go in to work and report it as a work-related injury in order to be covered by workers' compensation. In order to safeguard themselves to some extent, hotels keep sweep logs of the public areas; in the event of a guest slip and fall, the hotel can show that it does genuinely take preventative measures to protect its guests.

The U.S. Senate Bill 198, known as the Employee Right to Know, has heightened awareness of the storage, handling, and use of dangerous chemicals. Information about the chemicals must be made available to all employees. Great care and extensive training is required to avoid dangerous accidents.

The executive housekeeper must also maximize loss prevention. Strict policies and procedures are necessary to prevent losses from guest rooms. Some hotels require housekeeping associates to sign a form stating that they understand not to let any guest into any room. Such action would result in immediate termination of employment. Although this may seem drastic, it is the only way to avoid some hotel thefts.

Laundry

Increasingly, hotels are operating their own laundries. This subdepartment generally reports to the executive housekeeper. The modern laundry operates computerized washing/drying machines and large presses. Dry cleaning for both guests and employees is a service that may also come under the laundry department.

Houseperson

Some hotels, especially the smaller and older ones, contract out the laundry service. This is because it is costly to alter an existing hotel to provide space for laundry. Even space itself costs money because the space might be otherwise used for revenue-producing purposes, such as meetings, functions, and so on. In addition, by contracting out, the hotel does not have to own its own linen. It may rent linen and be charged for each piece used. However, operators frequently complain that they receive inferior linen and inconsistent service. Another alternative is for the hotel to purchase its own linen and have it laundered by contract. In either case, the executive housekeeper must ensure that strict control is maintained over linen.

The Chicago Hilton and Towers has installed a semicustomized linen-management and inventory-control system that is expected to save the 1,620-room property between $70,000 and $100,000 annually. The system reduces labor costs by eliminating the need to manually sort linen from the different properties that are served. In addition, because the system provides a perpetual inventory, needs can be anticipated better and overtime costs by housekeeping staff can be minimized.[34]

Much of the heavy work in the housekeeping department is conducted by housemen (housepersons). They clean public areas using heavy floor polishers for marble or tile floors, vacuum the corridors on the guest room floors, do carpet shampooing and moving of furniture, and, on occasion, take the linen from the linen room to the floors. The housemen may also assist the housekeepers with spring cleaning and the turning of mattresses.

Security/Loss Prevention

The protection of guests and their property is a crucial part of hotel operations. Owner and operators are charged under law to take all reasonable precautions to protect guests from robbery, arson, rape, and other kinds of assault. In addition, innkeepers may be held responsible for injuries to guests during the course of their stay. The courts have awarded huge sums of money to guests that hotels have failed to protect. When a serious incident occurs, it may cost the hotel not only dollars but also its reputation.

Hotel security has to deal with the following responsibilities:

➤ Emergency procedures
➤ Guest room security
➤ Key control
➤ Loss prevention/locks
➤ Access
➤ Alarm systems
➤ Perimeter control
➤ Lighting
➤ Closed circuit
➤ Safe deposit boxes
➤ Record keeping

Naturally, prevention is better than cure; thus, the essence of any security program should focus on preventing theft or damage to persons and property.

The security department is largely responsible for reacting to emergency situations. This is an awesome responsibility in today's crime-prevalent society. Most crimes occur between 6 p.m. and 3 a.m. During this time span, fewer hotel employees are on duty, especially on the guest room floors. Therefore, it is essential for hotels to have established procedures for each kind of emergency.

Guest room security has been upgraded in recent years by the introduction of the electronic room key. This plastic key is encoded at the front desk as the guests check in. These keys are only valid for the duration of the guests' stay and will not open the door after the guests check out. These keys are a definite improvement over a metal key that could easily fall into the wrong hands and allow a thief to gain access to the room at a later date.

Closed circuit television cameras have also helped reduce the number of thefts and assault cases in hotels. Strategically placed cameras will record movements in hotel lobbies, at the cashier's desk, and on the guest room floors. Hidden surveillance cameras are a valuable addition to the security defense. These cameras will also record people's movements without their realizing that they are being observed. These movements are displayed on monitor screens in the security office.

At the Mirage resort hotel in Las Vegas, security concerns are heightened by the cash-intensive casino operation. The Polaroid ID-2000 Plus computer-based electronic security management system plays a central role in supporting the Mirage's integrated security environment. The system combines advanced database computers and electronic-imaging technologies. This improves efficiency and helps minimize transaction discrepancies.[35]

Lack of security concerning guest room keys is the most serious problem faced by security professionals. In order to prevent problems, the front desk must take inventory of guest room keys whenever guests check out of the hotel. In addition, the front desk staff must verify identity before providing a new key. The most effective way to ensure the security of master keys is to conduct random key checks. Key logs with employees signing keys in and out should be maintained. Some hotels use a card exchange method, whereby employees who require keys are given laminated photo ID cards indicating which keys he or she is permitted to sign out.[36]

In order to reduce robberies, many hotels have installed a personal safe in every guest room in addition to centrally located safe deposit boxes. There are different types of locking devices available: plastic card locks with the combination encoded on it, digital locks with standard numerical keypad on the door of the safe, or standard key locks equipped with a biaxial key lock that can easily be replaced by hotel security.[37]

Summary

1. A big hotel is run by a general manager and an executive committee, which is represented by the key executives of all the major departments, such as rooms division, food and beverage, marketing, sales, and human resources.
2. The general manager represents the hotel and is responsible for its profitability and performance. Because of increased job consolidation, he or she also is expected to attract business and to empathize with the cultures of both guests and employees.
3. The rooms division department consists of front office, reservations, housekeeping, concierge, guest services, and communications.
4. The front desk, as the center of the hotel, sells rooms and maintains balanced guest accounts, which are completed daily by the night auditor. The front desk constantly must meet guests' needs by offering services such as mailing, faxing, and messages.

5. The property management system, centralized reservations, and yield management have enabled a hotel to work more efficiently and to increase profitability and guest satisfaction.
6. The communications department, room service, and guest services (such as door attendants, bellpersons, and the concierge) are vital parts of the personality of a hotel.
7. Housekeeping is the largest department of the hotel. The executive housekeeper is in charge of inventory, cleaning, employees, and accident and loss prevention. The laundry may be cleaned directly in the hotel or by a hired laundry service.
8. The electric room key, closed-circuit television cameras, and personal room safes are basic measures to protect the guests and their property.

Review Exercises

1. Briefly define the purpose of a hotel. Why is it important to empathize with the culture of guests?
2. List the main responsibilities of the front office manager.
3. Explain the terms *sell out, American plan,* and *rack rate.*
4. What are the advantages and disadvantages of yield management?

5. Why is the concierge an essential part of the personality of a hotel?
6. Explain the importance of accident and loss prevention. What security measures are taken in order to protect guests and their property?

Key Words and Concepts

Amenities
Average daily rate (ADR)
Central reservations system
Chief accountant/controller
City ledger
Concierge

Confirmed and guaranteed
  reservations
Daily report
Executive committee
Food and beverage director
General manager

Housekeeping
Human resources director
Inventory control
Marketing and sales director
Property management
  systems

Reservations
Room occupancy percentage
Room rates
Rooms division manager
Security/loss prevention
Yield management

Notes

[1] C. Nebel Eddystone III, *Managing Hotels Effectively: Lessons from Outstanding General Managers.* New York: Van Nostrand Reinhold, 1991, p. 13.

[2] Theodore R. Nathan, *Hotelmanship: A Guide to Hospitality Industry Marketing and Management.* Englewood Cliffs, N. J.: Institute for Business Planning, 1982, p. 16.

[3] Personal conversation with Steve Pelger, General Manager, Hyatt Regency, La Jolla, Calif., Nov. 1994.

[4] Eddystone, op cit., p. xviii.

[5] Stephen Michaelides, "Narrowing the Margins of Consistency," *Restaurant Hospitality, 76,* 10, October 1992, p. 26.

[6] Stephen G. Michaelides, "The First Resort," *Restaurant Hospitality, 74,* 8, August 8, 1990, pp. 162–166.

[7] Howard Feiertag, "GMs Should Assume Director-of-Sales Duties," *Hotel and Motel Management, 208,* 2, February 1, 1993, p. 14.

[8] Robert Selwitz, "Hoteliers Put Forth Spirited Efforts to Boost Profits," *Hotel and Motel Management, 206,* 15, September 9, 1991, pp. 2, 76.

[9] Ibid.

[10] Kathy Seal, "Westin Kauai Values Values," *Hotel and Motel Management, 206,* 6, April 8, 1991, pp. 2, 68, 82.

[11] PMS is a system of storing and retrieving information on reservations, room availability, room rates. The system may also interface with outlets (restaurants, bars, etc.) for recording guest charges. The accounting functions may also be integrated with a main system. Some hotels may have several systems that interface with one another.

[12] Michael L. Kasavana and Richard M. Brooks, *Managing Front Office Operations.* East Lansing, Mich.: The Educational Institute of the American Hotel and Motel Institute, 1991, p. 112.

[13] Resort Data Processing, Inc., Vail, Colorado 81657.

[14] Brian Katison, "The Politics of PMS," *Hotel and Motel Management, 207,* 11, June 22, 1992, pp. 33–35.

[15] Ibid.

[16] Maryfran Johnson, *Computerworld, 26,* 40, October 5, 1992, p. 6.

[17] Megan Row, "The PMS Wars: Holiday and Promos Are Chasing Each Other," *Lodging Hospitality, 48,* 6, June, 1992, p. 32.

[18] Alan Salomon, "Holiday Abuzz with HIRO/ENCORE," *Hotel and Motel Management, 207,* 7, April 27, 1992, pp. 33–34, 60.

[19] Richard Burns, "Lodging," *The American Hotel and Motel Association,* March 1993, p. 19.

[20] Ibid.

[21] Ibid.

[22] "Travel Agent Role Lessens as Business Redirects Bookings," *Hotel and Motel Management, 206,* 19, November 4, 1991, p. A-86.

[23] Pamela A. Weaver and Ken W. McCleary, "Basics Bring 'em Back: Extras Are Appreciated, but Business Travelers Still Value Good Service and Good Management," *Hotel and Motel Management, 206,* 11, June 24, 1991, pp. 29–32, 38.

[24] Joseph F. Durocher and Neil B. Niman, "Automated Guest Relations That Generate Hotel Reservations," *Information Strategy: The Executives Journal, 7,* 3, Spring 1991, pp. 27–30.

[25] Shirley Kimes, "The Basics of Yield Management," *The Cornell Hotel Restaurant Administration Quarterly, 30,* 3, November 1989, p. 14.

[26] Adapted from Michael L. Kasavana and Richard M. Brooks, *Managing Front Office Operations,* 3d ed. East Lansing, Mich.: The Educational Institute of the American Hotel and Motel Association, 1990, p. 390.

[27] William J. Quain, "Analyzing Sales-Mix Profitability," *The Cornell Hotel and Restaurant Administration Quarterly, 33,* 2, April 1992, pp. 56–62.

[28] McDowell Bryson and Adele Ziminski, *The Concierge: Key to Hospitality.* New York: John Wiley and Sons, 1992, p. 3.

[29] Betsy Wade, *The New York Times,* February 21, 1993.

[30] Nixon O. Jaso, "Your Secrets Are Safe with Me," *Conde' Nast Traveler, 5,* May 1993, p. 26.

[31] Leslee Jaquette, "St. Francis Caters to Japanese with Guest-Services Program," *Hotel and Motel Management, 207,* 13, July 27, 1992, pp. 6, 29.

[32] Michael Adams, "The Pleasure Is Theirs: A Day (or Two) in the Life of a Hotel Concierge," *Successful Meetings, 41,* 11, October 1992, pp. 69–75.

[33] Bryson and Ziminski, op cit., p. 194.

[34] Susan M. Bard, "Linen-Management System May Save a Bundle," *Hotel and Motel Management, 206,* 11, June 24, 1991, pp. 27–28.

[35] Juli Koentopp, "The Mirage Concerning Hotel Security," *Security Management, 36,* 12, December 1992, pp. 54–60.

[36] Phil Sunstrom, "Unlock the Secret to Key Control," *Security Management, 36,* 11, November 1992, pp. 59–61.

[37] Joanne A. Straub, "Safe Solution for Hotel Rooms," *Security Management, 36,* 12, December 1992, pp. 51–52.

Hotel Operations: Food and Beverage Division

After reading and studying this chapter you should be able to do the following:

➤ Describe the duties and responsibilities of a food and beverage director and other key department heads

➤ Describe a typical food and beverage director's day

➤ State the functions and responsibilities of the food and beverage departments

➤ Perform computations using key food and beverage operating ratios

Food and Beverage Management

In the hospitality industry, the food and beverage division is led by the director of food and beverage. She or he reports to the general manager and is responsible for the efficient and effective operation of the following departments:

➤ Kitchen/Catering/Banquet
➤ Restaurants/Room Service/Minibars
➤ Lounges/Bars/Stewarding

The position description for a director of food and beverage is both a job description and a specification of the requirements an individual needs to do the job. Figure 5–1 shows the duties and the average amount of time spent on each one.

In recent years, the list of skills needed by a food and beverage director have grown enormously, as shown by the following:

➤ Exceeding guests' expectations in food and beverage offerings and service
➤ Leadership
➤ Identifying trends
➤ Finding and keeping outstanding employees
➤ Training
➤ Motivation
➤ Budgeting
➤ Cost control
➤ Finding profit from all outlets
➤ Detailed working knowledge of the front of the home operations

These challenges are set against a background of stagnant or declining occupancies and the consequent drop in room sales. Therefore, greater emphasis has been placed on making food and beverage sales profitable. Traditionally, only about 20 percent of the hotel's operating profit comes from the food and beverage divisions. In contrast, an acceptable profit margin from a hotel's food and beverage division is generally considered to be 25 to 30 percent. This figure can vary according to the type of hotel. For example, according to Pannell Kerr Forster, an industry consulting firm, all-suite properties achieve a 7 percent food and beverage profit (probably because of the complimentary meals and drinks being offered to guests).

A typical food and beverage director's day might be like the following:

8:30 Check messages and read logs from outlets and security. Tour outlets, especially the family restaurant (a quick inspection)
Check breakfast buffet, reservations, and shift manager
Check daily specials
Check room service
Check breakfast service and staffing

POSITION TITLE: *Director of Food and Beverage: Food and Beverage*

REPORTS TO: *General Manager*

PURPOSE

Directs and organizes the activities of the food and beverage department to maintain high standards of food and beverage quality, service, and merchandising to maximize profits

EXAMPLES OF DUTIES

Average %
of time

10% Plan and direct planning and administration of the food and beverage department to meet the daily needs of the operation

10% Clearly describe, assign, and delegate responsibility and authority for the operation of the various food and beverage subdepartments, for example, room service, restaurants, banquets, kitchens, steward, and so on

10% Develop, implement, and monitor schedules for the operation of all restaurants and bars to achieve a profitable result

10% Participate with the chef and restaurant managers in the creation of attractive menus designed to attract a predetermined customer market

10% Implement effective control of food, beverage, and labor costs among all subdepartments

10% Assist area managers in establishing and achieving predetermined profit objectives and desired standards of quality for food, service, cleanliness, merchandising, and promotion

10% Regularly review and evaluate the degree of customer acceptance of the restaurant and banquet service, to recommend to management new operating and marketing policies whenever declining or constant sales imply (1) dissatisfaction by the customers, (2) material change in the make-up of the customer market, or (3) change in the competitive environment

10% Develop (with the aid of subdepartment heads) the operating tools necessary and incidental to modern management principles, for example, budgeting, forecasting, purchase specifications, recipes, portion specifications, menu abstracts, food production control, job descriptions, and so on

10% Continually evaluate the performance and encourage improvement of personnel in the food and beverage department. Planning and administering a training and development program within the department will provide well-trained employees at all levels and permit advancement for those persons qualified and interested in that career development.

Other

Regular attendance in conformance with standards established by management. Employees with irregular attendance will be subject to disciplinary action, up to and including termination of employment.

Due to the cyclical nature of the hospitality industry, employees may be required to work varying schedules to accommodate business needs.

On employment, all employees are required to fully comply with rules and regulations for the safe and efficient operation of facilities. Employees who violate rules and regulations will be subject to disciplinary action, up to and including termination of employment.

Supportive Functions

In addition to performance of the essential functions, employee may be required to perform a combination of the following supportive functions, with the percentage of time performance of each function to be determined solely by the supervisor:

Participate in manager-on-duty coverage program, requiring weekend stayover, constant monitoring, and trouble-shooting problems

Operate word processing program in computer

Perform any general cleaning tasks using standard cleaning products to adhere to health standards

SPECIFIC JOB KNOWLEDGE, SKILLS, AND ABILITIES

The employee must possess the following knowledge, skills, and abilities and be able to explain and demonstrate that he or she can perform the essential functions of the job, with or without reasonable accommodation, using some other combination of skills and abilities:

Considerable skill in complex mathematical calculations without error

Ability to effectively deal with internal and external customers, some of whom will require high levels of patience, information, and the ability to resolve conflicts

Ability to move throughout all food and beverage areas and hospitality suites and continually perform essential job functions

Ability to read, listen, and communicate effectively in English, both verbally and in writing

Ability to access and accurately input information using a moderately complex computer system

Hearing, smelling, tasting, and visual ability to observe and distinguish product quality and detect signs of emergency situations

QUALIFICATION STANDARDS

Education: College degree in related field required. Culinary skills and service background required

Experience: Extensive experience in restaurant, bar, banquet, stewarding, kitchen, sales, catering, and management required

License or certification: No special licenses required

Grooming: All employees must maintain a neat, clean, and well-groomed appearance (specific standards available)

Other: Additional language ability preferred

Courtesy Hilton Hotels.

Figure 5–1 *Job Description of Food and Beverage Director*

Visit executive chef and purchasing director

Visit executive steward's office to ensure that all the equipment is ready

Visit banquet service office to check on daily events and coffee break sequence

10:00 Work on current projects: new summer menu, pool outlet opening, conversion of a current restaurant with a new concept, remodeling of ballroom foyer, installation of new walk-in freezer, analysis of current profit-and-loss (P&L) statements. Plan weekly food and beverage department meetings

11:45 Visit kitchen to observe lunch service and check the "12:00 line," including banquets

Confer with executive chef

Check restaurants and banquet luncheon service

Have working lunch in employee cafeteria with executive chef, director of purchasing, or director of catering

1:30 Visit human resources to discuss current incidents

2:30 Check messages and return calls. Telemarket to attract catering and convention business

Conduct hotel daily menu meeting

3:00 Go to special projects/meetings

Tour cocktail lounges

Check for staffing

Review any current promotions

Check entertainment lineup

6:00 Check special food and beverage requests/requirements of any VIPs staying at the hotel

Tour kitchen

Review and taste

8:00 Review dinner specials

Check the restaurant and lounges

A food and beverage director's typical day usually starts at 8:00 a.m. and ends at 8:00 p.m., unless early or very late events are scheduled, in which case the working day is even longer. Usually, the food and beverage director works Monday through Saturday. If there are special events on Sunday, then she or he works on Sunday and takes Monday off. In a typical week, Saturdays are usually used to catch up on reading or specific projects.

The director of food and beverage eats in his or her restaurants at least twice a week for dinner and at least once a week for breakfast and lunch. Bars are generally visited with clients, at least twice per week. The director sees salespersons regularly, because they are good sources of information about what is

Food and Beverage Director and Executive Chef Discuss Operations

going on in the industry and can introduce leads for business. The director attends staff meetings, food and beverage meetings, executive committee meetings, interdepartmental meetings, credit meetings, and P&L statement meetings.

Food and Beverage Planning

Typically, the monthly forecast for a food and beverage department is prepared between the twelfth and the fifteenth of every month; a budget and forecast for the upcoming years is prepared between July and September. Every January, a planning meeting takes place with all the food and beverage department heads, and the year's special events are planned. These events include Easter, Mother's Day, St. Valentine's Day, St. Patrick's Day, Halloween, the summer program, Thanksgiving, Christmas, New Year's Eve, New Year's Day, and so on.[1]

To become a food and beverage director takes several years of experience and dedication. One of the best routes is to gain work experience or participate in an internship in several food and beverage departments while attending college. This experience should include full-time, practical kitchen work for at least one to two years followed by varying periods of a few months in purchasing, stores, cost control, stewarding,[2] and room service. Additionally, a year spent in each of the following work situations is helpful: restaurants, catering, and bars. After these departmental experiences, a person would likely serve as a department manager, preferably in a different hotel to the one in which the departmental experience was gained. This prevents the awkwardness of being manager of a department in which the person was once an employee, and also offers the employee the opportunity to learn different things at different properties. Figure 5–2 shows a career ladder for a food and beverage director.

Director of Food and Beverage Go-getters may rise to this position more quickly. It depends on the individual's capability, industry expansion, opportunities, and the labor market.	**9 to 15 years**
Assistant Food and Beverage Manager	**3 to 5 years**
Department Manager Kitchen restaurant, room service, stewarding, or cost control.	**3 to 5 years**
Department Experience kitchens, restaurants, lounges, purchasing, cost control, stewarding, room service, and catering	**3 to 5 years**

Figure 5–2   *Career Ladder to Director of Food and Beverage*

Kitchen

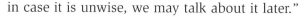

A hotel kitchen is under the charge of the executive chef; this person, in turn, is responsible to the director of food and beverage for the efficient and effective operation of kitchen food production. The desired outcome is to exceed guests' expectations in the quality and quantity of food, its presentation, taste, and portion size, and to ensure that hot food is served hot and cold food is served cold. The executive chef operates the kitchen in accordance with company policy and strives to achieve desired financial results.

Some executive chefs are becoming kitchen managers; they even serve as food and beverage directors in mid-sized and smaller hotels. This trend of "right sizing," observed in other industries, euphemistically refers to restructuring organizations to retain the most essential employees. Usually, this means cutting labor costs by consolidating job functions. For example, Michael Hammer is executive chef and food and beverage director at the 440-room Sheraton Grand Torrey Pines Hotel in La Jolla, California. Mike is typical of the new breed of executive chefs: His philosophy is to develop his sous chefs to make many of the operating decisions. Mike delegates ordering and hiring and firing decisions; sous chefs are the ones most in control of the group's production and the people who work on their teams. By delegating more of the operating decisions, Mike is developing the chefs de partie (or station chefs) and empowering them to make their own decisions. Mike says, "No decision is wrong—but in case it is unwise, we may talk about it later."

Executive Chef

Mike spends time maintaining morale, a vital part of the manager's job. The kitchen staff is under a great deal of pressure and frequently works against the clock. Careful cooperation is the key to success. Mike explains that he does not want his associates to "play the tuba"—he wants them to conduct the orchestra. He does not hold food and beverage department meetings; instead, he meets with groups of employees frequently and problems are handled as they occur. Controls are maintained with the help of software that costs out standard recipes, establishes perpetual inventories,[3] and calculates potential food cost per outlet. Today, executive chefs and food and beverage directors look past food cost to the actual profit contribution of an item. Contribution margin is the dollar differential between the cost and sales price of a menu item. For example, if a pasta dish costs $2.75 and sells for $8.75, the contribution is $6.00. If a chicken dish costs $3.25 and sells for $12.95 the contribution is $9.70, or $3.70 more. Labor cost benchmarks are measured by covers-per-person-hour. For example, in stewarding, it should take no more than one person hour to clean 37.1 covers.

Mike and his team of outlet managers have interesting challenges, such as staffing for the peaks and valleys of guests' needs at breakfast. Most guests want breakfast between 7 and 8:30 a.m., requiring organization to get the right people in the right place at the right time to ensure that meals are prepared properly and served in a timely manner.

At the Sheraton Grand Torrey Pines, executive chef Mike Hammer's day goes something like the following:

Breakfast Service

1. Arrive at 6 to 7 a.m., walk through the food and beverage department with the night cleaners
2. Check to make sure the compactor is working and the area is clean
3. Check that all employees are on duty
4. Ask people what kind of challenges they will face today
5. Sample as many dishes as possible, checking for taste, consistency, feel, smell, and overall quality
6. Check walk ins
7. Recheck once or twice a day to see where department stands production wise—this eliminates overtime
8. Approve schedules for food and beverage outlet
9. Keep a daily update of food and beverage revenues and costs
10. Forecast the next day's, week's, and month's business based on updated information
11. Check on final numbers for catering functions

Financial results are generally expressed in ratios, such as food cost percentage—the cost of food divided by the amount of food sales. In its simplest form, an example would be the sale of a hamburger for $1.00. If the cost of the food was $.30 then the food cost percentage would be 30 percent, which is about average for many hotels. The average might be reduced to 27 percent in hotels that do a lot of catering. As discussed later in this section, in determining the food and beverage department's profit and loss, executive chefs and food and beverage directors must consider not only the food cost percentage but also the contribution margin of menu items. Another important cost ratio for the kitchen is labor cost. The labor cost percentage may vary depending on the extent of convenience foods purchased versus those made from scratch (raw ingredients). In a kitchen, this may be expressed as a percentage of food sales. For example:

Food Sales $1,000

Labor Costs $250

The formula is cost/sales x 100 or 250/1,000 = 25 percent labor cost

Corporate Profile: ITT Sheraton Corporation

Mission statement:

At ITT Sheraton, we are committed to becoming the number one hospitality company in the world by attracting and retaining the best employees, and by providing total customer satisfaction in order to increase long-term profits and value for our owners and ITT.

Boston-based ITT Sheraton Corporation, a subsidiary of ITT Corporation, is a world-wide hospitality network focused on quality that owns, leases, manages, or franchises nearly 450 properties in sixty-four countries. ITT Sheraton has properties in more countries under a single brand than any other lodging company. The corporate facts are shown below:

ITT Sheraton's revenues in 1994: $3.9 billion
Total number of properties: 422
Projects under development: 50
Number of guest rooms: 131,555
Number of guests annually: 25 million
Number of employees: 104,000

ITT Sheraton has 266 properties in North America, 64 in Europe, 47 in the Asia/Pacific Division, 32 in Africa and the Middle East, and 13 in Latin America. The segments include 48 luxury properties, 278 upscale properties, and 98 mid-scale properties.

In addition to the sixty-four countries in which ITT Sheraton currently operates, new locations under development include Estonia, Ethiopia, Indonesia, Malaysia, Micronesia, Republic of Croatia, Tanzania, and Uruguay. ITT Sheraton's goals for the 1990s and beyond are to be the worldwide leader in hospitality and service and to extend its commanding lead in global presence to a minimum of ninety countries by the end of the century.

Sheraton began in 1937 when the company's founders, Ernest Henderson and Robert Moore, acquired their first hotel—the Stonehaven—in Springfield, Massachusetts. At the end of its first decade, Sheraton was the first hotel chain to be listed on the New York Stock Exchange.

The company began expanding internationally in 1949 with the purchase of two Canadian hotel chains. In 1968, Sheraton was acquired by ITT Corporation as a wholly owned subsidiary. Recognizing the advantages of international growth, ambitious development plans were put into place to create a truly global network of properties.

"Reservatron," launched in 1958, became the industry's first automated electronic reservations system. Sheraton was also the first chain to develop a toll-free 1-800 number system for direct consumer access.

The 1980s began a "new" Sheraton, a worldwide company with a global reputation for service excellence and quality. Under the leadership of John Kapioltas, the company received international recognition as an industry innovator.

In 1985, Sheraton became the first international hotel chain to operate a hotel bearing its own name in the People's Republic of China—The Great Wall Sheraton Hotel Beijing. This was followed by the 1986 signing of the first Western Management agreement in the East Bloc, the Sheraton Sofia Hotel Balkan in Bulgaria.

In the 1990s, ITT Sheraton has focused on improving the quality and service standards of its domestic operations. Over a billion dollars of renovation and construction work at Sheraton properties in North America was completed in 1992.

The projects—at motels in New York City, Toronto, Miami, Dallas, San Francisco, Los Angeles, Hartford, and Kauai—are part of an overall plan to strengthen ITT Sheraton's presence in important business centers across the country.

In 1992, ITT Sheraton increased its domestic and international presence through the acquisition of seven properties from Marriott Corporation. The transaction added six all-suite hotels in key U.S. metropolitan areas, as well as the Prince de Galles Hotel in the heart of Paris.

In 1994, ITT Sheraton acquired Ciga, making the

An executive chef has one or more sous chefs—*sous* is a French word meaning *under*. Because so much of the executive chef's time is spent on administration, sous chefs are often responsible for the day-to-day running of each shift. Depending on size, a kitchen may have several sous chefs: one or more for days, one for evenings, and another for banquets.

Under the sous chefs is the chef tournant. This person rotates through the various stations to relieve the station chef heads, also known as chefs de partie (see

company the leading supplier of luxury and upscale lodging in the world. The St. Regis, the flagship of The Luxury Collection, achieves five-diamond status from the Automobile Association of America (AAA), as does Lespinasse, its restaurant.[1]

ITT Sheraton spent $160 million to acquire the Desert Inn Hotel and Casino in Las Vegas, and then proceeded to spend nearly as much again to expand and renovate it. This marked a bold move by ITT Sheraton to become a major player in the U.S. gaming arena (the company already has casinos scattered from the Caribbean to Australia).

The company also has plans to create the Desert Kingdom, a 34-acre spectacular casino-hotel-entertainment complex to rival the extravagances already lined along the Las Vegas Strip. Desert Kingdom will bring guests in on boats floating on a river of gold through King Solomon's mines. The construction cost will be $750 million.

Another billion dollars or so is expected to be invested into a new riverboat-style casino at Tunica, Mississippi, and into buying and renovating top-tier hotels like New York's St. Regis and the Phoenician in Arizona. Internationally, the company plans to add twenty hotels to its forty-four in the Asia/Pacific region by 2000.

The company is putting up the capital it believes is required to execute a two-part strategy: to take a major place at the fast-growing American gaming table and to strengthen the position of its North American hotel oper-

ations in the higher-quality segments, where it believes the returns will be best in the foreseeable future. "We're going to walk our talk," says Sheraton president and chief operating officer, Dan Weadock. That means shaping up standards and operations as well. Weadock points to a new total quality management campaign that reaches from shortening the ninety-five-step process of booking a group's meeting by half to tasteful improvements at the bar. "Mondavi is now the Sheraton house wine, not plonk," declares Weadock.

The fundamental goal is to reestablish the quality image of the Sheraton brand, which top management admits has become soiled with second-rate properties. Franchisees who were not willing to put money into improving their appearance and safety equipment have lost their flags.[2]

If *globalization* is one Sheraton buzzword, definition is another. Weadock feels Sheraton has been perceived as a chain lacking in personality. He aims to alter that perception by providing high-profile imaging for each of its lines.[3]

Weadock says, "We expect to double our operating income this year over [last] and see another substantial increase after that. The industry started a turnaround the day after I took this job. I had nothing to do with it." Like a lucky poker player ready to cash in his chips, Weadock admits, "timing is everything."[4]

[1] This section draws on information provided by ITT Sheraton Corporation.

[2] "Navigating Change," *Lodging Hospitality,* July 1994.
[3] "Sheraton Goes for the Global Gold," *Lodging Hospitality,* November 1994.
[4] "Navigating Change."

Figure 5–3). These stations are organized according to production tasks, based on the classic "brigade" introduced by Escoffier. The brigade includes the following:

Sauce chef, who prepares sauces, stews, sautes, hot hors d'oeuvres
Roast chef, who roasts, broils, grills, and braises meats
Fish chef, who cooks fish dishes

Personal Profile: Jim Gemignani, Executive Chef

Jim Gemignani is executive chef at the fifteen-hundred-room Marriott Hotel in San Francisco.

Chef Jim, as his associates call him, is responsible for the quality of food, guest, and associate satisfaction and for financial satisfaction in terms of results. With over two hundred associates in eight departments, Chef Jim has an interesting challenge. He makes time to be innovative by researching food trends and comparative shopping. Currently, American cuisine is in, as are free-standing restaurants in hotels. An ongoing part of American cuisine is the healthy food that Chef Jim says has not yet found a niche.

Hotels are building identity into their restaurants by branding or creating their own brand name. Marriott, for example, has Pizza Hut pizzas on the room service menu. Marriott hotels have created their own tiers of restaurants. JW's is the formal restaurant, Tuscany's is a Northern Italian–themed restaurant, The American Grill has replaced the old coffee shop, and Kimoko is a Japanese restaurant. As a company, Marriott decided to go nationwide with the first three of these concepts. This has simplified menus and improved food quality and presentation, and yet regional specials allow for individual creativity on the part of the chef.

Jim Gemignani

When asked about his personal philosophy, Chef Jim says that in this day and age, one needs to embrace change and build teams; the guest is an important part of the team. Chef Jim's biggest challenge is keeping guests and associates happy. He is also director of food service outlets, which now gives him a front-of-the-house perspective. Among his greatest accomplishments are seeing his associates develop—twenty are now executive chefs—retaining 96 percent of his opening team, and being voted Chef of the Year by the San Francisco Chef's Association.

Chef Jim's advice: "It's tough not to have a formal education, but remember that you need a combination of 'hands on' and formal training. If you're going to be a leader, you must start at the bottom and work your way up; otherwise, you will become a superior and not know how to relate to your associates."

Soup chef, who prepares all soups

Cold larder/pantry chef, who prepares all cold foods: salads, cold hors d'oeuvres, buffet food, and dressings

Banquets chef, who is responsible for all banquet food

Pastry chef, who prepares all hot and cold dessert items

Vegetable chef, who prepares vegetables (This person may be the fry cook and soup cook in some smaller kitchens.)

(Soup, cold larder, banquets, pastry, and vegetable chefs' positions may be combined in smaller kitchens.)

English	French	Pronunciation
Sauce chef	Saucier	sau*see*ay
Fish chef	Poissonier	Pwa*so*neer
Roast chef	Rotisseur	Ro*tee*sur
Relief chef	Tournant	tour*nant
Vegetable chef	Entremetier	aun*tre*me*ker
Pastry chef	Patissier	pa*tis*seer
Pantry chef	Garde manger	gard*mon*zhay

Figure 5-3   *Chefs de Partie*

Restaurants

A hotel may have several restaurants or no restaurant at all; the number and type of restaurants varies as well. A major chain hotel generally has two restaurants: a signature or upscale formal restaurant and a casual coffee-shop type of restaurant. These restaurants cater to both hotel guests and to the general public. In recent years, because of increased guest expectations, hotels have placed greater emphasis on food and beverage preparation and service. As a result, there is an increasing need for professionalism on the part of the hotels' personnel.

Hotel restaurants are run by restaurant managers in much the same way as other restaurants. Restaurant managers are generally responsible for the following:

Exceeding guest service expectations
Hiring, training, and developing employees
Setting and maintaining quality standards
Marketing
Room service, minibars, or the cocktail lounge
Presenting annual, monthly, and weekly forecasts and budgets to the food and beverage director

Hotel Restaurant Lunch

Some restaurant managers work on an incentive plan with quarterly performance bonuses. Hotel restaurants present the manager with some interesting challenges because hotel guests are not always predictable. Sometimes they will use the hotel restaurants, and other times they will dine out. If they dine in or out to an extent beyond the forecasted number of guests, problems can arise. Too many guests for the restaurants results in delays and poor service. Too few guests means that employees are underutilized, which can increase labor costs unless employees are sent home early. Fortunately, over time, a restaurant manager keeps a diary of the number of guests served by the restaurant on the same night the previous week, month, and year. The number (house count) and type of hotel guest (e.g., the number of conference attendees who may have separate dining arrangements) should also be considered in estimating the number of expected restaurant guests for any meal. This figure is known as the *capture rate,* which when coupled with historic and banquet activity

Hotel Restaurant Dinner

and hotel occupancy will be the restaurant's basis for forecasting the number of expected guests.

Most hotels find it difficult to coax hotel guests into the restaurants. However, many continuously try to convert food service from a necessary amenity to a profit center. The Royal Sonesta in New Orleans offers restaurant coupons worth $5 to its guests and guests of nearby hotels. Another successful strategy, adopted by the Plaza Athenee in New York is to show guests the restaurants and explain the cuisine before they go to their rooms. This has prompted most guests to dine in the restaurant during their stay. At the Sheraton Boston Hotel and Towers, the restaurants self-promote by having cooking demonstrations in the lobby: The chefs offer free samples to hotel guests.[4]

Progressive hotels, such as the Kimco Hotel, San Francisco, ensure that the hotel restaurants look like free-standing restaurants with separate entrances. They also charge the restaurants rent and make them responsible for their own profit and loss statements.[5]

Compared with other restaurants, some hotel restaurants offer greater degrees of service sophistication. This necessitates additional food preparation and service skills and training. Compared to free-standing/independent restaurants, it is more difficult for hotel restaurants to operate at a profit. They usually are open from early morning until late at night, and are frequently underpatronized by hotel guests who tend to prefer to eat outside of the hotel at independent restaurants.

Bars

Hotel bars allow guests to relax while sipping on a cocktail after a hectic day. This opportunity to socialize for business or pleasure is advantageous for both guests and the hotel. Because the profit percentage on all beverages is higher than food items, bars are an important revenue source for the food and beverage departments. The cycle of beverages from ordering, receiving, storing, issuing, bar stocking, serving, and guest billing is complex, but, unlike restaurant meals, a beverage can be held over if not sold. An example of a world-famous hotel bar is The King Cole Bar in the St. Regis Hotel in New York City. This bar has been a favored New York "watering hole" of the rich and famous for many years. The talking point of the bar is a painted mural of Old King Cole, the nursery rhyme character.

Bar efficiency is measured by the pour/cost percentage. Pour cost is obtained by dividing the cost of depleted inventory by sales over a period of time. The more frequently the pour cost is calculated, the greater the control over the bar.[6]

Food and beverage directors expect a pour cost of between 16 and 24 percent. Generally, operations with lower pour costs have more sophisticated control systems and a higher volume catering operation. An example of this would be an automatic system that dispenses the exact amount of beverage requested via a pouring gun, which is fed by a tube from a beverage store. These systems are expensive, but they save money for volume operations by being less prone to pilferage, overpouring, or other tricks of the trade. Their greatest savings comes in the form of reduced labor costs; fewer bartenders are needed to make the same amount of drinks. However, the barperson may still hand pour premium brands for show.

Hotel bars are susceptible to the same problems as other bars. The director of food and beverage must set strict policy and procedure guidelines and see to it that they are followed. In today's litigious society, the onus is on the operator to install and ensure responsible alcohol service. If a guest becomes intoxicated and is involved in an accident, the server of the beverage, the bar person, and the manager may all be liable.

Another risk bars encounter is pilferage. Employees have been known to steal or tamper with liquor; they could, for example, dilute it with water or colored liquids, sell the additional liquor, and pocket the money. There are several other ways to defraud a bar. One of the better-known ways is to overcharge guests for beverages. Another is to underpour, which gives guests less for their money. Some bartenders overpour measures in order to receive larger tips. The best way to prevent these occurrences is to have a good control system, which should include shoppers—people who are paid to use the bar like regular guests, except they are closely watching the operation.

Old King Cole Bar

In a large hotel there are several kinds of bars:

The lobby bar: This convenient meeting place was popularized when Conrad Hilton wanted to generate revenue out of his vast hotel lobby. Lobby bars, when well managed, are a good source of income.

The restaurant bar: Traditionally, this bar is away from the hubbub of the lobby and offers a holding area for the hotel's signature restaurant.

The service bar: In some of the very large hotels, restaurants and room service have a separate backstage bar. Otherwise, both the restaurant and room service are serviced by one of the regular beverage outlets, such as the restaurant bar.

The catering and banquet bar: This bar is used specifically to service all the catering and banquet needs of the hotel. These bars can stretch any operator to the limit. Frequently, several cash bars must be set up at a variety of locations; if cash wines are involved with dinner, it becomes a race to get the wine to the guest before the meal, preferably before the appetizer. Because of the difficulties involved in servicing a large number of

Banquet Bar

guests, most hotels encourage inclusive wine and beverage functions in which the guests pay a little more for tickets that include a predetermined amount of beverage service. Banquet bars require careful inventory control. The bottles should be checked immediately after the function, and, if the bar is very busy, the bar manager should pull the money just before the bar closes. The breakdown of function bars should be done on the spot if possible to help prevent pilferage.

The banquet bar needs to stock not only large quantities of the popular wines, spirits, and beers but also a selection of premium spirits and after-dinner liqueurs. These are used in the ballroom and private dining rooms in particular.

The pool bars: Pool bars are popular at resort hotels where guests can enjoy a variety of exotic cocktails poolside. Resort hotels that cater to conventions often put on theme parties one night of the convention to allow delegates to kick back. Popular themes that are catered around the pool might be a Hawaiian Luau, a Caribbean reggae night, Mexican Fiesta, or Country and Western. Left to the imagination, one could conceive of a number of theme events.

Minibars: Minibars are small, refrigerated bars in guest rooms. They offer the convenience of having beverages available at all times. For security, they have a separate key, which may be either included in the room key envelope at check-in or withheld according to the guest's preference. Minibars are typically checked and replenished on a daily basis. Charges for items used are automatically added to the guest folio.

Night clubs: Some hotels offer guests evening entertainment and dancing. Whether formal or informal, these food and beverage outlets offer a full beverage service. Live entertainment is very expensive. Many hotels are switching to operations that operate with a DJ or where the bar itself is the entertainment (e.g., sports bar). Directors of food and beverage are now negotiating more with live bands, offering them a base pay (below union scale) and a percentage of a cover charge.

Sports bars: Sports bars have become popular in hotels. Almost everyone identifies with a sporting theme, which makes for a relaxed atmosphere that complements contemporary life-styles. Many sports bars have a variety of games such as pool, football, bar basketball, and so on, which, together with satellite televised sporting events, contribute to the atmosphere.

Stewarding Department

The chief steward is responsible to the director of food and beverage for the following functions:

Cleanliness of the back of the house (all the areas of the back stage that hotel guests do not see)

Maintaining clean glassware, china, and cutlery for the food and beverage outlets

Maintaining strict inventory control and monthly stock check

Maintenance of dishwashing machines

Inventory of chemical stock

Sanitation of kitchen, banquet isles, storerooms, walk ins/freezers, and all equipment

Pest control and coordination with exterminating company

Forecasting labor and cleaning supplies

A Chief Steward Checking the Silver Inventory

In some hotels the steward's department is responsible for keeping the kitchen(s) clean. This is generally done at night to prevent disruption of the food production operation. A more limited cleaning is done in the afternoon between the lunch and dinner services. The chief steward's job can be an enormous and thankless task. In hotels this involves cleaning up for several hundred people three times a day. Just trying to keep track of everything can be a headache. Some hotels have different patterns of glasses, china, and cutlery for each outlet. The casual dining room frequently has an informal theme, catering and banqueting a more formal one, and the signature restaurant, very formal place settings. It is difficult to ensure all of the pieces are returned to the correct places. It is also difficult to prevent both guests and employees from taking souvenirs. Strict inventory control and constant vigilance helps keep pilferage to a minimum.

Catering Department

Throughout the world's cultural and social evolution, numerous references have been made to the breaking of bread together. Feasts or banquets are one way to show one's hospitality. Frequently, hosts attempted to outdo one another with the extravagance of their feasts. Today, occasions for celebrations, banquets, and catering include the following:

➤ State banquets, when countries' leaders honor visiting royalty and heads of state

➤ National days

➤ Embassy receptions and banquets

➤ Business and association conventions and banquets

➤ Gala charity balls

➤ Company dinner dances

➤ Weddings

Catering has a broader scope than banquets. *Banquets* refers to groups of people who eat together at one time and in one place. *Catering* includes a variety of occasions when people may eat at varying times. However, the terms are often used interchangeably.

For example, catering departments in large, city-center hotels may service the following events in just one day:

➤ A Fortune 500 company's annual shareholders meeting
➤ An international loan signing ceremony
➤ A fashion show
➤ A convention
➤ Several sales and board meetings
➤ Private luncheons and dinner parties
➤ A wedding or two

Naturally each of these requires different and special treatment. Hotels in smaller cities may cater the local chamber of commerce meeting, a high school prom, a local company party, a regional sales meeting, a professional workshop, and a small exhibition.

Catering may be subdivided into on premise and off premise. In off-premise catering, the event is catered away from the hotel. The food may be prepared either in the hotel or at the event. The organization chart in Figure 5–4 shows how the catering department is organized.

The dotted lines show cooperative reporting relationships and continuous lines show a direct reporting relationship. For example, the banquet chef reports directly to the executive chef but must cooperate with the director of catering and the catering service manager.

Catering Office and Director

The director of catering is responsible to the food and beverage director for selling and servicing, catering, banquets, meetings, and exhibitions in a way that exceeds guests' expectations and produces reasonable profit. The director of catering has a close working relationship with the rooms division manager because the catering department often brings conventions, which require rooms, to the hotel. There is also a close working relationship with the executive chef. The chef plans the banqueting menus but the catering manager must ensure that they are suitable for the clientele and practical from a service point of view. Sometimes they work together in developing a selection of menus that will meet all the requirements, including cost and price.

The director of catering must be able to do the following:

1. Sell conventions, banquets, and functions
2. Lead a team of employees
3. Together with input from team members, make up departmental goals and objectives
4. Set individual and department sales and cost budget
5. Set service standards

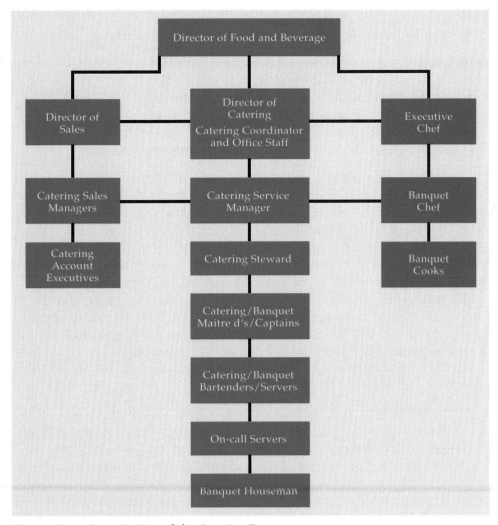

Figure 5–4   *Organization of the Catering Department*

6. Ensure that the catering department is properly maintained
7. Be extremely creative and knowledgeable of food, wine, and service
8. Be very well-versed in the likes and dislikes of various ethnic groups, especially Jewish, Middle Eastern, and European

Position Profile

The director of catering is required to have a variety of skills and abilities as shown in the following:

Technical

➤ A thorough knowledge of food and beverage management including food preparation and service

➤ Selling conventions, functions, and banquets

➤ The ability to produce profit
➤ Setting individual and department sales and costs budget

Leadership
➤ Leading a team of employees
➤ Setting departmental mission, goals, and objectives
➤ Training the department members in all facets of operations
➤ Setting service standards
➤ Ensuring that the catering department is properly maintained

The catering department is extremely complex and demanding; the tempo is fast and the challenge to be innovative is always present. The director of catering in a large city hotel should, over the years, build up a client list and an intimate knowledge of the trade shows, exhibitions, various companies, groups, associations, and SMERF organizations (social, military, education, religious, and fraternal market). This knowledge and these contacts are essential to the director of catering's success, as is the selection of the team members.

The main sales function of the department is conducted by the director of catering (DOC) and catering sales managers (CSMs). Their jobs are to optimize guest satisfaction and revenue by selling the most lucrative functions and exceeding guests' food and beverage and service expectations.

The DOC and catering sales managers obtain business leads from a variety of sources, including the following:

The hotel's director of sales. She or he is a good source of event bookings because she or he is selling rooms and catering is often required by meetings and conventions.

GMs. These are good sources of leads as they are very involved in the community.

The corporate office sales department. If, for example, a convention were held on the East coast one year at a Marriott hotel and by tradition the association goes to the West coast the following year, the Marriott hotel in the chosen city will contact the client or meeting planner. Some organizations have a selection of cities and hotels bid for major conventions. This ensures a competitive rate quote for accommodations and services.

The convention and visitors bureau. Here is another good source of leads because its main purpose is to seek out potential groups and organizations to visit that city. In order to be fair to all the hotels, they publish a list of clients and brief details of their requirements, which the hotel catering sales department may follow up on.

Reading the event board of competitive hotels. The event board is generally located in the lobby of the hotel and is frequently read by the competition. The CSM then calls the organizer of the event to solicit the business the next time.

Rollovers. Some organizations, especially local ones, prefer to stay in the same location. If this represents good business for the hotel, then the DOC and GM try to persuade the decision makers to use the same hotel again.

Enquiry: Incoming calls
    From prospective clients
    Director of marketing & sales
    Corporate sales office
    Cold calls by catering sales manager to seek prospective clients
Check for space available in the "bible"* or the computer program
Confirm availability and suggest menus & beverages. Invite clients to view hotel when it
    is set up for a similar function
Catering prepares a contract and creates a proposal and a pro-forma invoice for client.
    This enables client to budget for all costs with no surprise.
Catering manager makes any modifications and sends client a contract detailing events,
    menus, beverages, and costs.
Client confirms room booking, menus, and beverages by returning the signed contract.

*The bible is the function book in which a permanent record is maintained of each function room's availability, tentative booking, or guaranteed booking.

Figure 5–5 *Booking a Function*

Cold calls. During periods of relative quiet, the CSMs call potential clients to inquire if they are planning any events in the next few months. The point is to entice the client to view the hotel and the catering facilities. It is amazing how much information is freely given over the telephone.

Figure 5–5 shows the steps involved in booking a function.

The most frequent catering events in hotels are the following:

➤ Meetings
➤ Conventions
➤ Dinners
➤ Luncheons
➤ Weddings

For meetings, a variety of room set-ups are available, depending on a client's needs. The most frequently selected meeting room set-ups are as follows:

Theater style: Rows of chairs are placed with a center group of chairs and two aisles. Figure 5–6 shows a theater-style set-up with equipment centered on an audiovisual platform. Sometimes multimedia presentations, requiring more space for reverse image projections, reduce the room's seating capacity.

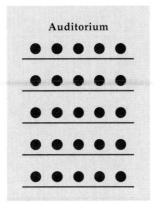

Figure 5–6 *Theater-Style Seating*

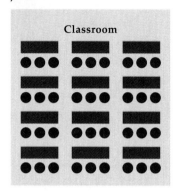

Figure 5–7   *Classroom-Style Seating*

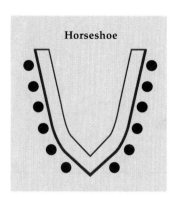

Figure 5–8   *Horseshoe-Style Seating*

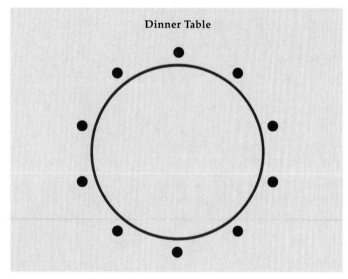

Figure 5–9   *Dinner-Style Seating*

Classroom style: As the name suggests, tables, usually slim 18" ones, are used because meeting participants need space to take notes. Classroom-style set-up usually takes about three times as much space as theater style, and takes more time and labor to set up and break down. Figure 5–7 shows a classroom-style set-up.

Horseshoe style: This type of meeting set-up (Figure 5–8) is frequently used when interaction is sought among the delegates, such as training sessions and workshops. The presenter or trainer stands at the open end of the horseshoe with a black or white board, flip chart, overhead projector, and video monitor and projector.

Dinner style: Dinners are generally catered at round tables of eight or ten persons for large parties and on boardroom-style tables for smaller numbers. Of course, there are variations of this set-up (see Figure 5–9).

Catering Event Order

A catering event order (CEO), which may also be called a banquet event order (BEO), is prepared/completed for each function to inform not only the client but also the hotel personnel about essential information (what needs to happen and when) to ensure a successful event.

The CEO is prepared based on correspondence with the client and notes taken during the property visits. Figure 5–10 shows a CEO and lists the rooms layout and decor, times of arrival, if there are any VIPs and what special attention is required for them, i.e., reception, bar times, types of beverages and service, cash or credit bar, time of meal service, the menu, wines, and service details. The catering manager or director confirms the details with the client. Usually, two copies are sent, one for the client to sign and return and one for the client to keep.

An accompanying letter thanks the client for selecting the hotel and explains the importance of the function to the hotel. The letter also mentions the guaranteed number policy. This is the number of guests for which the hotel will prepare, serve, and charge accordingly. The guaranteed number is given about seven days prior to the event. This safeguards the hotel from preparing for 350 people and having only 200 show up. The client naturally, does not want to pay for an extra 150 people—hence, the importance of a close working relationship with the client. Contracts for larger functions call for the client to notify the hotel of any changes to the anticipated number of guests in increments of ten or twenty.

SHERATON GRANDE TORREY PINES
BANQUET EVENT ORDER

POST AS:	U.S.I.U. WELCOME BREAKFAST		CHERI WALTER
EVENT NAME:	MEETING		
GROUP:	UNITED STATES INTERNATIONAL UNIVERSITY		
ADDRESS:	10455 POMERADO ROAD		BILLING:
	SAN DIEGO, CA 92131		
PHONE:	(619) 635-4627		DIRECT BILL
FAX:	(619) 635-4528		
GROUP CONTACT:	Dr. John Walker		Amount Received:
ON-SITE-CONTACT:	same		

DAY	DATE	TIME	FUNCTION	ROOM	EXP	GTE	SET	RENT
Wed	January 25, 1995	7:30 AM – 12:00 PM	Meeting	Palm Garden	50			250.00

BAR SET UP:

N/A

MENU:

7:30 AM CONTINENTAL BREAKFAST

Freshly Squeezed Orange Juice, Grapefruit Juice and
   Tomato Juice
Assortment of Bagels, Muffins and Mini Brioche
Cream Cheese, Butter and Preserves
Display of Sliced Seasonal Fruits
Individual Fruit Yogurt
Coffe, Tea and Decaffeinated Coffee

PRICE:_____

11:00 AM BREAK

Refresh Beverages as needed

WINE:

FLORAL:

MUSIC:

AUDIO VISUAL:
–OVERHEAD PROJECTOR/SCREEN
–FLIPCHART/MARKERS
–VCR/MONITORS

PARKING:

HOSTING PARKING, PLEASE PROVIDE VOUCHERS

LINEN:
HOUSE

SETUP:
–CLASSROOM STYLE SEATING
–HEAD TABLE FOR 2 PEOPLE
–APPROPRIATE COFFEE BREAK SETUP
–(1) 6' TABLE FOR REGISTRATION AT ENTRANCE
   WITH 2 CHAIRS, 1 WASTEBASKET

All food and beverage prices are subject to a 18% service charge and 7% state tax. Guarantee figures, cancellations, changes must be given 72 hours prior or the number of guests expected will be considered the guarantee. To confirm the above arrangements, this contract must be signed and returned.

ENGAGOR SIGNATURE _____   DATE _____

BEO # 003069

Figure 5–10   *Catering Event Order* (Courtesy of Sheraton Grande Torrey Pines.)

Experienced catering directors ensure that there will be no surprises for either the function organizer or the hotel. This is done by calling to check on how the function planning is going. One mistake catering directors sometimes make is accepting a final guest count without inquiring as to how that figure was determined. This emphasizes the fact that the catering director should be a consultant to the client. Depending on the function, the conversion from invitations to guests is about 50 percent. Some hotels have a policy of preparing for about 3 to 5 percent over the anticipated or guaranteed number. Fortunately, most events have a prior history. The organization may have been at a similar hotel in the same city or across the country. In either case, the catering director or manager will be able to receive helpful information from the catering director of the hotel where the organization's function was held previously.

The director of catering holds a daily or weekly meeting with key individuals who will be responsible for upcoming events. Those in attendance should be the following:

Director of catering
Executive chef and or banquet chef
Beverage manager or catering bar manager
Catering managers
Catering coordinator
Director of purchasing
Chief steward
Audiovisual representative

The purpose of this meeting is to avoid any problems and to be sure that all the key staff know and understand the details of the event and any special needs of the client.

Catering Coordinator

The catering coordinator has an exacting job in managing the office and controlling the "bible" or function diary. She or he must see that the contracts are correctly prepared and check on numerous last-minute details, such as whether or not flowers and menu cards arrive.

Catering Services Manager

The catering services manager (CSM) has the enormous responsibility of delivering higher-than-expected service levels to guests. The CSM is in charge of the function from the time the client is introduced to the CSM by the director of catering or catering manager. This job is very demanding because several functions always occur simultaneously. Timing and logistics are crucial to the success of the operation. Frequently, there are only a few minutes between the end of a day meeting and the beginning of the reception for a dinner dance.

The CSM must be liked and respected by guests and at the same time be a superb organizer and supervisor. This calls for a person of outstanding character and leadership—management skills essential for success. The CSM has several important duties and responsibilities including the following:

Directing the service of all functions

Supervising the catering housepersons in setting up the room

Scheduling the banquet captains and approving the staffing levels for all events

Cooperating with the banquet chef to check menus and service arrangements

Checking that the client is satisfied with the room set-up, food, beverages, and service

Checking last-minute details

Making out client bills immediately after the function. Adhering to all hotel policies and procedures that pertain to the catering department. This includes responsible alcoholic beverage service and adherence to fire code regulations

Calculating and distributing the gratuity and service charges for the service personnel

Coordinating the special requirements with the DOC catering manager and catering coordinator

Room Service/In-Room Dining

The term *room service* has for some time referred to all service to hotel guest rooms. Recently, some hotels have changed the name of room service to *in-room dining* to present the service as more upscale. The intention is to bring the dining experience to the room with quality food and beverage service.

A 1992 survey of members of the American Hotel and Motel Association showed that 56 percent of all properties offer room service and that 75 percent of airport properties provide room service. Generally, the larger the hotel and the higher the room rate the more likely that a hotel will offer room service.

Economy and several mid-priced hotels avoid the costs of operating room service by having vending machines on each floor and food items like pizza or Chinese food delivered by local restaurants. Conversely, some hotels prepare menus and lower price structures that do not identify the hotel as the provider of the food. As a result, the guests may have the impression that they are ordering from an "outside" operation when they are in fact ordering from room service.

The level of service and menu prices will vary from hotel to hotel. The Sheraton Grand at Torrey Pines, California, has butler service for all guest rooms without additional charge, which has become the trademark of the hotel.[7]

Butler Service

A few years ago, room service was thought of as a necessary evil, something that guests expected, but which did not produce profit for the hotel. Financial pressures have forced food and beverage directors to have this department also contribute to the bottom line. The room service manager has a difficult challenge running this department, which is generally in operation between sixteen and twenty-four hours a day. Tremendous effectiveness is required to make this department profitable. Nevertheless, it can be done. Some of the challenges in operating room service are as follows:

Delivery of orders on time—this is especially important for breakfast, which is by far the most popular room service meal

Making room service a profitable food and beverage department

Avoiding complaints of excessive charges for room service orders

There are many other challenges in room service operation. One is forecasting demand. Room service managers analyze the front desk forecast, which gives details of the house count and guest mix—convention, group, and others for the next two weeks. The food and beverage forecast will indicate the number of covers expected for breakfast, lunch, and dinner. The convention resumes will show where the convention delegates are having their various meals. For example, the number of in-house delegates attending a convention breakfast can substantially reduce the number of room service breakfast orders. Experience enables the manager to check if a large number of guests are from different time zones, such as the West or East coast or overseas. These guests have a tendency to either get up much earlier or much later. This could throw room service demands off balance. Demand also fluctuates between weekdays and weekends; for example, city hotels may cater to business travelers, who tend to require service at about the same time. However, on weekends, city hotels may attract families, who will order room service at various times. Resort guests, usually couples and families, are more relaxed and less likely to require twenty-four-hour room service. At airport hotels, however, people come and go and want to eat at all times.[8]

Once the forecast has been determined, the manager can begin to plan to meet the expected demand. The challenge of planning for the room service operation includes the following:

Planning the amount of equipment that will be required. Items like room service carts, trays, and cutlery need to be considered.

Staffing schedules need to be carefully planned so as to ensure maximum efficiency. A balance needs to be struck between having people standing around and being rushed off their feet. When planning the schedule, managers check the work load on the forecasts to determine how many different types of set-ups will be required (e.g., how many executive bars will have to be set up and replenished with fresh garnishes and ice, how many in-room dinners are expected, and how many amenities will need to be made up and placed in guestrooms).

The room-service menu requires careful planning. The challenge here is that the food must not only keep its presentation, but it must also have longevity. Room-service menus are generally quite mainstream because of the wide variety of guests. Even in a five-star hotel, it is virtually impossible to take hamburgers off the menu because hamburgers are a favorite food item for children. Most dishes that room service offers are items selected from the restaurant menu, thereby avoiding too much additional preparation.

Pricing the menu calls for judgment and a balancing act between charging a realistic amount and having prices appear too high, which might discourage guests from ordering.

In a structured environment, the organizational challenge of room-service management consists of mise en place, arranging everything in the correct place, and ready for action. The system for guests' ordering is organized in two main ways: by telephone and by doorknob hangers for breakfast orders. The room service order taker takes the order and makes out a bill, giving one copy to the kitchen and one to the servers. During quieter periods, the room service order taker helps with setting up the trays and carts. Running an operation in which each person has set duties contributes to the efficient running of the department.

To avoid problems with late delivery of orders, a growing number of hotels have dedicated elevators to be used only by room service during peak periods. At the 550-room Intercontinental hotel in London, up to 350 room service breakfasts are served per day; there the elevator is a mobile continental breakfast service kitchen. At the 565-room Stouffer Riviera Chicago, director of food and beverage Bill Webb has a solution: Rapid action teams (RAT) are designated food and beverage managers and assistants who can be called on when room service orders are heavy.

Westin Hotels recently introduced Service Express, an innovation that allows a customer to address all needs (room service, housekeeping, laundry, and other services) with a single call. In addition, new properties are designed with the room service kitchen adjacent to the main kitchen so that a greater variety of items can be offered.

Hotels are also looking at sous-vide (air-tight pouches of prepared food that can be quickly reheated). The food quality is good and the food can be prepared in advance during quiet times. Sous-vide works well for fish and almost anything except grilled dishes; it could streamline late-night service, especially at airport hotels, where a layover can mean one hundred people clamoring for dinner at midnight.

Some properties, in an effort to make room service more cost effective, have introduced more vending machines on guest floors. This gives guests a wider selection of food and beverage items at a lower cost without waiting.[9]

The challenge of speedy and accurate communication is imperative to a successful room service operation. This begins with timely scheduling and ends with happy guests. In between is a constant flow of information that is communicated by the guest, the order taker, the cook, and the server.

1. Make sure the table is properly set, and the order is correct before knocking on the door.

2. Knock on the door three times and immediately say "Good evening, This is room service."

3. As the guest opens the door, greet the guest appropriately. <u>Always ask if you may enter.</u>

4. On entering the room, ask the guest where she or he would like to dine this evening.

5. Present the order, and recommend other menu items.

6. Ask whether the guest would prefer the entrees to remain in the hot box if the order has salads or appetizers. If so, extinguish the sterno in the hot box and explain its use. If the guest would like you to take out the hot box, do so, but in a conservative manner. Never lift the hot box over the table and/or guest. Leave a service towel for the guest.

7. During this entire time it's important to mention that the room service server should be <u>reading</u> the customer they are servicing. Always remain courteous and friendly.

8. Ask the guest if he or she would like the wine opened and poured. Ask the same for beer, coffee/tea, soda, and so on.

9. On exiting, ask the guest to call room service for removal of tray/table, or if any further assistance is needed. <u>Thank them for using room serice.</u>

Figure 5–11   *Evening Room Service*

Another challenge is to have well-trained and competent employees in the room service department. From the tone of voice of the order taker and the courteous manner with which the order is taken to the panache of the server for the VIP dinners, training makes the difference between ordinary service and outstanding service. With training, which includes menu tasting with wine and suggestive selling, an order taker becomes a room service salesperson. This person is now able to suggest cocktails or wine to complement the entree, and can entice the guest with tempting desserts. The outcome of this is to increase the average guest check. Training also helps the set-up and service personnel hone their skills to enable them to become productive employees who are proud of their work.

An example of the steps of service for an evening room service associate is given in Figure 5–11.

Summary

1. The food and beverage department division is led by the director of food and beverage, who is responsible for the efficient operation of kitchen, catering, restaurants, bars, and room service; in addition, the director has to keep up with trends and preplan for special events.

2. A hotel kitchen is the responsibility of the executive chef, who is in charge of the quality and quantity of food, organization of the kitchen and his or her sous-chefs, administrative duties, and careful calculation of financial results.

3. A hotel usually has a formal and a casual restaurant, which are either directly connected to the hotel or operated separately.
4. Bars are an important revenue source for a hotel, but they must adhere to strict guidelines to be profitable. Commensurate with its size, a hotel might have several kinds of bars, such as a lobby bar, restaurant bar, minibar, or even a night club.
5. The chief steward has the often unrewarded job of cleaning the kitchen, cleaning the cutlery, plates, glasses, and backstage of the hotel and is in charge of pest control and inventory.
6. Catering is subdivided into on premise and off premise occasions, which may include meetings, conventions, dinners, luncheons, and weddings. According to the occasion, the type of service and room set-up may vary. It involves careful planning and the interaction and cooperation of many people.
7. Room service offers the convenience of dining in the room with quality food and beverage service at a price acceptable to both the guest and the hotel.

Review Exercises

1. Briefly describe the challenges a food and beverage director faces on a daily basis.
2. List the measures used to determine the food and beverage department's profit and loss.
3. Explain the problems a hotel faces in making the following departments profitable: restaurants, bars, and room service.
4. Explain the importance of the catering department for a hotel and list the responsibilities of a catering sales manager.

Key Words and Concepts

Capture rate
Catering
Chefs de partie
Chief steward
Contribution margin
Director of food and beverage
Executive chef/kitchen manager
Food cost percentage
Lounges/bars
Pilferage
Profit
Ratios
Room service/minibars
Sous chefs
Stewarding
Pour cost percentage
Responsible alcoholic beverage service

Notes

[1] Personal conversation with Evan Julian, director of food and beverage, San Diego Hilton, May 1993.
[2] Stewarding is responsible for back-of-the-house areas such as dishwashing, issuing and inventory of china, glassware, and cutlery. Stewarding duties include maintaining cleanliness in all areas.
[3] A perpetual inventory establishes a minimum inventory level at which time an order is automatically placed, avoiding shortages.
[4] Robert Selwitz, "Keeping Guests as Diners: Hotels Use a Variety of Efforts to Fill In-House Restaurants," *Hotel and Motel Management,* June 10, 1991, pp. 59–60.
[5] John Jesitus, "Hotels Take Various Approaches in Effort to Spice up Food-and-Beverage Profits," *Hotel and Motel Management,* September 7, 1992, pp. 47–48.
[6] Robert Plotkin, "Beverages: Stop Pouring Profits down the Drain," *Restaurant Hospitality,* February 1992, pp. 136–145.
[7] Ann Spiselman, "Speed and Quality in Room Service," *Hotels,* 27, 4, April 1993, p. 60.
[8] Ibid.
[9] This section draws on Spiselman, op cit.

The Restaurant Business: Development and Classification

6

After reading and studying this chapter you should be able to do the following:

➤ Trace the history and development of the restaurant business
➤ List factors that influence restaurant concept and marketing
➤ Discuss the important elements in menu planning
➤ List the classifications of restaurants
➤ Outline the development of a restaurant chain
➤ Describe the different characteristics of chain and independent restaurants
➤ Identify some of the top chain and independent restaurants

Restaurant Development

Restaurants play an important role in society. Dining out in restaurants fulfills an important sociological need. People need not only nourishment, but also the social interaction that takes place in a restaurant setting. Restaurants are one of the few places where we use all of our senses to enjoy the experience. Our taste, sight, smell, hearing, and touch are all employed to savor the food, service, and atmosphere of the restaurant.

The successful operation of a restaurant is dependent on a number of factors. From the restaurant's operating philosophy to controls, and all the factors in between, it is not easy to succeed in operating restaurants. This chapter covers many of the factors that are the necessary ingredients for the successful operation of a restaurant.

Operating Philosophy

At the heart of an enterprise is the philosophy of the owner or operator. The philosophy represents the way the company does business. It is an expression of the ethics, morals, and values by which the company operates.

Mission, Goals, and Objectives

Many companies have a formal mission statement that explains their reason for being in business. Red Lobster's mission statement (Figure 6–1) is a good example of a restaurant's mission.

Restaurant Market

The market is composed of those guests who will patronize the restaurant. A prospective restaurant owner will analyze the market to determine whether sufficient demand exists in a particular market niche, such as Italian or Southern cuisines. A *niche* is a marketing term used to describe a specific share or slot of a certain market. A good indication of the size of the market can be ascertained by taking a radius of from 1 to 5 miles around the restaurant. The distance will vary according to the type and location of the restaurant. In Manhattan, it may only be a few blocks, whereas in rural West Virginia it may be a few miles. The area that falls within the radius is called the *catchment area.* The demographics of the population within the catchment areas is

Red Lobster's mission is to provide every guest with a dining experience that exceeds expectations and ensures their return.

We serve a variety of attractive, excellent tasting food in a comfortable, inviting atmosphere.

We offer a wide range of competitive prices that provide exceptional value.

Our service is professional, knowledgeable, and friendly.

We are committed to the success of the individual, their quality of life, and to providing opportunities for recognition and professional growth and development.

We are an industry leader in providing growth and returns to our shareholders.

We are America's favorite seafood restaurant and a top choice for full-service dining.

Figure 6–1   *Mission Statement of Red Lobster's Restaurants*

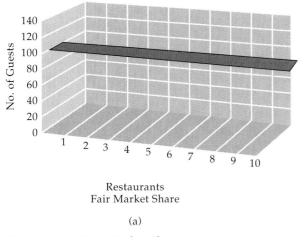

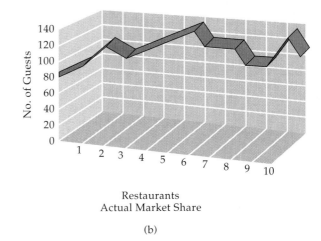

Restaurants
Fair Market Share

(a)

Restaurants
Actual Market Share

(b)

Figure 6–2 *Fair Market Share*

analyzed to reveal age, number of people in various age brackets, sex, ethnicity, religion, income levels, and so on. This information is usually available from the chamber of commerce or data at the local library or real estate offices.

One yardstick used to determine the potential viability of a restaurant is to divide the number of restaurants in the catchment area by the total population. The average number of people per restaurant in the United States is about five hundred. Perhaps this kind of saturation is one of the reasons for the high failure rate of restaurants. Obviously, each area is different; one location may have several Italian restaurants but no Southern restaurant. Therefore, a Southern restaurant would be unique in the market and, if properly positioned, may have a competitive advantage. If someone in the catchment area wanted to eat Italian food, he or she would have to choose among the various Italian restaurants. In marketing terms, the number of potential guests for the Italian restaurants would be divided by the number of Italian restaurants to determine fair market share (the average number of guests that would, if all other things were equal, eat at any one of the Italian restaurants). Figure 6–2a shows one thousand potential guests. If they all decided to eat Italian in the fair market share scenario, each restaurant would receive one hundred guests. In reality, we know this does not happen—for various reasons, one restaurant becomes more popular. The number of guests that this and the other restaurants receive then is called the *actual market share.* Figure 6-2b shows an example of the actual market share that similar restaurants might receive.

Restaurant Concept

Successful restaurant concepts are created with guests in mind. All too frequently someone thinks it would be a good idea to open up a particular kind of restaurant, only to find there are insufficient guests to make it viable.

For the winners, creating and operating a restaurant business is fun—lots of people coming and going, new faces, old friends. Restaurants provide a social gathering place where employees, guests, and management can get their adrenaline flowing in positive ways. The restaurant business is exciting and challenging; with the right location, food, atmosphere, and service it is possible to attract the market and make a good return on investment.

There are several examples of restaurant concepts that have endured over the past few decades. Appleby's, Chart House, Hard Rock Cafe, Olive Garden, Red Lobster, and TGI Friday's are some of the better-known U.S. chain restaurant concepts. Naturally, there are more regional and independent concepts.

The challenge is to create a restaurant concept and bring it into being, a concept that fits a definite market, a concept better suited to its market than that presented by competing restaurants.[1] Every restaurant represents a concept and projects a total impression or an image. The image appeals to a certain market—casual, formal, children, adults, ethnic, and so on. The concept should fit the location and reach out to its target market. A restaurant's concept, location, menu, and decor should intertwine.[2]

In restaurant lingo, professionals sometimes describe restaurants by the net operating percentage that the restaurant makes. TGI Friday's, for example, are usually described as 20 percent restaurants. A local restaurant may be only a 10 percent restaurant.

In order for the operation of a restaurant to be successful, the following factors need to be addressed:

➤ Mission
➤ Goals
➤ Objectives
➤ Market
➤ Concept
➤ Location
➤ Menu planning
➤ Ambiance
➤ Lease
➤ Other occupational costs

The odds in favor of being a big restaurant winner are not good. Approximately 540,000 commercial restaurants do business in the United States. Each year, thousands of new ones open and thousands more close, and even more change ownership for cents on the dollar. The restaurant business is relatively easy to enter, but it is deceptively difficult to succeed.[3]

The restaurant concept is undoubtedly one of the major components of any successful operation. Some restaurants are looking for a concept; some concepts are searching for a restaurant.

In New York, the Restaurant Associates own and operate Rockefeller Plaza's American Festival Cafe, SeaGrill, and Savories. The Associates' latest concept is Cucina & Co. located in the Pan Am Building in New York City. Restaurant Associates plans to create an 11,000-square-foot Grand Grill multiconcept restaurant. The theme depicts the great Pan Am Clipper terminals reminiscent of the roaring twenties, with a Grand Cafe with a Parisian brasserie concept adjacent to the restaurant.

The Associates also have in the works a scaled-down version of Panevino, a Tuscan Farmhouse concept. When asked what trends and opportunities are emerging in the industry, Restaurant Associate Nick Valenti says, "In urban locations, I'm thinking about high-quality takeout and elements of self-service in a concept. In both urban and suburban areas, it might be time to redefine the coffee shop. Stick with traditional fare but upgrade the ingredients considerably. For instance, club sandwiches should be served with fresh turkey, ripe tomatoes, and bread toasted to order."[4]

Restaurant Location

The restaurant concept must fit the location, and the location must fit the concept (see Figure 6–3). The location should appeal to the target market (expected guests). Other things being equal, prime locations cost more, so operators must either charge more for their menu items or drive sufficient volume to keep the rent/lease costs to between 5 to 8 percent of sales.

Key location criteria include the following:

➤ Demographics—How many people are there in the catchment area?
➤ The average income of the catchment area population

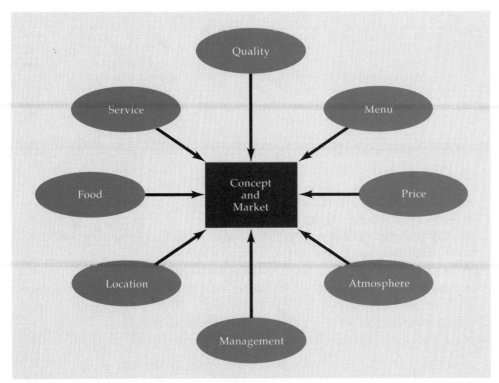

Figures 6–3 *Concept and Market* (Reprinted with permission from Donald E. Lundberg and John R. Walker, *The Restaurant from Concept to Operation*. New York: John Wiley and Sons, 1993, p. 16.)

Personal Profile:

Richard Melman and
The Lettuce Entertain You Enterprises Group, Chicago

Richard Melman is a genius among restaurant operators. He is the creator of a chain of some forty eclectic restaurants in Chicago. Each is unique and authentic, be it Italian, Greek, French, Spanish, or American. Some of the restaurants are co-owned by celebrities, such as the Eccentric, co-owned by Oprah Winfrey, which describes itself as a cosmopolitan American brasserie. Its bustling, creative atmosphere is highlighted by the artwork of more than one hundred Chicago artists. The restaurant features home-cooked meals worth leaving home for: fresh seafood, pastas, steaks, chicken, salads, and homemade desserts.

Richard Melman

Another of Melman's concepts is Papagus, an authentic Greek taverna that offers hearty Grecian delights in warm, friendly, rustic surroundings. Mezedes, a variety of bite-sized offerings, may be enjoyed with Greek wine and ouzo. The display kitchen adds an experiential atmosphere and offers specialties such as spit-roasted chicken, whole broiled red snapper, traditional braised lamb, spanikopita, and baklava.

Richard Melman's Lettuce Entertain You Enterprises Group also has other outstanding theme restaurants in the Chicago area. Scoozi recalls an artist's studio and serves Italian country cuisine; Cafe Ba-Ba-Reeba is a Spanish restaurant featuring tapas, the popular hot and cold little

dishes of Spain; Un Grand Cafe, an authentic Parisian cafe, features patés, salads, fresh grilled fish, and steak, as well as daily specials; and Gino's East serves a world-famous deep-dish pizza ranked number one by *People* magazine.

Richard Melman is often described as the Steven Spielberg or Andrew Lloyd Webber of restaurants. He brought Chicago the first salad bar, the first Spanish tapas, its most popular French restaurant, and more ways to eat Italian food than Caesar ever imagined. In the past, Melman traveled extensively to Europe, where he dreamed up his most inspired restaurants—Ambria (1980), Un Grand Cafe (1981), Avanzare (1982), and Scoozi (1986). Today, he works fewer hours and delegates more. At fifty-two, he has mellowed and his priorities have changed. Melman now concentrates on more healthful food and on being a good uncle instead of father figure to his staff. He prefers to be at home with his wife, three children, and dog. His passion is playing softball in an over-fifty league.

Richard Melman co-founded Lettuce Entertain You Enterprises in 1971. Now, twenty-plus years and thirty-six restaurants later, the company employs 3,650 and has annual revenues of $129 million. Lettuce has grown from a free-spirited den of entrepreneurs into a serious corporate player. One of Melman's strengths is his organiza-

➤ Growth or decline of the area
➤ Zoning, drainage, sewage, and utilities
➤ Convenience—How easy is it for people to get to the restaurant?
➤ Visibility—Can passersby see the restaurant?
➤ Accessibility—How accessible is the restaurant?
➤ Parking—Is parking required? If so, how many spaces are needed and what will it cost?
➤ Curbside appeal—How inviting is the restaurant?
➤ Location—How desirable is the neighborhood?

Several popular types of restaurant locations include the following:

➤ Stand-alone restaurants
➤ Cluster or restaurant row

tion. Currently, eleven restaurant divisions are organized around individual partners; some of them are chefs. Each partner has total operational control of his or her restaurant; divisions report to a ten-member executive committee that includes Melman and his earliest partners.

Further expansion is being considered for Maggiano's Little Italy and the Corner Bakery, a personal favorite of Melman's. Maggiano's is based on an Italian family-style theme, with big portions, red sauce, and Frank Sinatra music. Needless to say, Maggiano's is a big hit. Interestingly, according to Lettuce's corporate chef, Russel Bry, the food is prepared for Midwestern tastes—a little less spicy than other places, especially the coasts. A concept that works well in Chicago would not transplant well to New York or Los Angeles without adjusting the taste of the food.

Papagus

Over the years, Melman has stayed close to the customers by using focus groups and frequent-diner programs. The group's training programs are rated so highly by other restaurateurs that they are keen to hire former Lettuce employees.

Melman's management style is clearly influenced by team sports. He says, "There are many similarities between running a restaurant and a team sport. However, it's not a good idea to have ten all-stars; everybody can't bat fourth. You need people with similar goals—people who want to win and play hard."[1]

The Eccentric

[1] Marilyn Alva, "Does He Still Have It?," *Restaurant Business*, 93, 4, March 1, 1994, pp. 104–111.
The author gratefully acknowledges the courtesy extended by Lettuce Entertain You Enterprises.

➤ Shopping mall
➤ Shopping mall—free standing
➤ Downtown
➤ Suburban

Restaurant Ambiance

The atmosphere that a restaurant creates has both immediate conscious and subconscious effects on guests. The immediate conscious effect is how guests react to the ambiance on entering the restaurant—or even more importantly as an element in the decision-making process used in selecting a restaurant. Is it noisy? Are the tables too close? The subconscious is affected by mood, lighting, furnishings, and music; these play an important role in leaving a subtle impression on guests.

Restaurant guests are placing a greater emphasis on atmospherics (the design used to create a special atmosphere). Back in the 1970s, the majority of restaurants were quite plain. Today, atmospherics are built with the restaurant concept, which has an immediate sensory impact on customers.[5]

Perhaps the most noticeable atmospheric restaurants are those with a theme. The theme will use color, sound, lighting, decor, texture, and visual stimulation to create special effects for patrons.

Menu Planning

The menu may be the most important ingredient in the restaurant's success. The restaurant's menu must agree with the concept; the concept must be based on what the guest in the target market expects; and the menu must satisfy or exceed those expectations. The type of menu will depend on the kind of restaurant being operated.

There are six main types of menus:

A la carte menus offer items that are individually priced.
Table d' hote menus offer a selection of one ore more items for each course at a fixed price. This type of menu is used more frequently in hotels and in Europe. The advantage is the perception guests have of receiving good value.
Du jour menus list the items "of the day."
Tourist menus are used to attract tourists' attention. They frequently stress value and food that is acceptable to the tourists.
California menus are so named because, in some California restaurants, guests may order any item on the menu at any time of the day.
Cyclical menus repeat themselves over a period of time.

A menu generally consists of perhaps six to eight appetizers, two to four soups, a few salads—both appetizer and entree salads—eight to sixteen entrees, and about four to six desserts.

The many considerations in menu planning attest to the complexity of the restaurant business. Considerations include the following:[6]

➤ Needs and desires of guests
➤ Capabilities of cooks
➤ Equipment capacity and layout
➤ Consistency and availability of menu ingredients
➤ Price and pricing strategy (cost and profitability)
➤ Nutritional value
➤ Contribution margin
➤ Accuracy in menu
➤ Menu analysis
➤ Menu design

Needs and Desires of Guests

In planning a menu, the needs and desires of the guests are what is important—not what the owner, chef, or manager thinks. If it is determined that there is a niche in the market for a particular kind of restaurant, then the menu must harmonize with the theme of the restaurant.

The Olive Garden restaurants are a good example of a national chain that has developed rapidly over the past few years. The concept has been positioned and defined as middle of the road with a broad-based appeal. During the concept development phase, several focus groups were asked their opinions on topics from dishes to decor. The result has been extremely successful.

Several other restaurants have become successful by focusing on the needs and desires of the guest. Among them are Hard Rock Cafes, TGI Friday's, Red Lobster, Appleby's, and so on.

Capabilities of Cooks

The capabilities of the cooks must also harmonize with the menu and concept. An appropriate level of expertise must be employed to match the peak demands and culinary expertise expected by the guests. The length and complexity of the menu and the number of guests to be served are both factors in the determination of the extent of the cooks' capabilities.

The equipment capacity and layout will have an impact on the menu and the efficiency with which the cooks can produce the food. Some restaurants have several fried or cold items on the appetizer menu simply to avoid use of the stoves and ovens, which will be needed for the entrees. A similar situation occurs with desserts; by avoiding the use of the equipment needed for the entrees it makes it easier for the cooks to produce the volume of meals over peak periods.

One of the best examples of effective utilization of menu and equipment is Chinese restaurants. At the beginning of many Chinese restaurant menus there are combination dinners. The combination dinners include several courses for a fixed price. Operators of Chinese restaurants explain that about 60 to 70 percent of guests order those combinations. This helps the cooks because they can prepare for the orders and the food is produced quickly, which pleases the guests. It would create havoc if everyone ordered a la carte items because the kitchen and the cooks could not handle the volume in this way.

Equipment Capacity and Layout

All restaurant menus should be developed with regard to the capacity and layout of the equipment. Anyone who has worked in a busy kitchen on a Friday or Saturday night and been "slammed" will realize that part of the problem may have been too ambitious a menu (too many items requiring extensive preparation and use of too much equipment).

If the restaurant is already in existence, it may be costly to alter the kitchen. Operators generally find it easier to alter the menu to fit the equipment. The important thing is to match the menu with the equipment and production scheduling. A menu can be created to use some equipment for appetizers; for this one reason, the appetizers selections on the menu often include one or two cold cuts, possibly a couple of salads, but mostly some deep fried items or soups. This keeps the stove and grill areas free for the entrees. The desserts, if they are not brought in, are mostly made in advance and served cold or heated in the microwave.

Other considerations include the following:

➤ The projected volume of sales for each menu item
➤ Is the menu fixed or does it change with the seasons?
➤ Menu size. Large menus may call for a greater variety of equipment.
➤ Speed of service desired. Fast service may call for equipment of larger capacity.
➤ Nutritional awareness[7]

Most chefs are sufficiently adaptable to be able to prepare quality meals with the equipment provided. Some may prepare a more detailed mise en place,[8] and others will go further to partially cook items so that they can be furnished to order. Of course, there is always the old standby—the daily special—that can take the pressure off the production line.

Consistency and Availability of Menu Ingredients

In the United States, most ingredients are available year round. However, at certain times of the year, some items become more expensive. This is because they are out of season—in economic terms, the demand exceeds the supply so the price goes up. An example of this would be if a storm in the Gulf of Mexico disrupts the supply of fresh fish and shellfish and causes an increase in price. To offset this kind of situation some operators print their menus daily. Others may take advantage of purchasing a quantity of frozen items when the prices are low.

Price and Pricing Strategy

The target market and concept will to a large extent determine the menu price ranges. An example might be a neighborhood restaurant where the appetizers are priced from $3.25 to $6.95 and entrees are in the $6.95 to $11.95 price range. The selling price of each item must be acceptable to the market and profitable to the restauranteur. Factors that go into this decision include the following:

➤ What is the competition charging for a similar item?
➤ What is the item's food cost?
➤ What is the cost of labor that goes into the item?
➤ What other costs must be covered?
➤ What profit is expected by the operator?
➤ What is the contribution margin of the item?[9]

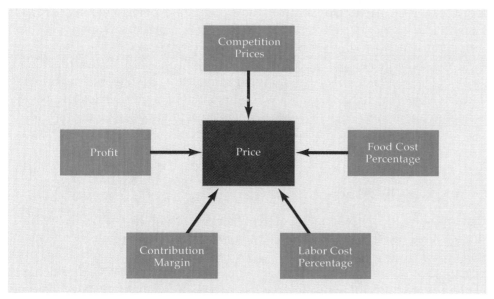

Figure 6–4 *Factors That Influence a Restaurant's Menu Prices*

Figure 6–4 illustrates the factors that influence a restaurant's menu prices.

There are two main ways to price menus. A comparative approach analyzes the price ranges of the competition and determines the price range for appetizers, entrees, and desserts. The second method is to cost the individual dish item on the menu and multiply it by the ratio amount necessary to achieve the desired food cost percentage. For example, to achieve a 30 percent food cost for an item priced at $6.95 on the menu, the food cost would have to be $2.09. Beverage items are priced the same way. This method will result in the same expected food cost percentage for each item. It would be great if we lived in such a perfect world. The problem is that if some items were priced out according to a 30 percent food cost they might appear to be overpriced according to customers' perceptions. For example, some of the more expensive meat and fish would price out at $18 to $21 when the restaurant would prefer to keep entree prices under $15. In order to balance this, restaurants lower the margin on the more expensive meat and fish items—as long as there are only one or two of them—and raise the price on some of the other items, such as soup, salad, chicken, and pasta. This approach is called the weighted average, whereby the factors of food-cost percentage, contribution margin, and sales volume are weighted.

Nutritional Value

A more health-conscious customer has prompted most restaurant operators to make changes not only to the menu selections but also to the preparation methods. Restaurant operators are using more chicken, fish, seafood, and pasta items on the menus today compared with a few years ago. Beef is now more lean than ever before. All of these items are being prepared in more healthful ways such as broiling, poaching, braising, casseroling, or rotisserieing instead of frying.

Increasingly, restaurants are publishing the nutritional value of their food. McDonald's has taken a leadership role in this. Other restaurants are utilizing a heart healthy symbol to signify that the menu item is suitable for guests with concerns about heart-healthy eating. Many restaurants are changing the oil used from the saturated fat, which is high in cholesterol, to 100 percent vegetable oil or canola oil, which is cholesterol free.

Accuracy in Menu

Laws prohibit misrepresentation of items being sold. In the case of restaurants, the so-called truth-in-menu laws refer to the fact that descriptions on the menu must be accurate. Prime beef must be prime cut, not some other grade, fresh vegetables must be fresh, not frozen, and Maine lobster had better actually come from Maine. Some restaurants have received sizable fines for violations of accuracy in menu.

Menu Analysis

One of the earliest approaches to menu analysis was developed by Jack Miller. He called the best-selling items *winners*; they not only sold more but were also at a lower food cost percentage. In 1982, Michael Kasavana and Donald Smith developed menu engineering, in which the best items are called *stars*—those that have the highest contribution margin and the highest sales. Later, David Pavesic suggested that a combination of three variables—food cost percentage, contribution margin, and sales volume—should be used.

Another key variable in menu analysis is labor costs. A menu item may take several hours to prepare, and it may be difficult to precisely calculate the time a cook spends in preparation of the dish. Operators add the total food and labor cost together to determine prime cost, which should not exceed about 60 to 65 percent of sales. The remaining 35 to 40 percent is for overhead and profit.

Menu Design and Layout

Basic menus can be recited by the server. Casual menus are sometimes written on a chalk or similar type board. Quick-service menus are often illuminated above the order counter. More formal menus are generally single page, or folded with three or more pages. Some describe the restaurant and type of food offered; most have beverage suggestions and a wine selection. The more upscale American-Continental restaurants have a separate wine list.

Some menus are more distinctive than others, with pictures of the items or at least enticing descriptions of the food. Research indicates that there is a focal point at the center of the right hand page; this is the spot to place the star or signature item.

Classifications of Restaurants

There is no single definition of the various classifications of restaurants, perhaps because it is an evolving business. Most experts would agree, however, that there are two main categories: full service and specialty. Other categories include such designations as quick service, ethnic, dinner house, occasion, casual, and so on. Some restaurants may even fall into more than one category. For instance, a restaurant could be both quick service and ethnic (Taco Bell). Another restaurant can be called specialty and dinner house (Chart House).

The National Restaurant Association's figures indicate that Americans are spending an increasing amount of food dollars away from home in various food service operations. Americans eat out about two hundred times a year, or about four times a week. Over 50 percent of all consumers visit a restaurant on their birthdays,[10] thereby making it the most popular day for eating out. Mother's Day and Valentine's Day are the second and third most popular days, respectively. The most popular meal eaten away from home is lunch, which brings in approximately 50 percent of fast food restaurant sales. Figure 6–5 illustrates the food-service industry sales by segments: full service, quick service, institutional, and other.

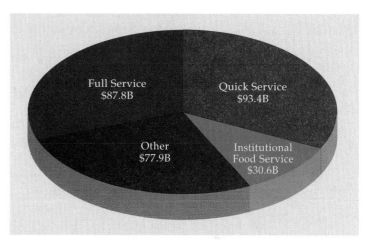

Figure 6–5   *1995 Food Service Industry Sales*

Full-Service Restaurants

A full-service restaurant is one where a good selection of menu items is offered, generally at least fifteen or more different entrees cooked to order, with nearly all the food being made on the premises from scratch from raw or fresh ingredients. Full-service restaurants may be formal or casual and may be further categorized by price, decor/atmosphere, level of formality, and menu. Most full-service restaurants may be cross-referenced into other categories as mentioned previously. Many of these restaurants serve haute cuisine (pronounced *hote*), which is a French term meaning elegant dining or *high food*. Many of the fine restaurants in the United States are based on French or northern Italian cuisine, considered by many Western connoisseurs to be the finest in the world.

Most full-service restaurants are independently owned and operated by an entrepreneur or a partnership. These restaurants are in almost every neighborhood. Today, with value-conscious customers expecting more for their money, it is becoming increasingly more difficult to make a profit in this segment of the business because of strong competition from other restaurants. Some companies, such as Marriott and Stouffer's, who had their early beginnings in the restaurant business, have since sold their restaurant chains because they could not yield the profit margin that management and investors expected.

Nation's Restaurant News (NRN) Fine Dining Hall of Fame, which was launched in 1980, now has over 130 restaurants. Most of them are full-service, independent restaurants. These restaurants are selected by the NRN's editors and published on the basis of excellence in food quality, service, innovation, and staff training and motivation. Over the years, many of America's finest independent restaurants have been honored. Among the early inductees into the hall of fame were the following:

New York—Lettuce, Four Seasons, The Quilted Giraffe, Shunlee Palace, Cafe des Artistes, Tommy Toy's Paroili Romanissimo
San Francisco—L'Etoile, Doros, La Bourgogne
Cincinnati—Maisonette
Tampa, Florida—Bern's Steak House and Columbia
Boston—Anthony's Pier 4
Chicago—Mortons, Jimmy's Place, Ambia, Le Perroquet
West Hollywood, California—Spago
New Orleans—K-Paul's
Washington—Germaine's
Houston—Rotisserie for Beef and Bird, Cafe Annie
St. Louis—Anthony's
Orlando, Florida—The Citrus Club
Philadelphia—Le Bec-Fin
Berkeley, California—Chez Panisse
Dallas—The Mansion on Turtle Creek, South Street Cafe, Zodiac

It is interesting to notice how many of these have a French influence in their names. In the United States, there are a number of restaurant cities, including New York, Chicago, Los Angeles, New Orleans, San Francisco, Boston, Atlanta, Houston, and Denver. Each of these cities has an example of a restaurateur extraordinaire.

The top independent restaurant in terms of sales is the Tavern on the Green in New York, which opened in 1976 and has sales of over $26 million from one thousand seats—including banquets, an average dinner check of $43.50—and serves 545,000 people a year.[11] Now that's cooking!

Other restaurants of interest are operated by celebrity chefs like Wolfgang Puck, co-owner of Spago and Chinois in Los Angeles, and Alice Waters of Chez Panisse in Berkeley, California. Both have done much to inspire a new generation of talented chefs. Alice Waters has been a role model for many female chefs and has received numerous awards and published several cookbooks, including one for children.

The level of service in full-service restaurants is generally high, with a hostess or host to greet and seat patrons. Captains and food servers advise guests of special items and assist with the description and selection of dishes during order taking. If there is no separate sommelier (wine waiter), the captain or food server may offer a description of the wine that will complement the meal and assist with the order taking. Some upscale or luxury full-service restaurants have table-side cooking and French service from a gueridon cart.[12]

The decor of a full-service restaurant is generally compatible with the overall ambiance and theme that the restaurant is seeking to create. These elements of food, service, and decor create a memorable experience for the restaurant guest.

Tavern on the Green (Courtesy Tavern on the Green.)

There is no national full-service luxury restaurant chain, possibly due to the following factors:

➤ Upscale full-service restaurants are not only labor intensive, but they also require a greater degree of skill to operate. The more sophisticated operation makes for a high labor cost.

➤ Only a small percentage of the population can afford the high prices that these restaurants need to charge by reason of their expensive location, decor, and labor. The restaurant is likely to be located in the high rent district and employ a highly skilled chef, kitchen, and service personnel who add to the labor costs. The luxurious furnishings and appointments of the restaurant may easily cost several million dollars. It takes more than a few dinners to pay for all these costs.

➤ The logistics of a national chain may prove difficult or costly to manage. Overhead costs may outweigh savings of economy of scale.

➤ Economies of scale are not as easily reaped with such a sophisticated product—a freshly prepared high quality meal.

➤ Consistency and quality are very difficult to maintain for such a sophisticated clientele.

➤ There is limited market appeal. This type of restaurant is more likely to succeed in major cities such as New York, Los Angeles, Boston, Chicago, New Orleans, Houston, Atlanta, and Philadelphia. There are a number of regional or greater metropolitan restaurants, each with a few locations in a city. There is an obvious benefit in both purchasing for and marketing a cluster of restaurants. In fact, most national chains have adopted the cluster concept as it increases customer awareness and builds traffic (customers).

The owner-operators of the upscale, white tablecloth restaurants have had more than their fair share of bad fortune in the past few years. First came the reduction in the tax deductibility for business entertainment from 100 percent to 80 percent, which then dropped to 50 percent: This reduced the so-called business lunch. A general decline in the consumption of alcohol also affected the success of fine dining establishments. In October 1987 the Wall Street stock market plunged. This forced the street-smart restaurateurs to re-examine every aspect of their business.

Success stories in such changing[13] times are hard to find, but here is an interesting one: One savvy restaurateur even managed to make a profit with sales of $1.1 million in 1990, whereas he had made a loss with sales of $2 million in 1987. This was achieved by the following survival tactics:

Renegotiating the restaurant's lease from $24,000 to $12,000 a month

Trimming payroll starting at the top from an annual payroll of $675,000 in May of 1989 to $200,000 in May of 1991—and it's still dropping

Using the same menu for lunch and dinner. This streamlined the mise en place—for example, the saucier (sauce chef) could come in the morning and prepare all of the sauces for the entire day. The special at lunch was always the special at dinner.

Simplifying menu terminology to speed service

Changing menu price structure

Building up private banquet business

Controlling cost. In 1986 food cost was 32 percent of sales and labor cost was 34 percent of sales; in 1991, food cost was 27 percent of sales and labor cost was 20 percent of sales.

These tactics are necessary for survival in the fiercely competitive restaurant business.

Specialty Restaurants

Under this general heading come fast food or quick service, family, ethnic, theme, casual dining, and dinner house restaurants. Be aware that some restaurants fall into more than one category, (ethnic [Italian] and full service like the Olive Garden, or specialty [seafood] and full service, like Red Lobster).

Pizza Hut (Photo Courtesy Pizza Hut.)

Quick Service/Fast Food

Quick-service or fast food restaurants offer limited menus featuring food such as hamburgers, fries, hot dogs, chicken (in all forms), tacos, burritos, gyros, teriyaki bowls, various finger foods, and other items for the convenience of people on the go. Customers order their food at a counter under a brightly lit menu featuring color photographs of food items. Customers are even encouraged to clear their own trays, which helps reduce costs. The following are examples of the different types of quick-service/fast food restaurants:

Hamburger—McDonald's, Burger King, Wendy's

Pizza—Pizza Hut, Domino's, Godfather's

Steak—Bonanza, Ponderosa

Seafood—Long John Silver's, Red Lobster

Chicken—KFC, Church's

Pancake—International House of Pancakes, Country Kitchen

Sandwich—Subway

Mexican—Taco Bell, El Torito, Chi Chi's

Figure 6–6 shows the top one hundred market shares by restaurant segment.

In some of the world's major cities, where space is expensive, stand-up restaurants open where busy office workers can eat a quick meal. Also found commonly in many major cities is "$1 Chinese Fast Food (no MSG)," whereby patrons select menu items and receive a small portion for one dollar. This is relatively quick and easy for the kitchen staff, because they can prepare a large serving of a particular dish, put it on low heat, and portion it out as necessary. For the customer, it is fast and affordable because they can have a taste of three or four different dishes for a cost of $3 or $4 (rice and noodles usually included free).

(of projected $19.2 billion aggregate sales total for 1994; in percentages)

Cafeteria 0.9%
Chicken 5.2%
Steak 3.1%
Hotel 5.4%
Other* 5.9%
Family 7.8%
Dinner House 8.3%
Pizza 10.3%
Contact 11.5%
Sandwich 41.7%

*Includes Buffet C–store, fish, in-store, snack, and theme park chains

Figure 6–6 *Top One Hundred Market Shares by Restaurant Segment* (Reprinted with permission from Bill Carlino, "Top One Hundred Market Shares by Restaurant," *Nation's Restaurant News, 27,* 11.)

Hamburger

The world's greatest fast food success story is undoubtedly McDonald's. Back in the 1950s, Ray Kroc was selling soda fountains. He received an order from Mr. McDonald for two soda fountains. Ray Kroc was so intrigued to find out why the McDonald brothers' restaurant needed two machines (everyone else ordered one) that he went out to the restaurant, where he saw the now-familiar golden arches and the hamburger restaurant. Ray persuaded the McDonalds to let him franchise their operation; billions of burgers later, the reason for the success may be summarized as follows: quality, speed, cleanliness, service, and value. This has been achieved by systemizing the production process and by staying close to the original concept—keeping a limited menu, heavy advertising, being innovative with new menu items, maintaining product quality, and consistency.

McDonald's is the giant of the entire quick-service/fast food segment with worldwide sales of $23.5 billion. This total is amazing because it is more than the next three megachains combined—KFC ($7.1 billion), Burger King ($6.7 billion),

Table 6–1
Top Ten Hamburger Chains

Name	1994 Sales ($ billion)
McDonald's	$25.00
Burger King	7.50
Wendy's	4.20
Hardee's	3.78
Jack in the Box	1.02
Sonic Drive-ins	.69
Carl's Jr.	.59
Whataburger	.43
Rally's	.35
White Castle	.30

and Pizza Hut ($6.3 billion).[14] McDonald's even has individual product items that are not the traditional burger—for example, chicken McNuggets and burritos as well as salads and fish, which all aim to broaden customer appeal.

In recent years, because traditional markets have become saturated, McDonald's has adopted a strategy of expanding overseas. More than two thirds of 1994's 334 new restaurants added by McDonald's were outside of the United States. McDonald's also seeks out nontraditional locations in the United States market, such as on military bases or smaller-sized units in the high-rent districts.

Customer appeal has been broadened by the introduction of breakfast and by targeting not only kids but also seniors. Innovative menu introductions have helped stimulate an increase in per-store traffic.

It is very difficult to obtain a McDonald's franchise in the United States because they have virtually saturated the primary markets. Carl's Jr., a California-based chain of 583 units has a franchising fee of $35,000, with a royalty fee of 4 percent and an advertising annuity of 4 percent. It often costs between $800,000 and $1 million to open a major brand fast food restaurant. Franchises for lesser-known chains are available for less money.

Each of the major hamburger restaurant chains has a unique positioning strategy to attract their target markets. Burger King hamburgers are flame broiled, and Taco Bell has a 59-, 79-, and 99-cent value menu-pricing strategy. Burger King experimented with offering table service to encourage evening business, but was unsuccessful.

Fuddruckers is a restaurant chain that describes itself as the "Cadillac of Burgers." Other gourmet burger restaurants may offer larger burgers with more side dishes to chose from, and they generally have decor that would attract the non-teenage market. Some of these restaurants have beer and wine licenses. Some smaller regional chains are succeeding in gaining market share from the big three burger chains because they provide an excellent burger at a reasonable price. In-and-Out Burger and Rally's are good examples of this. The top ten hamburger chains are listed in Table 6–1.

Pizza

The pizza segment continues to grow. By some estimates it is at least a $20 billion market,[15] with much of the growth fueled by the convenience of delivery. There are three main chains: Pizza Hut, Domino's, and Little Caesar's. There are several smaller regional chains. Pizza Hut, with system-wide sales of $6.3 billion, has broken into the delivery part of the business over which, until recently, Domino's had virtual monopoly. Little Caesar's, with 4,600 units and total sales of $2.1 billion, built a pizza empire on the perceived value of two pizzas for the price of one. Pizza Hut has now developed system-wide delivery units that also offer two pizzas at a reduced price. A Little Caesar's franchise fee is $20,000, with the cost to develop a store running between $120,000 and $160,000.

Chicken

Chicken has always been popular and will likely remain so because it is relatively cheap to produce and it is readily available and adaptable to a variety of preparations. In the 1990s, it also is perceived as a healthier alternative to burgers.

Kentucky Fried Chicken (KFC), with a total of 9,033 units and annual sales of around $7.1 billion, dominates the chicken segment. As a market leader that has almost saturated the United States market, KFC is seeking out nontraditional outlets, such as college campuses, schools, corporate cafeterias, and international locations. They are also attempting to build traffic by adding items to their menus such as Honey BBQ Chicken and Wings, Oriental Wings, Hot Wings, Kentucky Nuggets, and Rotisserie Gold. Other additions to their skin flavoring lineup include Skinfree Crispy, Extra Tasty Crispy, and Hot and Spicy.

Popeye's is next in the segment with 814 units and sales of $601 million. Popeye's signature menu item is a spicy Cajun-style chicken. There are a number of up-and-coming regional chains, such as El Pollo Loco, of Irvine, California. They focus on a marinated, flame-broiled chicken that is a unique, high-quality product. Boston Chicken, Kenny Rogers, and Cluckers are all expanding rotisserie chains.

KFC Restaurant and Rotisserie Gold, a Recent Popular Addition to Their Menu (Photos Courtesy KFC.)

Steak

The steak restaurant segment is quite buoyant in spite of nutritional concerns. The upscale dinner houses continue to attract the expense account and occasion diners. Some restaurants are adding additional value priced items like chicken and fish to their menus in order to attract more customers. Steak restaurant operators admit that they are not expecting to see the same customer every week, but hopefully every two or three weeks. The Chart House chain is careful to market their menus as including seafood and chicken, but steak is at the heart of the business, with 60 percent of sales from red meat.[16]

Both Ponderosa with 749 units and Bonanza with 483 units have sales of $769 million together, and are owned and operated by Metromedia Steak

House, Inc. They are both family concepts featuring counter service and food bars. These restaurants have also added additional items to their menu in order to broaden customer appeal. Some of these items are expansion of the Grand Buffet to include Mexican food items like Chimichangas, tamales, make-up-your-own burritos, barbecued ribs, and chicken.

Other chains in this segments include Sizzler, which is actually the number one volume steak sales restaurant, with sales of $905 million. Stewart Anderson's Black Angus, Golden Corral, Western Sizzlin', and Ryan's Family Steak Houses all have sales of over $100 million each. In fact, chains have the biggest stake in the segment.

Seafood

Red Lobster is widely regarded as the national chain of excellence in the seafood segment. The corporate profile of Red Lobster later in this chapter gives an indication of not only the corporation's success, but also the reasons for that success.

Red Lobster Food (Photo Courtesy Red Lobster.)

Seafood continues to be popular with consumers because of health concerns. A number of chains have introduced more baked and broiled items and dropped some of the fried ones. The seafood franchising segment is dominated by three chains—Long John Silver's with 1450 units, Red Lobster with 630 units, Captain D's (part of Shoney's Inc.) with 628 units, and Arthur Treacher's Fish & Chips with 96 units. There are, in addition, several regional chains such as Skipper's, a West Coast chain of 220 units based in Bellevue, Washington.

Pancake

Pancakes alone are not sufficient an attraction to sustain a restaurant operation. Therefore, each of the major franchised chains has added new menu items to increase customer interest and satisfaction.

The major force in this section is the International House of Pancakes (IHOP), with 490 units. Other major companies in this segment are Country Kitchen, a division of Minneapolis-based Carlson Companies with 245 units, and Village Inn, the 230-unit Denver-based subsidiary of Vicorp.

Each of the pancake chains is reacting to the health-conscious customer by using egg substitutes and a near cholesterol-free pancake. Pancake franchises cost approximately $50,000 for the franchise fee, a 4 to 5 percent annual royalty, and a 3 percent advertising fee.

Sandwich Restaurants

Sandwich restaurants are a popular way for a young entrepreneur to enter the restaurant business. The leader in this segment is Subway, which operates

Corporate Profile: Red Lobster

In 1968, a restaurant entrepreneur took a gamble on a new seafood restaurant concept in Lakeland, Florida. He was already in his midfifties, but Bill Darden decided to roll the dice at a time when most other men his age were looking toward retirement.

The gamble paid off—more than Darden could ever have imagined. His single seafood restaurant—Red Lobster—has since grown to become the largest seafood restaurant company in North America, with more than 630 restaurants in fortynine states and Canada.

Darden's restaurant career began in the 1930s in a tiny southern Georgia town called Waycross. It was there that nineteen-year-old Darden operated a small lunch counter called The Green Frog, where he served as manager, night cook, waiter, and counter server.

As he saved money from The Green Frog, he began to acquire other restaurants in Florida, Georgia, and South Carolina. In 1963, Darden and his partners bought an Orlando landmark, Gary's Duck Inn, a popular seafood restaurant.

It was so popular that Darden began to think about expanding the concept—creating a no-frills seafood restaurant that offered fast, efficient service. He collected several investors, hired an ad agency, and, as they say, the rest is history.

One constant in Red Lobster's twenty-five years of consistent growth and success has been change. Keeping pace with the ever-changing expectations of the dining-out public, North America's largest full-service seafood restaurant company continues to look for new ways to assure quality and value for its guests.

Innovative menu additions, enhanced service, and new, contemporary decor are recent examples of Red Lobster's commitment to not only meet, but also exceed, guest expectations.

This year, Red Lobster expects to serve more than 80 million pounds of seafood to more than 150 million guests. With seven hundred restaurants in the United States and over fifty in Canada, the company achieved sales in excess of $1.8 billion in fiscal year 1993.

"The Red Lobster concept is designed to offer quality seafood at moderate prices in a contemporary, nautical setting," says Red Lobster president Jefferey J. O'Hara. "Our commitment to quality, value and service for our guests has resulted in 25 years of consistent growth." All Red Lobster restaurants are company-owned and -operated, offering comfortable and efficient table service in an informal family atmosphere. Red Lobster menus feature a broad selection of shellfish and daily fresh fish entrees, in addition to beef, chicken, and seafood-steak combination platters.

The original restaurant in Lakeland, Florida, was such an immediate success that it was necessary to enlarge and remodel it within the first month of operation. Two years later, in 1970, Red Lobster's five restaurants attracted the attention of General Mills, which purchased the chain and provided the necessary resources for rapid nationwide expansion.

A Commitment to Quality

An important contributor to this successful climb is an uncompromising commitment to quality. "Through our rigorous inspection systems. . .from the seafood purchased directly from the world's best commercial fisherman to the food served in the restaurant, Red Lobster assures quality in purchasing, distribution and restaurant operations," O'Hara says. The Red Lobster quality assurance program is recognized as a food service industry leader. The program includes strict purchasing standards and inspections at various critical points. Ongoing laboratory testing of products before shipment to restaurants and quality control training for managers of each restaurant assure that quality is a priority—"from sea to table."

Additionally, in the United States, voluntary seafood inspection programs administered by the United States Department of Commerce (U.S.D.C.) are a further test of quality assurance for the restaurant chain. All Red Lobster seafood carries the U.S.D.C. and/or Canadian seafood inspection approval.

"We believe our success is the result of the strength of our original seafood concept, our commitment to quality, the job our employees consistently perform daily, and a dynamic menu that meets seafood lovers' changing tastes."

8,400 units. Cofounder Fred Deluca parlayed an initial investment of $1,000 into of one the largest and fastest-growing chains in the world. Franchise fees are $10,000 with a second store fee of $2,500. Average units sales are about $270,000 annually, with yearly costs of about $75,000.

The Subway strategy is to invest half of the chain's advertising dollars in national advertising. Franchise owners pay 2.5 percent of sales to the marketing fund. As with other chains, Subway is attempting to widen its core eighteen- to thirty-four-year-old customer base by adding Kids Packs and Value 4-inch Round sandwiches aimed at teens and women. Sandwich restaurants stress the health value of their restaurants.

Family Restaurants

Family restaurants evolved from the coffee shop style of restaurant. In this segment most restaurants are individually or family operated. Family restaurants are generally located in or with easy access to the suburbs. Most offer an informal setting with a simple menu and service designed to please all of the family. Some of these restaurants offer alcoholic beverages, which mostly consist of beer, wine, and perhaps a cocktail special. Usually, there is a hostess/cashier standing near the entrance to greet and seat guests while food servers take the orders and bring the plated food from the kitchen. Some family restaurants have incorporated salad and dessert bars to offer more variety and increase the average check.

Other restaurants that feature in this category include Marie Callender's, Baker's Square, and Howard Johnson.

Ethnic Restaurants

The majority of ethnic restaurants are independently owned and operated. The owners and their families provide something different for the adventurous diner or a taste of home for those of the same ethnic background as the restaurant. The traditional ethnic restaurants sprang up to cater to the taste of the various immigrant groups— Italian, Chinese, and so on.

Perhaps the fastest growing segment of ethnic restaurants in the United States, popularity-wise, is Mexican. Mexican food has a heavy representation in the southwestern states, although, because of near-market saturation, the chains are spreading east.

Taco Bell is the Mexican quick-service market leader with a 60 percent share. This PepsiCo., Fortune 500 company has achieved this incredible result with a value-pricing policy that has increased traffic in all units. Currently, there are 4,634 units with sales of $3.7 billion.[17]

Taco Bell (Courtesy Taco Bell.)

The next biggest chain in the Mexican quick-service segment, in terms of sales, is Chi-Chi's. Chi-Chi's 235 units have total sales of $433.1 million. The third largest quick-service chain is El Torito, with 145 restaurants and sales of 330 million. Del Taco Inc. of Costa Mesa, California, operates 275 restaurants. These Mexican food chains can offer a variety of items on a value menu, starting with 49 cents.

There are a great variety of ethnic restaurants in our major cities, and their popularity is increasing. For example, in 1985 in San Diego, America's sixth largest city, there were no Thai restaurants. Today there are twenty-two, in addition to new Afghan and Ethiopian restaurants.

Theme Restaurants

Many theme restaurants are a combination of a sophisticated specialty and several other types of restaurants. They generally serve a limited menu but aim to wow the guest by the total experience. Of the many popular theme restaurants, two stand out. The first highlights the nostalgia of the 1950s, as done in the T-Bird and Corvette diners. These restaurants serve all-American food such as the perennial meat loaf in a fun atmosphere that is a throw-back to the seemingly more carefree 1950s. The food servers appear in short polka-dot skirts with gym shoes and bobby socks. They will probably be chewing bubble gum; if you fill up on the main course and decline the dessert offerings, you are likely to receive an off-beat reply like "Thank God because my feet are killing me."

The second popular theme restaurant is the dinner house category; among some of the better-known national and regional chains are TGI Friday's, Houlihan's, and Bennigan's. These are casual American bistro-type restaurants that combine a lively atmosphere created in part by assorted bric-a-brac to decorate the various ledges and walls. These restaurants have remained popular over the past twenty years. In a prime location they can do extremely well.

People are attracted to theme restaurants because they offer a total experience and a social meeting place. This is achieved through decoration and atmosphere and allows the restaurant to offer a limited menu that blends with the theme. Throughout the United States and the world, there are numerous theme restaurants that stand out for one reason or another. Among other themes are airplanes, railway, dining cars, rock and roll, 1960s nostalgia, and many others.

Casual Dining and Dinner House Restaurants

As implied, casual dining is relaxed and could include restaurants from several classifications: chain or independent, ethnic, or theme. Hard Rock Cafe, TGI Friday's, The Olive Garden, and Red Lobster are good examples of casual dining.

Over the past few years, the trend in dinner house restaurants has been toward more casual dining. This trend merely reflects the mode of society. Dinner house restaurants have become fun places to let off steam. There are a

Chart House (Courtesy Chart House Restaurants.)

TGI Friday's (Courtesy TGI Friday's.)

Table 6–2
Dinner House Restaurant Chains

Name	1994 Sales ($ million)
1. Red Lobster	$1,820.0
2. Chili's Grill and Bar	837.8
3. TGI Friday's2	755.3
4. Applebee's	608.5
5. Chi Chi's	433.1
6. Bennigan's	424.0
7. Ruby Tuesday	338.4
8. The Ground Round	301.9
9. Red Robin	234.5
10. Hooter's	200.0
11. Hard Rock Cafe	197.1
12. Houlihan's	180.1
13. Chart House	150.0

Source: Reprinted with permission from "The Top 400 Ranking," *Restaurants and Institutions, 104,* 16, July 1, 1994, p. 54.

variety of restaurant chains that call themselves *dinner house restaurants.* Some of them could even fit into the theme category. Table 6–2 lists some of the better-known dinner house chains.

Many dinner house restaurants have a casual, eclectic decor that may promote a theme. Chart House, for example, is a steak and seafood chain that has a nautical theme.

TGI Friday's is an American Bistro dinner house with a full menu and a decor of bric-brac that contributes to the fun atmosphere. TGI Friday's is a chain that has been in operation for over twenty years, so the concept has stood the test of time. TGI Friday's is featured in Chapter 7, Restaurant Operations, as a corporation of excellence.

Summary

1. Restaurants offer the possibility of excellent food and social interaction. In general, restaurants strive to surpass an operating philosophy that includes quality food, good value, and gracious service.
2. In order to succeed, a restaurant needs the right location, food, atmosphere, and service to attract a substantial market. The concept of a restaurant has to fit the market it is trying to attract.
3. The location of a restaurant has to match factors such as convenience, neighborhood, parking, visibility, and demographics. Typical types of locations are downtown, suburban, shopping mall, cluster, or stand alones.

4. The menu and pricing of a restaurant have to match the market it desires to attract, the capabilities of the cooks, and the existing kitchen equipment.
5. The two main categories of restaurants are full ser-vice and specialty. Further distinctions can be made: quick service, ethnic, dinner house, occasion, and casual. In general, most restaurants fall into more than one category.

Review Exercises

1. What is understood by the term *catchment area,* and why is it essential for the success of a restaurant to concentrate on a certain market?
2. Explain why it is important that the location of a restaurant matches its concept.
3. The menu is another very important part of a restaurant. Explain the following terms: *table d'hote, accuracy in menu,* and *equipment capacity.*
4. Describe the two main ways to price a menu.
5. Explain why there is no full-service luxury restaurant chain. List tactics used by full-service restaurant owners to increase profitability.
6. Explain why there is no single definition of the various classifications of restaurants; give examples.

Key Words and Concepts

Actual market share
Casual dining
Classification of restaurants
Contribution margin
Dinner house restaurants
Ethnic restaurants
Fair market share
Food cost percentage
Full-service restaurants
Haute cuisine
Independent restaurants
Market segment
Quick-service restaurants
Restaurant concept
Specialty restaurants
Theme restaurants
Weighted average

Notes

[1] Donald E. Lundberg and John R. Walker, *The Restaurant from Concept to Operation,* 2d ed. New York: John Wiley and Sons, 1993, p. 12.
[2] Ibid.
[3] Lundberg and Walker, op cit., p. vii.
[4] This section draws on Jeff Weinstein and Brenda McCarthy, "Concept Creators," *Restaurants and Institutions, 103,* 15, June 15, 1993, pp. 34–59.
[5] Robert C. Lewis, and Richard E. Chambers, *Marketing Leadership in Hospitality: Foundations and Practices.* New York: Van Nostrand Reinhold, 1990, pp. 339–340.
[6] Lundberg and Walker, op cit., p. 63.
[7] Lundberg and Walker, op cit., p. 208.
[8] French for *everything in place.* It means all the preparation that goes into cooking before the actual cooking starts.
[9] Lundberg and Walker, op cit., p. 65.
[10] Rocco M. Angelo and Andrew N. Vladimir, *Hospitality Today: An Introduction.* East Lansing, Mich.: The Educational Institute of the American Hotel and Motel Association, 1991, p. 139.
[11] "R & I Top Independents," *Restaurants and Institutions, 102,* 10, April 1992, p. 90.
[12] A wheelable cart that is used to add flair to table-side service. It is also used for flambe dishes.
[13] Paul Fumkin, "Prunelle Thrives Despite Tough N.Y. Obstacles," *Nations Restaurant News, 25,* 20, May 20, 1991, p. 80.
[14] "The 1994 R & I 400: Overview," *Restaurants and Institutions, 104,* 16, July 1, 1994, p. 80.
[15] Ibid.
[16] "Market Share Report," *Restaurant Business, 91,* 9, June 10, 1992, p. 156.
[17] "The 1994 R & I 400: Overview," op cit.

Restaurant Operations

7

After reading and studying this chapter you should be able to do the following:

- ➤ Apply the forecasting technique used in the chapter to measure expected volume of business
- ➤ Describe the key points in purchasing, receiving, storing, and issuing
- ➤ Explain the important aspects of food production
- ➤ Name and describe the various types of services
- ➤ Contrast the difference between controllable expenses and fixed costs
- ➤ Explain the components of an income statement and operating ratios
- ➤ Describe the important aspects of a control system for a restaurant operation
- ➤ Outline the functional areas and tasks of a food service/restaurant manager

Restaurant Forecasting

Most businesses, including restaurants, operate by formulating a budget that projects sales and costs for a year on a weekly and monthly basis. Financial viability is predicated on sales, and sales budgets are forecasts of expected business.

Forecasting restaurant sales has two components: guest counts or covers and the average guest check. Guest counts or covers are the number of guests patronizing the restaurant over a given time period—a week, month, or year. To forecast the number of guests for a year, the year is divided into twelve twenty-eight-day and one twenty-nine-day accounting periods. The accounting periods then are broken down into four seven-day weeks (see Figure 7–1).

In terms of number of guests, Mondays usually are quiet; business gradually

Day	No. of Guests		Amount of Average Check		Amount of Food Sales		Amount of Beverage Sales		%	B	L	D	TOTAL SALES		%
	Forecast	Actual	Forecast	Actual	Forecast	Actual	Forecast	Actual					Forecast	Actual	
Mon															
Tues															
Wed															
Thur															
Fri															
Sat															
Sun															
Week's Total															

Figure 7–1   *Weekly Forecast of Restaurant Sales*

builds to Friday, which is often the busiest day. Friday, Saturday, and Sunday frequently provide up to 50 percent of revenue.

The average guest check is calculated by dividing total sales by the number of guests. Most restaurants keep such figures for each meal. The number of guests forecast for each day is multiplied by the amount of the average food and beverage check for each meal to calculate the total forecast sales. Each day, actual totals are compared with the forecasts. Four weekly forecasts are combined to form one accounting period; the thirteen accounting periods, when totaled, become the annual total. (Figure 7–2 shows a twenty-eight/twenty-nine-day period.)

Forecasting is used not only to calculate sales projections but also for predicting staffing levels and labor cost percentages. Much depends on the accuracy of forecasting. Once sales figures are determined, all expenditures, fixed and variable, have to be deducted to calculate profit or loss.[1]

Period	No. of Guests		Amount of Average Check		Amount of Food Sales		Amount of Beverage Sales		%	B	L	D	TOTAL SALES		%
	Forecast	Actual	Forecast	Actual	Forecast	Actual	Forecast	Actual					Forecast	Actual	
1															
2															
3															
4															
5															
6															
7															
8															
9															
10															
11															
12															
13															
Annual Total															

Figure 7–2   *Annual Forecast of Restaurant Sales*

Purchasing

Purchasing for restaurants involves procuring the products and services that the restaurant needs in order to serve its guests. Restaurant operators set up purchasing systems that determine the following:

Standards for each item (product specification)
Systems that minimize effort and maximize control of theft and losses from other sources
The amount of each item that should be on hand (par stock and reorder point)
Who will do the buying and keep the purchasing system in motion
Who will do the receiving, storage, and issuing of items[2]

It is desirable for restaurants to establish standards for each product, called *product specification.* When ordering meat, for example, the cut, weight, size, the percentage of fat content, and number of days aged are all factors that are specified by the purchaser.

Establishing systems that minimize effort and maximize control of theft may be done by computer or manually. However, merely computerizing a system does not make it theft-proof. Instead, employing honest workers is a top priority because temptation is everywhere in the restaurant industry.

An efficient and effective system establishes a stock level that must be on hand at all times. This is called a par stock. If the stock on hand falls below a specified reorder point, the computer system automatically reorders a predetermined quantity of the item.

In identifying who will do the buying, it is most important to separate task and responsibility between the person placing the order and the person receiving the goods. This avoids possible theft. The best way to avoid losses is to have the chef prepare the order, the manager or the manager's designee place the order, and a third person responsible for the stores receive the goods together with the chef (or the chef's designee).

Commercial (for-profit) restaurant and food service operators who are part of a chain may have the menu items and order specifications determined at the corporate office. This saves the unit manager from having to order individually; specialists at the corporate office can not only develop the menu but also the specifications for the ingredients to ensure consistency. Both chain and independent restaurants and food service operators use similar pre-purchase functions:

➤ Plan menus
➤ Determine quality and quantity needed to produce menus
➤ Determine inventory stock levels
➤ Identify items to purchase by subtracting stock levels from the quantity required to produce menus
➤ Write specifications and develop market orders for purchases

Professor Stefanelli at the University of Nevada–Las Vegas suggests a formal and an informal method of purchasing that includes the following steps:[3]

Formal	*Informal*
Develop purchase order	Develop purchase order
Establish bid schedule	Price quotation
Issue invitation to bid	Select vendor and place order
Tabulate and evaluate bids	
Award contract and issue delivery order	
Inspect/receive deliveries, inventory stores, and record transactions in inventory	Receive and inspect deliveries, store, and record transaction
Evaluate and follow up	Evaluate and follow up
Issue food supplies for food production and service	Issue food supplies for food production and service

The formal method is generally used by chain restaurant operators and the informal one by independent restaurant operators.

A purchase order comes as a result of the product specification. As it sounds, a purchase order is an order to purchase a certain quantity of an item at a specific price. Many restaurants develop purchase orders for items they need on a regular basis. These then are sent to suppliers for quotations, and samples are sent in for product evaluations. For example, canned items have varying amounts of liquid. Normally, it is the drained weight of the product that matters to the restaurant operator. After comparing samples from several vendors, the operator can choose the supplier that best suits the restaurant's needs.

Receiving

When placing an order, the restaurant operator specifies the day and time (for example, Friday, 10 a.m. to 12 noon) for the delivery to be made. This prevents deliveries from being made at inconvenient times.

Receiving is a point of control in the restaurant operation. The purpose of receiving is to ensure the quantity, quality, and price is exactly as ordered. The quantity and quality relate to the order specification and the standardized recipe. Depending on the restaurant and the type of food and beverage control system, some perishable items are issued directly to the kitchen, and most of the nonperishables items go into storage.

Storing/Issuing

Control of the stores is often a problem. Records must be kept of all items going into or out of the stores. If more than one person has access to the stores, it is difficult to know where to attach responsibility in case of losses.

Items should only be issued from the stores on an authorized requisition signed by the appropriate person. One restaurateur who has been in business for many years issues stores to the kitchen on a daily basis. No inventory is kept in the production area and there is no access to the stores. To some, this may be overdoing control, but it is hard to fault the results: a good food cost percentage. All items that enter the stores should have a date stamp and be rotated using the first in–first out (FIFO) system.

First in–first out is a simple but effective system of ensuring stock rotation. This is achieved by placing the most recent purchases, in rotation, behind previous purchases. Failure to do this can result in spoilage.

Food Production

Planning, organizing, and producing food of a consistently high quality is no easy task. The kitchen manager, cook, or chef begins the production process by determining the expected volume of business for the next few days. The same period's sales from the previous year will give a good indication of the expected volume and the breakdown of the number of sales of each menu item. As described earlier, ordering and receiving will have already been done for the day's production schedule.

The kitchen manager checks the head line cook's order, which will bring the prep (preparation) area up to the par stock of prepared items. Most of the prep work is done in the early part of the morning and afternoon. Taking advantage of slower times allows the line cooks to do the final preparation just prior to and during the actual meal service.

The kitchen layout is set up according to the business projected as well as the menu design. Most full-service restaurants have similar layouts and designs for their kitchens. The layout consists of the back door area, walk-ins, the freezer, dry storage, prep line, salad bar, cooking line, expediter, dessert station, and service bar area.

The cooking line is the most important part of the kitchen layout. It might consist of a broiler station, window station, fry station, salad station, saute station, and pizza station—just a few of the intricate parts that go into the set-up of the back-of-the-house. The size of the kitchen and its equipment are all designed according to the sales forecasted for the restaurant.

The kitchen will also be set up according to what the customers prefer and order most frequently. For example, if guests eat more broiled or sauteed

A Day in the Life of a TGI Friday's Kitchen Manager
Rob Plumbley, Kitchen Manager TGI Friday's, La Jolla, California

7 a.m.: Arrive. Check the work of cleaning crew (such as clogs in burners, stoves/ovens, etc.) for total cleanliness

7:15–7:40: Set production levels for all stations (broiler/hot sauce/expediter, cold sauce, vegetable preparation, baker preparation, line preparation: saute/noodles, pantry, fry/seafood portioning)

8:00: The first cooks begin arriving; greet them and allocate production sheets with priority items circled.

9:00: On a good day, the produce arrives at 9:00 a.m. Check for quality, quantity, accuracy (making sure the prices match the quotation sheet), and that the produce is stored properly

9:30–11:00: Follow up on production. The saute cook, who is last to come in, arrives. He or she is the closing person for the morning shift.
　　Follow up on cleanliness, recipe adherence, production accuracy
　　Check the stations to ensure the storage of prepped items (e.g., plastic draining inserts under poultry and seafood), the shelf life of products, general cleanliness, and that what is in the station is prepared correctly (e.g., turkey diced to the right size and portioned and dated correctly)

10:45: Final check of the line and production to ensure readiness. Did everyone prepare enough?

11:00–2:30: All hands on deck. Jump on the first ticket. Pretoast buns for burgers and hold in heated drawers. Precook some chicken breasts for salads. Monitor lunch until 2:30 p.m.
　　Be responsible for cleanliness
　　Determine who needs to get off the clock
　　Decide what production is left for the remainder of the day
　　Focus on changing over the line, change the food pan inserts (bar-b-que sauce, etc.)

2:30–3:15: Complete changeover of the line and check the stocking for the p.m. crew.
　　Final prep portioning
　　Check the dishwasher area and prep line for cleanliness
　　Check that the product is replaced in the store walk in or refrigerator
　　Reorganize the produce walk in. Check the storage of food, labels, and day dots, lids on.
　　Thank the a.m. crew and send them home

4:00–4:15: Welcome the p.m. crew
　　Place produce order (as a double check ask the p.m. crew what they might need)

5:00: Hand over to p.m. manager

Figure 7-3　*A Day in the Life of a T.G.I. Friday's Kitchen Manager*

items, the size of the broiler and saute must be larger to cope with the demand.

For example, T.G.I. Friday's has five rules of control for running a kitchen:

1. Order it well
2. Receive it well
3. Store it well
4. Make it to the recipe
5. Don't let it die in the window

Figure 7-3 shows a day in the life of a kitchen manager for T.G.I. Friday's.

Service

More than ever, what American diners really want to order when eating out is a side of good service. All too often, it is not on the menu. With increased competition, however, bad service may be going the way of Beef Wellington in American restaurants. Just as American cuisine came of age in the 1970s and 1980s, service is showing signs of maturing in the 1990s.

A new American service has emerged. A less formal—yet professional—approach is preferred by the 1990s restaurant guests. The restaurants' commitment to service is evidenced by the fact that most have increased training for new employees. For example, at Splendido in San Francisco's Embarcadero, the amount of time new servers spend in training has increased from forty to one hundred hours.

Servers are not merely order takers; they are the salespeople of the restaurant. A server undereducated about the menu can seriously hurt business. One would not be likely to buy a car from a salesperson who knew nothing about the car; likewise, customers feel uneasy ordering with an unknowledgeable waiter. Getting the waitstaff familiar with the menu can be a difficult task. Karen MacNeil, a restaurant service consultant and director of the New York Professional Service School, suggests two strategies: first, start from scratch and assume all servers know nothing about food; second, make learning fun—teach no more than three menu items a day and tell stories and use images to help things stick in servers' memories. It also is a good idea for the chef to coach the servers.[4]

Types of Restaurant Service

French Service

This form of service is generally reserved for haute cuisine (elegant) restaurants and complements an elegant ambiance. The food is attractively arranged on platters and presented to guests, after which the preparation of the food is completed on a gueridon table beside the guests' seats. A gueridon is a trolley-like table with a gas burner for table-side cooking. This is the most impressive and expensive form of service.

French service is conducted by an elaborate and formal staff comprised of the following:

➤ Maitre d' hotel: Restaurant manager
➤ Chef de rang: Station server in charge of service for approximately four tables. Greets guests, describes and takes menu orders, supervises service, and completes the preparation of some dishes on the gueridon and carves, slices, or debones dishes for guests

➤ Demi chef de rang: Assistant station server, assists the chef de rang, takes beverage orders, and serves food

➤ Commis de rang: Food server in training. Assists the demi chef de rang with serving of water, bread, butter, serving and cleaning of plates, taking orders to the kitchen, and bringing the food into the restaurant

French Service

Russian Service

With Russian service the food is cooked in the kitchen, cut, placed onto a serving dish, and beautifully garnished. The dish then is presented to the guests and served individually by lifting the food onto the guest's plate with a serving spoon and fork. Russian service can be used at a banquet or a dinner party, where the servers may wear white gloves.

American Service

This is a simplified version of Russian service techniques. The food is prepared and dished onto individual plates in the kitchen, carried into the dining room, and served to guests. This method of service is more popular because it is quicker and guests receive the food hot and beautifully presented by the chef.[5]

Russian Service

At Posterio, servers are invited to attend a one- and one-half-hour wine class in the restaurant; about three quarters of the forty-member staff routinely benefit from this additional training. The best employees are also rewarded with monthly prizes and with semiannual and annual prizes, which range from $100 cash, a limousine ride, dinner at Posterio, or a night's lodging at the Prescott hotel to a week in Hawaii. Servers at other San Francisco restaurants role play the various elements of service from greeting and seating guests, suggestive selling, correct methods of service, and guest relations to ensure a positive dining experience. A good food server in a top restaurant in many cities can earn about $40,000 a year.

Good servers quickly learn to gauge the guests' satisfaction levels and be sensitive to guests needs; for example, they check to ensure guests have everything they need as their entree is placed before them. Even better, they anticipate guests' needs. To take the preceding further, if the guest had used the entree knife to eat the appetizer, then a clean one should automatically be placed to the guest's right side. In other words, the guest should not receive the entree and then realize he or she needs another knife.

Another example of good service is when the server does not have to ask everyone at the table who is eating what. The server should either remember or do a seating plan so that the correct dishes are automatically placed in front of guests.

Danny Meyer, owner of New York City's celebrated Union Square Cafe and recipient of both the Restaurant of the Year and Outstanding Service Awards from the James Beard Foundation, gives each of the restaurant's ninety-five employees—from busboy to chef—a $600 annual allowance ($50 each a month) to eat in the restaurant and critique the experience.

At the critically acclaimed Inn at Little Washington in Washington, Virginia, servers are required to gauge the mood of every table and jot a number (one to ten) and sometimes a description ("elated, grumpy, or edgy") on each ticket. Anything below a seven requires a diagnosis. Servers and kitchen staff work together to try to elevate the number to at least a nine by the time dessert is ordered.

The Commander's Palace in New Orleans uses an elaborate system of color-coded tickets and hand signals in the dining room to ensure that everyone walks away a billboard for the restaurant. For example, when the maitre 'd touches the corner of his eye as he ushers guests to a table, it is a signal to the staff to take a good look, this is someone you should remember.

People are all impressed most by the use of their own names. Recognition of this kind is music to the ear and the ego. In upscale restaurants, guests' names are remembered by taking names from the reservation book and writing them on the meal check. This not only impresses the host and her or his guests, it may also increase the tip considerably.[6]

Marketing

Unhappy customers can be likened to hand grenades with pins pulled, ready to destroy waves of potential patrons. Unfortunately for restaurateurs, most guests do not voice their dissatisfaction at the time. However, they may write down what they will not say. Customer comment cards can be an effective way to hear what customers are thinking. *Restaurants and Institutions* magazine asked operators who use the comment cards to give some advice for success. The responses frequently included were creating a mailing list, making cards interactive, offering incentives, asking for specific comments, having customer-friendly designs (enough space for comments), locking the comment box, and not ignoring take-out customers.[7]

Suggestive Selling

Suggestive selling can be a potent weapon in the effort to increase food and beverage sales. Many restaurateurs can not think of a better, more effective, and easier way to boost profit margins. Servers admit that most guests are not offended or uncomfortable with suggestive selling techniques. In fact, cus-

Personal Profile: Herman Cain

Herman Cain, president and chief executive officer of Godfather's Pizza, Inc., is a living example of leadership and management successfully combined in one person. He was born in Atlanta, Georgia, from a humble family, yet rich in spirit. His mother's bible was a leading light throughout his life and career, and his father's optimism and sacrifices instilled in him the values and the principles that guided him from rural poverty to the crest of corporate America.

Cain has always been seeking challenges that could satisfy his profound need for accomplishments and achievement. He graduated from Morehouse College with a degree in mathematics, and later earned a master's degree in computer science while working as a mathematician for the Navy. However, government service did not seem to offer many entrepreneurial opportunities. Cain's competitive spirit led him to seek more challenges with Coca-Cola.

Herman Cain

In 1977, Cain began his experience in the food service industry, when he joined the Pillsbury Company. His exceptional abilities, both in terms of management, creativity, and, above all, hard work, were soon rewarded. Cain's career was well on its way to the top, when in only five years, at the age of thirty-four, he became vice president of corporate systems and services. Although such a position was the fulfillment of Cain's dream, as well as of his father's, Cain was not satisfied. He felt he was bound to achieve and move further beyond the limits.

After his many accomplishments with Pillsbury, he found himself hungering for new challenges and opportunities. At the age of thirty-six, Cain resigned his senior position and made a stunning move. He wanted to learn the restaurant business from the bottom up, and he accomplished this by tackling such tasks as broiling burgers at Burger King.

After only nine months, he had moved from being a trainee flipping burgers to regional vice president of the Philadelphia market. His next formidable accomplishment was the ultimate open door to today's success. He transformed his region from the worst performing area in Burger King's system to the best, which undoubtedly caught the attention of Pillsbury executives. The offer he received from Pillsbury was the ultimate challenge, one that a man with Cain's personality and skills could not refuse. His mission was to take over the presidency of a floundering pizza chain, Godfather's Pizza, and return it to profitability. Cain's dynamism, enthusiasm, and endless energy had finally found a way to be fully employed. In fact, Cain renewed Godfather's Pizza, breathing new life into a restaurant concept that had already been declared by many as terminated.

Within twelve months, the chain regained profitability. Two years later, Cain achieved corporate ownership, buying the chain from Pillsbury. Cain's success lies in the perfect combination of management and leadership skills. As a manager, he made use of his analytical abilities to diagnose the situation, make strategic plans, and develop tactics to return Godfather's Pizza to profitablitiy. He capitalized on every opportunity.

Cain realized that Godfather's goal was not to be a direct competitor to the industry's leaders—Pizza Hut and Domino's—but that he had to place a sharp focus on what the chain could do best—produce consistent quality products and maintain high standards of service, the driving force in any restaurant concept. A newly assembled management team helped him implement effectively the strategic actions designed to return the company to prosperity.

Cain's enthusiasm and leadership skills were transmitted to all segments of the company. Cain is a tremendously inspirational figure; his voice is one of those that cannot be ignored. It demands and obtains attention. He speaks powerfully and with a convincing self-confidence. "I'm a firm believer that we are put on this earth to make a difference," Cain said. This is undoubtedly his ultimate accomplishment.

tomers may feel special that the server is in tune with their needs and desires. It may be that the server suggests something to the guest that he or she may have never considered before. The object here is to turn servers into sellers. Guests will almost certainly be receptive to suggestions from competent servers for food and drink that complement each other.

Have you ever noticed how a server approaches your table and says, "Would you like a drink?" One way to increase sales is for a server to approach a table and ask if guests would prefer a glass of Fetzer Chardonnay, which is only so many dollars, or a Cowabunga. This approach not only describes the drinks, but also asks guests to choose which they would prefer, generating more sales than a question that can be answered "Yes, I want a . . . " or "No, thanks, I'll just have water."

The following are a few suggestions to change a restaurant's attitude toward suggestive selling:

1. Train servers as commissioned salespeople
2. Provide incentives and feedback
3. Teach servers to suggest pairings
4. Hire the sales type
5. Create students of food and wine
6. Encourage servers to upsell
7. Promote ear-grabbing phrasing
8. Recognize the unspoken suggestions
9. Incorporate role playing
10. Draw the line between sell and solicit[8]

Budgeting

Budgeting costs falls into two categories: fixed and variable. Fixed costs are constant no matter the volume of business. Fixed costs are rent/lease payments, interest, and depreciation. Variable costs fluctuate with the volume of business. Variable costs include controllable expenses such as payroll, benefits, direct operating expense, music and entertainment, marketing and promotion, energy and utility, administrative, and repairs and maintenance.

Regardless of sales fluctuations, variable or controllable expenses vary in some controllable proportion to sales. For example, if a restaurant is open on a Monday it must have a host, server, cook, dishwasher, and so on. The volume of business and sales total may be $750. However, on Friday that sales total might be $2250 with just a few more staff. The controllable costs increased only slightly in proportion to the sales, and the fixed costs did not change (see Table 7–1).

Lease and Controllable Expenses

Lease Costs

Successful restaurant operators will ensure that the restaurant's lease does not cost more than 5 to 8 percent of sales. Some chain restaurants will search for

Table 7–1
Controllable Costs versus Fixed Costs in Terms of Sales

	Restaurant A Monday		Restaurant A Friday	
Sales				
Food	$600	75.0%	$1800	75.0%
Beverage	150	25.0	450	25.0
Total Sales	$750	100.0	$2,250	100.0
Cost of Sales				
Food	198	26.0	540	30.0
Beverage	37.50	25.0	112.50	25.0
Total Cost of Sales	235.50		652.50	
Gross Profit	514.50		1,597.50	
Controllable expenses				
Salaries and wages	$195	26.0%	$472.50	21.0%
Employee benefits	30	4.0	90	4.0
Direct operating expense	45	6.0	90	4.0
Music	7.50	1.0	7.50	1.0
Marketing	30	4.0	30	4.0
Energy and utility	22.50	3.0	67.50	3.0
Administrative/general	30	4.0	90	4.0
Repairs and maintenance	15	2.0		2.0
Total controllable expenses	375.0		892.50	
Rent and other occupation costs				
Income before interest, depreciation, and taxes				
Interest				
Depreciation				
Total				
Net income before taxes				
Taxes				
Net income				

months or even years before they find the right location at the right price. Most leases are triple net, which means that the lessee must pay for all alterations, insurance, utilities, and possible commercial fees (e.g., landscaping or parking upkeep, security, etc.).

The best lease is for the longest time period with options for renewal and a sublease clause. The sublease clause is important because if the restaurant is not successful, the owner is still liable to pay the lease. With the sublease clause the owner may sublease the space to another restaurant operator or any other business.

Many leases are quoted at a dollar rate per square foot per month. Depending on the location, rates may range from $1.25 per square foot up to as high as $8.00 per square foot.

Some restaurants pay a combination of a flat amount based on the square footage and a percentage of sales. This helps protect the restaurant operator in the slower months and gives the landlord a bit extra during the good months.

Once a lease contract is signed, it is very difficult to renegotiate even a part of it. Only in dire circumstances is it possible to renegotiate lease contracts. The governing factor in determining lease rates is the market place. The market place is the supply and demand. If there is strong demand for space, then rates will increase. However, with a high vacancy rate, rates will be driven down by the owners in effort to rent space and gain income.

Controllable Expenses

Controllable expenses are all the expenses over which management and ownership has control. They include salaries and wages (payroll) and related benefits; direct operating expenses such as music and entertainment; marketing, including sales, advertising, public relations, and promotions; heat, light, and power; administrative and general expenses; and repairs and maintenance. The total of all controllable expenses is deducted from the gross profit. Rent and other occupation costs are then deducted to arrive at the income before interest, depreciation, and taxes. Once these are deducted, the net profit remains.

Successful restaurant operators are constantly monitoring their controllable expenses. The largest controllable expense is payroll. Because payroll is about 24 to 28 percent of a restaurant's sales, managers constantly monitor their employees not by the hour but by the minute. Bobby Hays, general manager of the Chart House restaurant in Solana Beach, California, says that he feels the pulse of the restaurant and then begins to send people home. Every dollar that Bobby and managers like him can save goes directly to the bottom line and becomes profit.

The actual sales results are compared with the budgeted amounts—ideally with percentages—and variances investigated. Most chain restaurant operators monitor the key result areas of sales and labor costs on a daily basis. Food and beverage costs are also monitored closely, generally on a weekly basis.

Restaurant Accounting

In order to operate any business efficiently and effectively, it is necessary to determine the mission, goals, and objectives. One of the most important goals in any enterprise is a fair return on investment, otherwise known as profit. In addition, accounting for the income and expenditures is a necessary part of any business enterprise. The restaurant industry has adopted a uniform system of accounts.

The uniform system of accounts for restaurants (USAR) outlines a standard classification and presentation of operating results. The system allows for easy comparison among restaurants because each expense item has the same schedule number.

Balance Sheet

A balance sheet shows the assets and liabilities of a restaurant or any business at a particular moment in time. The balance sheet is mainly used by owners and investors to verify the financial health of the organization. Restaurants are one of the few fortunate businesses to be on a cash basis for income receivables. There are no outstanding accounts receivable because all bills are paid in cash—even credit cards are treated as cash because of their prompt payment.

Operating or Income Statement

From an operational perspective, the most important financial document is the operating statement. Once a sales forecast has been completed, the costs of servicing those sales are budgeted on an income statement. Table 7–2 (next page) shows an example of an income statement for a hypothetical restaurant.

The income statement, which is for a month or a year, begins with the food and beverage sales. From this total the cost of food and beverage is deducted; the remaining total is gross profit. To this amount any other income is added (e.g., cigarettes, vending machines, outside catering, and telephone income). The next heading is controllable expenses, which includes salaries, wages, employee benefits, direct operating expenses (telephone, insurance, accounting and legal fees, office supplies, paper, china, glass, cutlery, menus, landscaping, and so on), music and entertainment, marketing, energy and utility, administrative and general, repairs and maintenance. The total of this group is called total controllable expenses. Rent and other occupation costs are then deducted from the total, leaving income before interest, depreciation, and taxes. Interest and depreciation are deducted leaving a total of net income before taxes. From this amount income taxes are paid leaving the remainder as net income.

Managing the money to the bottom line requires careful scrutiny of all key results, beginning with the big ticket controllable items like labor costs, food costs, and beverages, on down to related controllables.

Operating Ratios

Operating ratios are industry norms that are applicable to each segment of the industry. Experienced restaurant operators rely on these operating ratios to indicate the restaurant's degree of success. Several ratios are good barometers of a restaurant's degree of success. Among the better known ratios are the following:

- ➤ Food cost percentage
- ➤ Contribution margin
- ➤ Labor cost percentage
- ➤ Prime cost
- ➤ Beverage cost percentage

Table 7–2

Sample Income Statement

	Amount	Percentage
Sales		
Food		
Beverage		
Others		
Total sales	_____	100
Cost of Sales		
Food		
Beverage		
Others		
Total cost of sales	_____	
Gross profit	_____	
Controllable Expenses	_____	
Salaries and wages		
Employee benefits		
Direct operating expenses*		
Music and entertainment		
Marketing		
Energy and utility		
Administrative and general		
Repairs and maintenance		
Total controllable expenses	_____	
Rent and other occupation costs		
Income before interest, depreciation, and taxes		
Interest		
Depreciation		
Net income before taxes		
Income taxes	_____	
Net Income	=====	

Food Cost Percentage

The basic food cost percentage, for which the formula is cost/sales x 100 = the food cost percentage, is calculated on a daily, weekly, or monthly basis. The procedure works in the following manner:

1. An inventory is taken of all the food and the purchase price of that food. This is called the *opening inventory.*
2. The purchases are totaled for the period and added to the opening inventory.
3. The closing inventory (the inventory at the close of the week or period for which the food cost percentage is being calculated) and returns, spoilage, complimentary meals, and transfers to other departments are also deducted from the opening inventory plus purchases.
4. This figure is the cost of goods sold. The cost of goods sold is divided by the total sales. The resulting figure is the food cost percentage.

The following example illustrates the procedure:

Food Sales	$3,000
Opening Inventory	1,000
Add Purchases	500
	1,500
Less Spoilage and Complimentary Meals	100
Less Closing Inventory	500
Cost of Goods Sold	$900

$$\frac{\text{Food Cost } (\$900)}{\text{Sales } (\$3,000)} \times 100 = 30\% \text{ Food Cost Percentage}$$

The food cost percentage calculations become slightly more complicated when the cost of staff meals, management meals and entertaining (complimentary meals), and guest food returned are all properly calculated.

Food cost percentage has long been used as a yardstick of measuring the skill of the chef, cooks, and management to achieve a predetermined food cost percentage—usually 28 to 32 percent for a full-service restaurant and a little higher for a high-volume fast food restaurant.

Controlling food costs begins with cost-effective purchasing systems, a controlled storage and issuing system, and strict control of the food production and sales. The best way to visualize a food cost control system is to think of the food as money. Consider a $100 bill arriving at the back door: If the wrong people get their hands on that money, it does not reach the guest or the bottom line.

Contribution Margin

More recently, attention has focused not only on the food cost percentage but also on the contribution margin. The contribution margin is the amount that a menu item contributes to the gross profit, or the difference between the cost of the item and its sales price. Some menu items contribute more than others;

Corporate Profile: T.G.I. Friday's

In the spring of 1965, Alan Stillman, a New York perfume salesman, opened a restaurant located at First Avenue and 63rd Street. The restaurant boasted striped awnings, a blue exterior, and yellow supergraphics reading T.G.I. Friday's. Inside were wooden floors covered with sawdust, Tiffany-style lamps, bentwood chairs, red-and-white tablecloths, and a bar area complete with brass rails and stained glass.

T.G.I. Friday's was an immediate success. The restaurant on Manhattan's upper east side became the meeting place for single adults. In fact, *Newsweek* and the *Saturday Evening Post* called the opening of T.G.I. Friday's "the dawn of the singles' age."

In 1971, franchisee Dan Scoggin opened a T.G.I. Friday's in Dallas and in four other sites around the country. The success was instant; thus, began the company that is T.G.I. Friday's today.

By 1975, there were ten T.G.I. Friday's in eight states, but the great success that the company had seen was starting to diminish. Dan Scoggin began a country-wide tour to each restaurant; he talked with employees, managers, and customers to isolate the roots of successes and failures. This was the critical turning point for the company. The focus shifted from being just another restaurant chain to giving guests exactly what they wanted. The theories and philosophies Scoggin developed are the principles by which T.G.I. Friday's now does business.

T.G.I. Friday's goal was to create a comfortable, relaxing environment where guests could enjoy food and drink. Stained glass windows, wooden airplane propellers, racing sculls, and metal advertising signs comprised the elegant clutter that greeted guests when they entered a T.G.I. Friday's. Nothing was left to chance. Music, lights, air conditioning, decor, and housekeeping were all designed to keep guests comfortable. Employees were encouraged to display their own personalities and to treat customers as they would guests in their own homes.

As guests demanded more, T.G.I. Friday's provided more—soon becoming the industry leader in menu and drink selection. The menu expanded from a slate chalkboard to an award-winning collection of items representing every taste and mood.

T.G.I. Friday's also became the industry leader in innovation—creating the now famous potato skins and popularizing fried zucchini. This was the first restaurant chain to offer stone ground whole wheat bread, avocados, bean sprouts, and Mexican appetizers across the country. As guests' tastes continued to change, T.G.I. Friday's introduced pasta dishes, fettuccine, brunch items, and croissant sandwiches.

America owes the popularization of frozen and ice cream drinks to T.G.I. Friday's, where smooth, alcoholic and nonalcoholic drinks were made with fresh fruit, juices, ice cream, and yogurt. These recipes were so precise that T.G.I. Friday's drink glasses were scientifically designed for the correct ratio of each ingredient. These specially designed glasses have since become popular throughout the industry.

Through the years, T.G.I. Friday's success has been phenomenal. More than two hundred restaurants have opened in the United States and abroad, with average gross revenues of $3.5 million per year at each location, the highest per-unit sales volume of any national chain.

T.G.I. Friday's is now privately owned by Carlson Companies, Inc., of Minneapolis—one of the largest privately held companies in the country. Today, T.G.I. Friday's has come to be known as a casual restaurant where family and friends meet for great food, fun, and conversation. Everyone looks forward to Friday's!

What does it take to be successful in the restaurant business? and What does it take to be a leader? The answers to these questions are crucial to success as a restaurant company. The essentials of success in business are as follows:

1. Treat everyone with respect for their dignity
2. Treat all customers as if they are honored guests in your home
3. Remember that all problems result from either poor hiring, lack of training, unclear performance expectations, or accepting less than excellence
4. Remember that management tools are methods, not objectives

As you can see, these are principles to guide decision making as opposed to step-by-step actions. However, I would submit that if these principles are not followed, then actions have very short-term effects. And if you do choose to follow them, they form a base on which you can easily decide which specific actions are necessary in any given situation.

The basics of leadership are as follows:

1. Hire the right people
2. Train everyone thoroughly and completely
3. Be sure that everyone clearly understands the performance expectations
4. Accept only excellence

Here we are dealing with the very basics of how to provide strong, clear leadership. However, once again we are talking about only the minimum requirements, not all the qualities necessary to be a good leader. Individual success and that of the company, T.G.I. Friday's Inc., is predicated on understanding and following the essentials of success in business and the basics of leadership. Whether you are an hourly employee or a manager, it is critical that you manage your part of the business using these philosophies.

One of the things that makes T.G.I. Friday's unique is our philosophies and theories. These are principles that each employee understands to ensure we all stay focused on the same goals. T.G.I. Friday's philosophies and theories were first conceived in the mid-1970s. They are used to solve existing problems and enable us to be proactive to problems we have experienced in the past.

The Guest Focus

At most companies, it appears that senior management runs the company. The employees consider senior management to be the most important people with whom they interact. As a result, decisions are made in an effort to please senior management, and decisions that affect people lower in the hierarchy are viewed as less important. T.G.I. Friday's success is dependent on inverting the typical management pyramid. Guests are the most important element in the organization; immediately following them are the employees who are closest to the guests—those people who have the greatest impact on the guests' experience. The livelihood of each employee depends on one group of people: guests. It is critical we determine what guests' needs are and fill those needs. To the extent that we accomplish this objective, the needs of each person in our pyramid will be fulfilled. Every decision at T.G.I. Friday's is made with guests in mind.

The *"Five Easy Pieces Theory"* stresses T.G.I. Friday's deep concern for our guests' satisfaction. We will always cheerfully go out of our way to serve a quality product prepared to individual tastes. In the movie titled *Five Easy Pieces*, the star, Jack Nicholson, goes to a restaurant and orders a side order of whole wheat toast. The waitress makes it clear that they do not serve whole wheat toast. Nicholson notes on the menu that the chicken salad sandwich comes on whole wheat bread. The annoyed

waitress pointed to a sign in the restaurant that read "No substitutions" and "We reserve the right to refuse service to anyone." Jack Nicholson orders a chicken salad sandwich on whole wheat toast, but tells the waitress to hold the mayo, hold the lettuce, and hold the chicken salad, and just bring him the whole wheat toast. Unwisely, she asks where she should hold the chicken salad. Nicholson sarcastically responds, "Between your knees!" On that note, he leaves, a very dissatisfied guest. Our managers and employees are responsible for honoring any guest request within realistic possibilities. Many managers take a guest's request even further and get them exactly what they want—even if the ingredients are not in the restaurant.

The *"Triangle Theory"* explains the need to balance and expand upon the goals of the guest, employee, and company, and maximize the results to each. Managers make many decisions and must always consider the effect of those decisions on all three sides of the triangle—the guest, the employee, and the company. Some decisions can cause one side of the triangle to prosper (temporarily) at the expense of the other two. For example, if a company overprices its menu items, it can greatly improve the bottom line. However, guests will object to being cheated and will not return. This will ultimately result in lower staffing and will eventually kill the company. Management's responsibility is to balance the results among the three sides so all sides thrive. But this is only the first step. To grow and expand the business, decisions must be made that maximize or expand all three sides of the triangle at the same time.

These are just a few of the philosophies and theories on which T.G.I. Friday's is based. It is important we educate our people and we all are guided by the same principles.

Benefits

Starting compensation for managers is an individual issue, based on background and experience. In addition to a competitive base salary, T.G.I. Friday's also offers a bonus based on sales and/or profits to all restaurant employees, including general managers, kitchen managers, assistant general managers, and other managers. Management staffing is designed to meet volume needs and may number four to seven per store. Management generally works a five-day work week.

T.G.I. Friday's offers a complete benefits program for both hourly and management personnel. Among its features are health and dental coverage (dependent coverage is also available), vision care, life insurance, paid vacations, disability coverage, credit union, education assistance program, and a profit-sharing plan that allows employees to share in the success of the company. At T.G.I. Friday's Inc. they also believe that recognizing employees for their outstanding effort is our opportunity to acknowledge and reinforce the behavior we want to encourage.

Chris Yubanks is the general manager of a T.G.I. Friday's in San Diego. The typical day for Chris is a long and challenging experience. Chris usually comes in around 7:00 a.m. and will usually work until 6:00 or 7:00 p.m. Chris does routine paperwork on a daily basis; however, no day is the same as another in the restaurant business.

T.G.I. Friday's is one of the more successful restaurant concepts in the industry today. Management is taken very seriously in this restaurant. A typical day for Chris goes as follows:

➤ Chris usually works from 7 a.m. to 6 p.m.; however, leaving at 7:00 or 8:00 p.m. is not uncommon. He is scheduled to work five days a week, but sometimes this is not the case. If a manager calls in sick or there is a major problem at the restaurant, Chris must be there to cover the shift.

➤ The first thing Chris does in the morning is turn off the alarm. Next, he checks the sales from the previous day and compares them to previous week's numbers as well as the previous year's.

➤ The next thing is to boot up the computer. Chris runs the daily reports and counts the bank in the restaurant. If all of the drawers are correct and the store bank is correct, then Chris can do the daily walk around. This is done to check the cleanliness of the restaurant as well as to see if anything is needed to open.

➤ Following this, the produce usually arrives and is checked off accordingly.

➤ Then Chris checks for proper staffing for the day. If all employees have shown up for their shifts, then production is issued to the back of the house as well as opening duties to the front of the house.

➤ The final thing done prior to opening is having the employee meeting. This meeting is used to let the servers know what the daily specials are, the food and drinks to push, and a general pumping up for the employees.

➤ After all of the opening procedures are done the restaurant is ready to open for business.

➤ Now it is 11:30 and time to open the doors of the restaurant. Chris's job is simple—all he does for the remainder of the day is run the shift. Chris does this by constantly checking on the tables to make sure all of the guests are satisfied. When the guests are not satisfied, then Chris fixes the problem according to the guests' liking.

➤ After lunch, Chris counts out all of the employees cash drawers, cleans up the front of the house, and gets things ready for the closing manager. When the closing manager arrives at 4:30 p.m., the store bank is counted over to him or her. If the bank is correct, Chris and the closing manager go over the daily numbers for the day and discuss the closing shift.

Expectations of the General Manager

The expectations of the general manager are different in all restaurants; however, there are certain commonalities as well. Some of these commonalities are as follows:

➤ General managers answer directly to the owner, or to regional directors for major corporations.

therefore, restaurant operators focus more attention on the items that produce a higher contribution margin. It works like this:

The cost of the chicken dish is $2.00 and its selling price is $9.95, which leaves a contribution margin of $7.95. The fish, which costs a little more at $3.25 sells for $12.75 and leaves a contribution of $9.50. The pasta cost price of $1.50 and selling price of $8.95 leave a contribution margin of $7.45.

Under this scenario it world be better for the restaurants to sell more fish

> General managers are expected to run good numbers for the periods. The numbers analyzed are food cost, labor cost, beverage cost. These areas are controlled in order to produce sufficient profit for the restaurant.
> General managers promote good morale and teamwork in the restaurant. Having a positive environment in the restaurant is of utmost importance. This will not only keep the employees happy, but it will also contribute to providing better service to the guests.

Duties and Responsibilities

The general manager of a restaurant is directly in charge of all of the operations in the restaurant. General managers are also in charge of the floor managers, kitchen manager, and all of the remaining employees in the restaurant.

The general manager should always check on the floor managers to ensure that all policies and regulations are being met according to policy. This will keep operations running smoothly.

Another important duty is to organize and control the staffing of the restaurant. The floor managers usually write the employee schedule; however, the general manager is still directly responsible for proper staffing for the period. This will help control labor costs to around 20 percent of sales. The general manager is also in charge of conducting employee reviews and training.

Qualifications for a General Manager

To be hired as a general manager, the following qualifications are necessary:

> The general manager should be very knowledgeable in the restaurant business.
> He or she should have previously worked all the stations in a restaurant and be very familiar with them.

> The general manager should be able to get along with all people, be fair with all employees, and not discriminate.
> Having a degree is not the most important thing in becoming a general manager. However, a degree is very useful in moving up the ladder in a company to regional manager, regional director, and so on.

Budgeted Costs in a Restaurant

Running a good pace in the restaurant is of absolute importance. Every restaurant has different numbers to make. The following numbers came from a T.G.I. Friday's-type restaurant. These numbers reflect their goals versus actual numbers run for a given week.

	GOAL	ACTUAL	VARIANCE
Food Cost	27.0	27.2	+ .2
Labor Cost	19.9	20.8	+ .4
Beverage Cost	19.0	18.2	− .8

As can be seen, T.G.I. Friday's did well with the beverage cost; however, the food cost and the labor cost are two areas to focus on for the upcoming week.

Making good percentages for the restaurant is the most important focus, simply because this is where the restaurant makes or does not make a profit. When the general manager runs good numbers, then he or she will receive a large bonus check for contributing to the profit for the restaurant. This is why it is so important to focus on these three key areas.

Scheduling the Restaurant

Appropriate scheduling plays a key role in the success of the restaurant. For one thing, overscheduling and underscheduling have a direct effect on the labor cost. If there are too many employees working on a shift for the business acquired, then the labor cost will be high. In contrast, if there are not enough employees working, then the service will suffer and overtime will increase the labor cost.

because each plate will yield $1.55 more than if chicken were sold. Therefore, if we are operating a casual Italian restaurant, industry comparisons would show the following:

Labor costs at 20 to 24 percent of sales
Food costs at 28 to 32 percent of food sales
Beverage costs at 18 to 24 percent of beverage sales

Labor Cost Percentage

Labor costs are the highest single cost factor in staffing a restaurant. Fast food restaurants have the lowest labor costs (about 16 to 18 percent) with family and ethnic restaurants at about 22 to 26 percent, and upscale full-service restaurants at about 30 to 35 percent.

Prime Cost

Combined food and labor costs are known as prime cost. In order to allow for a reasonable return on investment, prime cost should not go above 60 to 65 percent of sales.

There are various methods of control, beginning with effective scheduling based on the expected volume of business. In reality, because of the high cost of labor, today's restaurateurs manage by the minute. Once a rush is over, the effective manager thanks employees for doing a great job and looks forward to seeing them again. This may appear to be micromanagement, but an analysis of restaurant operations does not leave any alternatives.[9]

Beverage Cost Percentage

The beverage cost percentage is calculated like the food cost percentage. The method used most often is first to determine the unit cost and then mark up by the required percentage to arrive at the selling price. This is rounded up or down to a convenient figure. The actual beverage cost percentage is then compared with the anticipated cost percentage; any discrepancy is investigated.

The National Restaurant Association publishes guidelines for restaurant operations. These valuable documents help provide a guide for operators to use when comparing their restaurants with other similar establishments. If the costs go above the budgeted or expected levels, then management must investigate and take corrective action.

Controls

Every dollar earned must be watched all the way to the bank, and every dollar spent must be analyzed to see if it is really necessary. Control provides information to management for operational decision-making purposes.

Industry experts describe the following losses resulting from a lack of controls:

➤ The food service industry loses approximately $20 billion a year to theft and cash mishandling.
➤ One out of every three employees will steal if given the opportunity. This includes theft of cash, merchandise, and time.

- ➤ Approximately 5 percent to 8 percent of gross sales is lost to internal theft.
- ➤ Thirty-five percent of all restaurants fail because of theft.
- ➤ Seventy-five percent of all missing inventory is from theft.
- ➤ Seventy-three percent of job applications are falsified.
- ➤ The majority of employees caught stealing have worked for an operation for an average of five to seven years.

Fred Del Marva, Chairman and CEO of Food and Beverage Investigations, loss management investigators in Novato, California, offers the following advice to reduce back-of-the-house theft:[10]

- ➤ Conduct frequent inventories
- ➤ Distribute receiving responsibilities
- ➤ Establish a par stock
- ➤ Refuse off-peak-hour deliveries
- ➤ Use insider accounting
- ➤ Designate an employee entry/exit
- ➤ Discourage duffel bags/reserve the right to search bags
- ➤ Oversee trash disposal

Another industry expert has the following suggestion: "Owners and managers could take expensive marketing plans that are designed to increase sales by 25 percent and toss them out the window if they would just make a minimal effort to control theft," says Francis D'Addario, director of loss prevention for Hardee's food systems, Rocky Mount, North Carolina. Many operators are reluctant to crack down on theft because they simply do not want to play cop. Other operators just refuse to believe they are being cheated because they trust their long-time employees. Spotting theft is a job in itself. A variance of more than half a percent in food cost should be considered odd enough to check out. An unusual food cost variance can mean cash is going out the front door or food is going out the back.[11]

Most restaurants rely on point of sale (POS) systems. These systems, such as a server's hand-held ordering device that automatically prints up the order in the kitchen or bar, have improved service efficiency. However, there is a cost involved and restaurant operators need to carefully select a point of sale system that is appropriate for their restaurants.

Buying a POS system for a restaurant can be a major investment. It is imperative that managers get the most value for their dollars. *Restaurants and Institutions* magazine surveyed a panel of experts from companies that use POS systems who suggested the following guidelines:

1. Buy from a reliable vendor
2. Decide what you need before buying
3 Don't get carried away with technology
4. Look for a computer company that knows restaurants
5. Buy standard software packages

6. Look for an adaptable piece of equipment
7. Try to use generic hardware
8. Find a system that simultaneously runs several programs
9. Consider quick credit card verification
10. Insist on a twenty-four-hour hot line
11. User-friendly systems can pay off.
12. Avoid downtime with a dual disk system
13. Find a system that helps control labor costs[12]

Food Service Manager Job Analysis

The National Restaurant Association (NRA) has formulated an analysis of the food service managers job by functional areas and tasks, which follows a natural sequence of functional areas from human resources to sanitation and safety.

Human Resource Management

Recruiting/Training
1. Recruit new employees by seeking referrals
2. Recruit new employees by advertising
3. Recruit new employees by seeking help from district manager/supervisors
4. Interview applicants for employment

Orientation/Training
1. Conduct on-site orientation for new employees
2. Explain employee benefits and compensation programs
3. Plan training programs for employees
4. Conduct on-site training for employees
5. Evaluate progress of employees during training
6. Supervise on-site training of employees that is conducted by another manager, employee leader, trainer, and so on
7. Conduct payroll sign up
8. Complete reports or other written documentation on successful completion of training by employees

Scheduling for Shifts
1. Review employee work schedule for shift
2. Determine staffing needs for each shift

3. Make work assignments for dining room, kitchen staff, and maintenance person(s)
4. Make changes to employee work schedule
5. Assign employees to work stations to optimize employee effectiveness
6. Call in, reassign, or send home employees in reaction to sales and other needs
7. Approve requests for schedule changes, vacation, days off, and so on

Supervision and Employee Development
1. Observe employees and give immediate feedback on unsatisfactory employee performance
2. Observe employees and give immediate feedback on satisfactory employee performance
3. Discuss unsatisfactory performance with an employee
4. Develop and deliver incentive for above-satisfactory performance of employees
5. Observe employee behavior for compliance with safety and security
6. Counsel employees on work-related problems
7. Counsel employees on nonwork-related problems
8. Talk with employees who have frequent absences
9. Observe employees to assure compliance with fair labor standards and equal opportunity guidelines
10. Discipline employees by issuing oral and/or written warnings for poor performance
11. Conduct employee and staff meetings
12. Identify and develop candidates for management programs
13. Put results of observation of employee performance in writing
14. Develop action plans for employees to help them in their performance
15. Authorize promotion and/or wage increases for staff
16. Terminate employment of an employee for unsatisfactory performance

Financial Management

Accounting
1. Authorize payment on vendor invoices
2. Verify payroll
3. Count cash drawers
4. Prepare bank deposits
5. Assist in establishment audits by management or outside auditors
6. Balance cash at end of shift
7. Analyze profit and loss reports for establishment

Cost Control
1. Discuss factors that impact profitability with district manager/supervisor
2. Check establishment figures for sales, labor costs, waste, inventory, and so on

Administrative Management

Scheduling/Coordinating
1. Establish objectives for shift based on needs of establishment
2. Coordinate work performed by different shifts, for example, clean up, routine maintenance, and so on
3. Complete special projects assigned by district manager/supervisor
4. Complete shift readiness checklist

Planning
1. Develop and implement action plans to meet financial goals
2. Attend off-site workshops and training sessions

Communication
1. Communicate with management team by reading and making entries in daily communication log
2. Prepare written reports on cleanliness, food quality, personnel, inventory, sales, food waste, labor costs, and so on
3. Review reports prepared by other establishment managers
4. Review memos, reports, and letters from company headquarters/main office
5. Inform district manager/supervisor of problems or developments that affect operation and performance of the establishment
6. Initiate and answer correspondence with company, vendors, and so on
7. File correspondence, reports, personnel records, and so on

Marketing Management

1. Create and execute local establishment marketing activities
2. Develop opportunities for the establishment to provide community services
3. Carry out special product promotions

Operations Management

Facility Maintenance
1. Conduct routine maintenance checks on facility and equipment
2. Direct routine maintenance checks on facility and equipment
3. Repair or supervise the repair of equipment
4. Review establishment evaluations with district manager/supervisor
5. Authorize the repair of equipment by outside contractor
6. Recommend upgrades in facility and equipment

Food and Beverage Operations Management
1. Direct activities for opening establishment
2. Direct activities for closing establishment
3. Talk with other managers at beginning and end of shift to relay information about ongoing problems and activities
4. Count, verify, and report inventory
5. Receive, inspect, and verify vendor deliveries
6. Check stock levels and submit orders as necessary
7. Talk with vendors concerning quality of product delivered
8. Interview vendors who wish to sell products to establishment
9. Check finished product quality and act to correct problems
10. Work as expediter to get meals served effectively
11. Inspect dining area, kitchen, rest rooms, food lockers, storage, and parking lot
12. Check daily reports for indications of internal theft
13. Instruct employees regarding the control of waste, portion sizes, and so on
14. Prepare forecast for daily or shift food preparation

Service
1. Receive and record table reservations
2. Greet familiar customers by name
3. Seat customers
4. Talk with customers while they are dining
5. Monitor service times and procedures in the dining area
6. Observe customers being served in order to correct problems
7. Ask customers about quality of service
8. Ask customers about quality of the food product
9. Listen to and resolve customer complaints
10. Authorize complimentary meals or beverages
11. Write letters in response to customer complaints
12. Telephone customers in response to customer complaints
13. Secure and return items left by customers

Sanitation and Safety
1. Accompany local officials on health inspections on premise
2. Administer first aid to employees and customers
3. Submit accident, incident, and OSHA reports
4. Report incidents to police
5. Observe employee behavior and establishment conditions for compliance with safety and security procedures

Summary

1. Most restaurants forecast a budget on a weekly and monthly basis that projects sales and costs for a year in consideration of guest counts and the average guest check.
2. In order to operate a restaurant, products need to be purchased, received, and properly stored.
3. Food production is determined by the expected business for the next few days. The kitchen layout is designed according to the sales forecasted.
4. Good service is very important. A distinction is made among Russian, American, and French service. In addition to taking orders, servers act as salespersons for the restaurant.
5. Budgeting costs are divided into fixed costs (such as lease or rent) and variable costs, which include controllable expenses such as salaries, entertainment, and promotion.
6. Accounting for the income and expenditures is necessary in order to gain a profit. Measures of accounting are the uniform system of accounts for restaurants, a balance sheet, and an income statement.
7. Restaurant operators rely on ratios such as food cost percentage, contribution margin, labor cost percentage, and prime cost to indicate the restaurant's degree of success.
8. The point-of-sales system is one form of control that restaurants use to protect themselves from theft.

Review Exercises

1. Briefly describe the two components of restaurant forecasting.
2. Explain the key points in purchasing, receiving, and storing.
3. Why is the kitchen layout an important aspect of food production?
4. Explain the purpose of suggestive selling. What characteristics make up a good server?
5. Accounting is important in order to determine the profitability of a restaurant. Briefly describe the following terms:
   a. controllable expenses
   b. uniform system of accounts
   c. prime cost
6. What is the point-of-sales system, and why is a control system important for a restaurant operation?

Key Words and Concepts

Average guest check	First in–first out	Menu	Receiving
Balance sheet profit	Fixed costs	Operating ratios	Reorder point
Beverage cost percentage	Food cost percentage	Par stock	Restaurant accounting
Budgeting	Gross profit	Prime Cost	Restaurant forecasting
Contribution margin	Income statement	Product specification	Uniform system of accounts
Control	Labor cost percentage	Purchasing	Variable costs
Controllable expenses			

Notes

[1] This section draws on Donald E. Lundberg and John R. Walker, *The Restaurant from Concept to Operation.* New York: John Wiley and Sons, 1993, pp. 86–87.

[2] Ibid., p. 275.

[3] Ibid.

[4] This section draws on Beth Lorenzini, "Turn Servers into Menu Masters, *Restaurants and Institutions, 103,* 6, March 1, 1993, pp. 93–100.

[5] T. Suji, *Professional Restaurant Service.* New York: John Wiley and Sons, 1992, p. 14.

[6] This section draws on Tom Sietseima, "Restaurants Trying Harder to Please," *San Francisco Chronicle,* July 14, 1993, p. A-1.

[7] This section draws on Rajan Chaudhry, "Use Customers as Consultants," *Restaurants and Institutions, 103,* 5, February 15, 1993, pp. 97–104.

[8] This section draws on Pat DiDomenico, "The Power of Suggestions: Turn Servers into Sellers," *Restaurants USA, 13, 2,* February 1993, pp. 20–23.

[9] Personal conversation with Bobby Hays, general manager, Chart House Restaurant, Solana Beach, California, January 1994.

[10] Personal conversation with Fred Del Marva, May 1994.

[11] This section draws on Beth Lorenzini, "The Secure Restaurant," *Restaurants and Institutions, 102,* 25, October 21, 1992, pp. 84–102.

[12] This section draws from Jeff Weinstein, "13 Things You Need to Know before Buying a POS System," *Restaurants and Institutions, 103,* 3, February 1, 1993, pp. 131–134.

Non-commercial Food Service Management

After reading and studying this chapter you should be able to do the following:

➤ Outline the different noncommercial food service segments

➤ Describe the five factors that distinguish noncommercial food service operations from commercial ones

➤ Explain the need for and trends in elementary and secondary school food service

➤ Describe the complexities in college and university food service

➤ Identify characteristics and trends in health care and business and industry food service

Overview

Noncommercial food service consists of all food service operations that are classified as not-for-profit and includes the following segments:

➤ Airlines
➤ Military
➤ Elementary and secondary schools
➤ Colleges and universities
➤ Health care facilities
➤ Business and industry

Several features distinguish noncommercial food service operations from commercial ones:

1. In a restaurant, the challenge is to please the guest. In noncommercial food service, it is necessary to meet both the needs of the guest and the client (i.e., the institution itself).
2. In some operations, the guests are a captive clientele. These guests may be eating at the food service operation only once or on a daily basis.
3. Many noncommercial operations are housed in host organizations that do not have food service as their primary business.
4. Most noncommercial food service operations produce food in large-quantity batches for service and consumption within fixed time periods. (For example, batch cooking means to produce a batch of food to serve at 11:30 a.m., another batch to serve at 12:15 p.m., and a third batch to serve at 12:45 p.m., rather than putting out all of the food for the whole lunch period at 11:30 a.m. This gives the guests who come to eat later in the serving period a better quality meal.)
5. The volume of business is more consistent and therefore easier to cater. Because it is easier to predict the number of meals and portion sizes, it is easier to plan, organize, produce, and serve meals; therefore, the atmosphere is less hurried than that of a restaurant. Weekends tend to be quieter than weekdays in noncommercial food service, and, overall, the hours and benefits may be better than those of commercial restaurants.

Airlines

In-Flight Food Service

Fred Martin, president of Dobbs International, believes—rightfully—that food has become a major competitive factor with the airlines. Airlines constantly are striving to be more efficient, demanding better food at the same or lower costs. Airlines may either provide meals from their own in-flight business or have the service provided by a contractor. In-flight food may be prepared in a factory mode at a facility close to but outside of the airport. In these cases, the food is prepared and packaged; it then is transported to the departure gates for the appropriate flights. Once the food is loaded onto the aircraft, flight attendants take over serving the food and beverages to passengers.

In-flight food service is a complex logistical operation: The food must be able to withstand the transport conditions and the extended hot or cold holding period from the time it is prepared until the time it is served. If a food item is to be served hot, it must be able to re-thermalize well on the plate. In addition, the meal needs to look appealing, be tasty, and be able to fit with the limited space available.[1] Finally, all food and beverage items must be delivered on time and correctly to each departing aircraft.

Caterair International is the largest in-flight caterer in terms of sales, with $1.1 billion in 1993. The company was founded in 1990 after an employee-leveraged buyout from Marriott Corporation. Marriott had been a pioneer in in-flight catering, but the corporation made a strategic decision to focus its resources on areas in which the return on investment was greater.

Dobbs International, based in Phoenix, Arizona, is the third largest in-flight caterer in its segment, with sales of $475 million in 1993. However, Dobbs is recognized as the quality service leader in airline catering.

Another major player in the in-flight food service market is Sky Chefs, headquartered in Dallas, Texas. Sky Chefs was part of American Airlines, but was sold in a strategic move to reduce debt and to allow the airline to focus on its core business.

The industry is experiencing a period of considerable growth, which has led these companies to seek new ventures. In 1993, for example, Dobbs International purchased fifteen of United Airlines' flight kitchens, which increased the company's volume by 61 percent. Sky Chefs reached a marketing agreement with Lufthansa, thus further expanding the company's operations in Europe.

Food being Prepared, Loaded, and Served on an Aircraft (Courtesy Dobbs International.)

AMERICAN FLAGSHIP SERVICE

TO START

An assortment of warm mixed Nuts
to accompany your preferred Cocktail or Beverage

APPETIZER

Basil-cured Salmon
Served with Tomato Caper Relish, Lemon and a Crouton

THE SALAD CART

A zesty Caesar Salad with Romaine Lettuce, Croutons,
Parmesan Cheese and Caesar Dressing
Anchovies are available for those who wish

ENTREES

CHATEAUBRIAND
Chateaubriand served with a fresh Herb and Cabernet Sauvignon Sauce,
offered with Mashed New Potatoes and Carrots seasoned with Thyme

GRILLED CHICKEN WITH FETTUCCINE
Breast of Chicken presented over Fettuccine tossed with Pesto,
Bacon, Tomato and enhanced by a Four Cheese Sauce

PACIFIC PRAWNS WITH THAI CURRY SAUCE
Jumbo Prawns served on a spicy Thai Curry Sauce, presented with
Jasmine Pineapple Rice and Black Bean and Mango Relish

BREAD BASKET
Sourdough and Multigrain Rolls

THE DESSERT CART

ICE CREAM SUNDAE
Häagen-Dazs Vanilla Ice Cream with a choice of Hot Fudge,
Butterscotch or seasonal Fruit Toppings and fresh Whipped Cream

FRUIT AND CHEESE
A sampler of Cheese
complemented by fresh Fruit and Crackers

PRIOR TO ARRIVAL

Pecan Chocolate Chip Cookies, freshly baked on board

Figure 8–1 *In-Flight Menu* (Courtesy American Airlines.)

The in-flight food service management operators plan the menus, develop the product specifications, and arrange the purchasing contracts. They also are involved with galley, design, development of in-flight service procedures, and equipment logistics.[2]

Each airline has a representative who oversees one or more locations and checks on the quality, quantity, and delivery times of all food and beverage items. Airlines regard in-flight food service as an expense that needs to be controlled. The cost for the average in-flight meal is just over $6.00. The cost had been higher, but in order to trim costs, many airlines now offer snacks instead of meals on a number of short flights and flights that do not span main meal times. Some airlines try to stand out by offering superior food and beverages in hopes of attracting more passengers. Others reduce or eliminate food service as a strategic decision to support lower fares. Generally, international flights have better-quality food and beverage service.

On board, each aircraft has two or three categories of service, usually coach, business, and first class. First- and business-class passengers usually receive free beverages and upgraded meal items and service. These meals may consist of items like fresh salmon or filet mignon. Figure 8–1 shows an in-flight menu. On international flights, the per-passenger food cost ranges from about $10.32 for Northwest Airlines to $37.10 for American Airlines.[3]

A number of smaller regional and local food service operators contract to a variety of airlines at hundreds of airports. Most airports have caterers or food service contractors who compete for airline contracts. With several international and U.S. airlines all using U.S. airports, each airline must decide whether to use its own food service (if it has one) or to contract with one of several independent operators.

Airport Food Service

Food service at most airports is operated by management companies like ARAMARK Leisure Services or Host International (a division of Marriott Corporation). More recently, airports have begun to use branded concepts, whereby a Pizza Hut or other branded restaurant is located in the airport.

Pizza Hut at an Airport (Courtesy Pizza Hut.)

Military

Military food service is a large and important component of noncommercial food service. There are about 1.8 million soldiers, sailors, and aviators in active duty in the United States. Even with the military downsizing, food service sales top $6 billion. Base closings have prompted many military food service organizations to rediscuss services and concepts in order to better meet the needs of their personnel. In particular, it was noticed that the food delivery methods needed considerable adjustment. In fact, complaints by the operators focused on excessively long times for orders, delayed delivery, and poor product and inventory control. The Department of Defense thus introduced direct vendor delivery, which proved to be a satisfactory choice. On the whole, reports indicate excellent service and product.

Recent trends in military food service call for services such as officers' clubs to be contracted out to food service management companies. This change has reduced military costs because many of the officers' clubs lost money. The clubs now have moved the emphasis from fine dining to a more casual approach with family appeal. Many clubs are renovating their base concept even further, restyling according to theme concepts, such as sports or country-western, for example. Other cost-saving measures include menu management, such as the use of a single menu for lunch and dinner (guests seldom eat both meals at the clubs). With proper plating techniques and portion size manipulation, a single menu can be created for lunch and dinner, meaning one inventory for both meals and less stock in general. To make this technique work successfully, the menu features several choices for appetizers, entrees, and desserts.

Another trend is the testing of prepared foods that can be reheated and served without much labor. Technological advances mean that field troops do not eat out of tin cans anymore; instead, they receive their food portions in plastic-and-foil pouches called MREs, or meals ready-to-eat. Today, mobile field kitchens can be run by just two people, and bulk food supplies have been replaced by preportioned, precooked food packed in trays, which then are reheated in boiling water.

Feeding military personnel includes feeding troops and officers in clubs, dining halls, and military hospitals, as well as in the field. As both the budget and the numbers of personnel decrease, the military is downsizing by consolidating responsibilities. With fewer people to cook for, fewer cooks are required.

A model for such downsizing is the U.S. Marine Corps. Since 1986, the marines have been contracting out food service. With smaller numbers, they could not afford to take a marine away from training to work in the dining facilities without affecting military operations.

In addition, fast food restaurants like McDonald's and Burger King have opened on well over two hundred bases; they are now installing Express Way kiosks on more bases.[4] The fast food restaurants on base offer further alternatives for military personnel on the move.

One problem that may arise as a result of the downsizing and contracting out of military food service is that it is not likely that McDonald's could set up on the front line in a combat situation. The military will still have to do their own food service when it comes to mobilization.

Elementary and Secondary Schools

The United States government enacted the National School Lunch Act in 1946 in response to concern about malnourishment in military recruits.[5] The rationale was that if students received good meals, the military would have healthier recruits. In addition, such a program would make use of the surplus food farmers produced.

Today, about twenty-five million children are fed breakfast or lunch—or both—each day in approximately eighty-seven thousand schools, at a cost of about $6 billion annually.

Many concerns currently face school food service. One major challenge is to balance salability with good nutrition. Apart from cost and nutritional value, the broader social issue of the universal free meal arises. Proponents of the program maintain that better nourished children have a better attention span and are less likely to be absent from school and will stay in school longer. Offering a free meal to all students also removes the poor kid stigma from school lunch. Detractors from the universal program say that if we learned anything from the social programs that were implemented during the 1960s, it was that throwing money at problems is not always the answer. Although these detractors believe conceptually in a universal program, they do not believe that it will solve the hunger problems in America.

Both sides agree that there is serious concern about what young students are eating. The recent news about the fat and cholesterol in the popcorn served at movie theaters shocked many adults. More shocking is what school children are eating, as one recent survey illustrates.[6] A U.S. Department of Agriculture survey found that school lunches, on average, exceeded dietary guidelines for fat by 25 percent, for saturated fat by 50 percent, and for sodium by 85 percent. Equally shocking is the percentage of children who eat one serving or less of fruits and vegetables each day (not counting french fries), as shown in Figure 8–2.

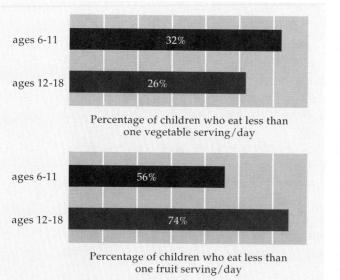

Percentage of children who eat less than one vegetable serving/day

Percentage of children who eat less than one fruit serving/day

Source: National Cancer Institute

Figure 8–2   *Children and the Servings of Fruit and Vegetables They Eat*

The preparation and service of school food service meals varies. Some schools have on-site kitchens where the food is prepared, and dining rooms where the food is served. Many large school districts operate a central commissary that prepares the meals and then distributes them among the schools in that district. A third option is for schools to purchase ready-to-serve meals that require only assembly at the school.

Schools may decide to participate in the national school lunch program (NSLP) or operate on their own. In reality, most schools have little choice because participating in the program means that federal funding is provided in the amount of approximately $1.75 per meal per student.

Meeting dietary guidelines is also an important issue. Much work has gone into establishing the nutritional requirements for children. It is difficult to achieve a balance between healthy food and costs, taking children's eating habits into account. Under the national school lunch program regulations, students must eat from what is commonly known as the type A menu. All of the items in the type A menu must be offered to all children at every meal. The children have to select a minimum of three of the five meal components in order for the school to qualify for funding. However, USDA regulations have established limits on the amount of fat and saturated fat that can be offered. Fat should not exceed 30 percent of calories per week, and saturated fat was cut down to 10 percent of calories per week. Figure 8–3 illustrates school lunch menus and Figure 8–4 shows the school lunch menu pattern requirements.

The government-funded NSLP, which pays $4.7 billion per year for the meals given or sold at a discount to school children, is a huge potential market for fast food chains. Chains are extremely eager to penetrate into the elementary and secondary school markets, even if it means a decrease in revenues. "We do reduce the price of our product, and we do make less margin than in our normal operations," says Joy Wallace, national sales director/nontraditional sales for Pizza Hut. However, they believe that it is to their benefit to introduce Pizza Hut to young people very early—in other words, the aim is to build brand loyalty. As a matter of fact, in Duluth, Minnesota, James Bruner, food service director for the city schools, was forced into offering branded pizza in several junior high and high schools. The local principals, hungry for new revenue, began offering Little Caesar's in direct competition to the cafeteria's frozen pizzas.

Taco Bell is in nearly 3,000 schools, Pizza Hut in 4,500, Subway in 650; Domino's, McDonald's, Arby's, and others are well established in the market as well.

Philadelphia schools fulfill nutritional requirements and also bring brand-name food to school: Domino's prepares pizzas to the school district's specifications at a cost that is much lower than if the school made the pizza from scratch or bought it frozen. At Broward County high schools in Florida, Pizza Hut, Domino's, or a local pizzeria (depending on students' vote) delivers pizza twice a week. Two other days a week, Subway delivers sandwiches; again, the cost is lower than making similar sandwiches at school.[7]

The San Juan Capistrano high school in California has gone one step further. The high school is a franchisee of Taco Bell, KFC, and Pizza Hut. Food

WINTER ELEMENTARY LUNCH PORTION GUIDE
January 2 – April 17, 1995

DATE	MONDAY		TUESDAY		WEDNESDAY		THURSDAY		FRIDAY	
Jan 2 Jan 30 Feb 27 Mar 27	1717 Bean & Cheese Burrito 139 Green Beans 29 Chilled Fruit Cup 693 Milk	1 #16 #16 1	648 Chicken Nuggets 118 Catsup 651 Celery Sticks 96 Ranch Dip 979 WW Bread & Butter 40 Orange Wedges 693 Milk	4 ea 1 tbsp 1 oz #40 1 sl 2 ea 1	406 (Turkey) Ham w/ Melted Mozzarella on Bun 229 French Fries 118 Catsup 253 Apple Wedges 693 Milk	1 7/# 1 Tbsp 2 ea 1	188 Party Pizza 381 Mixed Green Salad w/ 1117 Ranch Dressing 1343 Golden State Cookie 693 Milk	12/sh #12 #30 1	650 Cheese Quesadilla 181 Spanish Rice 651 Celery Sticks 1219 Jello w/ Pears 693 Milk	1 #12 1 oz #12 1
Jan 9 Feb 6 Mar 6 Apr 13	712 Corn Dog 118 Catsup 372 Mustard 652 Potato Rounds 521 Carrot Sticks 693 Milk	1 2 Tbsp 1 Tbsp 7/# 1 oz 1	1802 Stuffed Potato 381 Mixed Green Salad w/ 1117 Ranch Dressing 979 WW Bread w/ Butter 29 Chilled Fruit Cup 693 Milk	1 ea #12 1 sl #16 1	812 Spaghetti w/Pork and Turkey 1191 WW Dinner Roll 85 Creamy Coleslaw 269 Chilled Peaches 693 Milk *	#8 32/pan #12 #16 1	462 Cheese Pizza 92 Corn 31 Gingerbread 693 Milk	1 #16 50/pan 1	1370 Tostada Boat 253 Apple Wedges 693 Milk	1 2 ea 1
Jan 16 Feb 13 Mar 13	418 Char Patty on WW Bun 333 Shredded Lettuce 229 French Fries 118 Catsup 269 Chilled Peaches 693 Milk	1 #16 7/# 2 Tbsp #16 1	1779 Seafood Salad Sandwich 746 Carrot Coins 96 Ranch Dip 1652 Brownie 693 Milk	1 1 oz #40 2 Tbsp 1	587 Ham & Cheese Roll-up (Pork) 652 Potato Rounds 118 Catsup 29 Chilled Fruit Cup 693 Milk *	1 7/# 1 Tbsp #16 1	1793 Pizza Bagel 1273 Celery Pieces 96 Ranch Dip 1304 Trail Mix 693 Milk	1 ea 1 oz #40 #12 1	1717 Bean & Cheese Burrito 381 Mixed Green Salad w/ 1117 Ranch Dressing 40 Orange Wedges 693 Milk	1 #40 2 ea 1
Jan 23 Feb 20 Mar 20	538 Turkey Hot Dog 118 Catsup 372 Mustard 521 Carrot Sticks 273 Chilled Pineapple 693 Milk	1 1 Tbsp 1 Tbsp 1 oz #16 1	691 Turkey & Gravy 173 Whipped Potatoes 1714 Bernies Breadsticks 40 Orange Wedges 693 Milk	1 #16 60/pan 2 ea 1	1805 Salisbury Steak 92 Niblet Corn 605 Nutribun 1395 Kiwi Wedge 693 Milk	1 ea #16 40/pan 2 ea 1	686 Sausage Pizza (Pork) 139 Green Beans 130 Cherry Jello Dessert 693 Milk *	12/sh #16 #12 1	403 Grilled Cheese Sandwich 652 Potato Rounds 118 Catsup 179 Pear Wedges 693 Milk	1 7/# #12 2 ea 1

LUNCH

HOLIDAYS: Monday, January 2 - Use Monday's menu on Tuesday, January 3
Tuesday, January 3 - Use Tuesday's menu on Wednesday, January 4
Monday, January 16 - Use Monday's menu on Wednesday, January 18: Delete #333 Shredded Lettuce
Tuesday, January 17 - Staff Development Day
Friday, February 17 - Omit Friday's menu
Monday, February 20 - Use Monday's menu on Tuesday, February 21: Delete #521 Carrot Sticks; add #183 Cowboy Beans #16

F254

Figure 8–3 *Sample Elementary School Lunch Menu*

School Lunch Patterns
For Various Age/Grade Groups

USDA recommends, but does not require, that you adjust portions by age/grade group to better meet the food and nutritional needs of children according to their ages. If you adjust portions, Groups I-IV are minimum requirements for the age/grade groups specified. If you do not adjust portions, the Group IV portions are the portions to serve all children.

			Minimum Quantities				Recommended Quantities[2]
	COMPONENTS		Preschool		Grades K-3	Grades 4-12[1]	Grades 7-12
			ages 1-2 (Group I)	ages 3-4 (Group II)	ages 5-8 (Group III)	age 9 & over (Group IV)	ages 12 & over (Group V)
SPECIFIC REQUIREMENTS • Must be served in the main dish or the main dish and only one other menu item. • Vegetable protein products, cheese alternate products, and enriched macaroni with fortified protein may be used to meet part of the meat/meat alternate requirement. Fact sheets on each of these alternate foods give detailed instructions for use.	Meat or Meat Alternate	A serving of one of the following or a combination to give an equivalent quantity:					
		Lean meat, poultry, or fish (edible portion as served)	1 oz	1-1/2 oz	1-1/2 oz	2 oz	3 oz
		Cheese	1 oz	1-1/2 oz	1-1/2 oz	2 oz	3 oz
		Large egg(s)	1/2	3/4	3/4	1	1-1/2
		Cooked dry beans or peas	1/4 cup	3/8 cup	3/8 cup	1/2 cup	3/4 cup
		Peanut butter or other nut or seed butters	2 Tbsp	3 Tbsp	3 Tbsp	4 Tbsp	6 Tbsp
		Peanuts, soy nuts, tree nuts, or seeds, as listed in program guidance, meet no more than 50% of the requirement and must be combined in the meal with at least 50% of other meat or meat alternate. (1 oz of nut/seeds=1 oz of cooked lean meat, poultry, or fish.)	1/2 oz=50%	3/4 oz=50%	3/4 oz=50%	1 oz=50%	1-1/2 oz=50%
• No more than one-half of the total requirement may be met with full-strength fruit or vegetable juice. • Cooked dry beans or peas may be used as a meat alternate or as a vegetable but not as both in the same meal.	Vegetables and/or Fruits	Two or more servings of vegetables or fruits or both to total	1/2 cup	1/2 cup	1/2 cup	3/4 cup	3/4 cup
• At least 1/2 serving of bread or an equivalent quantity of bread alternate for Group I, and 1 serving for Groups II-V, must be served daily. • Enriched macaroni with fortified protein may be used as a meat alternate or as a bread alternate but not as both in the same meal. NOTE: Food Buying Guide for Child Nutrition Programs, PA-1331 (1984) provides the information for the minimum weight of a serving.	Servings of bread or Bread Alternate	A serving is: • 1 slice of whole-grain or enriched bread • A whole-grain or enriched biscuit, roll, muffin, etc. • 1/2 cup of cooked whole-grain or enriched rice, macaroni, noodles, whole-grain or enriched pasta products, or other cereal grains such as bulgur or corn grits • A combination or any of the above	5 per week	8 per week	8 per week	8 per week	10 per week
The following forms of milk must be offered: • Whole milk • Unflavored lowfat milk NOTE: This requirement does not prohibit offering other milk, such as flavored milk or skim milk, along with the above.	Milk	A serving of fluid milk	3/4 cup (6 fl oz)	3/4 cup (6 fl oz)	1/2 pint (8 fl oz)	1/2 pint (8 fl oz)	1/2 pint (8 fl oz)

[1]Group IV is highlighted because it is the one meal pattern which will satisfy all requirements if no portion size adjustments are made.
[2]Group V specifies recommended, not required, quantities for students 12 years and older. These students may request smaller portions, but not smaller than those specified in Group IV.

Figure 8–4 *School Lunch Menu Pattern Requirements* (U.S. Department of Agriculture, National School Lunch Program.)

service director Bill Caldwell says that this has created a win-win situation: Students get the food they like and also gain valuable work experience in the restaurants.[8]

Despite the positives, although it is not hard to convince the children, chains need to convince the adults. Much debate has arisen as to whether chains should enter the schools or not. Many parents feel that the school environment should provide a standard example for what sound nutrition should be, and they believe that with fast food as an option, that will not be the case.

At a recent school lunch challenge at the American Culinary Federation (ACF) Conference, chefs from around the country developed nutritious menus geared to wean children away from junk food to healthy foods. An 80-cent limit on the cost of raw ingredients was placed on the eleven finalists. Innovation and taste, as well as healthfulness, were the main criteria used to evaluate the winning entry: turkey taco salad, sausage pizza bagel, and stuffed potatoes.

Professional chefs are now working with the Department of Agriculture's Food and Consumer Services to develop healthful recipes and menus with increased appeal without an increase in cost.[9]

Nutrition Education Programs

Nutrition education is now a required part of the nation's school lunch program. As a result of this program, children are learning to improve their eating habits, which, it is hoped, will continue for the rest of their lives. To support the program, nutritional education materials are used to decorate the dining room halls and tables. Perhaps the best example of this is the food pyramid developed by the Food and Nutrition Service of the United States Department of Agriculture. Figure 8–5 shows this food pyramid, which is a guide of what to choose to eat each day for a healthy diet.

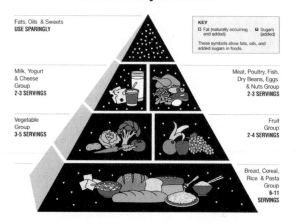

Figure 8–5   *Food Pyramid* (U.S. Department of Agriculture and U.S. Department of Health and Human Services.)

Colleges and Universities

College and university food service operations are complex and diverse. Among the various constituents of food service management are residence halls, cafeterias/student unions, faculty clubs, convenience stores, administrative catering, and outside catering.

On-campus dining is a challenge for food service managers because the clientele lives and eats all of its meals at the campus dining facility. Students, staff, and faculty may quickly become bored with the sameness of the sur-

Personal Profile: Manuel Lorenzo

Manuel Lorenzo

Manuel Lorenzo is a supervisor for Marriott Food Services and arrives at United States International University (USIU) to begin his shift at 9:00 a.m. Manuel's first duty is to check the catering board where he will find a list of scheduled catering events for the day. Manuel then plans the food preparation and starts gathering the necessary equipment.

By 10:00 a.m., Manuel goes around to all the food service outlets that are open during the night hours and collects money and receipts. The cash must then be immediately transported to the bank for deposit. The figures must also be entered into the company computer.

After Manuel completes handling the money, he talks with Sheri Henderson, the director of food services at USIU. She keeps him abreast of information for the day. This is the time any problems or concerns can be addressed. At 11:00 a.m., Manuel walks around to make sure the cafeteria is ready to serve lunch. Manuel supervises the lunch operation until it ends at 1:30. After lunch, Manuel continues working on catering functions and makes sure everything flows and is ready for dinner.

Before Manuel leaves for the day, he must check to see that all catering vehicles are tanked and running properly. Then, the storerooms must be cleaned and organized. Sheri will also have a list of projects for Manuel to complete. These tasks usually consist of maintaining sanitation standards. Last, Manuel checks staffing levels for the rest of the week and deals with basic human resource functions.

Manuel sees time management as one of the major challenges of his career. Events are constantly pending, and he has only a very limited amount of time to plan, organize, and carry out those functions. Manuel contends that the only way to be successful, in this respect, is to be highly organized. Also, Manuel says that success requires one to be a "people-person." This skill helps him deal with employees effectively and helps him understand the people he serves, so that he can serve them better.

Keeping the customer satisfied is another challenge for Manuel. University food service operations have the unique and difficult task of keeping long-term boarding residents happy with food quality. Manuel solves this problem by serving a wide variety of entrees, yet keeping consistent with daily staples.

Each catering event is different because of the variety in food served. With each new function, Manuel learns something about food and/or culture. Manuel admits that this is one of the most interesting, exciting, and rewarding aspects of his job.

roundings and menu offerings. Most campus dining is cafeteria style and offers cyclical menus that rotate on a predetermined schedule.

However, a college food service manager does have some advantages when compared with a restaurant manager. Budgeting is made easier because the on-campus students have already paid for their meals and their numbers are easy to forecast. When the payment is guaranteed and the guest count is predictable, planning and organizing staffing levels and food quantities is relatively easy and should ensure a reasonable profit margin. For instance, the daily rate is the amount of money required per day from each person to pay for the food service. Thus, if food service expenses for one semester of ninety-eight days amount to $650,000 for an operation with one thousand students eating, the daily rate will be

$$\frac{\$650,000 \div 98,000}{1,000} = \$6.63$$

College Food Service (Courtesy ARAMARK.)

College food service operations now offer a variety of meal plans for students. Under the old board plan, when students paid one fee for all meals each day—whether they ate them or not, the food service operator literally made a profit from the students who did not actually eat the meals they had paid for. More typically now, students match their payments to the number of meals eaten: Monday–Friday, breakfast, lunch, dinner; dinner only; and prepaid credit cards that allow a student to use the card at any campus outlet and have the value of the food and beverage items deducted from his or her credit balance.

Student Unions

The college student union offers a variety of food service that caters to the needs of a diverse student body. Among the services offered are cafeteria food service, beverage services, branded quick-service restaurants, and take-out food service.

The cafeteria food service operation is often the "happening" place in the student union where students meet to socialize as well as to eat and drink. The cafeteria is generally open for breakfast, lunch, and dinner. Depending on the volume of business, the cafeteria may be closed during the nonmeal periods and weekends, and the cafeteria menu may or may not be the same as the residence food service facility. Offering a menu with a good price value is crucial to the successful operation of a campus cafeteria.

On campuses at which alcoholic beverage service is permitted, beverage services mainly focus on some form of a student pub where beer and perhaps wine and spirits may be offered. Not to be outdone, the faculty will undoubtedly have a lounge that also offers alcoholic beverages. Other beverages may be served at various outlets such as a food court or convenience store. Campus beverage service provides opportunities for food service operators to enhance profits.

In addition, many college campuses have welcomed branded, quick-service restaurants as a convenient way to satisfy the needs of a community on the go. Such an approach offers a win-win situation for colleges. The experience and brand recognition of chain restaurants like Pizza Hut, McDonald's, Subway, and Wendy's attract customers; the restaurants pay a fee, either to the food service management company or the university directly. Obviously, there is a danger that the quick-service restaurant may attract customers that the cafeteria might then lose, but competition tends to be good for all concerned.

Take-out food service is another convenience for the campus community. At times, students—and staff—do not want to prepare meals and are thankful for the opportunity to take meals with them. And, it is not just during examination time that students, friends, and staff have a need for the take-out option. For example, tailgate parties prior to football and basketball games or concerts and other recreational/sporting events allow entrepreneurial food service operators to increase revenue and profits.

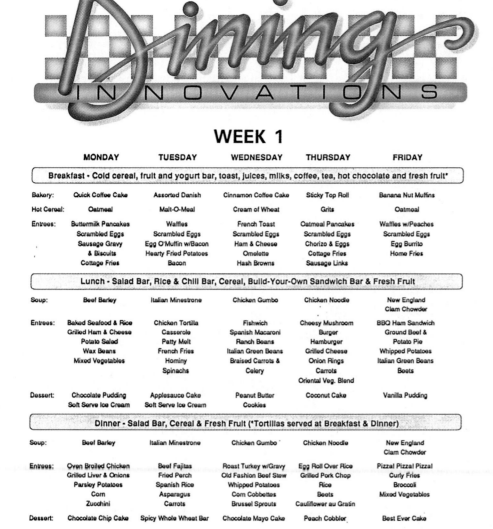

Figure 8–6   *Sample College Menu* (Courtesy Marriott Foodservice Management.)

The type of contract that a food service management operator signs varies depending on the size of the account. If the account is small, a fee generally is charged. With larger accounts, operators contract for a set percentage (usually about 5 percent) or a combination of a percentage and a bonus split.

Figure 8–6 shows a typical college menu for the dining hall where students usually eat on campus.

Trends in College Food Service Management

College and university food service managers face increasing challenges. *Restaurants and Institutions* magazine asked selected managers to identify some of those challenges. In general, managers mentioned trying to balance rising costs with tighter dollars. Bill Rigan, food service center manager at

Corporate Profile: ARAMARK

In the 1950s, Dave Davidson and Bill Fishman, both in the vending business, realized that they shared the same dreams and hopes of turning vending into a service and combining it with food service. The two entrepreneurs joined forces to become the first truly national vending and food service company. Automatic Retailers of America (ARA) was born in 1959. Fishman and Davidson had the management skills, the capital, and the expertise to expand. And this they did— ARAMARK is the world's leading provider of quality managed services. It operates in all fifty states and in ten foreign countries, offering a very diversified and broad range of services.

ARAMARK's emphasis on the quality of service management was evident from the very beginning of its operations. ARAMARK entered new markets by researching the best-managed local companies, acquiring them, and persuading key managers to stay with the company.

The company's vision, in fact, states that ARAMARK is "a company where the best people want to work." This is one fundamental constant in ARAMARK's early success: It grew its business by focusing on growing its management. The company's guiding principles reaffirm such a concept:

"Because we succeed through performance, we encourage the entrepreneur in each of us, and work always to improve our service.

Because we thrive on growth, we seek new markets and new opportunities, and we innovate to get and keep new customers."

With the 1961 acquisition of Slater System, Inc., the largest food service business in the country, ARAMARK began the diversification process, and has continued since to amplify the portfolio of services it now offers. The focus on management skills at every level, especially the local one, gave ARAMARK an invaluable resource.

In fact, with every acquisition, local managers were encouraged and rewarded for becoming multiskilled entrepreneurs. This approach to outsourcing is, put more simply, the ability of the company to take the best management skills and apply them to all the lines of business the company uses to diversify.

Among ARAMARK operations are the following:

Food, leisure and support services: The company provides food, specialized refreshments, dietary services, and operation support to businesses, educational facilities, government, and medical institutions. ARAMARK also manages food, lodging, hospitality, and support services at national parks and other recreational facilities that serve the general public.

Health and education services: ARAMARK provides specialized management services for hospitals and medical services. It also specializes in providing early-childhood and school-age education services.

Uniform services: The company is America's largest provider of uniform services and work apparel for virtually all types of institutions.

Magazine and book services: ARAMARK is the leading wholesale distributor of magazines, newspapers, and books.

ARAMARK successfully manages the diversity of segment concepts under the guideline of one single purpose: to be the world leader in managed services. With annual revenues in excess of $5 billion, the company is among the market leaders in all of its businesses, and it is in an ideal position for further market growth. Joseph Neubauer, chairman and CEO, realizes this:

"I am energized by the bright prospects for the journey ahead. . . . I can't wait to get started."

Adapted courtesy of ARAMARK.

Oklahoma State University–Stillwater pointed out two main challenges: a reduction of revenues from board-plan sales, combined with increased costs, such as food and utilities. He dealt with these challenges by recognizing that inasmuch as he could not change the utilities or hourly rates for employees, he would have to maximize purchasing potential. He also made optimal usage of scratch cooking, convenience foods, and more efficient labor scheduling.

Martha Willis, food service director at Tennessee Technological University–Cookeville, sees declining enrollment and a reduction in state funding. This translates to a cutback in services and more pressure to produce a bigger bottom line. Martha intends to achieve this by filling vacant full-time positions with part-time and student employees. The savings made by not having to pay full-time employee benefits can amount to 30 percent of a person's wage.

A food service manager's responsibilities in a small or midsize operation are frequently more extensive than those of managers of the larger operations. This is because larger units have more people to whom to delegate certain functions, such as human resources. For example, following are some of the responsibilities that the food service manager in a small or midsize operation might have in addition to strictly food service responsibilities:

Employee Relations
➤ Business vs. personal needs, family problems
➤ Rewards/recognition
➤ Drug alcohol abuse/prevention
➤ Positive work environment
➤ Coaching/facilitating vs. directing

Human Resource Management
➤ Recruitment/training/evaluating
➤ Wage/salary administration
➤ Benefits administration
➤ Compliance with federal/state laws/EEO/Senate Bill 198
➤ Harassment/OSHA
➤ Disciplinary actions/terminations
➤ Unemployment/wrongful disclosure

Financial/Budgeting
➤ Project budgets
➤ Actual vs. budget monitoring (weekly)
➤ Controlling food cost, labor, expenses, and so on
➤ Record keeping requirements/audit
➤ Monitoring accounts payable/receivable
➤ Billing/collecting
➤ Compliance to contracts
➤ Cash procedures/banking

Safety Administration
➤ Equipment training/orientation
➤ Controlling workers compensation
➤ Monthly inspections/audits (federal/state/OSHA requirements/Senate Bill 198)

Safety Budget
➤ Work on the expensive injuries

Food Production/Service
➤ Menu/recipe development
➤ Menu mix vs. competition

DESCRIPTION		%	STUDENT UNION	%	TOTAL	%
SALES						
FOOD REGULAR	951178				951178	
FOOD SPECIAL FUNCTIONS	40000				40000	
PIZZA HUT EXPRESS			100000		100000	
BANQUET & CATERING	200000				200000	
CONFERENCE	160000				160000	
BEER			80000		80000	
SNACK BAR			300000		30000	
ALA CARTE CAFE	60000				60000	
** TOTAL SALES	1411178		480000	100.0%	1891178	100.0%
PRODUCT COST						
BAKED GOODS	9420		4700		14120	
BEVERAGE	10000		8000		18000	
MILK & ICE CREAM	11982		2819		14801	
GROCERIES	131000		49420		180420	
FROZEN FOOD	76045		37221		113266	
MEAT SEAFOOD, EGGS & CHEESE	129017		48000		177017	
PRODUCE	65500		26000		91500	
MISCELLANEOUS					0	
COLD DRINK	0		0		0	
** TOTAL PRODUCT COST	432964		176160	36.7%	609124	32.2%
LABOR COST						
WAGES	581000		154000		735000	
LABOR—OTHER EMPLOYEES	101500		545000		156000	
BENEFITS + PAYROLL TAXES	124794		50657		175451	
MANAGEMENT BENEFITS	58320		6000		64320	
WAGE ACCRUALS	0				0	
** TOTAL LABOR COST	865614		265157	55.2%	1130771	59.8%
FOOD OPERATING COST-						
CONTROLABLE	24000		6000		30000	
CLEANING SUPPLIES	9000		46000		55000	
PAPER SUPPLIES					0	
EQUIPMENT RENTAL					0	
GUEST SUPPLIES	4500		2500		7000	
PROMOTIONS	35000		5000		40000	
SMALL EQUIPMENT					0	
BUSINESS DUES & MEMBERSHIP	3000				3000	
VEHICLE EXPENSE	3600		700		4300	
TELEPHONE	17000		5000		22000	

Figure 8–7 *Sample Operating Statement*

> Food waste/leftovers utilization
> Production records
> Production control
> Presentation/merchandising

Sanitation/FBI Prevention
> FBI (food-borne illness) prevention
> Sanitation/cleaning schedule
> Proper food handling/storage
> Daily prevention/monitoring
> Monthly inspection
> Health department compliance

DESCRIPTION		%	STUDENT UNION	%	TOTAL	%
LAUNDRY & UNIFORMS					0	
MAINTENANCE & REPAIRS	1200		200		1400	
FLOWERS	10000		4000		140000	
TRAINING					0	
SPECIAL SERVICES	18000		3000		21000	
MISCELLANEOUS						
** TOTAL CONTROLLABLE SUPPLIES	125300	8.9%	72400	15.1%	197700	10.5%
OPERATING COSTS-NON CONTROLLABLE						
AMORTIZATION & DEPRECIATION	13500		7000		20500	
INSURANCE	55717		14768		70485	
MISCELLANEOUS EXPENSE	12400		4100		16500	
ASSET RETIREMENTS					0	
RENT/COMMISSIONS	48000		40000		88000	
PIZZA HUT ROYALTIES			7000		7000	
PIZZA HUT — LICENSING MARKETING			7000		7000	
TAXES, LICENSE & FEES	5000		500		5500	
VEHICLE — DEPRECIATION & EXPENSE	4000				4000	
ADMINSTRATION & SUPERVISION						
** TOTAL NON-CONTROLLABLE COST	138617	9.8%	80368	16.7%	218985	11.6%
** TOTAL COST OF OPERATIONS	**1562495**	**110.7%**	**594085**	**123.8%**	**2156580**	**114.0%**
EXCESS OR (DEFICIT)	**(151317)**	**(10.7%)**	**(114085%)**	**(23.8)**	**(265402)**	**(14.0%)**
PARTICIPATION-CONTRACTOR *** NET EXCESS OR (DEFICIT)						
STATISTICS						
CUSTOMER COUNT						
HOURS WORKED						
AVERAGE FOOD-SALES/CUSTOMER						

Figure 8–7 *(continued)*

Purchasing/Recruiting
➤ Ordering/receiving/storage
➤ Food and beverage specifications/quality
➤ Inventory control
➤ Vendor relation/problems

Staff Training/Development
➤ On-the-job vs. structured
➤ Safety/sanitation/food handling, and so on
➤ Food preparation/presentation

A sample operating statement is shown in Figure 8–7. It shows a monthly statement for a college food service operation.

Health Care Facilities

Health care food service operations are remarkably complex because of the necessity of meeting the diverse needs of a delicate clientele. Health care food service is provided to hospital patients, long-term care and assisted-living residents, visitors, and employees. The service is given by tray, cafeteria, dining room, coffee shop, catering, and vending.

The challenge of health care food service is to provide the many special meal requirements to patients with very specific dietary requirements. Determining which meals need to go to which patients and ensuring that they reach their destinations employs especially challenging logistics. In addition to the patients, health care employees need to enjoy a nutritious meal in pleasant surroundings in a limited time (usually thirty minutes). Because employees typically work five days in a row, care must be taken to keep the area and the menu changing with themes and specials that maintain interest.

The main focus of hospital food service is the tray line. Once all of the requirements for special meals have been prepared by a registered dietician, the line is set up and color coded for the various diets. The line begins with the tray, a mat, cutlery, napkin, salt and pepper, and perhaps a flower. As the tray moves along the line, various menu items are added according to the color code for the particular patient's diet. Naturally, each tray is double- and triple-checked, first at the end of the tray line and then on the hospital floor. The line generally goes floor by floor at a rate of about five trays a minute; at this rate, a large hospital with six hundred beds can be served within a couple of hours. This is time consuming for the employees, because three meals a day represent up to six hours of line time. Clearly, health care food service is very labor intensive, with labor accounting for about 55 to 66 percent of operating dollars. In an effort to keep costs down, many operators have increased the number of help-yourself food stations, buffets, salads, desserts, and topping bars.

Patient counts and lengths of stay are declining, which emphasizes the importance of finding new ways of generating revenues. According to 1994's ten largest self-operated hospitals, one of the basic service areas, the cafeteria, is generating the biggest revenue-producing opportunities.[10]

Health Care Food Service (Courtesy ARAMARK.)

Hospital food service has evolved to the point

where the need for new revenue sources has changed the traditional patient and nonpatient meal-service ratios at many institutions. This situation was imposed by the federal government when it narrowed the treatment-reimbursement criteria; originally 66 percent of a typical acute-care facility's food service budget went towards patients' meals, with the remainder allocated for feeding the employees and visitors. In the past few years, as cash sales have become more important, the $^{66}/_{33}$ percent ratio has reversed.

Dolly Strenko

Ever resourceful, managers of health care operations, like Dolly Strenko of Southwestern General Hospital in Middleburg Heights, Ohio, have created such concepts as a medical mall with a retail pharmacy, flower and gift shops and boutique, a retail bakery, with an exhibition conveyor oven and a 112-seat restaurant deli with take-out services for adjacent medical offices and outside catering for weddings, bar mitzvahs, and other functions. Dolly has also been instrumental in elevating culinary standards, the result of hiring an executive chef who was a graduate of the Culinary Institute of America.

Experts agree that because economic pressures will increase, food service managers will need to use a more high-tech approach, incorporating labor-saving sous vide and cook-chill methods. This segment of the industry, which currently is dominated by self-operated food service, will continue to see contract specialists, such as Monson Custom management, Marriott, and ARAMARK Services, increase their market share at the expense of self-operated health care food services. One reason for this is that the larger contract companies have the economy of scale and a more sophisticated approach to quantity purchasing, menu management, and operating systems that help to reduce food and labor costs. A skilled independent food service operator has the advantage of being able to introduce changes immediately without having to support layers of regional and corporate employees.

Another trend in health care food service is the arrival of the major quick-service chains. McDonald's, Pizza Hut Express, Burger King, and Donuts are just a few of the large companies that have joined forces with the contract food service operators. Using branded quick-service leaders is a win-win situation for both the contract food service operator and the quick-service chain. As one operator put it, "The new McDonald's can be a training facility for future employees—in effect, a potential resource for our staff needs. Our union scale of $7.22 per hour could entice some 'cross-overs.' The branded image also helps the overall retail side of the food service operation."

The chains benefit from long-term leases at very attractive rates compared with a restaurant site. Chains assess the staff size and patient and visitor count to determine the size of unit to install. Thus far, they have found that weekday lunches and dinners are good, but the numbers on weekends are disappointing.

In contrast, several hospitals are entering the pizza-delivery business: They hook up phone and fax ordering lines, and they hire part-time employees to deliver pizzas made on the premises. This ties in with the increasing emphasis on customer service. Patients' meals now feature "comfort foods," based on the concept that the simpler the food is, the better. Hence, the resurgence of meat loaf, pot pies, meat and potatoes, and tuna salad, which contribute to customer satisfaction, makes them feel at home and comfortable.

Business and Industry

Business and industry (B&I) food service is one of the most dynamic segments of the food service industry. In recent years, B&I food service has improved its image by becoming more colorful, with menus as interesting as commercial restaurants.

There are important terms to understand in B&I food service:[11]

1. *Contractors:* Companies that operate food service for the client on a contractual basis. Most corporations contract with food service management companies because they are in manufacturing or some other service industry. Therefore, they engage professional food service management corporations to run their employee dining facilities. Contract food service operators have one main advantage over self-operators: They do not have to give as high a compensation and benefit package as the corporation itself.
2. *Self-operators:* Companies that operate their own food service operations. Self-operators are corporations who decide to operate their own food service. In some cases, the reason is that it is easier to control one's own operation; for example, it is easier to make changes to comply with special nutritional or other dietary requests.
3. *Liaison personnel:* A liaison is responsible for translating corporate philosophy to the contractor and for overseeing the contractor to make certain that he or she abides by the terms of the contract.

Contractors have approximately 80 percent of the B&I market. The remaining 20 percent is self-operated, but the trend is for more food service operations to be contracted out. The size of the B&I sector is approximately thirty thousand units. In order to adapt to corporate downsizing and relocations, the B&I segment has offered food service in smaller units rather than huge full-sized cafeteria. Another trend is the necessity for B&I food service to break even or, in some cases, make a profit. An interesting twist is the emergence of multi-tenant buildings, the occupants of which may all use a central facility. However, in today's turbulent business environment, there is a high vacancy rate in commercial office space. This translates into fewer guests for B&I operators in multi-tenant office buildings. As a result, some office buildings have leased space to commercial branded restaurants.

B&I food service operators have responded to requests from corporate employees to offer more than the standard fast food items of pizza and hamburgers; they want healthier foods offered, such as make-your-own sandwiches, salad bars, fresh fruit stations, and ethnic foods.

Business and Industry Food Service
(Courtesy ARAMARK.)

Most B&I food service operators offer a number of types of service. The type of service is determined by the resources available: money, space, time, and expertise. Usually these resources are quite limited, which means that most operations use some form of cafeteria service.

B&I food service may be characterized in the following ways:

1. Full-service cafeteria with either straight line, scatter, or mobile systems
2. Limited-service cafeterias offering parts of the full-service cafeteria, fast food service, cart and mobile service, fewer dining rooms, and executive dining rooms

Summary

1. Noncommercial food service operations have a non-profit orientation and include segments such as airlines, military, schools and colleges, health care facilities, and businesses.

2. Quality food has become a major competitive factor among airlines, which either provide meals from their own in-flight business or have it prepared by a contractor, such as Caterair or Sky Chefs.

3. Service to the military includes feeding troops and officers in clubs, dining halls, and hospitals as well as out in the field. Direct vendor delivery, menu management, prepared foods, and fast food chains directly on the base have met new trends in military food service.

4. Schools are either equipped with on-site kitchens and dining rooms or receive food from a central commissary. They try to balance salability with good nutrition. Today, nutrition education is a required subject in school.

5. College and university food service operations include residence halls, cafeterias, student unions, faculty clubs, convenience stores, and catering.

6. The responsibilities of a food service manager are very complex. He or she is in charge of employee relations, human resource management, budgeting, safety administration, sanitation, and inventory.

7. Health care food service operations need to provide numerous special meals to patients with very specific dietary requirements and nutritious meals in a limited time for employees. The main areas of concern for health care food service operations are tray lines and help-yourself food stations.

8. Business and industry food service operations either operate with a full-service cafeteria or limited-service cafeteria. The type of service is determined by money, space, and time available.

Review Exercises

1. What are noncommercial food service operations?

2. List and explain features that distinguish noncommercial food service operations from commercial ones.

3. Describe the issues that schools are currently facing concerning school food service.

4. Explain the term *national school lunch program* (NSLP).

5. Identify recent trends in college food service management.

6. What are the pros and cons concerning fast food chains on campus?

7. Briefly explain the complex challenges for health care food service operations.

Key Words and Concepts

Airline
Batch cooking
Board plan
Business
Colleges and universities

Commercial food service
Dietary guidelines
Elementary and secondary schools
Health care

In-flight meal costs
Military
National School Lunch Program
Noncommercial food service

Nutrition education programs
Tray line

Notes

[1] A. McCool, F. L. Smith, and D. L. Tucker, *Dimensions of Noncommercial Foodservice Management.* New York: Van Nostrand Reinhold, 1994, p. 278.

[2] Ibid., p. 281.

[3] Ibid., p. 282.

[4] *Restaurant Business, 104,* 21, September 20, 1992, p. 118.

[5] Susie Stephensen, "School Lunch: One Correct Answer? Or Multiple Choice?" *Restaurants and Institutions,* September 1, 1993, p. 114.

[6] *U.S. News and World Report, 116,* 8, May 9, 1994, p. 18.

[7] "Schools," *Restaurants and Institutions, 103,* 20, August 15, 1993, p. 44.

[8] Jeff Weinstein, "Free-Flow Style Star in Kitchen Design Award," *Restaurants and Institutions, 104,* 21, September 1, 1993, p. 120.

[9] "School Lunch Challenge: Nutritious Food," *Restaurants and Institutions, 102,* 23, October 1, 1994, p. 29.

[10] Personal conversation with Dolly Strenko, November 1994.

[11] Philip S. Cooke. In Joan B. Bakos and Guy E. Karrick (eds.), *Dining in Corporate America: Handbook of NonCommercial Management.* Rockville, Md.: Aspen Publishers, 1989, p. xvii.

Beverages

After reading and studying this chapter you should be able to do the following:

➤ List the types of spirits and how they are made
➤ Describe the wine-making process and the major wine-growing regions of the world
➤ Distinguish various types of beer
➤ Outline the history of coffee
➤ Explain a restaurant's liability in terms of serving alcoholic beverages

$\mathcal{S}$erving beverages is traditional throughout the world. According to his or her culture, a person might welcome a visitor with coffee or tea—or bourbon. Beverages are generally categorized into two main groups: alcoholic and nonalcoholic. Alcoholic beverages are further categorized as wines, beer, and spirits.

Wines

Wine is the fermented juice of freshly gathered ripe grapes. Wine may also be made from other sugar-containing fruits, such as blackberries, cherries, or elderberries. In this chapter, however, we will confine our discussion to grape wines. Wine may be classified first by color: red, white, or rose. Wines are further classified as light beverage wines, sparkling wines, fortified wines, and aromatic wines.

Light Beverage Wines

White, red, or rose table wines are light beverage wines; such table wines may come from a variety of growing regions around the world. In the United States, the premium wines are named after the grape variety, such as Chardonnay and Cabernet Sauvignon. In Europe, they are primarily named after their region of origin, such as Pouilly Fuisse and Chablis.

Sparkling Wines

Champagne, sparkling white wine, and sparkling rose wine are called the *sparkling wines.* Sparkling wines sparkle because they contain carbon dioxide. The carbon dioxide may be either naturally produced or mechanically infused into the wine. The best-known sparkling wine is champagne, which has become synonymous with celebrations and happiness. Champagne may, by

Wine	Beer	Spirits
Still	Top fermenting	Grapes/fruit
Natural	Lager	Grains
Fortified	Bottom fermenting	Cactus
Aromatic	Ale	Sugar
Sparkling	Stout	cane/Molasses
	Lager	
	Pilsner	
	Porter	

Figure 9–1   *Alcoholic Beverages*

law, only come from the Champagne region of France. Sparkling wines from other countries have *Method Champenoise* written on their labels to designate that a similar method was used to make that sparkling wine.

Fortified Wines

Sherries, ports, madeiras, and marsalas are fortified wines, meaning that they have had brandy or wine alcohol added to them. The brandy or wine alcohol imparts a unique taste and increases the alcohol content to about 20 percent. Most fortified wines are sweeter than regular wines. Each of the groups of fortified wines has several subgroups with myriad tastes and aromas.

Aromatic Wines

Vermouths and aperitifs are aromatic wines. Aromatized wines are fortified and flavored with herbs, roots, flowers, and barks. These wines may be sweet or dry. Aromatic wines are also known as aperitifs, which generally are consumed before meals as digestive stimulants. Among the better known brands of aperitif wines are Dubonnet Red (sweet), Dubonnet White (dry), Vermouth Red (sweet), Vermouth White (dry), Byrrh (sweet), Lillet (sweet), Punt e mes (dry), St. Raphael Red (sweet), and St. Raphael White (dry).

The History of Wine

Wine has been produced for centuries. The ancient Egyptians and Babylonians recorded the fermentation process. The first records about wine making date back about seven thousand years. The Greeks received the vine from the Egyptians and later the Romans contributed to the popularization of wine in Europe by planting vines in the territories they conquered.

The wine produced during these times was not the Cabernet or Chardonnay of today. The wines of yesteryear were drunk when they were young and likely to be highly acidic and crude. To help offset these deficiencies, people added different spices and honey, which made the wine at least palatable. To this day, some Greek and German wines have flavoring added.

The making of good wine is dependent on the quality of the grape variety, the type of soil, climate, preparation of vineyards, and the method of wine making. Thousands of grape varieties exist, thriving in a variety of soil and climatic conditions. Different plants thrive on clay, chalky, gravelly, and sandy soil. The most important wine-making grape variety is the Vitis Vinifera, which yields cabernet sauvignon, gamay, pinot noir, pinot chardonnay, and riesling. Figure 9–2 tells an interesting story about wine.

In Europe, during the Middle Ages, it was considered a good thing to make a pilgrimage to Rome once in a lifetime. There is a delightful story of a German bishop who liked his wine and food so much that he sent a servant to seek out the best tavern. (The tavern door was to be marked est, meaning it is.) Est was painted on the best tavern door in the town they would reach that evening. After traveling across Germany and into northern Italy, the bishop's group came across a tavern door with Est! Est! Est! painted on it. Well, the bishop liked the wine and food at that tavern so much he never actually made it to Rome.

Figure 9–2   *Est! Est! Est!*

The Making of Wine

Wine is made in six steps: crushing, fermenting, racking, maturing, filtering, and bottling (see Figure 9–3). Grapes are harvested in the autumn, after they have been scientifically tested for maturity, acidity, and sugar concentration. The freshly harvested grapes are taken to pressing houses where the grapes are destemmed and crushed. The juice that is extracted from the grapes is called *must*.

The second step of the process is the fermentation of the must, a natural phenomenon caused by yeasts on the skin of the grapes. Additional yeasts also are added either environmentally or by formula. When exposed to air in the proper environment, the yeast multiplies. Yeast converts the sugar in the grapes to ethyl alcohol, until little or no sugar remains in the wine. The degree of sweetness or dryness in the wine can be controlled at the end of the fermentation process by the addition of alcohol, removing the yeast by filtration, or by adding sulphur dioxide.

Red wine gains its color during the fermentation process from the coloring pigments of the red grape skins, which are put back into the must.

After fermentation has ceased, the wine is transferred to racking containers, where it settles before being poured into oak barrels or large stainless steel containers for the maturing process. Some of the better wines are aged in oak barrels, from which they acquire additional flavor and character during the barrel aging. Throughout the aging process, red wine extracts tannin from the wood, which gives longevity to the wine. Some white wine and most red wine is barrel aged for periods ranging from months to more than two years. Other white wines that are kept in stainless steel containers are crisp, with a youthful flavor; they are bottled after a few months for immediate consumption.

After maturing, the wine is filtered to help stabilize it and remove any solid particles still in the wine. This process is called *fining*. The wine is then *clarified* by adding either egg white or bentonite, which sinks to the bottom of the vat. The wine then is bottled.

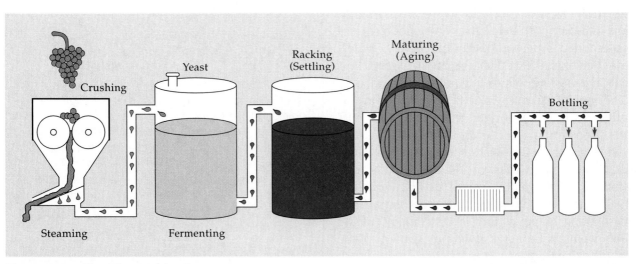

Figure 9–3   *The Wine-Making Process*

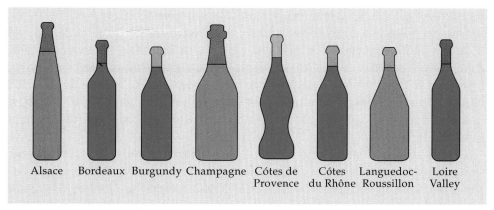

Figure 9–4   *Wine Bottles*

Fine vintage wines are best drunk at their peak, which may be a few years—or decades—away. Red wines generally take a few more years to reach their peak than do white wines. In Europe, where the climate is more variable, the good years are rated as vintage. The judgment of experts determines the relative merits of each wine-growing district and awards merit points on a scale of one to ten. The bottle shapes used are shown in Figure 9–4.

Matching Wine with Food

The combination of food and wine is one of life's great pleasures. We eat every day, so a gourmet will seek out not only exotic foods and vintage wines, but also simple food that is well prepared and accompanied by an unpretentious, but quality, wine.

Over the years, traditions have developed a how-to approach to the marrying of wines and food. Generally speaking, the following traditions apply:

➤ White wine is best served with white meat (chicken, pork, or veal), shellfish, and fish.
➤ Red wine is best served with red meat (beef, lamb, duck, or game).
➤ The heavier the food, the heavier and more robust the wine can be.
➤ Champagne can be served throughout the meal.
➤ Port and red wine go well with cheese.
➤ Dessert wines best complement desserts and fresh fruits that are not highly acidic.
➤ When a dish is cooked with wine, it is best served with that wine.
➤ Regional food is best complemented by wines of the region.
➤ Wines should never accompany salads with vinegar dressings, chocolate dishes, or curries; the tastes will clash or be overpowering.
➤ Sweet wines should be served with foods that are not too sweet.

Food and wine are described by texture and flavor. Textures are the qualities in food and wine that we feel in the mouth, such as softness, smoothness, roundness, richness, thickness, thinness, creaminess, chewiness, oiliness, harshness, silkiness, coarseness, and so on. Textures correspond to sensations of touch and temperature, which can be easy to identify—for example, hot, cold, rough, smooth, thick, thin. Regarding the marrying of food and wine, light food with light wine is always a reliable combination. Rich food with rich wine can be wonderful as long as the match is not too rich. The two most important qualities to consider when choosing the appropriate wine are richness and lightness.

Flavors are food and wine elements perceived by the olfactory nerve as fruity, minty, herbal, nutty, cheesy, smoky, flowery, earthy, and so on. A person often determines flavors by using the nose as well as the tongue. The combination of texture and flavor is what makes food and wine a pleasure to enjoy; a good match between the food and wine can make occasions even more memorable.

Major Wine-Growing Regions of Europe and North America

Europe

Germany, Italy, Spain, Portugal, and France are the main European wine-producing countries. Germany is noted for the outstanding riesling wines from the Rhine and Moselle river valleys. Italy produces the world-famous chianti. Spain makes good wine, but is best known for sherry. Portugal also makes good wine, but is better known for its port.

Burgundy Vineyard

France is the most notable of the European countries, producing not only the finest wines but also champagne and cognac. The two most famous wine-producing areas in France are the Bordeaux and Burgundy regions. The vineyards, villages, and towns are steeped in the history of centuries devoted to the production of the finest quality wines. They represent some of the most beautiful countryside in Europe and are well worth visiting.

In France, wine is named after the village in which the wine is produced. The name of the wine grower is also important; because the quality may vary, reputation understandably is very important. A vineyard might also include a chateau in which wine is made.

Within the Bordeaux region, wine growing is divided into five major districts: Medoc, Graves, St. Emilion, Pomerol, and Sauternes. The wine from each of these districts has its own characteristics.

There are several other well-known wine producing regions of France, such as the Loire Valley, Alsace, and Cotes du Rhone. French people regard wine as an important part of their culture and heritage.

United States

In California, viticulture began in 1769 when Junipero Serra, a Spanish friar, began to produce wine for the missions he started. At one time the French considered California wines to be inferior. However, California is blessed with a perfect climate and excellent vine-growing soil. In the United States, the name of the grape variety is used to name the wine, not the village or chateau used by the French. The better known varietal white wines in the United States are chardonnay, sauvignon blanc, riesling, and chenin blanc; varietal red wines are cabernet sauvignon, pinot noir, merlot, and zinfandel.

California viticulture areas are generally divided into three regions:

1. North and central coastal region
2. Great central valley region
3. Southern California region

The north and central coastal region produces the best wines in California. A high degree of use of mechanical methods allows for efficient, large-scale production of quality wines. The two best-known areas within this region are the Napa and Sonoma Valleys. The wines of the Napa and Sonoma valleys resemble those of Bordeaux and Burgundy. In recent years, the wines from the Napa and Sonoma valleys have rivaled and even exceeded the French and other European wines. The chardonnays and cabernets are particularly outstanding.

The Napa and Sonoma valleys are the symbols as well as the centers of the top-quality wine industry in California. The better-known wineries of California include those shown in Figure 9–5.

Napa Valley

Diamond Creek
Inglenook
Heitz
Krug
Louis Martini
Moet & Chandon
Robert Mondavi
Stag's Leap
Sterling

Sonoma Valley

Chateau St. Jean
Clos du Bois
De Loach
Dry Creek
Gundlach Bundschu
Iron Horse
Kenwood
Preston
Sebastiani

South of San Francisco

Concannon
Paul Masson
Mirassou
Ridge
Calloway
Thornton

Figure 9–5 *Better-Known California Wineries*

Napa Valley

Personal Profile: Robert Mondavi

Since its founding in 1966, the Robert Mondavi Winery has established itself as one of the world's top wineries. Robert Mondavi, now in his eighties, still continues his activity as wine's foremost spokesperson, having greatly contributed to the wine industry throughout his successful life.

Robert Mondavi was born in 1913 to an Italian couple who had emigrated from the Marche region of Italy in 1910. His father, Cesare, became involved in shipping California wine grapes to fellow Italians. Extremely pleased with California, Cesare Mondavi decided to move to the Napa Valley and set up a firm that shipped fruit east. Robert Mondavi grew up among wines and vines and remained in his father's business.

Robert began by improving the family enterprise, adding to it the management, production, and marketing skills he learned at Stanford University, from which he graduated in 1936. Robert acknowledged the great business potential of the Napa valley in the broader context of the California wine industry. What the firm needed was to be upgraded with innovations in technology, to keep up with the changes in the overall business environment.

Robert Mondavi

Mondavi had an ambitious dream that found its chance to come into reality when the Charles Krug Winery was offered for sale in 1943. The facility was purchased, and Robert knew that the strategy toward success included well-planned marketing as well as the crucial wine-making expertise that the family traditionally had.

Mondavi understood also the importance of the introduction of innovative processes that could place the winery in a competitive position. From the 1950s to the 1960s, he performed many experiments and introduced pivotal innovations. For example, Robert popularized new styles of wine, such as the chenin blanc, which was previously known as white pinot and was not doing well in the market. Mondavi changed the fermentation, turning the wine into a sweeter and more delicious wine. The name was also changed, and sales increased four-fold the following year.

Similarly, he noticed that the sauvignon blanc was a slow-selling wine. He began producing it in a drier style, called it fume blanc, and turned it into an immediate success. Although the winery's operations were successful, Mondavi was still looking for a missing link to the chain. A trip to Europe, designed to study the finest wineries' techniques, convinced him to adopt a new, smaller type of barrel to age the wine, which he believed added a "wonderful dimension to the finished product."

In 1966, Robert Mondavi opened the Robert Mondavi Winery, which represented the fulfillment of the family's vision to build a facility that would allow them to produce truly world-class wines. In fact, since its establishment, the winery has led the industry, standing as an example of continuous research and innovation in winemaking, as well as a "monument to persistence in the pursuit of excellence."

Throughout the years of operation, the original vision remained constant: to produce the best wines that were the perfect accompaniments to food and to provide the public with proper education about the product. As a matter of fact, the Robert Mondavi Winery sponsors several educational programs, such as seminars on viticulture, a totally comprehensive tour program in the Napa Valley wineries, and the great chefs program.

All of the family members are actively involved in the implementation of the winery, united and guided by a shared determination to continue the winery's tradition of excellence.

Several other states and Canadian provinces provide quality wines. New York, Oregon, and Washington are the other major U.S. wine-producing states. In Canada, the best wineries are in British Columbia's Okanagan Valley and southern Ontario's Niagara peninsula. Both of these regions produce excellent wines.

Wine also is produced in many other temperate parts of the world, most notably Australia, New Zealand, Chile, Argentina, and South Africa. Figure 9–6 shows that there may be a connection between wine and health.

A glass of wine may be beneficial to health. This perspective was featured in the CBS news magazine program "60 Minutes," which focused on a phenomenon called the French paradox. The French eat 30 percent more fat than Americans, smoke more, and exercise less, yet they suffer fewer heart attacks—about one third as many as Americans. Ironically, the French drink more wine than people of any other nationality—about 75 liters per person a year. Research indicates that wine attacks platelets, which are the smallest of the blood cells and which cause the blood to clot, preventing excess bleeding. However, platelets also cling to the rough, fatty deposits on arterial walls, clogging and finally blocking arteries and causing heart attacks. Wine's flushing effect removes platelets from the artery wall. Needless to say, after the "60 Minutes" program was broadcast, sales of wine, particularly red wine, in the United States increased dramatically.

Figure 9–6 *Wine and Health*

Beer

Beer is a brewed and fermented beverage made from malted barley and other starchy cereals and flavored with hops. Beer is a generic term, embracing all brewed malt beverages with a low alcohol content, varying from 4 to 16 percent.[1] The term *beer* includes the following:

- ➤ Lager, the beverage that is normally referred to as beer, is a clear light-bodied refreshing beer.
- ➤ Ale is fuller bodied and more bitter than lager.
- ➤ Stout is a dark ale with a sweet, strong, malt flavor.
- ➤ Pilsner is not really a beer. The term *pilsner* means that the beer is made in the style of the famous beer brewed in Pilsen, Bohemia.

The Brewing Process

Beer is brewed from water, malt, yeast, and hops. The brewing process begins with water, an important ingredient in the making of beer. The mineral content and purity of the water largely determine the quality of the final product. Water accounts for 85 to 89 percent of the finished beer.

Next, grain is added in the form of malt, which is barley that has been ground to a course grit. The grain is germinated, producing an enzyme that converts starch into fermentable sugar.

The yeast is the fermenting agent. Breweries typically have their own cultured yeasts, which, to a large extent, determine the type and taste of the beer. See Figure 9–7 for a description of the brewing process.

Mashing is the term for grinding the malt and screening out any bits of dirt. The malt then goes through a hopper into a mash tub, which is a large stainless steel or copper container. Here the water and grains are mixed and heated.

The liquid is now called *wort* and is filtered through a mash filter or lauter tub. This liquid then flows into a brewing kettle, where hops are added and the

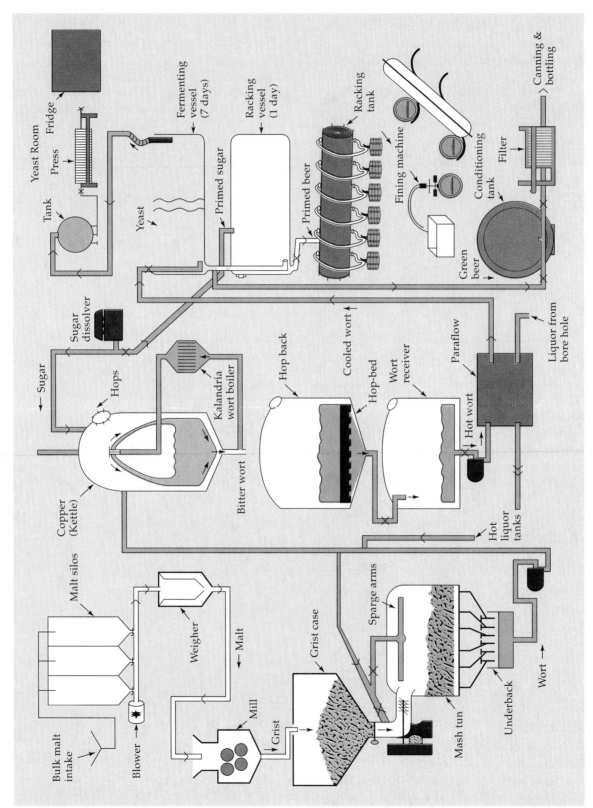

Figure 9-7 *The Beer-Making Process*

244

mixture is boiled for several hours. After the brewing operation, the hop wort is filtered though the hop separator or hop jack. The filtered liquid then is pumped though a wort cooler and flows into a fermenting vat where pure-culture yeast is added for fermentation.[2] The brew is aged for a few days prior to being barreled for draught beer or pasteurized for bottled or canned beer. Table 9–1 shows the major U.S. and Canadian brewers.

Spirits

A spirit or liquor is made from a liquid that has been fermented and distilled. Consequently, a spirit has a high percentage of alcohol, gauged in the United States by its proof content. *Proof* is equal to twice the percentage of alcohol in the beverage; therefore, a spirit that is 80 proof is 40 percent alcohol. Spirits traditionally are enjoyed before or after a meal, rather than with the meal. Many spirits can be consumed straight or neat, or they may be enjoyed with water, soda water, juices, or cocktail mixes.

Fermentation of spirits takes place by the action of yeast on sugar-containing substances, such as grain or fruit. Distilled drinks are made from a fermented liquid that has been put through a distillation process (see Figure 9–8).

Table 9–1
Top U.S. and Canadian Brewers

U.S. BREWERS

Company	Percent of Market
Anheuser-Busch	48.8
Miller	22.8
Coors	10.7
Stroh	6.4
Helleman	4.4
Other	6.9

Greg W. Prince, "All They Wanna Do is Sell Some Beer," *Beverage World*, March 1995, 1587, vol. 114, p. 82.

CANADIAN BREWERS

Company	Percent of Market
Molson	50.0
Labatt	44.0
U.S. Imports	3.0
Others	3.0

Wall Street Journal, March 16, 1993, p. B4.

Whiskeys

Among the better known spirits is whiskey, which is a generic name for the spirit first distilled in Scotland and Ireland centuries ago. The word *whiskey* comes from the Celtic word *visgebaugh* meaning *water of life*. Whiskey is made from a fermented mash of grain to which malt, in the form of barley, is added. The barley contains an enzyme called diastase that converts starch to sugars. After fermentation, the liquid is distilled. Spirits naturally are white or pale in color, but raw whiskey is stored in oak barrels that have been charred (burnt), which gives whiskey its caramel color. The whiskey is stored for a period of time, up to

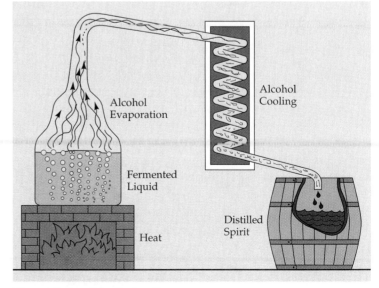

Figure 9–8   *Distillation Process*

a maximum of twelve to fifteen years. However, several good whiskeys reach the market after three to five years. Most whiskeys are blended to produce a flavor and quality that is the characteristic of the brand. Not surprisingly, the blending process at each distillery is a closely guarded secret. There are four distinct whiskey types that have gained a worldwide acknowledgment throughout the centuries: Scotch whiskey, Irish whiskey, bourbon whiskey, and Canadian whiskey.

Scotch Whiskey

Scotch whiskey, or Scotch, has been distilled in Scotland for centuries, and has been a distinctive part of the Scots' way of life. From its origins in remote and romantic Highland glens, scotch whiskey has become a popular and international drink, its flavor appreciated throughout the world. Scotch became popular in the United States during the days of Prohibition (1919 to 1933) when it was smuggled into the country from Canada. It is produced like other whiskeys, except that the malt is dried in special kilns that give it a smokey flavor. Only whiskey made with this process can be called Scotch whiskey. Some of the better-known quality blended Scotch whiskeys are Chivas Regal and Johnnie Walker Black Label.[3]

Irish Whiskey

Irish whiskey is produced from malted, unmalted barley, corn, rye, and other grains. The malt is not dried like the Scotch whiskey, which gives Irish whiskcy a milder character, yet an excellent flavor. Two well-known Irish whiskeys are Old Bushmill's Black Bush and Jameson's 1780.[4]

Bourbon Whiskey

Liquor was introduced in America by the first settlers, who used it as a medicine. Bourbon has a peculiar history. In colonial times in New England, rum was the most popular distilled spirit. After the break with Britain, settlers of Scottish and Irish background predominated. They were mostly grain farmers and distillers, producing whiskey for barter. When George Washington levied a tax on this whiskey, the farmers moved south, and continued their whiskey production. However, the rye crop failed, so they decided to mix corn, particularly abundant in Kentucky, with the remaining rye. The result was delightful. This experiment occurred in Bourbon county; hence the name of the new product.

Bourbon whiskey is produced mainly from corn; other grains are also used, but they are of secondary importance. The distillation processes are similar to those of other types of whiskey. Charred barrels provide bourbon with its distinctive taste. It is curious to notice that barrels can only be used once in the United States to age liquor. Aging therefore occurs in new barrels after each distillation process. Bourbon may be aged up to six years to improve its mellowness. Among the better-known bourbon whiskeys are Jack Daniels, Makers Mark, and George Dickle.

Canadian Whiskey

Like bourbon, Canadian whiskey is produced mainly from corn. It is characterized by a delicate flavor that nonetheless pleases the taste. Canadian

Corporate Profile: The Seagram Company, Ltd.

In simpler times, consumers met around a market square to make their purchases. In our century, the process has grown infinitely more complex. The challenge for Seagram and its customers is to continue developing channels of trade for the consumer's ultimate benefit, enhancing choice convenience, and service. That is why we take time to understand our customers' business and make our technologies fit theirs ... why we maintain the flexibility to create strategies for individual customers.[1]

The Seagram Company, Ltd. is a leading global producer and marketer of distilled spirits, wines, coolers, fruit juices, and mixers. The company operates worldwide through two major units: The Seagram Spirits and Wine Group and The Seagram Beverage Group. The Seagram Spirits and Wine Group, the company's largest operating unit, produces, markets, and distributes more than 230 brands of distilled spirits and 195 brand of wines, champagnes, ports, and sherries. Some of Seagram's best-known names, such as Chivas Regal Premium Scotch whiskey, Martell cognac, and Mumm champagne, are sold throughout the world, and others are produced primarily for sale in specific markets. The company operates on a global scale: Spirits and wines are produced by the group at facilities located in twenty two countries in North America, South America, Europe, and Australia. Regardless of this sweepingly broad scale, the sale of Seagram spirits and wines to its customers is far from mass operation. The company focuses on cultivating individual and personalized contact with its customers, either directly or through representatives of the company. This well-organized network of "ambassadors" (wholesalers or distributors) extends Seagram's reach to the public and allows for a closer interaction between the company and its clients.

This strong focus on customers gives Seagram's a truly competitive advantage in the industry. The close interaction has been further emphasized with the adoption of an electronic data interchange (EDI) system, which provides direct, paperless exchange of order information with the customers.

In addition to this state-of-the-art technology, Seagram's business success is given by other remarkable factors, such as differentiation of product lines and effective exploitation of business areas that represent a future potential. The company believes that the wide range of the Spirit and Wine Group's product portfolio, and the broad diversity of its geographic markets, reduce Seagram's vulnerability to changes in the industry's environment, such as consumers' preferences, social trends, and economic conditions.

Recent emphasis of product development, in fact, has resulted in the introduction of several new brands in 1993. In the Scotch whiskey category, for example, the increased portfolio of brands has allowed the company to compete at a premium level.

Just as the creation of new brands represents an investment in the company's future, the expansion into new geographies gives Seagram's a valid and broad base for future growth. In particular, the company is devoting a great deal of attention to China, which is considered to be the single most important market opportunity of the decade. Seagram has captured a significant share of this potential market by expanding its operations and increasing its presence. Infrastructures and facilities are being established and particular emphasis is placed on strengthening business relationships with its customers.

Seagram's shows a great deal of diversity in its channels of trade. The concentration of penetrating individual hotels and restaurants has proven to be particularly effective. Spirits and wines selections offered at fine hotels and restaurants set an influential standard of taste and brand perception. Seagram's brands have obtained a strong, worldwide predominance in this segment; the all-over presence of Seagram's on wine and cocktail lists greatly influences consumers' home consumption. In order to guarantee a continuity to this process, Seagram's must nurture each individual relationship with future hosts over time. To this end, the company is working with major hotels and catering schools today, to reach the great sommeliers and chefs of tomorrow.

[1] Courtesy of The Seagram Company, Ltd.

whiskey must be at least four years old before it can be bottled and marketed. It is distilled at 70 to 90 percent alcohol by volume. Among the better-known Canadian whiskeys are Seagrams and Canadian Club.

White Spirits

Gin, rum, vodka, and tequila are the most common of the spirits that are called *white spirits.* Gin, first known as Geneva, is a neutral spirit made from juniper berries. Although gin originated in Holland, it was in London that the word *Geneva* was shortened to gin, and almost anything was used to make it. Often, gin was made in the bathtub in the morning and sold in hole-in-the-wall dramshops all over London at night. Obviously, the quality left a lot to be desired, but the poor drank it to the point of national disaster.[5] Gin also was widely produced in the United States during Prohibition. In fact, the habit of mixing something else with it led to the creation of the cocktail. Over the years, gin became the foundation of many popular cocktails. (e.g., martini, gin and tonic, gin and juice, and Tom Collins).

Rum can be light or dark in color. Light rum is distilled from the fermented juice of sugarcane, and dark rum is distilled from molasses. Rum comes mainly from the Caribbean Islands of Barbados (Mount Gay), Puerto Rico (Bacardi), and Jamaica (Myers). Rums are mostly used in mixed frozen and specialty drinks such as rum and Coke, rum punches, daiquiris, and piña coladas.

Tequila is distilled from the agave tequilana (a type of cactus), which is called *mezcal* in Mexico. Official Mexican regulations require that tequila be made in the area around the town of Tequila, because the soil contains volcanic ash, which is especially suitable for growing the blue agave cactus. Tequila may be white, silver, or golden in color. The white is shipped unaged; silver is aged up to three years; and golden is aged in oak between two and four years. Tequila is mainly used in the popular margarita cocktail or in the tequila sunrise made popular in a song by the Eagles rock group.

Vodka can be made from many sources, including barley, corn, wheat, rye, or potatoes. Because it lacks color, odor, and flavor, vodka generally is combined with juices or other mixers whose flavors will predominate.

Other Spirits

Brandy is distilled from wine in a similar fashion to other spirits. American brandy comes primarily from California, where it is made in column stills and aged in white-oak barrels for two years or more. The best known American brandies are made by Christian Brothers and Ernest and Julio Gallo. Their brandies are smooth and fruity with a touch of sweetness. The best brandies are served as after-dinner drinks, and ordinary brandies are used in the "well for mixed drinks.

Cognac is regarded by connoisseurs as the best brandy in the world. It is only made in the Cognac region of France, where the chalky soil and humid climate combine with special distillation techniques to produce the finest brandy. Only brandy from this region may be called *cognac.* Most cognac is aged in oak casks from two to four years or more.

Because cognacs are blends of brandies of various ages, no age is allowed on the label; instead, letters signify the relative age and quality:

VSOP   =   very superior old pale
VVSOP =   very, very superior old pale

E	=	extra or special
F	=	fine
X	=	extra
VS	=	very special
VO	=	very old
VVO	=	very, very old
XO	=	extra old

Brandies labeled as *VSOP* must be aged at least four years. All others must be aged in wood at least five years. Five years then is the age of the youngest cognac in a blend; usually several others of older age are added to lend taste, bouquet, and finesse. About 75 percent of the cognac shipped to Canada and the United States is produced by four companies: Courvoisier, Hennessy, Martell, and Remy Martin.

Nonalcoholic Beverages

Nonalcoholic beverages are increasing in popularity. The 1990s have been a radical shift from the free love 1960s and the singles bars of the 1970s and early 1980s. People are, in general, more cautious about the consumption of alcohol. Life-styles have become more health conscious, and organizations like MADD have pricked the social conscience about being responsible in consuming alcohol. Overall consumption of alcohol has decreased in recent years, with spirits declining the most.

The healthful 1990s have seen the introduction of several new beverages to the nonalcoholic list.

Coffee

Coffee is the drink of the present. People who used to frequent bars are patronizing coffee houses. Sales of specialty coffees are expected to exceed $3 billion by 1999. By 1999, the Specialty Coffee Association of America predicts that there will be more than twenty-five hundred coffee cafes nationwide and another three thousand espresso bars.[6]

Coffee first came from Ethiopia and Mocha, which is in the Yemen Republic. Legends say that Kaldi, a young Abyssinian goatherd, accustomed to his sleepy goats, noticed that after chewing certain berries, the goats began to prance about excitedly. He tried the berries himself, forgot his troubles, lost his heavy heart, and became the happiest person in "happy Arabia." A monk from a nearby monastery surprised Kaldi in this state, decided to try the berries too, and invited the brothers to join him. They all felt more alert that night during prayers![7]

In the Middle Ages, coffee found its way to Europe via Turkey, but not without some objections. In Italy, priests appealed to Pope Clement VIII to have the use of coffee forbidden among Christians. Satan, they said, had forbidden his followers, the infidel Moslems, the use of wine because it was used in the Holy

Communion and given them instead his "hellish black brew." Apparently the pope liked the drink, for his reply was, "Why, this Satan's drink is so delicious that it would be a pity to let the infidels have exclusive use of it." So his Holiness decided to baptize the drink, after which it quickly became the social beverage of Europe's middle and upper classes.[8]

In 1637, the first European coffee house opened in England; within thirty years, coffee houses had replaced taverns as the island's social, commercial, and political melting pots.[9] The coffee houses were nicknamed *penny universities,* where any topic could be discussed and learned for the price of a pot of coffee. The men of the period not only discussed business but also actually conducted business. Banks, newspapers, and the Lloyd's of London Insurance Company began at Edward Lloyd's coffeehouse.

Coffee houses were also popular in Europe. In Paris, Cafe Procope, which opened in 1689 and still operates today, has been the meeting place of many a famous artist and philosopher, including Rousseau and Voltaire (who are reputed to have drunk forty cups of coffee a day).

The Dutch introduced coffee to the United States. Coffeehouses became the haunts of the revolutionary activists plotting against King George of England and his tea tax. John Adams and Paul Revere planned the Boston Tea Party and the fight for freedom at a coffeehouse, which established coffee as the traditional democratic drink of Americans.

Brazil produces more than 30 percent of the world's coffee, most of which goes into canned and instant coffee. Coffee connoisseurs recommend beans by name, such as Arabaca and Robusta Beans. In Indonesia, coffee is named for the island on which it grows; the best is from Java and is rich and spicy with a full-bodied flavor. Yemen, the country in which coffee was discovered, names its best coffee for the port of Mocha. Its fragrant, creamy brew has a rich, almost chocolatey aftertaste. Coffee beans are frequently blended by the merchants who roast them; one of the best blends, Mocha Java, is the result of blending these two fine coffees.

Coffee may be roasted from light to dark according to preference. Light roasts are generally used in canned and institutional roasts, and medium is the all-purpose roast most people prefer. Medium beans are medium brown in color, and their surface is dry. Although this brew may have snappy, acidic qualities, its flavor tends to be flat. Full, high, or Viennese roast is the roast preferred by specialty stores, where balance is achieved between sweetness and sharpness. Dark roasts have a fancy rich flavor, with espresso the darkest of all roasts. Its almost black beans have shiny, oily surfaces. All of the acidic qualities and specific coffee flavor are gone from espresso, but its pungent flavor is a favorite of espresso lovers.

Decaffeinating coffee removes the caffeine with either a solvent or water process. In contrast, many specialty coffees have things added. Among the better-known specialty coffees are café au lait or

Bernini's Coffee House, La Jolla, California

caffé latte. In these cases, milk is steamed until it becomes frothy and is poured into the cup together with the coffee. Cappuccino is made by adding steamed hot milk to an espresso, which may then be sprinkled with powdered chocolate and cinnamon.[10]

Tea

Tea is a beverage made by steeping in boiling water the leaves of the tea plant, an evergreen shrub, or a small tree native to Asia. Tea is consumed as either a hot or cold beverage by approximately half of the world's population, yet it is second to coffee in commercial importance because most of the world's tea crop is consumed in the tea-growing regions. Tea leaves contain 1 to 3 percent caffeine. This means that weight for weight, tea leaves have more than twice as much caffeine as coffee beans. However, a cup of coffee generally has more caffeine than a cup of tea because one pound of tea leaves makes 250 to 300 cups of tea whereas one pound of coffee makes only forty cups.

The following is a list of where the different types of tea come from:

Chinese—Oolong, Orange pekoe
India—Darjeeling, Assams, Dooars
Indonesia—Java, Sumatra

Carbonated Soft Drinks

Coca Cola and Pepsi have long dominated the carbonated soft drink market. In the early 1980s, diet coke and diet Pepsi were introduced and quickly gained in popularity. The diet colas now command about a 10-percent market share. Caffeine-free colas offer an alternative, but they have not, as yet, become as popular as diet colas.

Inasmuch as U.S. market sales tend to be flat now, companies are expanding internationally. Indeed, as much as 80 percent of Coca Cola's profits in 1993 came from international sales.[11]

Juices

Popular juice flavors include orange, cranberry, grapefruit, mango, papaya, and apple. Nonalcoholic versions of popular cocktails made with juices have been popular for years and are known as virgin cocktails.

Juice bars have established themselves as places for quick, healthy drinks. Lately, "smart drinks" have become popular, which are supposed to boost energy and improve concentration. The smart drinks are made up of a blend of juices, herbs, amino acids, caffeine, and sugar, and are sold under names such as Energy Plasma Blast and IQ Booster.

Other drinks have jumped on the healthy drink bandwagon, playing on the consumer's desire to drink something refreshing, light, and healthful. Often, these drinks are fruit flavored, giving the consumer a feeling of drinking something healthy, instead of sugar-filled sodas. Unfortunately, these drinks usually just add the flavor of the fruit and rarely have any nutritional value whatsoever. Also, some drinks are created by mixing different fruit flavors to come up with new, exotic flavors such as Passion-Kiwi-Strawberry and Mango-Banana Delight. Some examples of such drinks are Snapple and Tropicana Twister.

Sport enthusiasts also find drinks available in stores that professional athletes use and advertise. These specially formulated *isotonic beverages* help the body regain the vital fluids and minerals that are lost during heavy physical exertion. The National Football League sponsors Gatorade and encourages its use among its athletes. The appeal of being able to drink what the professionals drink is undoubtedly one of the major reasons for the success of Gatorade's sales and marketing. Other brands of isotonic beverages include Powerade and All Sport, which is sponsored by the National Collegiate Athletics Association.

Bottled Water

Bottled water was popular in Europe years ago when it was not safe to drink tap water. In North America, the increased popularity of bottled water has coincided with the trend toward healthier life-styles.

In the 1980s, it was chic to be seen drinking Perrier or some other imported bottled water. Perrier, which comes from France, lost market share a few years ago when an employee tampered with the product. Now the market leader is Evian, which is also French. Domestic bottled water is equally as good as imported and is now available in various flavors that offer the consumer a greater selection.

Bottled waters are available as sparkling, mineral, and spring waters. Bottled water is a refreshing, clean-tasting, low-calorie beverage that will likely increase in popularity as a beverage on its own or to accompany another beverage such as wine or whiskey.

Bars and Beverage Management

From an operating perspective, bar and beverage management follows much the same sequence of steps as food, as shown in the following:

➤ Forecasting
➤ Determining what to order
➤ Selecting the supplier
➤ Placing the order
➤ Receiving the order
➤ Storing
➤ Issuing
➤ Serving
➤ Accounting
➤ Controlling

Taverns

Taverns are informal, unpretentious bars that mostly serve beer, with some spirits and an occasional glass of wine. Taverns generally serve food at meal times and offer patrons a good atmosphere in which to relax and socialize.

Restaurant Bars

In restaurants, the bar is often used as a holding area to allow guests to enjoy a cocktail or aperitif before sitting down to dinner. This allows the restaurant to space out the guests' orders so that the kitchen can cope more effectively; it also increases beverage sales. The profit margin from beverages is higher than the food profit margin.

In some restaurants, the bar is the focal point or main feature. Guests feel drawn to having a beverage because the atmosphere and layout of the restaurant encourage them to have a drink. Beverages generally account for about 25 to 30 percent of total sales. Many restaurants used to have a higher percentage of beverage sales, but the responsible consumption of alcoholic beverages has influenced people to decrease their consumption of alcoholic beverages.

Bars carry a range of each spirit, beginning with the "well" package. The well package is the least expensive pouring brand that the bar uses when guests simply ask for a "Scotch and water." The "call" package is the group of spirits that the bar offers to guests who are likely to ask for a particular name brand. For example, guests call for Johnnie Walker Red Label. An example of a premium Scotch is Johnnie Walker Black Label, and a super premium Scotch is Chivas Regal.

A popular method of costing each of the spirits poured is calculated according to the following example:

With quantity purchasing discounts, a well-brand bottle of vodka might cost $5.00. A bottle yields twenty-five one-ounce shots, each sold for $2.50; this means that the $5.00 bottle brings in $62.50.

The profit margins produced by bars may be categorized as follows:

Liquor Pouring Cost % (approx.)	12
Beer	25
Wine	38

When combined, the sales mix may have an average pouring cost of 16 to 20 percent.

Most bars operate on some form of par stock level, which means that for every spirit bottle in use, there is a minimum par stock level of one, two, or more bottles available as a back up. As soon as the stock level falls to a level below the par level, more is automatically purchased.

Night Clubs

There are several types of night clubs. In big cities, some cater to the upscale crowd that goes to clubs to see and be seen. These clubs have bars and may have live or recorded music. Some clubs feature a single type of music; other clubs feature rock 'n roll one night, soul the next, and rhythm and blues or reggae the following night. These clubs charge an entrance fee and a higher price for drinks than restaurants. However, the night club business is fickle; what is in one year may be out the next.

Sports Bars

Sports bars have always been popular, but have become more so with the decline of disco and singles bars. Many people relax in the sporting atmosphere, so bar/restaurants like Trophies in San Diego or Characters at Marriott hotels have become popular "watering holes." Satellite television coverage of the top sporting events helps sports bars to draw crowds.

Liquor Liability and the Law

Owners, managers, bartenders, and servers may be liable under the law if they serve alcohol to minors and to persons who are intoxicated. The extent of the liability can be very severe. The legislation that governs the sale of alcoholic beverages is called dram shop legislation. The dram shop laws or civil damage acts were enacted in the 1850s and dictated that owners and operators of drinking establishments are liable for injuries caused by intoxicated customers.[12]

Some states have reverted back to the eighteenth century common law, removing liability from vendors except in cases involving minors. Nonetheless, most people recognize that as a society, we are faced with major problems of under-age drinking and drunk driving.

To combat under-age drinking in restaurants, bars, and lounges, a major brewery distributed a booklet showing the authentic design and layout of each state's drivers license. Trade associations, like the National Restaurant Association and the American Hotel and Motel Association, have, together with a number of major corporations, produced a number of preventive measures and programs aimed at responsible alcohol beverage service. The major thrust of these initiatives are awareness programs and mandatory training programs like TIPS (training for intervention procedures by servers) to promote responsible alcohol service. TIPS is sponsored by the National Restaurant Association and is a certification program that informs participants about alcohol and the effects of alcohol on people, the common signs of intoxication, and how to help customers avoid drinking too much.

Other programs include designated drivers, who only drink nonalcoholic beverages and ensure that friends return home safely. Some operators give free nonalcoholic beverages to the designated driver as a courtesy.

One positive outcome of the responsible alcohol service programs for operators is a reduction in the insurance premiums and legal fees that had skyrocketed in previous years.

Summary

1. Beverages are categorized into alcoholic and nonalcoholic beverages. Alcoholic beverages are further categorized into spirits, fortified wines, wines, and beer.
2. Spirits have a high percentage of alcohol and are served before or after a meal. Fermentation and distillation are parts of their processing. The most popular white spirits are rum, gin, vodka, and tequila.
3. Wine is the fermented juice of ripe grapes. It is classified into red, white, and rose, and we distinguish between light beverage wines, sparkling wines, and aromatic wines.
4. The six steps in making wine are crushing, fermenting, racking, maturing, filtering, and boiling. France, Germany, Italy, Spain, and Portugal are the main European wine-producing areas, and California is the main American wine-producing area.
5. Beer is a brewed and fermented beverage made from malt. Different types of beer include ale, stout, lager, and pilsner.
6. Today people have become more health conscious about consumption of alcohol; nonalcoholic beverages such as coffee, tea, soft drinks, juices, and bottled water are increasing in popularity.
7. Beverages make up 20 to 30 percent of total sales in a restaurant, but managers are liable if they serve alcohol to minors. Programs such as designated driver, TIPS, and virgin cocktails have increased.

Review Exercises

1. What are spirits? Explain the process of fermentation and distillation and the origin of Scotch whiskey and brandy.
2. What is the difference between fortified and aromatic wines? In what combination is it suggested to serve food and wine and why?
3. Describe the brewing process of beer. What is the difference between a stout and a pilsner?
4. Why have nonalcoholic drinks increased in popularity and what difficulties do bar managers face when serving alcohol?
5. Describe the origin of coffee.

Key Words and Concepts

Alcohol	Dram shop legislation	Must	TIPS
Aperitif	Fermenting	Prohibition	Vintage
Beer, malt, hops, and yeast	Fortified wines	Sparkling wines	Wines
Champagne			

Notes

[1] H. J. Grossman, *Grossman's Guide to Wines, Spirits, and Beers.* New York: Charles Scribner's Sons, 1955, p. 293.

[2] *Encyclopedia Americana*, 1991, p. 452.

[3] Michael M. Coltman, *Beverage Management.* New York: Van Nostrand Reinhold, 1989, p. 160.

[4] Ibid.

[5] C. Katsigris and M. Porter, *The Bar and Beverage Book*, 2d ed. New York: John Wiley and Sons, 1991, p. 139.

[6] *Food Arts, 6,* 10, December 1993, p. 54.

[7] Claudia Roden, *Coffee.* Middlesex, England: Penguin Books, 1987, p. 20.

[8] Ibid.

[9] This section draws on Sara Perry, *The Complete Coffee Book,* San Francisco: Chronicle Books, 1991, p. 8.

[10] Ibid.

[11] Coca Cola's 1993 annual report.

[12] Gerald D. Robin, "Alcohol Service Liability: What the Courts Are Saying," *The Cornell Hotel and Restaurant Administration Quarterly, 31,* 1, February 1991, p. 102.

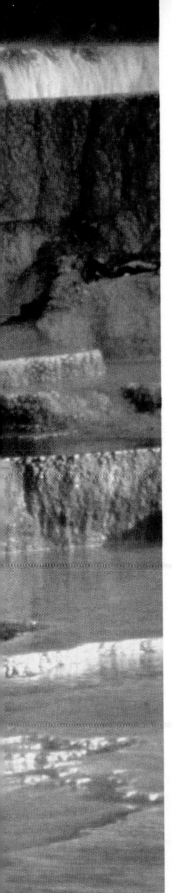

Recreation and Leisure

After reading and studying this chapter you should be able to do the following:

➤ Discuss the relationship of recreation and leisure to wellness
➤ Explain the origins and extent of government-sponsored recreation
➤ Distinguish between commercial and noncommercial recreation
➤ Name and describe various types of recreational clubs

he fundamental truth that recreation is essential to the cultural, moral, and spiritual well-being of our people has been reaffirmed. . . . The challenge to use leisure time effectively and constructively demands full development of our national, state, and local recreational resources.

—JOHN F. KENNEDY

Recreational activities include all kinds of sports, both team and individual. Baseball, softball, football, basketball, volleyball, tennis, swimming, jogging, skiing, hiking, aerobics, rock climbing, and camping are all active forms of recreation. Passive recreational activities include reading, fishing, playing and listening to music, gardening, playing computer games, and watching television or movies.

Recreation is an integral part of the nation's total social, economic, natural resource, and urban environment. It is a basic component of individual and social behavior and aspiration.[1]

Recreation, Leisure, and Wellness

As post-industrial society has become more complex, life has become more stressed. The need to develop the wholeness of the person has become increasingly important. Compared to a generation ago, the stress levels of business executives are much higher. The term *burnout*—and indeed, the word *stress*—have only become a part of our everyday vocabulary in recent years. Recreation is all about creating a balance, a harmony in life that will maintain wellness and wholeness.

Recreation allows people to have fun together and to form lasting relationships built on the experiences they have enjoyed together. This recreational process is called *bonding*. Bonding is hard to describe, yet the experience of increased interpersonal feeling for friends or business associates as a result of a recreational pursuit is common. These relationships result in personal growth and development.

Biking, Swimming, Hiking

The word *recreation* is defined in the dictionary as "the process of giving new life to something, of restoring something."[2]

Recreation is synonymous with life-style and the development of a positive attitude. An example of this is the increased feeling of well-being experienced after a recreational activity. Some people make the mistake of trying to pursue happiness as a personal goal. It is not enough for a person to say, "I want to be happy; therefore, I will recreate." Nathaniel Hawthorne wrote in the mid-nineteenth century: "Happiness in this world, when it comes, comes incidentally. Make it the object of pursuit, and it leads us on a wild goose chase, and it is never attained. Follow some other object, and very possibly we may find that we have caught happiness without dreaming of it."[3]

Recreation is a process that seeks to establish a milieu conducive to the discovery and development of characteristics that can lead to happiness. Happiness and well-being, therefore, are incidental outcomes of recreation. Thus, happiness may be enhanced by the pursuit of recreational activities.

The setting of personal recreational goals is equally as important as any other business or personal goal. These goals might include running a mile in under six minutes or maintaining a baseball batting average above .300. The fact that a person sets and strives to achieve goals requires personal organization. This helps improve the quality of life.

History shows again and again a direct linkage between leisure and the advancement of civilization. Hard work alone leaves no time for becoming civilized. Ironically, however, the opportunity to be at leisure is the direct result of increased technological and productivity advancements.

Government-Sponsored Recreation

Various levels of government are intertwined, yet distinct, in their parks, recreation, and leisure services. The founding fathers of America said it best when they affirmed the right to life, liberty, and the pursuit of happiness in the Declaration of Independence. The general welfare clause of the Constitution has become a legal basis for federal action affecting leisure pursuits.4

Government raises revenue from income taxes, sales taxes, and property taxes. Additionally, government raises special revenue from recreation-related activities such as automobile and recreational vehicles, boats, motor fuels, transient occupancy taxes (TOT) on hotel accommodations, state lotteries, and others.

The monies are distributed among the various recreation- and leisure-related organizations at the federal, state/provincial, city, and town levels.

New York Marathon

Recreation and leisure activities are extremely varied, ranging from cultural pursuits like museums, arts and crafts, music, theater, and dance to sports (individual and team), outdoor recreation, amusement parks, theme parks, community centers, playgrounds, libraries, and gardens.

A number of demographic factors affect participation in recreational activities: personality, sex, age, health, cultural background, upbringing, education, environment, occupation, and social contacts.[5]

Perceptions and attitudes play a major role in determining whether or not individuals participate in recreation, and if so, how much they enjoy their experiences. People's perceptions and attitudes are products of the total environment. All of the stimuli received throughout life mold an individual's outlook and feelings. These stimuli, in turn, are controlled by the person's demographics.[6] In the end, people select recreational pursuits based on their interests and capabilities.

Recreation professionals face a number of policy and legal concepts,[7] among them the following:

➤ Comprehensive recreation planning
➤ Land classification systems
➤ Federal revenue sharing
➤ Acquisition- and development-funding programs
➤ Land-use planning and zoning
➤ State and local financing
➤ Off-road vehicle impacts and policy
➤ Use of easements for recreation
➤ Designation of areas (such as wilderness, wild and scenic rivers, national trails, nature preserves)
➤ Differences in purposes and resources (of the numerous local, state/provincial, and federal agencies that control more than one third of the nation's land, much of which is used for recreation)

National Parks in the United States

National Parks are the best idea we ever had. Absolutely American, absolutely democratic, they reflect us at our best rather than our worst
—WALLACE STEGNER, 1983

The prevailing image of a national park is one of grand natural playgrounds, such as Yellowstone national park; but there is much more to it than that. The United States has designated 367 national park units throughout the country, comprising a rich diversity of places and settings.

The National Parks Service was founded in 1916 by Congress to conserve park resources and to provide for their use by the public so as to leave them unimpaired for the enjoyment of future generations.

In addition to the better known parks such as Yellowstone and Yosemite, the Parks Service also manages many other heritage attractions, including the Freedom Trail in Boston, Independence Hall in Philadelphia, the Antietam

National Battlefield in Sharpsburg, Maryland, and the U.S.S. Arizona Memorial at Pearl Harbor in Hawaii. The Parks Service is also charged with caring for myriad cultural artifacts, including ancient pottery, sailing vessels, Colonial-period clothing, and civil war documents.

> *There is nothing so American as our National Parks . . . the fundamental idea behind the parks . . . is that the country belongs to the people.*
> —FRANKLIN D. ROOSEVELT

The ever-expanding mandate of the Parks Service also calls for understanding and preserving the environment. It monitors the ecosystem from Arctic tundra to coral atolls, researches the air and water quality around the nation, and participates in global studies on acid rain, climate change, and biological diversity.

The idea of preserving exceptional lands for public use as national parks arose after the Civil War when America's receding wilderness left unique national resources vulnerable to exploitation. Recent years have seen phenomenal growth in the system, with three new areas created in the last twenty years. These include new kinds of parks, such as urban recreational areas, free flowing rivers, long-distance trails, and historic sites honoring our nation's social achievements. The system's current roster of 367 areas covers more than 80 million acres of land, with individual areas ranging in size from the thirteen-million-acre Wrangell–St. Elias National Park and Preserve in Alaska to the Thaddeus Kosciuszko National Memorial (a Philadelphia row house commemorating a hero of the American Revolution), which covers two one-hundredths of an acre.

More than 272 million visitors go to the parks each year and take advantage of the full range of services and programs. The focus once placed on preserving the scenery of the most natural parks has shifted as the system has grown and changed. Today emphasis is placed on preserving the vitality of each park's ecosystem and on the protection of unique or endangered plant and animal species.[8]

Yellowstone National Park (Courtesy Yellowstone National Park.)

National Parks in Canada

Canada has twenty-nine large national parks and more than 20 national historical parks and sites. Banff National Park, known for the world's most beautiful mountain peaks, was the first park of the system, founded in 1885. Jasper, Kootenay, Yoho Glacier, and Mt. Revelstoke National Parks, several provincial

Banff Springs Hotel and Park

parks, and the extensive Rocky Mountain Forest Reserve combine to make an immense complex of public lands along the spine of the spectacularly scenic Rocky Mountains of Alberta and British Columbia. These parks are accessed by the Canadian Pacific Railway, the Trans-Canada Highway, and small aircraft.[9]

The Canadian National Parks act states that "The parks are hereby dedicated to the people of Canada for their benefit, education, and enjoyment—and shall be maintained and made use of, so as to leave them unimpaired for the enjoyment of future generations."

The Canadian parks have highly developed tourist service islands (such as the town of Banff), well-appointed lodges and chalets, ski resorts, sports centers, and retreats, mostly natural in character. The largest of Canada's—and perhaps the world's—national parks is Wood Buffalow in Alberta and the Northwest Territories. Its 4,481,000 hectares (17,300 square miles) serve as home to the world's largest herd of bison roaming wild. The park is not developed for the public, but serves strictly as a wildlife preserve.

In Canada, recreation programming became a serious concern of the government after World War II. Provincial responsibility for recreation comes under several headings: outdoor activities, sports and physical recreation, arts and culture, social activities, tourism, and travel. Within each category, the government may have differing levels of responsibility: primary, in which a department or agency is required to provide a given service; secondary, in which an agency specifically is permitted (although not required) to provide a service; and tertiary, in which an agency performs a recreation function because it is related to another primary responsibility.[10]

In the past few decades, the federal government of Canada, in response to perceived needs, has created activities themes. During the 1950s, it was physical fitness; in the 1960s, it was youth; and in the 1970s, it was cultural and multicultural expression. The 1980s and 1990s have brought a combination of previous programs, with family themes.

Public Recreation and Parks Agencies

During the early part of the nineteenth century, the parks movement expanded rapidly as a responsibility of government and voluntary organizations. By the early 1900s, fourteen cities had made provisions for supervised play facilities, and the playground movement gained momentum. Private initiative and

Public Golf Course

Public Basketball Court

financial support were instrumental in convincing city government to provide tax dollars to build and maintain new play areas.

About the same time, municipal parks were created in a number of cities. Boston established the first metropolitan park system in 1892. In 1898, the New England Association of Park Superintendents (predecessor of the American Institute of Park Executives) was established to bring together park superintendents and promote their professional concerns.

Increasingly, the concept that city governments should provide recreation facilities, programs, and services became widely accepted. Golf courses, swimming pools, bathing beaches, picnic areas, winter sports facilities, game fields, and playgrounds were constructed.

Commercial Recreation

Recreation management came of age in the 1920s and 1930s, when recreation and social programs were offered as a community service. Colleges and universities began offering degree programs. Both public and private sector recreation management has grown rapidly since 1950.

Commercial recreation has been defined as "recreation for which the consumer pays and for which the supplier expects to make a profit."[11] Commercial recreation includes theme parks, attractions, and clubs.

Theme Parks

Visiting theme parks has always been a favorite tourist activity. Theme parks create an atmosphere of another place and time and usually concentrate on one dominant theme around which architecture, landscaping, costumed personnel, rides, shows, food services, and merchandise are coordinated.[12]

Personal and Corporate Profile: Walt Disney

A Man with a Vision and a Dream That He Was Able to Turn into Reality

To all who come to this happy place: Welcome! Disneyland is your land; here, age relives fond memories of the past, and here youth may savor the challenge and promise of the future.

Disneyland is dedicated to the hard facts that have created America, with the hope that it will be a source of joy and inspiration to all the world.

—*Disneyland Dedication Plaque, July 17, 1955*

In 1923, at the age of twenty-one, Walt Disney arrived in Los Angeles from Kansas City to start a new business. The first endeavor of Walt Disney and his brother Roy was a series of "shorts" called *Alice Comedies,* which featured a child actress playing with animated characters. Realizing that something new was needed to capture the audience, Walt Disney conjured up the concept of a mouse. In 1927, Disney began a series called *Oswald The Lucky Rabbit.* It was well received by the public, but Disney lost the rights due to a dispute with his distributor.

Mickey and Minnie Mouse first appeared in *Steamboat Willie* on November 8, 1928, which also incorporated music and sound. Huge audiences were ecstatic about the Disney Brothers, who became overnight successes.

In the next few years, Walt and Roy made many Mickey Mouse films, which earned them enough to develop other projects, including full-length motion pictures in Technicolor. Their first film was *Snow White and the Seven Dwarfs,* which opened in 1937. The success of *Snow White* led to other hits: *Pinocchio* and *Fantasia* in 1940, *Dumbo* in 1941, *Bambi* in 1942, and *Saludos Amigos* in 1943. Disney also was successful with live-action films such as *The Reluctant Dragon, Song of the South,* and *20,000 Leagues Under the Sea.* In 1954, Disney entered the television revolution with the Disneyland television series; in 1955, "The Mickey Mouse Club" debuted on the ABC network.

Cinderella Castle. © *The Walt Disney Company.*

Walt Disney said that Disneyland really began when his two daughters were very young. Saturday was always daddy's day, and he would take them to the merry-go-round and sit on a bench eating peanuts while they rode. Sitting there, he felt that there should be something built, some kind of a family park where parents and children could have fun together.[1]

Walt's original dream was not easy to bring to reality. During the bleak war years, not only was much of his overseas market closed, but also the steady stream of income that paid for innovation dried up. However, even during the bleak years, Walt never gave up. Instead, he was excited to learn of the public's interest in the movie studios and the possibility of opening the studios to allow the public to visit the birth place of Snow White, Pinocchio, and other Disney characters.

Gradually the concept of Disneyland came into focus. The clincher was Walt's fascination for trains and the need for a new home with a large yard for the train. Walt had to negotiate with more than three hundred bankers before he could raise the capital necessary to open Disneyland. He never gave up. Disney later wrote, "I could never convince the financiers that Disneyland was feasible, because dreams offer too little collateral."[2]

Disneyland had its growing pains—larger-than-expected opening day crowds, long lines at the popular rides, and a cash flow that was so acute that the cashiers had to rush the admission money to the bank in order to make payroll. Fortunately, since those early days, Disneyland and the Disney characters have become a part of not only Walt Disney, but also of the American dream.

By the early 1960s, Walt had turned most of his attention from film to real estate. Because he was upset to see

---

[1] Randy Bright, *Disneyland: Inside Story.* New York: Abrams, 1987, p. 33.

[2] Ibid, p. 34.

cheap motels and souvenir shops pop up around Disneyland, he made sure that for his next venture, Walt Disney World, he bought 27,500 acres around the park. The center of Walt Disney World was to be the Experimental Prototype Community of Tomorrow (EPCOT Center). Regrettably, EPCOT and Walt Disney World were his dying dreams, as Walt Disney succumbed to cancer in 1966.

The ensuing years have given Disney phenomenal successes with EPCOT Center movies, a TV station, The Disney Channel, Disney stores, and Disney-MGM Studios theme park. In April 1992, EuroDisneyland opened, close to Paris. In 1994, his Royal Highness, Prince Al Waleed Bin Talal Bin Abdula of Saudi Arabia, purchased 25 percent of The EuroDisneyland Paris Resort.

The Tokyo Disneyland continues to be successful; since its opening in 1983, about 140 million people have spent an average of $85 per visit (compared with $60 at Disneyland and $70 at Walt Disney World).

The Walt Disney Co. had revenues of $10.1 billion in 1994 with movies like *The Lion King,* which netted more than $1 billion.

The adjacent list of theme parks shows the phenomenal success of the Disney Theme Parks—they are the most visited parks in the world.

Both Walt Disney World and Disneyland have a great college program that enables selected students to work over the summer months in a variety of hotel, food service, and related park positions. Disney has also introduced a faculty internship that allows faculty to intern in a similar variety of positions.

Walt Disney World is composed of three major theme parks: Magic Kingdom, EPCOT, and Disney-MGM Studios, with more than one hundred attractions, twenty-two resort hotels themed to far-away lands, spectacular nighttime entertainment as well as vast shopping, dining, and recreation facilities that cover thousands of acres in this tropical paradise.

The Walt Disney World includes twenty-five lighted tennis courts, ninety-nine holes of championship golf, marinas, swimming pools, jogging and bike trails, water skiing, and motor boating. The resort also offers a unique zoological park and bird sanctuary on Discovery Island in the middle of Bay Lake, alive with birds, monkeys, and alligators, 226 restaurants, lounges, and food courts, a nightclub metropolis to please about any musical palate, a starry-eyed tribute to 1930s Hollywood, and even bass fishing. Walt Disney World is always full of new surprises: It now features the world's most unusual water adventure park, a "snow-covered" mountain with a ski-resort theme called Blizzard Beach.

1.	Walt Disney World's Magic Kingdom, EPCOT Center, Disney-MGM Studios, Buena Vista, Florida	*30.2 million*
2.	Tokyo Disneyland, Japan	*16.9 million*
3.	Disneyland, Anaheim, California	*11.6 million*
4.	EuroDisneyland, France	*8.7 million*
5.	Universal Studios, Orlando, Florida	*6.7 million*
6.	Blackpod Pleasure Beach, England	*6.5 million*
7.	Lotte World, Seoul, Korea	*6.0 million*
8.	Universal Studios, Hollywood, California	*4.8 million*
9.	Sea World of Florida, Orlando, Florida	*4.1 million*
10.	Sea World of California, San Diego, California	*4.0 million*

Source: Hotels, September, 1994

World's Most Popular Amusement/Theme Parks Attendance

Three new Disney hotels are architecturally exciting and more affordable than ever, with the fun-filled Disney's All-Star Sports Resort and Disney's colorful All-Star Music Resort (categorized as value-class hotels). The newly opened Disney's Wilderness Lodge is the park's jewel, with its impressive tall-timber atrium-lobby and rooms built around a Rocky Mountain geyser pool.

For nighttime fun, there is Planet Hollywood's newest entertainment restaurant (opened in December 1994) near Pleasure Island nightclubs. Overall, the park has a cast of thirty-seven thousand hosts, hostesses, and entertainers famous for their warm smiles and commitment to making every night an especially good one for Disney guests.

There is more to enjoy than ever: ExtraTERRORestrial Alien Encounter, developed in collaboration with George Lucas, and Transportarium in New Tomorrowland. Already open are Fantasyland's Legend of the Lion King, EPCOT's INNOVENTIONS, the mind-blowing 3-D adventure, Honey, I Shrunk the Audience in Future World, and at the Disney-MGM Studios, the ultimate thriller, The Twilight Zone Tower of Terror™.

Magic Kingdom

The heart of Walt Disney World and its first famous theme park is the Magic Kingdom, the "happiest land on earth," where "age relives fond memories" and "youth savors the challenge of the future." It is a giant theatrical stage where guests are part of exciting Disney adventures. It is also the home of Mickey Mouse, Snow White, Peter Pan, Tom Sawyer and Davy Crockett, Captain Nemo, and Swiss Family Robinson.

More than forty major shows and ride-through attractions, not to mention shops and unique dining facilities, fill its seven lands of imagination. Each land carries out its theme in fascinating detail—architecture, transportation, music, costumes, dining, shopping, and entertainment are designed to create a total atmosphere where you can leave the ordinary world behind.

Main Street, USA—Turn-of-the-century charm with horsedrawn street-cars, horseless carriages, Penny Arcade, and grand-circle tour on Walt Disney World Steam Railroad

Adventureland—Explore with Pirates of the Caribbean, wild animal Jungle Cruise, Swiss Family Treehouse, Tropical Serenade by birds, flowers, and tikis

Frontierland—Thrills on Splash Mountain and Big Thunder Mountain Railroad, musical fun in Country Bear Jamboree, Shooting Gallery, Tom Sawyer's Island caves and raft rides

Liberty Square—Steamboating on the Rivers of America, mystery in the Haunted Mansion, whooping it up in Diamond Horseshoe Saloon, viewing the impressive Hall of Presidents with addition of President Bill Clinton in a speaking role

Fantasyland—Cinderella Castle is gateway to new Legend of the Lion King plus Peter Pan's Flight, newly enhanced Snow White's Adventure, Mr. Toad's Wild Ride, 20,000 Leagues Under the Sea submarines, Flying Dumbo, Alice's Mad Tea Party, musical cruise with doll-like dancers in It's a Small World, Cinderella's Golden Carousel, and Skyway cable car to Tomorrowland

Mickey's Starland—Mickey's House, Grandma Duck's Farm, Mickey's Treehouse playground, Mickey's Magical TV World show, and private photo session in Mickey's Dressing Room

New Tomorrowland—Sci-Fi city of future, new frightening Alien Encounter, Transportarium time machine travel in Circle-Vision 360, new whirling Astro-Orbiter, speedy Space Mountain, new production of Carousel of Progress, Grand Prix Raceway, elevated Transit tour, Delta Dreamflight, new Disney Character show on Tomorrowland Stage

EPCOT

EPCOT is a unique, permanent and ever-changing world's fair with two major themes in Future World and World Showcase. Highlights include Illumi-Nations, nightly spectacle of fireworks, fountains, lasers, and classical music.

Future World shows amazing exposition of technology of the near future for home, work, and play now in INNOVENTIONS, which continually adds newest consumer products. Major pavilions exploring past, present, and future are shown in Spaceship Earth story of communications. Universe of Energy giant dinosaurs help explain origin and future of energy. There are also the Wonders of Life with spectacular Body Wars, Cranium Command and other medical health subjects, World of Motion exploring transportation, Journey into Imagination, The Land with spectacular agricultural research and environmental growing areas, and The Living Seas, the world's largest indoor ocean with thousands of tropical sea creatures.

The World Showcase shows international pavilions around World Showcase Lagoon that enable guests to see world-famous landmarks, sample native foods, entertainment, and culture of eleven nations:

> Mexico—Mexico's fiesta plaza and boat trip on El Rio Del Tiempo plus San Angel Inn for authentic Mexican cuisine

Theme parks and attractions vary according to theme, which might be historical, cultural, geographical, and so on. Some parks and attractions focus on a single theme, like the marine zoological Sea World parks. Other parks and attractions focus on multiple themes, like King's Island in Ohio, a family entertainment center divided into six theme areas: International Street, October First, River-Town, Hanna-Barbera Land, Coney Mall, and Wild Animal Habitat. Another example is Great America in California, a hundred-acre family entertainment center that evokes North America's past in five themes: Home Town Square, Yukon Territory, Yankee Harbor, Country Fair, and Orleans Place.[13]

Norway—With a thrilling Viking boat journey and Restaurant Akershus

China—Wonders of China Circle-Vision 360 film tour from the Great Wall to the Yangtze River plus Nine Dragons Restaurant

Germany—With an authentic Biergarten restaurant

Italy—With St. Mark's Square street players and L'Originale Alfredo di Roma Ristorante

United States—The American Adventure's stirring historical drama

Japan—Re-creating an Imperial Palace plus Teppanyaki Dining Rooms

Morocco—Morocco's palatial Restaurant Marrakesh

France—With Impressions de France film tour of the French country-side, Chefs de France and Bistro de Paris restaurant

United Kingdom—With Shakespearean street players plus Rose & Crown Pub

Canada—Featuring a Halifax to Vancouver Circle-Vision 360 tour.

Each showcase has additional snack facilities and a variety of shops featuring arts, crafts, and merchandise from each nation.

Disney–MGM Studios

With fifty major shows, shops, restaurants, ride-through adventures, and backstage tours, the Disney–MGM Studios combines real working motion picture, animation, and television studios with exciting movie attractions. Newest adventure in Sunset Boulevard theater district is Twilight Zone Tower of Terror(tm), with stunning thirteen-story elevator fall. The famous Chinese Theater on Hollywood Boulevard houses The Great Movie Ride.

Other major attractions include Backstage Studio Tour of production facilities, Catastrophe Canyon, and New York Street; tour of Walt Disney Animation Studios, Florida; exciting shows at Indiana Jones Epic Stunt Spectacular and Jim Henson's Muppet*Vision 3-D, plus thrilling space flight on Star Tours.

Especially entertaining for movie/TV fans are SuperStar Television and Monster Sound Show, where audience members take part in performances. Favorite Disney films become entertaining stage presentations in the Voyage of the Little Mermaid theater and Beauty and the Beast, a live, twenty-five-minute musical revue at Theater of the Stars. Best restaurants include the Hollywood Brown Derby, 1950s Prime Time Cafe, Sci-Fi Dine-In Theater, Mama Melrose's Ristorante Italiano, and Studio Commissary.

All this—and much more!—is what helps make Walt Disney World the most popular destination resort in the world. Since its opening in 1971, more than five hundred million guests, including kings and celebrities from around the world and all six U.S. presidents in office since the opening, have visited the parks. What causes the most comment from guests is the cleanliness, the friendliness of its cast, and the unbelievable attention to detail—a blend of showmanship and imagination that provides an endless variety of adventure and enjoyment.

Sunny beaches, exciting new adventures, and a fabulous resort and outdoor recreation facilities make a Walt Disney World excursion in Florida the ultimate dream vacation. There is a special Disney magic that frees guests from everyday cares to enjoy this unique world of fantasy, fun, thrills, and relaxation. There is something special for every age and every taste.[3]

---

[3] Pamela S. Weiers, "Escape to Disney's Fun and Sunshine Now,"*The New York Times* Advertising supplement, February 5, 1995.

Clubs

Private clubs are places where members only gather for social, recreational, professional, or fraternal reasons. Many of today's clubs are adaptations of their predecessors, mostly from England and Scotland. For example, the North American Country Club is largely patterned after the Royal and Ancient Golf Club of St. Andrews, Scotland, founded in 1758, and recognized as the birthplace of golf.

Club management is similar in many ways to hotel management. Managers are responsible for forecasting, planning, budgeting, human resource development, food and beverage facility management, and maintenance. The main differences between club management and hotel management is that with clubs, the guests feel as if they are the owners (in many cases they are), and frequently they behave as if they are the owners. Their emotional attachment is stronger than that of hotel guests who do not use hotels with the same frequency that members use clubs. Another difference is that most clubs do not offer sleeping accommodations.

Club members pay fees to belong to the club (an initiation fee) and as annual membership dues thereafter. Some clubs also charge a set utilization fee, usually related to food and beverages, which is charged whether or not those services are used. There are approximately fourteen thousand private clubs in America,[14] including both country clubs and city clubs.

The Club Manager's Association of America (CMAA) is the professional organization to which many of the club managers of the six thousand private country clubs belong.[15] The association aims to keep managers abreast of current practices and procedures. The professional guidelines that club managers set for themselves include the following:

➤ Club managers shall be judicious in their relationships with club members, aware of the need to maintain a line of professional demarcation between manager and the club membership.

➤ Club managers shall set an example by their demeanor and behavior that employees can use as a guide in their conduct with club members and guests.

➤ Club managers shall serve the community in every way possible.

➤ Club managers shall pursue their quest for knowledge through educational seminars and meetings that will improve their ability to manage their clubs.

➤ Club managers shall actively participate in local and national association meetings and activities.

➤ Club managers shall be above reproach. There can be no half measure of integrity in their obligations to their clubs, their employees, their club members, or in their dealings with purveyors.

➤ Club managers shall be ready at all times to offer assistance to their associates, their club officials, and all others engaged in the maintenance and conduct of their club operations.

➤ Club managers shall not be deterred from compliance with the law as it applies to their clubs.[16]

Figure 10–1 is a sample job description for a club general manager, and Figure 10–2 lists the club management competencies.

Club Management Structure

The internal management structure of a club is governed by a constitution and bylaws. These establish election procedures, officer positions, a board of directors, and standing committees. Guidance and direction also are provided as to what and how each office and committee will function.[17]

I. **Position:** General Manager
II. **Related Titles:** Club Manager; Club House Manager
III. **Job Summary:** Serves as chief operating officer of the club; manages all aspects of the club including its activities and the relationships between the club and its board of directors, members, guests, employees, community, government, and industry coordinates and administers the club's policies as defined by its board of directors. Develops operating policies and procedures and directs the work of all department managers. Implements and monitors the budget, monitors the quality of the club's products and services, and ensures maximum member and guest satisfaction. Secures and protects the club's assets, including facilities and equipment
IV. **Job Tasks (Duties):**
 1. Implements general policies established by the board of directors; directs their administration and execution
 2. Plans, develops, and approves specific operational policies, programs, procedures, and methods in concert with general policies
 3. Coordinates the development of the club's long-range and annual (business) plans
 4. Develops, maintains, and administers a sound organizational plan; initiates improvements as necessary
 5. Establishes a basic personnel policy; initiates and monitors policies relating to personnel actions and training and professional development programs
 6. Maintains membership with the Club Managers Association of America and other professional associations. Attends conferences, workshops, and meetings to keep abreast of current information and developments in the field
 7. Coordinates development of operating and capital budgets according to the budget calendar; monitors monthly and other financial statements for the club; takes effective corrective action as required.
 8. Coordinates and serves as ex-officio member of appropriate club committees
 9. Welcomes new club members; meets and greets all club members as practical during their visits to the club
 10. Provides advice and recommendations to the president and committees about construction, alterations, maintenance, materials, supplies, equipment, and services not provided in approved plans and/or budgets
 11. Consistently ensures that the club is operated in accordance with all applicable local, state, and federal laws
 12. Oversees the care and maintenance of all the club's physical assets and facilities
 13. Coordinates the marketing and membership relations programs to promote the club's services and facilities to potential and present members
 14. Ensures the highest standards for food, beverage, sports and recreation, entertainment, and other club services
 15. Establishes and monitors compliance with purchasing policies and procedures
 16. Reviews and initiates programs to provide members with a variety of popular events
 17. Analyzes financial statements, manages cash flow, and establishes controls to safeguard funds. Reviews income and costs relative to goals; takes corrective action as necessary
 18. Works with subordinate department heads to schedule, supervise, and direct the work of all club employees
 19. Attends meetings of the club's executive committee and board of directors
 20. Participates in outside activities that are judged as appropriate and approved by the board of directors to enhance the prestige of the club; broadens the scope of the club's operation by fulfilling the public obligations of the club as a participating member of the community
V. **Reports to:** Club President and Board of Directors
VI. **Supervises:** Assistant General Manager (Club House Manager); Food and Beverage Director; Controller; Membership Director; Director of Human Resources; Director of Purchasing; Golf Professional (Director of Golf); Golf Course Superintendent; Tennis Professional; Athletic Director; Executive Secretary

Courtesy: Club Managers Association of America

Figure 10–1 *Job Description, Club Manager*

The members elect the officers and directors of the club. The officers represent the membership by establishing policies by which the club will operate. Many clubs and other organizations maintain continuity by having a succession of officers: from secretary to vice president, president, and board of directors. The per-

Private Club Management
History of Private Clubs
Types of Private Clubs
Membership Types
Bylaws
Policy Formulation
Board Relations
Chief Operating Officer Concept
Committees
Club Job Descriptions
Career Development
Golf Operations Management
Golf Course Management
Tennis Operations Management
Swimming Pool Management
Yacht Facilities Management
Fitness Center Management
Locker Room Management
Other Recreational Activities

Food and Beverage Operations
Sanitation
Menu Development
Nutrition
Pricing Concepts
Ordering/Receiving/Controls/Inventory
Food and Beverage Trends
Quality Service
Creativity in Theme Functions
Design and Equipment
Food and Beverage Personnel
Wine List Development

**Accounting and Finance
   in the Private Club**
Accounting and Finance Principles
Uniform System of Accounts
Financial Analysis
Budgeting
Cash Flow Forecasting
Compensation and Benefit
   Administration
Financing Capital Projects
Audits
Internal Revenue Service
Computers
Business Office Organization
Long-Range Financial Planning

Human and Professional Resources
Employee Relations
Management Styles
Organizational Development
Balancing Job and Family
   Responsibilities
Time Management
Stress Management
Labor Issues
Leadership vs. Management

Building and Facilities Management
Preventive Maintenance
Insurance and Risk Management
Clubhouse Remodeling and
   Renovation

Contractors
Energy and Water Resource
   Management
Housekeeping
Security
Laundry
Lodging Operations

**External and Governmental
   Influences**
Legislative Influences
Regulatory Agencies
Economic Theory
Labor Law
Internal Revenue Service
Privacy
Club Law
Liquor Liability
Labor Unions

Management and Marketing
Communication Skills
Marketing Through In-House
   Publications
Professional Image and Dress
Effective Negotiation
Member Contact Skills
Working with the Media
Marketing Strategies in a Private
   Club Environment

Courtesy: Club Managers Association of
   America

Figure 10–2   *Club Management Competencies*

son elected president is the person the membership feels is the most qualified person to lead the club for that year. Regardless of who is elected president, the club manager must be able to work with that person and the other officers.

The president presides at all official meetings and is a leader in policy making.[18] The vice president will, in the absence of the president, perform the presidential duties. If the club has more than one vice president, then the title *first, second, third,* and so on may be used. Alternatively, vice presidents may be assigned to chair certain functions, such as membership. Vice presidents usually chair one or more committees.

The treasurer obviously must have some financial/accounting background because an integral part of his or her duties is to give advice on financial matters such as employing external auditors, preparing budgets, and installing control systems.

The secretary records the minutes of meetings and takes care of club-related correspondence. This position can be combined with that of treasurer, in which case the position is titled *secretary-treasurer.* The secretary may also serve on or chair certain committees.

Committees play an important part in the club's activities. If the committees are effective, the operation of the club is more efficient. The term of committee membership is specified, and committee meetings are conducted in accordance with Robert's Rules of Order, which are procedural guidelines on the correct way to conduct meetings. Typical committees include the following: house, membership, finance/budget, entertainment, sports, special/ad hoc, and so on.

Country Clubs

A country club offers recreational facilities; the focus generally is on golf, but tennis and swimming are frequently included. Occasionally, other activities, such as horseback riding, pool rooms, card rooms, aerobic facilities, and other activities are also provided for the members' enjoyment.

Nearly all country clubs have one or more lounges and restaurants, and most have banquet facilities. Members and their guests enjoy these services and can be billed monthly. The banquet facilities are used for formal and informal parties, dinners, dances, weddings, and so on by members and their personal guests. Some country clubs charge what might seem to be an excessive amount for the initiation fee in order to maintain exclusivity—as much as $250,000 in some cases.

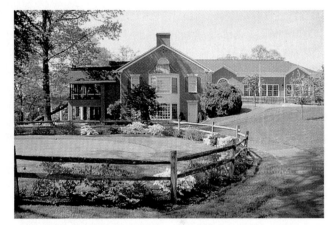

Country Club (Photo courtesy of The Club Managers Association.)

Country clubs have two or more types of membership: full and social membership. Full membership enables members to use all of the facilities all of the time. Social membership only allows members to use the social facilities: lounges, bars, restaurants, and so on and perhaps the pool and tennis courts. Other forms of membership can include weekday and weekend memberships.

A few years ago, country clubs were often considered to be bastions of a social elite. Although that description still may be somewhat true, today there are numerous examples of new clubs that have opened without the "stuffy" waiting list and what's-your-pedigree? approach to would-be-members. Additionally, at the newer clubs, the cost of initiation and membership may be considerably less than at some of the more-established clubs.

City Clubs

City clubs are predominantly business oriented; they vary in size, location, types of facility, and services offered. Some of the older, established clubs own their own buildings, and others lease space. Clubs exist to cater to the wants and needs of members. Clubs in the city fall into the following categories:

➤ Professional
➤ Social

Personal Profile: Sally Burns Rambo:

A Giver of the First Order

General Manager
Lakewood Country Club Dallas
Voted 1991 Club Manager of the Year

After graduating from high school at sixteen, Sally Burns Rambo began her professional career working in a bank. The actual launch in the business environment came when she began to work at the local newspaper. Her talent earned her the promotion to office manager. Working as office manager gave her an opportunity to become well known in the community. This led to her being offered a club's office manager position by the Eastern Hills Country Club members.

During the first six months of her working at the club, two club managers were fired, so leaders of the club persuaded Sally to serve as interim manager until someone else was appointed. However, nobody else was ever appointed for that position, and Sally was to be the general manager of the club for the next twenty-one years.

Her talents and skills were not forgotten after her retirement. In fact, she was again persuaded to manage a club that was in serious decline. Sally recalls that she regretted taking this position for about four months, because the club was in extremely bad condition. But she accepted the challenge with enormous determination: "You've never been a quitter and you're not going to quit now," she told herself. By improving the quality of food and service, she made Lakewood a fun place to be. Members and guests enjoyed themselves and looked forward to visiting the club.

Sally has always been a risk-taker and an innovator. She introduced a novel concept in her club, which was initially not approved by some members. She decided to feature a country western band, that, regardless of the warnings against the idea she had received from the members, proved to be a great success. Many other successes followed with some of the top names in entertainment. Sally believed that the important thing was that the club gave its members something they could take pride in with their friends. The quality of these parties helped the club regain membership. Sally is a hands-on manager who makes sure all details are attended to. She adds that "you make your money on member-sponsored parties" and that "you have to get your business volume that way rather than through regular dining room business because most members will not dine at the club every day."

Key ingredients in Sally's success are continually educating herself and her caring enthusiasm to staffing: "Hire the right people, pay them well, let them show what they know, and they will make you look good." Sally has a staff of 102 full-time employees, and the club serves fourteen hundred members, including families—up from less than four hundred when she took over as manager.

Sally is a firm believer of the fact that you need to be dedicated, with a willingness to work hard. In fact, she often works twelve hours a day and she never drinks on the job![1]

[1] Eldon Miller, "1991 Club Manager of the Year," *Club Management*, December 1991.

➤ Athletic
➤ Dining
➤ University
➤ Military
➤ Yachting
➤ Fraternal
➤ Proprietary

Professional clubs, as the name implies, are clubs for people in the same profession. The National Press Club in Washington, D.C., the Lawyer's Club in

New York City, and the Friars Club for actors and other theatrical people in Manhattan are good examples.

Social clubs allow members to enjoy one another's company; members represent many different professions, yet they have similar socioeconomic backgrounds. Social clubs are modeled after the famous men's social clubs in London, such as Boodle's, St. James's, and White's. At these clubs, it is considered bad form to discuss business. Therefore, conversation and social interaction is focused on companionship or entertainment unrelated to business.

The oldest social club in America is thought to be the Fish House in Philadelphia, founded in 1832. To ensure that the Fish House would always be socially oriented rather than business oriented, it was formed as a men's cooking club with each member taking turns preparing meals for the membership.[19]

Other social clubs exist in several major cities. The common denominator is that they all have upscale food and beverage offerings and have club managers to manage them.

Athletic clubs give city workers and residents an opportunity to work out, swim, play squash and/or racquetball, and so on. Some of the downtown athletic clubs provide tennis courts and running tracks on the roof. Athletic clubs also have lounges, bars, and restaurants at which members may relax and interact socially. Some athletic clubs also have meeting rooms and even sleeping accommodations.

Dining clubs are generally located in large city office buildings. Memberships are often given as an inducement to tenants who lease space in the office building. These clubs are always open for lunch and occasionally for dinner.

University clubs are private clubs for alumni. With a few exceptions, they are for one university's alumni. University clubs are generally located in the high rent district and offer a variety of facilities and attractions focusing on food and beverage service.

Military clubs cater to both NCOs (noncommissioned officers) and enlisted officers. Military clubs offer similar facilities as other clubs for recreation and entertainment and food and beverage offerings. Military clubs are located on base and have in recent years given over their club management to civilians.

Yacht clubs provide members with moorage slips, where their boats are kept secure. In addition to moorage facilities, yacht clubs have lounge, bar, and dining facilities similar to other clubs. Yacht clubs are based on a sailing theme and attract members with various backgrounds who have sailing as one of their common interests.

Fraternal clubs include many special organizations such as the Veterans of Foreign Wars, Elks, and Shriners. These organizations foster camaraderie and often assist charitable causes. They generally are less elaborate than other clubs, but have bars and banquet rooms that can be used for various activities.

Proprietary clubs operate on a for-profit basis. They are owned by corporations or individuals; people wanting to become members purchase a membership, not a share in the club. Proprietary clubs became popular with the real estate boom in the 1970s and 1980s. As new housing developments were planned, clubs were included in several of the projects. Households paid a small initiation fee and monthly dues between \$30 and \$50, allowing the whole family to participate in a wide variety of recreational activities.

Clearly, the opportunities for recreation and leisure abound. The goal must be to achieve a harmony between work and leisure activities and to become truly professional in both giving and receiving these services. The next few years will see a substantial increase in the leisure and recreational industries.

Noncommercial Recreation

Noncommercial recreation includes voluntary organizations, campus, armed forces, and employee recreations as well as recreation for special populations.

Voluntary Organizations

Voluntary organizations are nongovernmental, nonprofit agencies, serving the public-at-large or selected elements with multiservice programs that often include a substantial element of recreational opportunity. The best-known voluntary organizations include the Boy Scouts, Girl Scouts, YMCA, YWCA, and YM-YWHA.

In the early 1900s, YMCAs began to offer sporting facilities and programs. The Ys, though nonprofit, were pioneers in basketball, swimming, and weight training. Later, commercial health clubs also began to evolve, offering men's and women's exercise on alternating days. As the sports and fitness movement grew, clubs became oriented toward special interests. Now, clubs can be classified as follows: figure salons, health clubs, body-building gyms, tennis clubs, racquetball centers, or multipurpose clubs.[20]

A multipurpose club has more exclusive recreation programs than a health club. Leagues, tournaments, and classes are common for racquet sports, and most clubs offer several types of fitness classes. Some innovative clubs offer automatic bank tellers, stock market quote services, computer matching for tennis competition, auto detailing, laundry and dry cleaning services, and wine-cellar storage.

Club revenue comes from membership fees, user fees, guest fees, food and beverage sales, facility rental, and so on. Human resources accounts for about 66 percent of expenses at most clubs.

It is amazing to realize that in the center of a city, there may be several voluntary organizations, each serving a particular segment of the population. Richard Kraus writes that a study of the city of Toronto that examined various land uses and leisure programs in the city's core found the following organizations: a Boy's Club, a Mission, the Center of the Metropolitan Association for the Retarded, a Catholic settlement house, a day care center, an Indian center, a YM-YWHA, a service center for working people, a Chinese center, a

Ukrainian center, and several other organizations meeting special needs and interests. These were all in addition to public parks, recreation areas, and nineteen churches.

Campus, Armed Forces, and Employee Recreation

Campus Recreation

North America's colleges and universities provide a major setting for organized leisure and recreational programs with services involving millions of participants each year. The programs include involvement by campus recreation offices, intramural departments, student unions, residence staffs, or other sponsors. The activities have heavy components of the following types: competitive sports and games; outdoor recreation trips and events; cultural programs such as music, drama, dance, and films; and leisure-oriented activities.[21]

The various recreational activities help in maintaining good morale on campus. Some use recreational activities such as sports or orchestras or theater companies as a means of gaining alumni support. Students look for an exciting and interesting social life. For this reason, colleges and universities offer a wide range of recreational and social activities that may vary from campus to campus.

Armed Forces Recreation

It is the official policy of the Department of Defense to provide a well-rounded morale, welfare, and recreational program for the physical, social, and mental well-being of its personnel. Each of the services sponsors recreational activities under the auspices of the Morale, Welfare, and Recreation Program (MWR), which reports to the Office of the Assistant Secretary of Defense for Manpower, Reserve Affairs, and Logistics. MWR activities are provided to all military personnel and civilian employees at all installations.

MWR programs include the following types of activities:

➤ Sports, including self-directed, competitive, instructional, and spectator programs
➤ Motion pictures
➤ Service clubs and entertainment
➤ Crafts and hobbies
➤ Youth activities for children of military families
➤ Special interest groups, such as aero, automotive, motorcycle, and power boat clubs, or hiking, skydiving, or rod and gun clubs
➤ Rest centers and recreation areas
➤ Open dining facilities
➤ Libraries

Recreation is perceived as an important part of the employee benefits package for military personnel, along with the G.I. Bill, medical services, commissaries, and exchanges.

Employee Recreation

Business and industry have realized the importance of promoting employee efficiency. Human resource experts have found that workers who spend their free time at constructive recreational activities have less absenteeism resulting from emotional tension, illness, excessive use of alcohol, and so on. Employee recreation programs may also be an incentive for a prospective employee to join a company.

In the United States and Canada, almost all of the leading corporations have an employee recreation and wellness program. Some companies include recreation activities in their team building and management development programs.

Recreation for Special Populations

Recreation for special populations involves professionals and organizations that have a responsibility for serving special populations, such as the mentally ill, mentally retarded, or physically disabled. In recent years, there has been increased recognition of the need to provide recreational programs for special populations. These programs have evolved with therapeutic recreation as a form of treatment. Programs have been developed for each of the special population groups.

One of the sports programs for people with disabilities that has received considerable attention in recent years is the Special Olympics, an international program of physical fitness, sports training, and athletic competition for children and adults with mental retardation. The program is unique because it accommodates competitors at all ability levels by assigning participants to competition divisions based on both age and actual performance.[22]

Today, the Special Olympics serves more than one million individuals in the United States and more than seventy other countries. Among the official sports are track and field events, swimming, diving, gymnastics, ice skating, basketball, volleyball, soccer, softball, floor hockey, poly hockey, bowling, frisbee disk, downhill skiing, cross-country skiing, and wheelchair events. The National Recreation and Park Association and numerous state and local agencies and societies work closely with Special Olympics in promoting programs and sponsoring competitions.[23]

Summary

1. Recreation is free time that people use to restore, rest, and relax their minds and bodies. Recreational activities can be passive or active, an individual or a group activity.

2. Recreational activities range from cultural pursuits such as museums or theaters, to sports or outdoor recreation such as amusement parks, community centers, playgrounds, and libraries. These services involve various levels of government.

3. National parks preserve exceptional lands for public use, emphasizing the protection of its ecosystem and endangered plant and animal species and honoring historical sites. Two of the best-known of the current 367 parks include Yellowstone and Yosemite national parks.

4. Today, city governments are increasingly expected to provide recreational facilities such as golf courses, swimming pools, picnic areas, and playgrounds as a community service.
5. Commercial recreation—for example, theme parks, clubs, and attractions—involves a profit for the supplier of the recreational activity.
6. Clubs are places where members gather for social, recreational, professional, or fraternal reasons. There are many different types of clubs such as country clubs or city clubs, according to the interests they represent to their members.
7. Noncommercial recreation are nongovernmental and nonprofit agencies, including voluntary organizations, campus, armed forces, employee recreation, and recreation for special population such as the physically disabled.

Review Exercises

1. Define recreation and its importance to human wellness. What factors affect an individual's decision to participate in recreational activities?
2. Describe the origin of government-sponsored recreation in consideration of the origin and purpose of national parks.
3. Briefly describe the difference between commercial and noncommercial recreation.
4. Briefly explain the purpose of a theme park and the purpose of clubs.
5. Explain the concept of recreation for special populations.

Key Words and Concepts

Clubs
Commercial recreation
Government-sponsored recreation
Leisure
National parks
National Parks Service
Noncommercial recreation
Recreation
Recreation for special populations
Theme parks
Voluntary organizations
Wellness

Notes

[1] Douglas M. Knudson, *Outdoor Recreation*. New York: Macmillan, 1980, p. 1.
[2] Bruno Hans Geba, *Being at Leisure, Playing at Life: A Guide to Health and Joyful Living*. La Mesa, California: Leisure Science Systems International, 1985, p. 19.
[3] Ibid., p. 66.
[4] Janet R. MacClean, J. Peterson, and D. Martin, *Recreation and Leisure: The Changing Scene*, 4th ed. New York: John Wiley and Sons, 1985, p. 72.
[5] Michael Chubb and Holly R. Chubb, *One Third of Our Time: An Introduction to Recreation Behavior and Resources*. New York: John Wiley and Sons, 1981, p. 191.
[6] Ibid.
[7] Knudson, op. cit., p. 7–8.
[8] This section draws on information supplied by the National Parks Service.
[9] Knudson, op. cit., p. 261.
[10] Richard Kraus, *Recreation and Leisure in Modern Society*, 3d ed. Glenview, Ill.: Scott, Foresman, 1984, pp. 159–160.
[11] MacLean, op. cit., p. 220.
[12] Ady Milman, "Theme Parks and Recreation," *VNR'S Encyclopedia of Hospitality and Tourism*. New York: Van Nostrand Reinhold, 1993, p. 934.
[13] Other prominent theme parks and attractions are Knott's Berry Farm, Universal Studios, and Six Flags over America.
[14] Richard, Martin, "Tradition Gives Way to Reform," *Nation's Restaurant News, 23*, 4, January 23, 1989, p. F-7.
[15] Personal interview with Joe Purdue, Club Managers Association of America, January 1995.
[16] Ted E. White, *Club Operations and Management*. Boston: CBI Publishing, 1979, pp. 6–7.
[17] Ibid., p. 17.
[18] Ibid.
[19] Stephen Birmingham, *America's Secret Aristocracy*. New York: Berkeley Books, 1990, p. 209.
[20] John C. Crossley and Lynn M. Jamieson, *Introduction to Commercial Recreation*. Champaign, Ill.: Sagamore Publishing, 1988, p. 248.
[21] Kraus, op cit., p. 213.
[22] Richard Kraus and John Shank, *Therapeutic Recreation Service: Principles and Practices*, 4th ed. Dubuque, Iowa: Wm C. Brown, 1983, p. 143.
[23] Ibid.

Meetings, Conventions, and Expositions

After reading and studying this chapter you should be able to do the following:

- ➤ Name the main hospitality industry associations
- ➤ Describe the various types of meetings
- ➤ Explain the difference among meetings, expositions, and conventions
- ➤ Describe the role of a meeting planner
- ➤ Explain the primary responsibilities of a convention and visitors bureau or authority
- ➤ List the steps in event management

Historical Review

People have gathered to attend meetings, conventions, and expositions since ancient times, mainly for social, sporting, political, or religious purposes. As cities became regional centers, the size and frequency of such activities increased, and various groups and associations set up regular expositions.

Associations go back many centuries to the Middle Ages and before. The guilds in Europe were created during the Middle Ages to secure proper wages and maintain work standards. Associations began in the United States at the beginning of the eighteenth century, when the Rhode Island candle makers organized themselves.

Today, according to the American Society of Association Executives (ASAE), in the United States, associations operate at the national level, and a hundred thousand more function at the regional, state, and local levels. The association business is big business. Associations spend about $53.5 billion holding 215,000 meetings and conventions that attract approximately 22.6 million attendees (see Figure 11–1).

The hospitality and tourism industry itself consists of a number of associations, including the following:

➤ The American Hotel and Motel Association
➤ The National Restaurant Association
➤ The International Association of Convention and Visitors Bureaus
➤ Hotel Sales and Marketing Association
➤ Meeting Planners Association
➤ Association for Convention Operation Management
➤ Club Managers Association
➤ Professional Convention Management Association

In reality, associations are the only independent political force for industries like hospitality, offering the following benefits:[1]

➤ Governmental/political voice
➤ Marketing avenues
➤ Education
➤ Member services
➤ Networking

Thousands of associations hold annual conventions at various locations across North America and the rest of the world. Some associations alternate their venues from east to central to west; others meet at fixed locations such as the NRA show in Chicago or the American Hotel and Motel Association (AH&MA) convention and show in New York.

As Figure 11–1 indicates, professional and trade associations hold 70 percent of the conventions market, totaling $75 billion a year.[2]

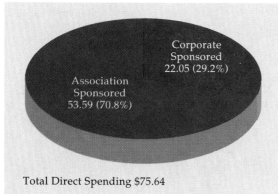

Corporate Sponsored 22.05 (29.2%)

Association Sponsored 53.59 (70.8%)

Total Direct Spending $75.64

Figure 11–1   *The Conventions Market*

Types of Meetings

Meetings are conferences, workshops, seminars, or other events designed to bring people together for the purpose of exchanging information.[3] Meetings can take any one of the following forms:

Clinic: A workshop-type educational experience whose attendees learn by doing. A clinic usually involves small groups interacting with each other on an individual basis.

Forum: An assembly for the discussion of common concerns. Usually experts in a given field take opposite sides of an issue in a panel discussion, with liberal opportunity for audience participation.

Seminar: A lecture and a dialogue that allow participants to share experiences in a particular field. A seminar is guided by an expert discussion leader, and usually thirty or fewer persons participate.

Symposium: An event at which a particular subject is discussed by experts and opinions are gathered.

Workshop: A small group led by a facilitator or trainer. It generally includes exercises to enhance skills or develop knowledge in a specific topic.

Meetings are mostly organized by corporations, associations, social, military, educational, religious, and fraternal groups (SMERF). The reasons for having a meeting can range from the presentation of a new sales plan to a total quality management workshop. The purpose of meetings is to affect behavior. For example, as a result of attending a meeting, a person should know or be able to do certain things. Some outcomes are very specific; others may be less so. For instance, if a meeting were called to brainstorm new ideas, the outcome might be less concrete than for other types of meetings.

Meeting attendance can vary in size. Successful meetings require a great deal of careful planning and organization. In San Francisco, a major convention city, convention delegates spend approximately $300 per day,[4] almost twice that of vacation travelers. Figure 11-2 shows convention delegates' spending in San Francisco in 1993.

Meetings are set up according to the wishes of the client. The three main types of meeting set ups are theater style, classroom style, and boardroom. Theater style generally is intended for a large audience that does not need to make a lot of notes or refer to documents. This style usually consists of a raised platform and a lectern from which a presenter addresses the audience. Classroom set-ups are used when the meeting format is more instructional. Participants need to take detailed notes or refer to documents. A workshop-type meeting often uses this format. Boardroom set ups are made for small numbers of people. The meeting takes place around one block rectangular table.

Expositions are events designed to bring together purveyors of products, equipment, and services in an environment in which they can demonstrate

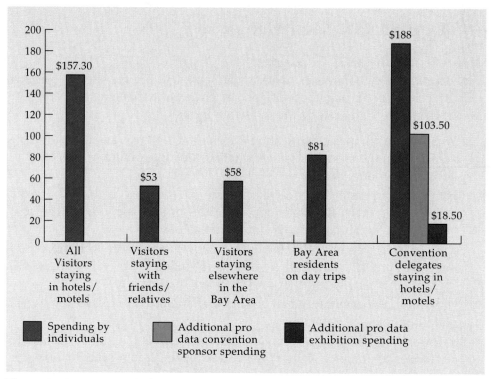

Figure 11–2   *Average Daily Visitor Spending in San Francisco* (Reprinted with permission from the *San Fransisco Examiner*. August 28, 1994, p. B2.)

their products and services to a group of attendees at a convention or trade show.[5] Exhibitors are an essential component of the industry because they pay to exhibit their products to the attendees. Exhibitors interact with attendees with the intention of making sales or establishing contacts and leads for follow up. Expositions can take up several hundred thousand square feet of space, divided into booths for individual manufacturers or their representatives. In the hospitality industry, the two largest expositions are the American Hotel and Motel Association's (AH&MA) annual New York Show (held in November at the Javits Center) and the National Restaurant Association's Annual Exposition held every May in Chicago. Both events are well worth attending.

Conventions are meetings combined with expositions. Conventions are generally larger meetings with some form of exposition or trade show included. A number of associations have one or more conventions per year. These conventions raise a large part of the association's budget. A typical convention follows a format like this:

➤ Welcome/registration
➤ Introduction of president
➤ President's welcome speech, opening the convention
➤ First keynote address by a featured speaker
➤ Exposition booths open (equipment manufacturers and trade suppliers)

NRA Show (Photo courtesy of the National Restaurant Association.)

➤ Several workshops or presentations on specific topics
➤ Luncheon
➤ More workshops and presentations
➤ Demonstrations of special topics (e.g., culinary arts for a hospitality convention)
➤ Vendors' private receptions
➤ Dinner
➤ Convention center closes

Figure 11–3 on pages 284–85 shows a convention event profile for a trade show.

Conventions are not always held in convention centers; in fact, the majority are held in large hotels over a three- to five-day period. The headquarters hotel is usually the one in which most of the activity takes place. Function space is allocated for the registration, convention, expositions, meals, and so on.

Associations used to be viewed as a group that held an annual meeting and convention with speeches, entertainment, an educational program, and social events. They have changed in activity and perception.

Key Players in the Industry

The need to hold face-to-face meetings and attend conventions has grown into a multibillion dollar industry. Many major and some smaller cities have convention centers with nearby hotels and restaurants.

San Diego
Convention Center Corporation
EVENT PROFILE

EVENT STATISTICS

Event Name:	/6/San Diego Apartment Association Trade Show	ID:	9506059
Sales Person:	Joy Peacock	Initial Contact:	8/3/1994
Event Manager:	Trish A. Stiles	Move In Date:	6/22/1995
ConVis Contact:		Move In Day:	Thursday
Food Person:		Move In Time:	6:01 am
Event Tech.:		First Event Date:	6/23/1995
Event Attend.:		First Event Day:	Friday
Nature of Event:	LT Local Trade Show	Start Show Time:	6:01 am
Event Parameter:	60 San Diego Convention Center	End Show Time:	11:59 pm
Business Type 1:	41 Association	# of Event Days:	1
Business Type 2:	91 LOCAL	Move Out Date:	6/23/1995
Booking Status:	D Definite	Move Out Day:	Friday
Rate Schedule:	III Public Show, Meetings and Location	Out Time:	11:59 pm
Open to Public:	No	Date Confirmed:	8/3/1994
Number Sessions:	1	Attend per Sesn:	3000
Event Sold By:	F Facility (SDCCC)	Tot Room Nights:	15
Abbrev. Name:	/6/Apartment Assn	Public Release:	Yes
Est Bill Amount:	Rent - 6,060.00 Equip –	0.00 Food –	0.00
Last Changed on:	8/20/94 in: Comment Maintenance	By – Joy Peacock	

This Event has been in the facility before

CLIENT INFORMATION

Company: San Diego Apartment Assn, a non-profit Corporation
Contact Name: Ms. Leslie Cloud, Sales and Marketing Coord.
ID: SDAA
1011 Camino Del Rio South, Suite 200, San Diego, CA 92108
Telephone Number: (619) 297-1000
Fax Number: (619) 294-4510
Alternate Number: (619) 294-4510

Company: San Diego Apartment Assn, a non-profit Corporation
Alt Contact Name: Ms. Pamela A. Trimble, Finance & Operations Director
1011 Camino Del Rio South, Suite 200, San Diego, 92108
Telephone Number: (619) 297-1000
Fax Number: (619) 297-4510

EVENT LOCATIONS

ROOM	MOVE IN	IN USE	ED	MOVE OUT	BS	SEAT	RATE	EST. RENT	ATTEND
A	6/22/95 6:01 am	6/23/95	1	6/23/95 11:59 pm	D	E	III	6,060.00	5000
AS	6/22/95 6:01 am	6/23/95	1	6/23/95 11:59 pm	D	E	III	0.00	10
R01	6/22/95 6:01 am	6/23/95	1	6/23/95 11:59 pm	D	T	III	0.00	450
R02	6/22/95 6:01 am	6/23/95	1	6/23/95 11:59 pm	D	T	III	0.00	350
R03	6/22/95 6:01 am	6/23/95	1	6/23/95 11:59 pm	D	T	III	0.00	280
R04	6/22/95 6:01 am	6/23/95	1	6/23/95 11:59 pm	D	T	III	0.00	280
R05	6/22/95 6:01 am	6/23/95	1	6/23/95 11:59 pm	D	T	III	0.00	460

FOOD SERVICES

ROOM	DATE	TIME	BS ATTEND	EST. COST FOOD SERVICE

There are No Food Services booked for this event

Figure 11–3 *Convention Program* (Courtesy of the San Diego Convention Center.)

San Diego
Convention Center Corporation

EVENT PROFILE

EVENT EQUIPMENT/SERVICES

ROOM	MOVE IN	INUSE	ED MOVE OUT	QUANTITY EQUIPMENT

There are No Equipment booked for this event

FOLLOW-UP/CHECKLIST ITEMS

FOLLOW-UP	DATE	ITEM	COMPLETED DATE	ASSIGN TO
	9/26/94	C DUE/date contracted		Vincent R. Magana
	8/22/94	c from sales	8/23/94	Sonia Michel
	8/22/94	c to licensee	8/23/94	Sonia Michel
	8/22/94	date c 1st printed	8/22/94	Sonia Michel

EVENT COMMENTS

8/3/94–JMP–This is a very strong hold for this group. CAD is pursuing a release of Hall A from Group Health and then this will be confirmed on a first option. Also holding an alternate date in April until this is released. All other rooms are clear.

200 BOOTHS – have used Carden in the past.
This is a trade show for the Apartment industry — products and services needed to keep a rental property in shape. Use Rooms 1–5 as seminar rooms. Trish has been the Event Coordinator for '93 – '94.

8/18/94 - JMP-CAD has been able to clear Hall A on a first option for move-in on 22nd from Group Health. Made definite and requested Sonia produce a contract. NOTE TO SONIA: Contract should be signed and mailed to alternate contact Pam Trible. Meeting logistics only will go through Leslie. Note to housekeeping: we did the cleaning for the 1994 show.

LICENSE AGREEMENT REQUEST

EVENT COMMENTS

Requested:	Saturday, 08/20/94, 2:56 pm
License #:	9506059
Sales Person:	JMP
Nature of Event:	Local Trade
Full Legal Name of Licensee:	Yes
Insurance Y/N:	Yes
Deposit Schedule:	50-50
Special Arrangements or Directions:	Contract should be signed and sent to alternate contact Pam Trimble. Leslie is responsible for meeting logistics only.
Gross Revenues F/B Revenue:	$1000 concessions
In House A/V Revenue:	$600
Security Revenue:	$200
Telecom. Revenue:	$220

(Below, identify MI/MO or event days and attendance for each event).
Other business in Center: GROUP HEALTH, definite, Hall B-1 (m/o 22nd), 3000ppl; ALCOHOLICS ANON, definite, Hall B, move-in; SECURITY EXPO, tentative, Hall C (m/i 22nd, show 23rd), 6600ppl; ENTRP. EXPO, contracted, Ballroom (m/i 23rd), 2000ppl.

Figure 11–3 *(continued)*

Personal Profile: Carol C. Wallace

Executive Vice President/General Manager, San Diego Convention Center Corporation

Carol grew up in a single-parent household in Cincinnati, Ohio. Her mother was an excellent role model who shared her experiences with Carol, stressing education and a strong work ethic. Carol began work at age thirteen selling penny candy, and ever since has aspired to be the best that she can be.

The road to the achievement of this goal began by completing her education. After graduating from Ohio State University with a degree in English and Journalism, Carol intended to go to graduate school and become a teacher. It was while she was working at the university that she began to plan meetings. This led to involvement with the Ohio Lung Association in a public relations capacity. Carol not only planned meetings but also special events, like the 1973 Run for Life and Breath, and the first statewide "Go Cold Turkey" no-smoking campaigns.

Carol was invited to speak about the success of these events at a national conference in Dallas. She found the resultant career challenge that she was offered in Dallas too tempting to pass up; besides, she adds, the 80-degree weather was much better than the 30-degree weather she had left in Ohio! In 1976, she began working in the Public Affairs Department, Office of Special Events planning meetings. In 1980, Carol noticed a career announcement for the Dallas Convention Center, which was looking for an entry-level convention services representative. She applied, was accepted, and began working at what was then the fifth largest convention center in the United States. Carol says that this was like being an intern in a hospital where you worked hard to support the senior staff.

After two years at the Dallas Convention Center, Carol spoke with her manager about career prospects and was soon promoted to assistant manager of the facility. In 1989, Carol was recruited by an executive search firm to become the opening executive director of the Denver Convention Complex. Carol recalls that the opportunity of opening a new convention complex allowed her to develop personal-

Carol Wallace

ly, as she was responsible for the hiring of complex staff and for a successful inauguration. Carol had gone quite a long way from the beginnings in Ohio. But, there was still more to come. In 1991, Carol was again approached by an executive recruiter, who offered to move her to San Diego's new convention center. Carol's performance at the San Diego Convention Center has been very successful, thus continuing her outstanding career journey.

Carol's day is mainly taken up with meetings, such as the following:

➤ Meetings with staff deal with the renovation of the concourse and civic theater, which are both run by the convention center.

➤ Meetings with the food service operations staff: the concourse outlets are run by the center.

➤ Meetings with City Hall, necessary for the planning and preparation of the Republican National Convention

➤ Meetings with the architects on the center's expansion

➤ Meetings with meeting planners who are considering San Diego as a site for their clients' events

Carol also has to travel in order to represent the center and the city at the major meeting planners conventions. Carol's philosophy is that a job is not a mere 8 to 5 routine: "If the job is not done, then stay until it is." Her focus is not, "I'm doing this because I want to be successful"—success will come as a result of doing excellent work. A story illustrating this happened back in Dallas one Saturday—a day that Carol was not usually in the office. Just as Carol was about to leave, she got a call from a man, whose flight had been delayed three hours, requesting a tour of the center. After giving the man a comprehensive tour, her boss received a call on Monday morning from the same man. Apparently, he was the big decision maker for a major convention that they had been trying to book for months. Yes, you guessed, Carol had impressed him so much be booked the convention.

The major players in the convention industry are convention and visitors' bureau (CVBs) meeting planners and their clients, the convention centers, specialized services, and exhibitions. The wheel diagram in Figure 11–4 shows the

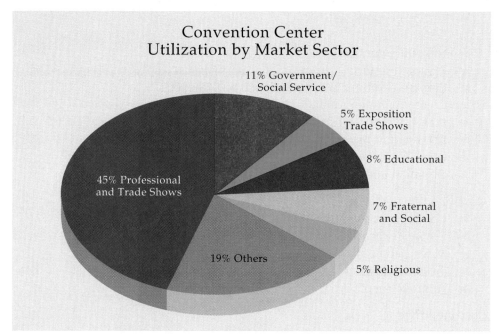

Figure 11–4 *Major Players in the Convention Industry*

number of different people and organizations involved with meetings, conventions and expositions.

Meeting Planners

Meeting planners may be independent contractors who contract out their services to both associations and corporations as the need arises or they may be full-time employees of corporations or associations. In either case, meeting planners have interesting careers. According to the International Convention Management Association (ICMA), about 212,000 full- and part-time meeting planners work in the United States.

The professional meeting planner not only makes hotel and meeting bookings but also plans the meeting down to the last minute, always remembering to check to ensure that the services contracted for have been delivered. In recent years, the technical aspects of audiovisual and simultaneous translation equipment have added to the complexity of meeting planning.

The meeting planner's role varies from meeting to meeting, but may include some or all of the following activities:[6]

Premeeting Activities
➤ Plan meeting agenda
➤ Establish meeting objectives
➤ Predict attendance
➤ Set meeting budget
➤ Select meeting site

➤ Select meeting facility
➤ Select hotel(s)
➤ Negotiate contracts
➤ Plan exhibition
➤ Prepare exhibitor correspondence and packet
➤ Create marketing plan
➤ Plan travel to and from site
➤ Arrange ground transportation
➤ Organize shipping
➤ Organize audiovisual needs

On-site activities
➤ Conduct pre-event briefing
➤ Prepare executive plan
➤ Move people in/out
➤ Troubleshoot
➤ Approve invoices

Post meetings
➤ Debrief
➤ Evaluate
➤ Provide recognition and appreciation
➤ Arrange shipping
➤ Plan for next year

Fortunately for most meeting planners, once they have taken care of a meeting one year, subsequent years typically are very similar.

Meeting Planner at Site Inspection

Convention centers and hotels provide the meeting space and accommodations as well as the food and beverage facilities and service. The convention center and a hotel team from each hotel capable of handling the meeting will attempt to wow the meeting planner. The hotel sales executive will send particulars of the hotel's meeting space and a selection of banquet menus and invite the meeting planner for a site inspection. During the site inspection, the meeting planner is shown all facets of the hotel, including the meeting rooms, guest-sleeping rooms, the food and beverage outlets, and any special facility that may interest the planner or the client.

Convention and Visitors Bureaus (CVB)

Convention and visitors bureaus (CVBs) are a major player in the meetings conventions and expositions market. The International Association of Conventions and Visitors Bureaus (IACVB) describes a CVB as a not-for-profit umbrella organization that represents an urban area that tries to solicit business- or pleasure-seeking visitors.

The convention and visitors bureau comprises a number of visitor industry organizations representing the various industry sectors:

➤ Transportation
➤ Hotels and motels
➤ Restaurants
➤ Attractions
➤ Suppliers

The bureau represents these local businesses by acting as the sales team for the city. A bureau has four primary responsibilities:

1. To encourage groups to hold meetings, conventions, and trade shows in the area it represents
2. To assist those groups with meeting preparations and to lend support throughout the meeting
3. To encourage tourists to visit the historic, cultural, and recreational opportunities the city or area has to offer
4. To develop and promote the image of the community it represents[7]

The outcome of these four responsibilities is for the cities' tourist industry to increase revenues. Bureaus compete for business at trade shows, where interested visitor industry groups gather to do business. For example, a tour wholesaler who is promoting a tour will need to link up with hotels, restaurants, and attractions in order to package a vacation. Similarly, meeting planners are able to consider sev-

Figure 11–5 *Average Expenditure per Delegate per Stay* (Reprinted with permission from *Hotel and Motel Management*, *209*, 3, February 22, 1994, p. 6. Copyright by Advanstar Communications, Inc.)

eral locations and hotels by visiting a trade show. Bureaus generate leads (prospective clients) from a variety of sources. One source, associations, have national/international offices in major cities like Washington, D.C. (so that they can lobby the government), New York, Chicago, and San Francisco.

A number of bureaus have offices or representatives in these cities or a sales team who will make follow up visits to the leads generated at trade shows. Alternatively, they will make cold calls on potential prospects such as major associations, corporations, and incentive houses. The sales manager will invite the meeting, convention, or exposition organizer to make a familiarization (FAM) trip to do a site inspection. The bureau assesses the needs of the client and organizes transportation, hotel accommodations, restaurants, and attractions accordingly. The bureau will then let the individual properties and other organizations make their own proposals to the client. Figure 11–5 shows the average expenditure per delegate per stay by the convention type; Figure 11–6

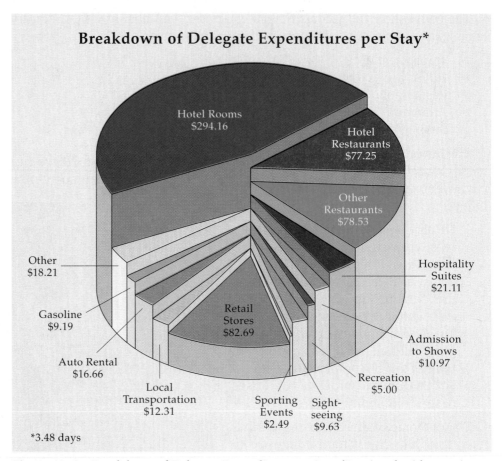

Figure 11–6 *Breakdown of Delegate Expenditure per Stay* (Reprinted with permission from *Hotel and Motel Management*, 209, 3, February 22, 1994, p. 6. Copyright by Advanstar Communications, Inc.)

shows the breakdown of delegate expenditures per stay; and Figure 11–7 indicates the percentage of each item of expenditure.

Convention Centers

Convention centers are huge facilities where meetings and expositions are held. Parking, information services, business centers, and food and beverage facilities are all included in the centers.

Usually convention centers are corporations owned by county, city, or state governments and operated by a board of appointed representatives from the various groups having a vested interest in the successful operation of the center. The board appoints a president or general manager to run the center according to a predetermined mission, goals, and objectives.

Convention centers have a variety of exposition and meeting rooms to accommodate both large and small events. The centers generate revenue from the rental of space, which frequently is divided into booths (one booth is about 100 feet square). Large exhibits may take several booths' space. Additional revenue

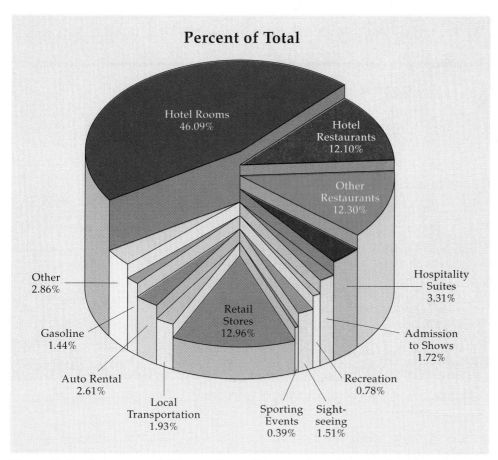

Percent of Total

Hotel Rooms
46.09%

Hotel
Restaurants
12.10%

Other
Restaurants
12.30%

Hospitality
Suites
3.31%

Other
2.86%

Retail
Stores
12.96%

Gasoline
1.44%

Admission
to Shows
1.72%

Auto Rental
2.61%

Recreation
0.78%

Local
Transportation
1.93%

Sporting
Events
0.39%

Sight-
seeing
1.51%

Figure 11–7 *Percentage of Delegate Expenditure per Item* (Reprinted with permission from *Hotel and Motel Management, 209,* 3, February 22, 1994, p. 6. Copyright by Advanstar Communications, Inc.)

is generated by the sale of food and beverages, concession stand rentals, and vending machines. Many centers also have their own subcontractors to handle staging, construction, lighting, audiovisual, electrical, and communications.

In addition to the megaconvention centers, a number of prominent centers also contribute to the local, state, and national economies. One good example is the Rhode Island Convention Center. The $82 million center, representing the second largest public works project in the state's history, is located in the heart of downtown Providence, adjacent to the 14,500-seat Providence Civic Center. The 365,000-square foot center offers a 100,000-square-foot main exhibit hall, a 20,000-square-foot ballroom, eighteen meeting rooms, and a full-service kitchen that can produce five thousand meals per day. The exhibit hall divides into four separate halls, and the facility

Jacob K. Javits Convention Center in New York City

Providence Convention Center (Courtesy Providence R. I. Convention Center.)

features its own telephone system, allowing individualized billing. A special rotunda function room at the fore of the building features glass walls that offer a panoramic view of downtown Providence for receptions of up to 365 people. Extensive use of glass on the facade of the center provides ample natural light throughout the entrance and prefunction areas.

A convention center can draw millions of new dollars into the economy of the city in which it is located. Figure 11–8 shows the average center income from delegate spending at conventions, trade shows, and congresses held at north American gateway cities, north American national/regional cities, European gateway cities, European national cities, and other cities.

Event Management

The larger convention center events are planned years in advance. As stated earlier, the convention and visitors bureau is usually

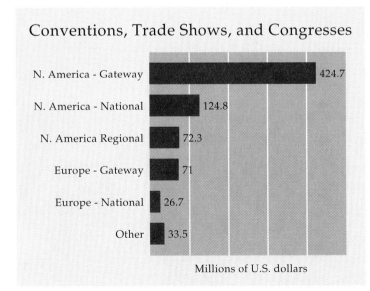

Figure 11–8 *Average Convention Center Income from Delegate Spending* (Courtesy of San Diego Convention Center.)

Corporate Profile:

Las Vegas Convention and Visitors Authority (LVCVA)

The LVCVA is one of the top convention and visitors bureaus, charged with the following mission: "To attract to the Las Vegas area a steadily increasing number of visitors to support the hotel and motel room inventory in Clark County."[1]

In the 1994 financial year, the Las Vegas Convention and Visitors Authority hosted over 290 convention attended by over one million delegates. The LVCVA is organized in the following way: State law establishes the number, appointment, and terms of the authority's board of directors. A twelve-member board provides guidance and establishes policies to accomplish the LVCVA mission.

Seven members are elected officials of the county, and each represents one of the incorporated cities therein; the remaining five members are nominated by the Las Vegas Chamber of Commerce and represent different segments of the industry. The board is one of the most successful public/private partnerships in the country. Under the presidency of Manuel J. Cortez, the Las Vegas Convention and Visitors Authority and its board of directors have received numerous awards, among them the following:

Organizational Chart, Las Vegas Convention and Visitors Authority
(Courtesy of The Las Vegas Convention and Visitors Authority)

World Travel Awards
- ➤ World's Leading Tourist and Convention Board
- ➤ World's Leading Conference and Convention Center
- ➤ World's Leading Gaming Destination
- ➤ Top North American Tourist and Convention Board

The Las Vegas Convention and Visitor's Authority's organizational structure is shown above. The board of directors employs a president (executive) to serve as chief executive officer. Other members of the executive staff are: vice president marketing, vice president operations, and vice president facilities. The marketing division's first priority is to increase visitors to Las Vegas and southern Nevada. The division is composed of eight teams that specialize in various market segments to increase visitors and convention attendance. The teams are also shown above.

The marketing services team is responsible for providing visitor services including research, registration, convention housing, hotel/motel reservations, and visitor information. The research team tracks the dynamics of the Las Vegas and Clark County tourism marketplace, along with the competitive gaming and tourism environment. The registration department coordinates and pro-

[1] Las Vegas Convention and Visitors Authority

vides temporary help for conventions and trade shows being held in Las Vegas. The housing division receives and processes hotel and motel housing forms from convention and trade show delegates, forwarding the reservations to participating hotels daily. The reservations department operates toll-free telephone lines, transferring the calls of travel agents, tourists, conventioneers, and special event attendees to hotels and motels within a requested location and price range.

Five visitor centers operate in Jean, Boulder City, Mesquite, Laughlin, and Las Vegas seven days a week and serve more than thirty-eight thousand visitors a month. A brochure room supports the visitor centers by answering thousands of telephone calls and letters requesting a variety of information on Las Vegas including recreation, weddings, entertainment, and special events. The staff sends out posters, brochures and other information.

The convention sales team coordinates convention sales efforts at the Authority, as well as contributes to the success of convention sales citywide by providing sales leads to the hotels. Sales managers travel throughout the United States and the world, meeting with association meeting planners selling the benefits of holding conventions in Las Vegas. Members of the team also attend numerous convention and trade shows where they host or sponsor special events and functions to entice conventions and trade shows to Las Vegas.

With a market share of 88 percent of leisure travelers visiting Las Vegas, travel promotion is vital to the LVCVA. The tour and travel team is responsible for positioning Las Vegas as a complete and affordable destination, and the preeminent gaming and entertainment capital in the world. Because 39 percent of all leisure travelers use a travel agent, the tour and travel team aggressively markets Las Vegas with travel agents.

Familiarization trips for travel agents are conducted by team members to generate enthusiasm and excitement around Las Vegas bookings. Travel agent presentations are also scheduled in both primary and selected secondary airline market cities. To generate excitement with travel agents, familiarization trips, travel agent presentations, and promotions are also scheduled for Laughlin. Additionally, a Laughlin 1-800 number is advertised for tourism information.

The corporate and incentive markets are traditionally considered the high end of the travel industry. These buyers are extremely sophisticated and value conscious, and are looking for the highest quality facilities and amenities. Corporate and Incentive team members increase the use of Las Vegas as a corporate meeting site and as a destination for the incentive marketplace. Team members attend various trade shows throughout the United States and Canada as well as selected cities in Europe and Asia, promoting Las Vegas as a complete, value-oriented, flexible, and accessible resort destination for corporate meetings.

With increases in visitation from almost every country, the LVCVA's international team is charged with maintaining a high profile in the international marketplace, positioning Las Vegas and southern Nevada as the preferred destination, and the gateway to the West. Team members travel throughout the world from the Pacific Rim countries of Japan, Korea, and Taiwan to the European countries of Germany, Switzerland, France, and Austria, as well as Canada and South America. Team sales executives provide information, brochures, and sales material in foreign languages emphasizing Las Vegas as a world-class, full-service resort destination.

The team also serves on an air service task force through McCarran International Airport, and provides a steady flow of current information to key airline executives seeking support for nonstop service to Las Vegas when considering new destinations. In November 1994, the LVCVA, in partnership with McCarran International Airport, welcomed the first regularly scheduled international nonstop flight to Las Vegas. Condor Airlines' inaugural flight from Cologne, Germany, to Las Vegas is an example of the work of the joint air service task force.

Since 1992, wholesale travel is one of the fastest-growing segments of the Las Vegas tourism market. During the past three years, the wholesale market has increased over 75 percent, and the wholesaler team positions Las Vegas as a destination without limits for the variety of packages and activities that can be arranged. To provide education on the variety of activities offered by Las Vegas, the wholesaler team plans and implements several annual familiarization tours for wholesalers.

Annual Special Events
➤ Las Vegas Senior Classic
➤ Las Vegas Invitational
➤ National Finals Rodeo
➤ Big League Weekend
➤ Las Vegas Bowl
➤ Laughlin River Days
➤ Laughlin River Flight
➤ Laughlin Rodeo Days

In recent years, special event planners have also showed increased interest in Las Vegas and Laughlin as event destinations. Team members travel to several special event trade shows and conferences to maximize the opportunities for special events to be held in Las Vegas. The team works in cooperation with Las Vegas Events and the Laughlin Marketing Partners to aggressively pursue events that provide television exposure and draw large numbers of participants, spectators, and visitors.

Las Vegas Territory Matching Grant Funds

The Las Vegas Territory grants program provides funding for the advertising and promotion of special events in rural Clark County to attract visitors to the outlying areas. These events create a more enhanced vacation experience and provide a variety of additional activities for the Las Vegas visitor. Some examples are Boulder City Art in the Park, Henderson Industrial Days, Mesquite Arts Festival, NLV Parade of Many Cultures, and Mt. Charleston Festival in the Pines.

Travelers responded to the new advertising theme— "A World of Excitement in One Amazing Place"—and the Las Vegas tourism and convention business continues to flourish despite a slow-growing domestic travel demand and increased competition last year. Although many destinations report flat visitor volume, Las Vegas is experiencing double-digit increases.

The advertising team is responsible for developing the general marketing strategy that provides a blueprint for the development of specific marketing initiatives, advertisements, and public relations efforts. These strategies are incorporated into each division of the marketing department.

During fiscal year 1993, the Las Vegas News Bureau became a part of the LVCVA. The news bureau provides information about Las Vegas and southern Nevada through direct contact with national and international free-lance journalists and working members of print and broadcast media. The bureau also maintains a complete photographic collection of Las Vegas, depicting the resort

```
                        /Finance
                        /Security
OPERATIONS ——  Materials Management
                        /Information Technology
                        /Community Service and Involvement
```

Activities within Operations Department

and entertainment growth of the area over a period of almost fifty years.

The operations department provides administrative support services to the marketing and facilities divisions, as well as security for the entire authority. Activities within operations are shown above.

Finance

The finance division maintains a general accounting system for the authority to ensure accountability in compliance with legal provisions and in accordance with generally accepted accounting principles. Finance is composed of financial services, accounting, and payroll activities. Additional responsibilities include the preparation of the authority's annual financial report (CAFR) and the annual budget. The CAFR has received the Government Finance Officers Association (GFOA) Excellence in Financial Reporting Award from 1985 through 1994. The budget has also been honored by GFOA, receiving the Distinguished Budget Presentation award from 1990 through 1994.

Materials Management

Materials management supports the marketing, operations, and facilities divisions by providing for purchasing of materials, services, and goods needed to meet its goals and objectives. Materials management is responsible for the storage and distribution of various supply items through an extensive warehousing program, as well as through printing and mail distribution.

Security

The security division provides protection of authority property, equipment, employees, and convention attendees twenty-four hours a day, 365 days a year, and also oversees paid parking and fire safety functions. The team patrols both the convention center and Cashman Field properties, and is trained in first aid assistance. Several officers have been recognized by the authority board and convention organizations for providing life-saving measures to convention attendees.

Information Technology

The information technology division (ITD) is responsible for efficiently and effectively meeting the automation and information needs of the authority. ITD sustains a staff of technically competent professionals to design, maintain, implement, and operate the systems necessary to support the goals of the authority.

Rental Waiver Program

The LVCVA successfully runs an annual rental waiver program that provides $100,000 in grant money for in-kind use of Cashman Field facilities and equipment. Dozens of legitimate registered Nevada nonprofit groups use the facility each year, transforming Cashman Field into a virtual civic center.

The LVCVA's research division tracks trends and statistics that

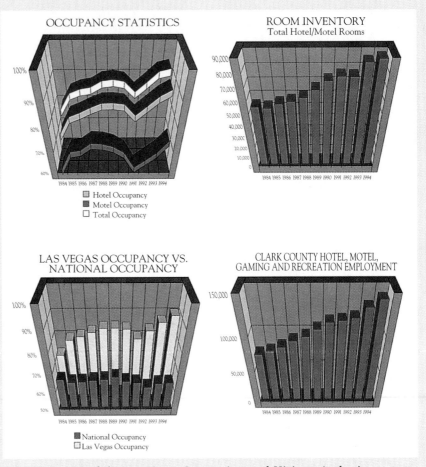

Success Factors of the Las Vegas Convention and Visitors Authority
(Courtesy of The Las Vegas Convention and Visitors Authority)

responsible for the booking of conventions beyond eighteen months ahead. Obviously, both the convention and visitors bureau and the convention center marketing and sales teams work closely together. Once the booking becomes definite, the senior event manager assigns an event manager to work with the client throughout the sequence of pre-event, event, and postevent.

The booking manager is critical to the success of the event by booking the correct space and working with the organizers to help them save money by allocating only the space really needed and allowing the client to begin setting up on time. A contract is written up based on the event profile. The event profile stipulates in writing all of the client's requirements and will give relevant information (such as which company will act as decorator subcontractor to install carpets and set up the booths).

give an accurate picture of the tremendous growth in

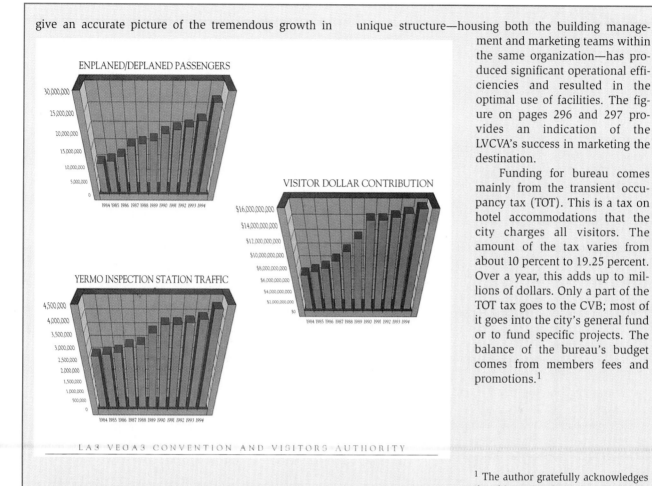

LAS VEGAS CONVENTION AND VISITORS AUTHORITY

southern Nevada from 1984 through 1994. The LVCVA's

unique structure—housing both the building management and marketing teams within the same organization—has produced significant operational efficiencies and resulted in the optimal use of facilities. The figure on pages 296 and 297 provides an indication of the LVCVA's success in marketing the destination.

Funding for bureau comes mainly from the transient occupancy tax (TOT). This is a tax on hotel accommodations that the city charges all visitors. The amount of the tax varies from about 10 percent to 19.25 percent. Over a year, this adds up to millions of dollars. Only a part of the TOT tax goes to the CVB; most of it goes into the city's general fund or to fund specific projects. The balance of the bureau's budget comes from members fees and promotions.[1]

[1] The author gratefully acknowledges that this section draws on information given by the Las Vegas Convention and Visitors Authority.

The contract requires careful preparation because it is a legal document and will guarantee certain provisions. For example, the contract may specify that the booths may only be cleaned by center personnel or that food may be prepared for samples only, not for retail. After the contract has been signed and returned by the client, the event manager will from time to time make follow-up calls until about six months from the event when arrangements such as security, business services, and catering will be finalized.

The event manager is the key contact between the center and the client. She or he will help the client by introducing approved subcontractors who are able to provide essential services. Figure 11–9 shows a job description for an event manager.

SAN DIEGO CONVENTION CENTER

EVENT MANAGER

DEFINITION

Under moderate direction from the services manager, plans, directs, and supervises assigned events and represents services manager on assigned shifts.

KEY RESPONSIBILITIES

- Plans, coordinates, and supervises all phases of the events to include set ups, move ins and outs, and the activities themselves
- Prepares and disseminates set-up information to the proper departments well in advance of the activity, and ensures complete readiness of the facilities
- Responsible for arranging for all services needed by the tenant
- Coordinates facility staffing needs with appropriate departments
- Acts as a consultant to tenants and the liaison between in-house contractors and tenants
- Preserves facility's physical plant and ensures a safe environment by reviewing tenants plans; requests and makes certain they comply with facility, state, county, and city rules and regulations
- Prepares accounting paperwork of tenant charges, approves final billings, and assists with collection of same
- Resolves complaints, including operational problems and difficulties
- Assists in conducting surveys, gathering statistical information, and working on special projects as assigned by services manager
- Conducts tours of the facilities.

MINIMUM REQUIREMENTS

- Bachelor's degree in hospitality management, business, or recreational management from a fully accredited university or college, plus two (2) years of experience in coordinating major conventions and trade shows
- Combination of related education/training and additional experience may substitute for bachelor's degree
- An excellent ability to manage both fiscal and human resources
- Knowledge in public relations; oral and written communications
- Experienced with audiovisual equipment

225 Broadway, Suite 710 • San Diego, CA 92102 • (619) 239-1989
FAX (619) 239-2030
Operated by the San Diego Convention Center Corporation

Figure 11–9 *Job Description for an Event Manager* (Courtesy of San Diego Convention Center.)

EVENT DOCUMENT
REVISED COPY
/6/SAN DIEGO INTERNATIONAL BOAT SHOW
Monday, January 2, 1995 – Monday, January 9, 1995

SPACE: Combined Exhibit Halls AB, Hall A - How Manager's Office, Box Office by Hall A, Hall B –
Show Manager's Office, Mezzanine Room 12, Mezzanine Room 13, Mezzanine Rooms 14 A&B, AND
Mezzanine Rooms 15 A&B

CONTACT: Mr. Jeff Hancock
National Marine Manufacturers Association, Inc.
4901 Morena Blvd.
Suite 901
San Diego, CA 92117
Telephone Number: (619) 274-9924
Fax Number: (619) 274-6760
Decorator Co.:   Greyhound Exposition Services
Sales Person: Denise Simenstad
Event Manager: Jane Krause
Event Tech.:   Sylvia A. Harrison

SCHEDULE OF EVENTS:

Monday, January 2, 1995
  5:00 am – 6:00 pm   Combined Exhibit Halls AB
                            Service contractor move in GES,
                            Andy Quintena

Tuesday, January 3, 1995
  8:00 am – 6:00 pm   Combined Exhibit Halls AB
                            Service contractor move in GES,
                            Andy Quintena

 12:00 pm – 6:00 pm   Combined Exhibit Halls AB
                            Exhibitor move in

Wednesday, January 4, 1995
  8:00 am – 6:00 pm   Combined Exhibit Halls AB
                            Exhibitor move in
                            Est. attendance: 300

Thursday, January 5, 1995
  8:00 am – 12:00 pm   Combined Exhibit Halls AB
                            Exhibitor final move in

 11:30 am – 8:30 pm   Box Office by Hall A
                            OPEN: Ticket prices, Adults $6, Children 12 & under $

Figure 11–10   *Event Document, International Boat Show* (Courtesy of the San Diego Convention Center.)

Two weeks prior to the event an event document is distributed to department heads. The event document has all the detailed information that each
department needs to know in order for the event to run smoothly. About ten

days ahead, a WAG meeting (week at a glance) is held. The WAG meeting is one of the most important meetings at the convention center because it provides an opportunity to avoid problems—like two event groups arriving at the same time or additional security for concerts or politicians. About this same time a preconvention or pre-expo meeting is held with expo managers and their contractors—shuttle bus managers, registration operators, exhibit floor managers, and so on.

Once the set up begins, service contractors marshall the eighteen-wheeler trucks to unload the exhibits by using radio phones to call the trucks from a nearby depot. Once the exhibits are in place, the exposition opens and the public is admitted. Figure 11–10 shows an event document for the Sixth International Boat Show at the San Diego Convention Center. It gives information regarding the exact amount of space allocated, the contact person, and the schedule of events.

Specialized Services

A number of companies offer specialized services such as transportation, entertainment, audiovisual, escorts and tour guides, convention set up, and destination management.

Summary

1. Conventions, meetings, and expositions serve social, political, sporting, or religious purposes. Associations offer benefits such as a politic voice, education, marketing avenues, member services, and networking.
2. Meetings are events designed to bring people together for the purpose of exchanging information. Typical forms of meetings are conferences, workshops, seminars, forums, and symposiums.
3. Expositions serve the purpose of bringing together purveyors of products, equipment, and services in an environment in which they can demonstrate their products. Conventions are meetings that include some form of exposition or trade show.
4. Meeting planners contract out their services to associations and corporations. Their responsibilities include pre-meeting, on-site, and post-meeting activities.
5. The convention and visitors bureaus are non-profit organizations that assess the needs of the client and organize transportation, hotel accommodations, restaurants, and attractions.
6. Conventions centers are huge facilities, usually owned by the government, where meetings and expositions are held. Events at convention centers require a lot of planning ahead and careful event management. A contract based on the event profile and an event document are parts of effective management.

Key Words and Concepts

Associations
Boardroom style
Classroom style
Clinic
Convention

Convention centers
Convention and visitors bureaus
Exposition
Familiarization trip

Forum
Incentive market
Meeting
Meeting planner
Seminar

Site inspection
Symposium
Theater style
Trade show
Workshop

Review Exercises

1. What are associations and what is their purpose?
2. Explain the term SMERF.
3. Describe the main types of meeting set ups.
4. What is a workshop and a seminar?
5. Explain the difference between an exposition and a convention.

6. What is a convention center?
7. List the duties of CVBs.
8. Conventions require careful planning. Explain the purpose of an event profile and an event document.

Notes

[1] John Hogan, *Lodging*, December 1993.

[2] From Deloitte and Touche, Convention Liaison Council, as quoted in *USA Today*, April 5, 1994.

[3] Rhonda J. Montgomery and Sandra K. Strick, *Meetings, Conventions, and Expositions: An Introduction to the Industry*. New York: Van Nostrand Reinhold, 1995, p. 13.

[4] Wendy Tanaka, "Convention Attendees Spend More," *San Francisco Examiner*, August 28, 1994, p. B2.

[5] Deny G. Rutherford, *Introduction to the Conventions, Expositions, and Meeting Industry*. New York: Van Nostrand Reinhold, 1990, p. 44.

[6] Montgomery and Strick, op. cit., pp. 171–172.

[7] Montgomery and Strick, op. cit., p. 19.

Marketing, Human Resources, and Culture

After reading and studying this chapter you should be able to do the following:

➤ Discuss the importance of environmental scanning as it relates to marketing and sales

➤ List and explain each of the steps in the marketing process

➤ Show how a competitor analysis is conducted

➤ Explain the term *product life cycle*

➤ State the difference between marketing and sales

➤ List and explain the steps in human resources management and development process

➤ Describe culture and ethnic diversity

$\mathcal{E}$ach segment of the hospitality industry uses the services of the marketing, sales, and human resources departments.

Marketing

Marketing and sales are critically important to the success of hospitality organizations. Without guests, there is no need for front line employees or anyone else for that matter! Marketing is all about finding out what guests' wants and needs are and providing them at a reasonable cost and profit.

Marketing begins with a corporate philosophy and a mission. But, the philosophy and mission should not just hang on an office wall; it should be practiced every day by everyone. Peter Drucker, highly respected management guru, says that the only valid definition of business purpose is to create customers. In the hospitality industry, we would quickly add "and keep them coming back." Creating a customer means finding a product or service that a number of people want or need. When Kemmons Wilson began Holiday Inns, he was successful because he fulfilled a need that many families and business people had: a quality lodging experience at a value. Ray Kroc is another example of giving the American public what they wanted. Through McDonald's quick-service restaurants, he met the need for food on the run.

Alastair Morrison identifies eleven characteristics of marketing or customer orientation.[1]

1. Customer needs are the first priority.
   ➤ Answering customer needs produces more satisfied customers.
   ➤ All departments, managers, and staff share a common goal.
2. Understanding customers and their needs is a constant concern and research activity.
   ➤ Knowing customers and their needs increases the ability to satisfy these needs.
3. Marketing research is an ongoing activity that should be assigned a very high priority.
   ➤ Changes in customer needs and characteristics are identified.
   ➤ Viability of new services and products are determined.
4. Frequent reviews are made of strengths and weaknesses relative to competitors.
   ➤ Strengths are accentuated and weaknesses addressed.
5. The value of long-term planning is fully appreciated.
   ➤ Changes in customer needs are anticipated and acted on; marketing opportunities are realized.

6. Customers' perceptions of the organization are known.
   ➤ Services, products, and promotions are designed to match customers' image.
7. Interdepartmental cooperation is valued and encouraged.
   ➤ Increased cooperation leads to better services and greater customer satisfaction.
8. Cooperation with complementary organizations is recognized as worthwhile.
   ➤ Increased cooperation generates greater customer satisfaction.
9. Change is seen as inevitable and not as being unnecessary.
   ➤ Adaptations to change are made smoothly and are not resisted.
10. The scope of business or activities is broadly set.
    ➤ Opportunities that serve customers more comprehensively, or those that tap into related fields, are capitalized upon.
11. Measurement and evaluation of marketing activities is frequent.
    ➤ Effective marketing programs or tactics are repeated or enhanced; ineffective ones are dropped.
    ➤ Marketing expenditures and human resources are used effectively.

Large corporations, and small independent hospitality operators both go through similar decision-making processes to seek out new market opportunities and to increase market share in existing markets.

Environmental Analysis

Before the first decisions about marketing can be made, it is advisable to gain background information on topics such as environmental analysis. Environmental analysis means studying the economic, social, political, and technological influences that could affect the hospitality business. Figure 12–1 illustrates the environmental scanning process.

Economic Impacts

The economy can affect hospitality corporations in a macro way (the big picture) or in a micro way (the local picture). In a macro sense, interest rates affect the cost of borrowing money, and exchange rates affect the number of tourists visiting specific destinations. Some economists suggest that the economy goes through cycles. We can all agree that the mid-1980s seemed like boom times compared to the recession of the early 1990s. As a result, people today are more value conscious, which is why the economy segment of the lodging industry has grown in recent years.

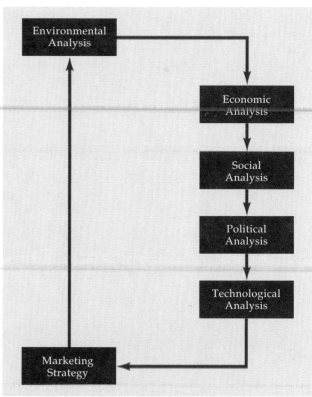

Figure 12–1 *The Environmental Analysis Process*

The importance of environmental analysis should not be underestimated. The knack of being at the right place at the right time may be luck for some, but it is a carefully calculated move for others. There are many good examples of hospitality leaders who saw the environment changing and with it the wants, needs, and expectations of guests: Ray Kroc, with quick-service restaurants; Richard Melman, with table dining; Robert Hazard, with hotels; and Herb Kelleher, with the airline business, were all trail blazers with one thing in common—the ability to scan the environment and be leaders in the path of progress by developing products and services that anticipated and provided for peoples' wants and needs.

To many who come across a good idea, it may seem like common sense to exploit an opportunity. Still, many corporations are struggling today because they have not done a good environmental scan.

Social Analysis

A survey of our social landscape reveals that life-styles in the 1990s are more hectic. With more two-income families, additional stresses are placed on those families who must juggle parenting and work. Higher divorce rates have led to more single-parent families and increased female careerism. A greater emphasis on fitness and wellness has led to more of a grazing approach to eating. Food service trends are definitely toward healthier eating. In this and other sectors of the hospitality industry, customers have become more knowledgeable and, as a consequence, have higher expectations; these higher expectations, coupled with a quest for value, add up to ever-changing scenarios for hospitality operators.

Demographics are a part of social analysis. Demographics are a profile of society in a given area and include age, sex, household and per capita income, family size, occupation, education, religion, race/ethnicity, and national origin. Demographic information is used by marketing specialists to identify groups of people with similar characteristics and problems for which the marketers may develop a solution.

We all know that people living in the more expensive areas are more likely to go on a cruise than those in the low-income neighborhoods. Cruise lines therefore know to whom to send promotional materials and which television and radio programs are popular with the various target markets. A target market, just as it sounds, is a market that is targeted for the product or service that a company is planning to offer or already offers.

In general, consumers in the 1990s have developed a taste for instant gratification. People are taking more vacations, but shorter ones, to destinations that are closer to home. Life-styles have become more casual; hence, the increase in casual-theme restaurants. As a nation, approximately 30 percent of our food dollar is eaten away from home.

Political Analysis

Both federal and state legislators and judiciary affect the hospitality industry in a number of ways: employment legislation, minimum wage, health care, taxes on benefit packages, the tax deduction of business meals dropping to 50 percent from 80 percent, and city-wide no-smoking ordinances. Much may also depend on the political party in control.

Technological Analysis

Given that labor is the single highest cost in hospitality business, any technology that leads to greater efficiency is worth investigating. In all sectors of the industry, technological advances are benefiting guests and businesses alike. Consider how much more safe a guest feels with an electromagnetic room door opener than a key. The key was easy to duplicate, but the plastic card becomes invalid as soon as the guest checks out. In restaurants, hand-held remote ordering devices have helped speed up service to guests from both the bar and kitchen. Computers are now able to store hundreds of menus

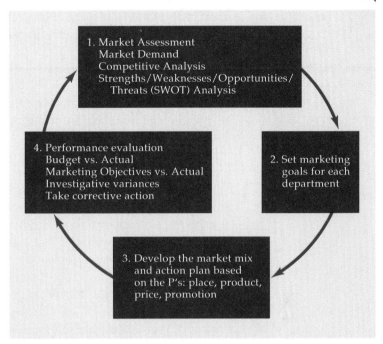

Figure 12–2 *Marketing Planning*

and, at the push of a button, convert the ingredients for a recipe for any number of guests. Some can even make out purchase orders as well.

The benefit of environmental scanning is to focus the attention of the top management prior to the formulations of the next steps in the marketing process, namely, the following:

- ➤ Marketing planning
- ➤ Market assessment
- ➤ Market demand
- ➤ Competitive analysis
- ➤ Positioning
- ➤ Marketing goals and objectives
- ➤ Marketing mix
- ➤ Action plan based on the P's (place, product, price, promotion)
- ➤ Performance evaluation
- ➤ Budget vs. actual
- ➤ Investigate variance
- ➤ Take corrective actions

Figure 12–2 illustrates the elements of marketing planning.

Market Assessment

Market assessment simply tries to determine if there is a need for a product or service in the market and to assess its potential. This is done by examining the existing market, its size, demographics, the key players, the customers' wants and needs, and general conditions and trends.

Market Demand

Market demand is not always so easy to quantify. However, by doing our best to gather all available information we can guesstimate the demand for a particular product or service.

Within the hospitality industry, there is obviously considerable variation among the different components: travel and tourism, lodging, food service, leisure, and recreation. To assess the market for Amtrak or a discount airline, it would be necessary to consider peoples' travel habits: Who are the potential users, how many are there, and where are they located?

For a lodging company that might want to determine the number of female business travelers, information is available from organizations like the American Hotel and Motel Association or consultants and research organizations such as Pannel Kerr Forster. Some surveys have indicated that approximately 40 percent of all business travel is by females. Therefore, we can deduce that if there are ten thousand hotel rooms in a city center and that they were on average 70 percent occupied with a 40 percent business versus conventions and family mix there would be:

10,000 x .7 x .4 = 2,800 women business travelers visiting that city

Competitor Analysis

Analyzing the competitions' strengths and weaknesses will help us determine which strategies to use in the marketing action plan. All hospitality businesses have competitors. The competition may be across the street or across the country or the world. Usually in the lodging, restaurants, and food service sectors, the competition is close; for example, most people going to New Orleans for Mardi Gras will stay at a hotel in the city. The question is which one. Similarly, guests selecting restaurants and food service establishments will usually choose one within a given radius of about ten miles—give or take a few miles. Therefore, most restaurants realize that their competition is either other restaurants of a similar nature or those within a similar price range; in some cases, such as quick-service restaurants, the competition may also convenience stores, or even take-out meals.

Competition may be farther away when it comes to destination vacation spots. A family living in St. Louis may want a winter vacation in Mexico, but may also consider the Caribbean or even Hawaii or Florida or Southern California.

For the purpose of comparison with competitors, marketers make a matrix of the important elements. In each case, the elements may be selected by the marketing person, owner/operators, and top management/department heads. Figure 12–3 shows a comparison matrix form. The appropriate elements are

		Competitors					
Benefit	Our Operation	1	2	3	4	5	6

Figure 12-3 *Comparison Matrix*

listed in the left-hand column under the heading of benefit. Then, our operation is compared with others using a 1–10 or 1–100 scoring system and/or written comments.

One of the benefits of a comparison matrix is that it helps to focus attention on where our operations are better or worse compared to the competition. Obviously, some elements are beyond owner's and management's control. For example, you cannot move a hotel or restaurant over a few blocks because you don't like its current location.

The elements that are controllable are those to be given the greatest attention; service and quality of food are good examples. Another benefit of a comparison matrix is to identify the market segments that we and the competition are best suited to serve. An example of this is Hyatt hotels and resorts introducing Camp Hyatt in order to attract families at a time when their usual business guests are not using the hotels much. By targeting regular Hyatt hotel business guests, Camp Hyatt has been successful in offering a benefit and a service to a specific target market.

Positioning

Positioning means to occupy a specific place in the market and project that position to the target market. In the process of doing the competitive analysis of the strengths and weakness of the competition, it usually becomes apparent which position a corporation or independent hospitality business should occupy and project. Some companies are deliberately adopting the new concept of positioning in several market segments. Marriott and Choice Hotels are good examples.

Because McDonald's is so strong in the children's market, Wendy's and Burger King position themselves as more adult quick-service burger restaurants. Motel 6 operations position themselves as the least expensive national chain where guests will receive a clean comfortable room for about $26. Positioning statements help get the message across to the target market (e.g., "What you want is what you get at McDonald's today!").

Marketing Goals and Objectives

Setting marketing goals gives a measure by which progress toward the goals can be monitored. Goals are set both for the total enterprise and each department. An example of a marketing goal for a hotel might be to increase weekend occupancy from 43.2 percent to 48.2 percent by a specified date. Another could be to increase the average daily rate from $76 to $80. Other goals target each market segment, such as corporate meetings and conventions, sport, leisure, and so on. Goals are set for each of the hospitality operations' units or departments. Campus food service managers would set sales goals for outside catering, satellite restaurants, tailgate parties, and so on.

Objectives are the how-to tactics used in order to meet or exceed the goals. Using the preceding examples, management would plan and organize specific activities that would result in a 5 percent increase in weekend occupancy. Objectives must be planned for each goal.

Marketing Mix

The *marketing mix* is the term used to focus on the pertinent Ps: place, product, price, promotion, partnership, packaging, programming, and people.

Place means the location, which is extremely important for hospitality businesses. The expression "In business, the three most important things are location, location, location!" stresses that importance. Hotels, motels, restaurants, tourist attractions, and destinations to a large extent either thrive or perish based on their location.

The only problem is that owners and managers must, if they have a prime location, produce the revenue to keep the mortgage or lease payments to a certain percentage of total sales. In a restaurant, for example, operators aim to keep mortgage or lease payments to about 6 to 8 percent of sales in order to allow an appropriate amount to cover other costs and produce a reasonable profit.

The *product* must suit the wants and needs of the target market. The product is positioned to meet those wants and needs as a result of the previous steps in the marketing process. Additionally, surveys and focus groups (small groups that are a representative sample of the target market) provide feedback on the extent to which the product meets their wants and needs.

A great example of ensuring that the product suits the needs of the target market was Marriott's development of Courtyard Inns, which they developed after extensive research on what their target market wanted. They constructed prototype rooms on which focus groups were invited to comment. This careful product development led to the launch of a very successful new type of lodging concept.

All products and services are at some stage in the product life cycle, just as humans go through the life cycle from birth/introduction, growth, maturity, and declining period. Figure 12–4 shows the stages in the product life cycle. An example of a product that was introduced a few years ago and had a very quick growth rate, an early maturity, and rapid decline was the disco. To a large extent, sports bars and coffee houses have taken over.

Price plays an important role in purchasing decisions, as we all know from experience. Most guests are price sensitive—as the old expression says, there is no loyalty that $.25 won't change. In other words, if the fast food restaurant across the street offers the same product for $.25 less, then (other things being equal) they will get the business.

Obviously, things like value are closely linked with price. People will only purchase a particular product or service if they perceive that it is a good value—hence the value-meal packs and real-meal deals. The closer price is to value, the more likely the guest will be satisfied and will return.

In recent years, pricing in the hospitality industry has had an interesting effect on consumer behavior. In the early 1980s, hospitality enterprises increased prices and found that

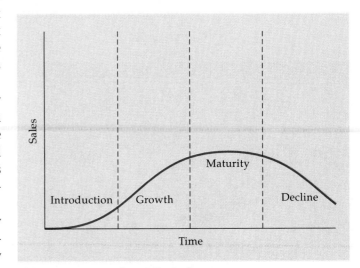

Figure 12–4 *Product Life Cycle*

guests kept on coming. Many businesses were liberal with expense accounts that enabled executives to stay in better hotels and entertain clients in expensive restaurants.

At that time these costs were all tax deductible. Then, in 1986, tax deductions of business expenses for restaurant meals were reduced to 80 percent (they subsequently were reduced to 50 percent). These measures, combined with the recession, had a profound effect on restaurants, especially upscale restaurants.

Quite naturally, business dropped off as guests who were spending money on dining traded down to the mid-priced restaurants, and mid-priced clientele moved into the quick-service segment. Quick-service restaurants flourished, and convenience stores and supermarkets began to put delicatessens into the stores.

Price also played a part in the surge of economy and mid-price hotels and motels that have come on line in recent years. Guests resisted paying more than what they considered to be a reasonable price for hotel accommodations. The fact that the luxury hotel market was overbuilt also helped.

Price may be determined in the main ways: the comparative approach and the cost-plus approach. The comparative approach assesses what other similar operations are charging for the same or similar service/product. The cost-plus approach means that all the costs are accounted for and a selling price is determined after an amount for profit is allocated. As you can likely already determine, both methods have advantages.

Performance Evaluation

Evaluating the actual operations against expected performance is ongoing and lets an organization see how well it has done compared with how well it said it would do. Providing performance feedback enables management to plan future marketing strategies. If expected and actual performance vary, then the discrepancy is examined and alternative strategies are developed. Having established the results and the reasons for any variances, the final step in the marketing process is to take the necessary corrective action to achieve the company's goals.

Director of Marketing and Sales Meeting

Sales

Sales is an important part of marketing. The difference between marketing and sales is that with marketing, the focus is on the guest. With sales the focus is on the product or service for sale.

More people have the title *sales manager* or *account executive* than *marketing director*. The sales department is responsible for making sales to guests in the target market. Sales can be to new accounts or existing ones. Each sales department is organized in a way that best suits the organization. Some companies have national—even international—sales offices in addition to unit sales depart-

Personal Profile: Carroll R. Armstrong

Marketing Director, San Diego Convention Center

Twenty-five years ago, Carroll Armstrong was well on his way to becoming a successful jazz musician when he changed careers. Since that time, his career has progressed to his present position of marketing director at the San Diego Convention Center. Carroll has been a force in the success in four major convention centers. A colleague describes Carroll as the number one convention center marketing professional in the country. However, his biggest challenge was opening the San Diego Convention Center.

In 1987, when Carroll arrived in San Diego, he looked at the existing convention centers. Carroll concluded that if San Diego was to be successful, the center must compete for business in several markets; in addition to the traditional convention center markets, two nontraditional convention center markets, incentive business and the corporate markets, were increasingly important. These additional market segments would help maximize the property and create additional revenue.

Carroll Armstrong

In the 1980s, many of the convention centers operated in an institutional mode. Because they were state or city owned, they were expected to lose money. The challenge of the San Diego Convention Center was that it could not open and operate in the same way as others did. The convention center would have to be more economically self-sufficient. The center would have to be the pump primer and operate like any other business.

The philosophy that Carroll created was that the center would operate like a fine hotel. Whereas many other centers contract out their food service and consequently have mediocre reputations, the San Diego Convention Center's catering has white-glove "Escoffier" food preparation and service. Carroll realized that the me-generation wants service with style, and, if they are getting value, they will pay the few extra costs.

The strategy of differentiating the center by service has been successful because the center has won the meeting planners' choice award from *Meeting News Magazine*. This recognizes that one of the major goals of the convention center is to run the center like a first-class hotel, so that delegates can walk from the hotels to the convention center without noticing any difference. To achieve this, the center has uniformed doorpersons and concierge-like guest-relations staff to answer questions and offer suggestions about everything from a meeting room location to city-wide entertainment. Additionally, guest-service guides stand near elevators to direct attendees to appropriate rooms.

Carroll is moving toward his ultimate goal of being able to choose which organizations can use the center by

ments. The sales team may then be split up according to the various target markets: association, corporate, catering, and so on, and by region—Northeast, Midwest, West, and so on. The sales team maintains account files with follow-up ticklers. It also prospects for new business by making cold calls on potential clients (usually by telephone) or in the form of a sales blitz, whereby the team will cover given areas of a city and pound the pavement. In a sales blitz, the team asks companies about their accommodations and restaurant needs and which hotels/restaurants they currently use; the team also obtains the names of the people responsible for booking hotels/restaurants so that they may be invited to the hotel for a personal tour (usually including lunch). During the tour, the sales account executive quantifies the demand and type of accommodations/meals required and the number of room nights per month/restaurant meals in order to be able to quote competitive rates.

Each member of the sales team has a quota of dollar sales to achieve. Therefore, sales professionals guard their clients very carefully. Making a sale and influencing the guest to become a repeat guest is vital in today's competitive marketplace. About 80 percent of a hotel's and some restaurants' business comes from about 20 percent of the guests.

Human Resources Management

It is precisely because the hospitality industry offers intangible services and products that human resources management is so critical to the success of the organization. One hotel restaurant or tourism enterprise is often much the same as the other; what makes the difference is service and professionalism.

As we already know, the hospitality industry is the largest in the world, employing some seventy million people. No other industry has as much frontline guest contact between employees and guests—especially entry-level employees. Employment ranges from entry-level positions to specialized positions, supervisory positions, and managerial/executive positions. Human resources is all about attracting, selecting, orienting, training, developing, and evaluating the performance of an organization's most important resources, the human ones.

In addition to these activities, several other functions are part of the human resources process, including job descriptions, job specifications, advertising, payroll and benefits, grievances, and ensuring conformance to federal and state or provincial legislation.

The complexity of human resources management and development in the hospitality industry is increased by the fact that many unskilled workers are employed for entry-level positions, often with little or no training. Also, there is enormous and increasing cultural diversity within the industry. Figure 12–5 shows the human resources management and development process.

Each segment of the hospitality industry follows the human resources functions. In this section, we will examine them sequentially. The business and economic conditions of recent years necessitated what has been called re-engineering, downsizing, or right-sizing.

Task Analysis

Because human resource or labor costs are the highest single cost of being in business, it has become necessary to examine each task of each employee to determine its outcome on the guest experience. A good example of analyzing a task from a guest's viewpoint is to start when a guest arrives at a hotel. Traditionally, one person acted as a greeter/door person and took the guest's luggage; that person gave the luggage to a bellperson, who in turn transport-

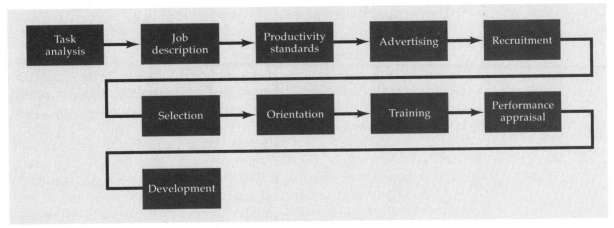

Figure 12–5 *Human Resources Management and Development Process*

ed it to the front desk. After the guest had registered, it was quite possible that another bellperson transported the guest's luggage to the assigned room. This not only involved the guest interacting with three or four different individuals, but it also annoyed the guest because of the amount of tipping involved.

Ordinarily, task and job analysis examines the tasks necessary to perform the job; when approved and listed, these tasks become the job description. An example is that the job description of a hotel door person would include greeting an arriving automobile, opening the passenger or driver door, welcoming the guests to the hotel, offering to remove the guests' luggage from the car, transporting it to the front desk (or holding it on the cart) while the guest registers, and then escorting the guest and transporting the luggage to the allocated room. Some innovative hotels have cross-trained their employees to the point that the person who greets guests outside the hotel actually rooms the guest by handling the check in, allocating the room, and then escorting the guests. This means that the guest only comes in contact with one or two employees; the program has been extremely well received by guests.

Job Description

A job description is a detailed description of the activities and outcomes expected of the person performing the job (see Figure 5-1, page 129). The job description is important because it can become a legal document. Some cases have come before the courts and administrative agencies in which an employee who was dismissed has sued the former employer, claiming that he or she did not know or were not properly informed of the duties required.

Today, many companies have employees sign their job descriptions to avoid any confusion or misunderstandings about their job and its responsibilities. The job description specifies the specific knowledge, qualifications, and skills necessary to do the job successfully. Job descriptions can be used as good performance measurement tools.

Productivity Standards

With today's high labor costs, increasing employee productivity has become a major issue. Productivity standards may be established for each position within the organization. Productivity standards are determined by measuring or timing how long it takes to do a given task. Departments then are staffed according to forecasted demand, be it restaurant covers, hotel occupancy, or attendance at a theme park.

Employee productivity is measured in dollar terms by dividing sales by labor costs. If sales totaled $46,325 and labor costs were $9,265, productivity would be measured as a factor of 5. This means that for every dollar in labor costs, $5 in sales was generated. Another way of expressing employee productivity is to divide sales by the number of employees to arrive at the sales generated per employee.

Other measures of productivity might be the number of covers served by a food service employee or the number of guest checked in by a front-desk agent.

Recruitment and Selection

Recruitment and selection is the process of finding the most suitable employee for the available position. The process begins with announcing the vacancy; sometimes this is done first within the organization, then outside. Applications are received from a variety of sources:

> ➤ Internal promotion
> ➤ Employee referrals
> ➤ Applicant files
> ➤ Transfers within the company
> ➤ Advertising
> ➤ Colleges and universities
> ➤ Government-sponsored employment services

Human Resources Manager Checking References

Application forms and resumes are accepted and screened by the human resources department. Many companies require applicants to come to the property and personally fill out the application form. The human resources department then reviews the application form and resumé for accuracy and to ensure that the prospective employee is legally entitled to work in the country. It is advisable to do extensive background checks, although most previous employers will, for legal reasons, generally only give the beginning and ending dates of employment. See Figure 12–6 for a description of the recruitment and selection process.

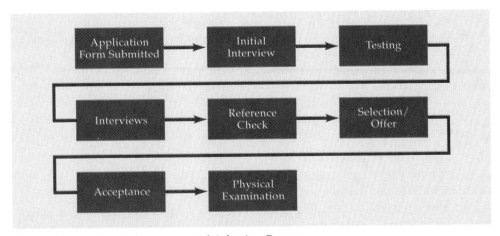

Figure 12–6 *The Recruitment and Selection Process*

Applicants are invited to attend an interview with the employment manager. This is a general screening interview to determine that the applicant is suitable for employment in a general way. Employment managers look for dress, mannerisms, attentiveness, attitude, and interest; they also ask questions that encourage the applicant to answer in some detail. This necessitates asking open-ended questions such as "What did you like most and least about your last job?" Questions like this invite the applicant to open up. The two-way exchange of information allows the prospective employee to ask or learn about the job and the corporation. Assuming the applicant makes a favorable impression, she or he will be invited for a second interview with the department head. The interview with the department head will assess the candidate's ability to do the job and his or her interpersonal suitability to join the department team.

Selection means to select the most suitably qualified candidate for the available position. Providing candidates meet the minimum requirements stated in the job specification, then the best individual may be selected from the qualified applicants. Part of the selection process might involve tests (personality, aptitude, skill, psychological) to ensure that candidates possess the requisite interpersonal skills or knowledge to do the job. In addition, some companies, as a condition of employment, require new employees to take a drug-screening test.

Assuming the reference and background checks are positive, a formal offer is made in writing to the prospective employee. The offer outlines the terms and conditions of employment and has a date by which the offer must be accepted. The last step in the recruitment and selection process is a medical examination. The medical examination acts as a precaution for both the employee and the corporation.

Orientation

Either prior to, beginning or during the first few days of employment, new hires are required to attend an orientation session. At the orientation, new employees learn details about the corporation's history and about compensation and benefits. Safety and fire prevention are also introduced as well as the property's service philosophy. Department heads and the general manager usually introduce themselves to the new employees and wish them well in their new positions.

Training

Training in many organizations is an ongoing activity that is conducted by a training department, a training manager, or by line management or specially selected individuals within each department. The first step in establishing a training program is to identify the training needs and then set training objectives. Because the training must be geared toward guest expectations, training often focuses on areas where current service falls short of guest expectationas.

There are five main types of employee training: apprentice, simulation, certification, on-the-job, and off-the-job. Apprentice training is given to people who are new to a particular job. The training is specially designed to teach participants the correct way to do a particular task. This often follows the "tell me, show me, let me do it" routine.

Simulation training simulates the actual workplace. For example, there are specially prepared simulation exercises for travel agents on the Sabre and Apollo airline reservation systems. Once the trainee has reached the required level of proficiency, she or he then is allowed to do real ticketing.

Certification training enables individuals to gain corporate or professional certification by attaining passing scores on practical or theoretical tests. These tests are generally job specific and are helpful in motivating employees to develop in a professional manner. The Culinary Federation of America operates a certification program, as does the National Restaurant Association and the American Hotel and Motel Association.

On-the-job-training (OJT) helps maintain standards by having managers, supervisors, trainers, or fellow employees coach individuals in the most effective way to do the required work. OJT allows the trainee to quickly learn the best way to do the work based on the experience of trial and error. New hotel housekeepers may work with an experienced employee for a few days to learn the preferred way to do rooms.

Off-the-job-training is done away from the workplace and is usually used for nontechnical training, such as effective communications, team-building, motivation, and leadership. These topics often are handled by outside experts. These training methods help individuals to quickly learn the job and to improve their performance in doing the work. Some interesting anonymous industry comments heard in training sessions include the following:

➤ People in the organization are a reflection of the leadership.
➤ We don't run restaurants, we manage associations.
➤ We hire cheerleaders.
➤ What do you do to get your employees to smile? SMILE! I'm lucky if they don't look as if they are in pain!!

➤ We are hiring people today that we wouldn't have let in as customers a few years ago.
➤ You can teach nice people, but you can't teach people to be nice.
➤ You achieve what you inspect, not what you expect.

Performance Appraisal

The purpose of performance appraisal is to compare an employee's actual performance to pre-established standards as described in the job description. Performance appraisal has been viewed by the industry as positive as well as negative. The positive attributes of performance appraisal include giving feedback to employees, building the appraisal into a personal development plan, establishing a rationale for promotion and wage/salary increases, and helping to establish objectives for training programs.

Some of the negative aspects of performance reviews include the following:

➤ Too many appraisals expect only the immediate supervisor to take sole responsibility for doing the appraisal.
➤ Managers often do a poor job of giving feedback to employees.
➤ Managers save up incidents to dump on employees at evaluation times.
➤ Managers are biased in their appraisals.
➤ Managers may be either too hard or too soft on employees.
➤ Too many employees are not aware of the performance criteria that they will be evaluated against.

Another major difficulty with most performance appraisal systems is that the judgments involved are frequently subjective, relating primarily to personality traits or observations that cannot be verified. Three common distortions in performance appraisals include the following:

➤ Recent behavior influence. An evaluator's judgment may be influenced by the employee's recent behavior (good or bad). It is important to guard against giving recent behavior greater emphasis in the appraisal.
➤ The halo effect. The halo effect occurs when a supervisor is overly concerned with one particular aspect of the overall job, such as punctuality. If an employee is punctual, he or she will likely receive a better evaluation than one who is occasionally late even if his or her productivity is somewhat less.
➤ Like-me syndrome. We all tend to like people who are similar to ourselves; naturally, there is a tendency to give a better appraisal to those employees who are most like ourselves.

There is an inherent weakness in all appraisals. Any system by which a superior rates a subordinate is likely to cause resentment in the person being rated or anxiety in the rater. The basic answer to the anxiety problem is to develop a supportive social system aimed at reducing individual anxiety and thus freeing up energies for constructive purposes. The supportive system includes help from peers and supervisors that will make the employee feel more positive toward the experience and offer a real chance for improvement.

Job Analysis	Describes the job and personal requirements for a particular job.
Performance Standards	State expected performance.
Performance Appraisal	Appraises the level of employee performance and compares each element to standards.

Figure 12–7   *Linkages among Job Analysis, Job Description, and Performance Appraisal*

One of the best analogies about managerial feedback to employees was given by Dr. Ken Blanchard in *The One Minute Manager,* who said that there is no such thing as an unmotivated person. An unmotivated employee may be a superstar at the local bowling alley. But imagine that as Fred rolls the ball down the alley, a supervisor stands there and says "You only knocked down seven pins; why didn't you knock them all down?" Then, to make matters worse, the manager places a curtain in front of the pins so that Fred will not know what to aim for or how well he bowled. Finally, the supervisor removes both the curtain and the pins. When Fred is asked to bowl again, he replies, "I can't; I don't have anything to aim at!" This is analogous to the many people who work for organizations without knowing job performance expectations and the criterion for appraisal.

Performance appraisals make the link between performance standards and organizational goals. Another critical element is the linkage between the job analysis, job description, and the appraisal form. Figure 12–7 shows the importance of the linkage among job analysis, job description, and performance appraisal.

Performance appraisals need to be fair, equal, and nondiscriminatory. Performance—not personality—needs to be judged. Although a variety of ways to judge employee performance exist, the graphic scale is the most widely used rating scale. Such scales generally have either five or seven numbers (see Figure 12–8).

Appearance

Neat and in good taste	Neat but occasionally not in good taste	Sometimes careless	Untidy	Not suitable for the job
1	2	3	4	5

Ability to Learn

Learns with exceptional rapidity	Grasps instructions readily	Average ability to learn new things	Somewhat slow in learning	Limited in new duties
1	2	3	4	5

Figure 12–8   *Graphic Rating Scales*

An alternative format is shown in Figure 12–9.

The biggest advantage of the graphic rating scale is that it saves time for the person completing it, time that should be spent on other things.

Self-appraisal is a form of appraisal that lets employees evaluate their own performance. This may then become the basis of discussion with the supervisor/manager. It also complements an MBO program as it enables employees to have a say in setting their own objectives. Obviously, the supervisor/manager will also complete an appraisal form and sit down to compare notes with the employee.

Accuracy:

1. ( ) Rarely makes mistakes
2. ( ) Above average
3. ( ) Average
4. ( ) Below average
5. ( ) Highly inaccurate

Figure 12–9 *Performance Appraisal Checklist*

Developmental appraisal is a progressive appraisal technique, aimed at helping the employee to develop and to improve in the performance of his or her duties. A specific employee development plan will stipulate the kind of development that will help the employee to improve performance. An example of this form is shown in Figure 12–10 on page 322.

The important thing to remember when considering performance appraisal and the law is that managers must run a tight ship. Appraisals must not only be fair but must also be seen to be fair. This means that when appraisals are used as a criteria for promotion (or in extreme circumstances, the release of an employee), the appraisal system must withstand careful scrutiny. It only takes one disgruntled employee to file a grievance with the Equal Employment Opportunity Commission for a substantial amount of management time and money to be spent. Even if the company were to win the case it would still lose money. Team appraisals are becoming popular because most people don't want to let the team down, so each member encourages others to excel.

Compensation

Compensation is the term used to describe what most people call a pay check. Actually, however, compensation is more than a pay check; it is the total reward system, consisting of established policies and procedures to govern the compensation package. The compensation package includes wages, salaries, and benefits. The term *wages* is generally used with hourly employees, and the term *salaries* usually is used for employees who work for a set rate of pay.

The Fair Labor Standards Act (FLSA) requires industries to distinguish not between management and nonmanagement, but between exempt and nonexempt employees. Exempt employees are those who fall under section 13 (a) (1) of the federal minimum wage law. Exempt employees are not paid overtime because they are performing managerial supervisory duties a minimum of 60 percent of their work time. Nonexempt employees are paid overtime for any hours worked beyond the thirty-five- or forty-hour work week.

Appropriate levels of compensation are set once the job is evaluated for skill levels, responsibility, competencies, knowledge, and working conditions. Frequently, a range is set, with increments allowing for progression after a

MBO – DEVELOPMENTAL TYPE APPRAISAL FORM

Priority Urgency	Duties	Performance Expectations	Performance Appraisal				
			Far Below Standard	Below Standard	Meets Standard	Above Standard	Well Above Standard

EMPLOYEE DEVELOPMENT PLAN:

1. What kind of development will help improve performance?
    (_____) a. on the job training
    (_____) b. training course
    (_____) c. self-development
    (_____) d.

2. How will this developmental training be arranged? _____
    _____
    _____

3. How long will it take? _____
    _____
    _____

Figure 12–10   *MBO/Development Appraisal Form*

specified time. Jobs then are graded and priced, taking into account items such as tips or service charges.

Some companies offer bonuses or other incentives based on achieving certain results; others have instituted employee stock ownership plans (ESOP). The idea of employee ownership of a company is not new, but it does improve commitment and performance, as does the concept of profit sharing.

Over the years, various legislative acts have been enacted that have affected hospitality human resources. The Fair Labor Standards Act (1938 and as amended) is a broad federal statute that mandates the following:

- ➤ Federal minimum wage law
- ➤ Employee meals and meal credit
- ➤ Equal pay
- ➤ Child labor
- ➤ Overtime
- ➤ Tips, tip credits, and tip-pooling procedures
- ➤ Uniforms and uniform maintenance
- ➤ Record keeping
- ➤ Exempt versus nonexempt employees

The Equal Pay Act of 1963 prohibits companies from paying different salaries on the basis of sex. The Civil Rights Act of 1964 went further and established the Equal Employment Opportunity Commission (EEOC). This act makes it unlawful to discriminate with respect to hiring, compensating, working condition, privileges, or terms of employment. In 1967, the Age Discrimination Act was passed, prohibiting employment discrimination against those over forty years of age. Compensation and benefits can amount to 25 to 39 percent of payroll, making them the highest single cost factor in the hospitality industry.

Employee safety has become significantly more important because of the large increase in workers' compensation claims. This increase has resulted in large increases in insurance premiums. Employers have been forced to pay special attention to employee safety, including the use and handling of dangerous chemicals.

Employee Assistance Programs (EAP) have been instituted at many progressive companies. Employees who have problems may request help (assistance) in confidence, without losing their jobs. The emphasis of most EAPs is on prevention and intervening before the crisis stage is reached.

Employee Development

Employee development is a natural progression from appraisal. A development plan is made by the employee and his or her supervisor. The plan will outline the development activity and indicate when the development will take place. In well-run corporations, employee development is ongoing; it may take the form of in-house training or workshops and seminars on specific topics.

Certification is an excellent form of employee development because it validates a person's ability to do an excellent job and become more professional. Certification can be internal or external. Internal certification occurs when a company has stipulated certain criteria associated with a position (such as knowing the menu, being able to describe each item, and so on). External certification occurs when an employee takes courses toward a professional designation such as the National Restaurant Association's Foodservice Management Professional (FMP).

Corporate Profile:

Marriott International, Inc./Host Marriott Corporation

Marriott International became a public company in October 1993, when Marriott Corporation split into two separate companies. Marriott International manages lodging and service businesses. It has operations in fifty states and twenty-four countries, with approximately 170,000 employees. It has annual sales of about $8 billion.

Host Marriott Corporation focuses on two basic businesses—real estate ownership and airport and tollroad concessions. Host Marriott has operations or properties in thirty-eight states and six countries, with approximately twenty-three thousand employees. The company has annual sales of approximately $1.3 billion, with significant operating cash flow.

Marriott International, Inc.

> "We are committed to being the best lodging and management services company in the world by treating employees in ways that create extraordinary customer service and shareholder value."—Mission statement

Marriott International owns the trademarks, trade names, and reservation and franchise systems that were formerly owned by Marriott Corporation. The new company has two operating groups. Their divisions are leaders in their respective businesses, and enjoy strong customer preference.

The Lodging Group is composed of Marriott's four hotel management divisions: Marriott Hotels, Resorts, and Suites manages or franchises 254 full-service hotels (plus six managed hotels under construction); Courtyard, the company's moderately priced lodging division (229 hotels); Residence Inn, the leader in the extended-stay segment (186 inns); and Fairfield Inn, Marriott's economy lodging division (161 inns). In total, the group manages or franchises 830 hotels with approximately 177,600 rooms. Also included are Marriott Ownership Resorts, which operates twenty-eight timesharing properties with over fifty-nine thousand interval owners and Marriott Golf, which presently manages seventeen golf facilities.

The service group has three principal divisions: Marriott Management Services provides food and facilities management for business, education, and health care clients, with over three thousand accounts; Marriott Senior Living Services manages nineteen retirement communities (plus eight under construction), offering independent and assisted living for older Americans. Marriott Distribution Services provides food and related products to the company's operations and external clients through seven distribution centers. J. W. Marriott, Jr., is chairman, president, and chief executive officer of Marriott International.

Host Marriott Corporation

The leading operator of airport and tollroad food, beverage, and merchandise concessions, Host Marriott expanded in 1992 by acquiring the airport operations of Dobbs Houses, Inc. Host Marriott now serves approximately seventy-five airports, primarily in the United States, with some concessions in Australia, New Zealand, and Pakistan. The company also operates ninety-three food and merchandise units on fourteen U.S. tollroads, and has concessions at forty-two sports and entertainment attractions. Host is a licensee of seventeen major nationally branded food and merchandise concepts.

The company owns 130 Marriott lodging properties (including two hotels now under construction) and fourteen retirement communities, located in thirty-three states and three countries, which are managed under long-term agreements with Marriott International, Inc. Host Marriott or its subsidiaries act as general or limited partners in a number of Marriott lodging partnerships, and own certain parcels of land.

Host Marriott's lodging portfolio includes twenty-eight full-service hotels, among them the San Francisco Marriott and the New York Marriott Marquis; fifty-four Courtyard hotels (moderate price segment); eighteen Residence Inn properties (extended-stay segment); and thirty Fairfield Inn properties (economy segment). Richard E. Marriott is chairman of Host Marriott.

Employee Retention

Employee retention is the exact opposite of employee turnover. Whether it is called retention or turnover, the subject is still a major concern for the hospitality industry in general and human resources directors in particular.

It is frustrating for management to spend the time and effort on employees who go through the employment process only to leave a short time later. Retention is expressed as a percentage; if a department has one hundred employees on January 1 and sixty-three stay throughout the year, then the retention rate is 63 percent. This means that thirty-seven people left the organization and had to be replaced. Experts estimate that the turnover of one hourly position per week costs between $150,000 and $213,000 per year.[2]

Peter Yu, president of Richfield Hotel Management, estimated that the entire industry loses $1.8 billion per year because of employee turnover. Each turnover costs Richfield about $1,400. Richfield has a 35 to 40 percent retention rate, which has improved by 10 percent since beginning an employee-maintenance program; the next goal is to achieve 40 percent retention.[3]

To reduce losses, Ritz-Carlton intensified its employee-selection process. Then the company encouraged employees' input in creating their work environment. Within a few years, the company lowered its turnover rate from 90 percent to 30 percent. Ritz-Carlton aspires to maintain a 20 percent turnover rate by 1996.[4]

Equal Employment Opportunity (EEO)

Equal employment opportunity is the legal right of all individuals to be considered for employment and promotion on the basis of their ability and merit. The intent of this legislation is to prevent discrimination against applicants for the reasons given in the Civil Rights Act. The EEOC is the organization that individuals may turn to if they feel that they have been discriminated against. If it agrees, the commission will file charges against individuals or organizations.

Americans with Disabilities Act (ADA)

The ADA has two components: Employment and Public Accommodations. The ADA prohibits discrimination against persons with disabilities and stipulates that employers must make "readily achievable" modifications to their premises and to the work practices and working conditions for the disabled. Existing facilities need not be retrofitted to provide full accessibility. However, barrier removal that is readily achievable and easily completed without significant difficulty or expense is required in all existing buildings.

Harassment

Employers are responsible for creating and maintaining a working environment that is pleasant, avoiding hostile, offensive, intimidating, or discriminatory conduct or statements. In other words, the workplace must be kept free from all forms of harassment, including those based on sex, race, religious choice, ethnic background, and age. Sexual harassment, in particular, has occurred frequently over the past few years. Although very controversial in its identification and definition, sexual harassment does include unwanted sexual advances, requests for sexual favors, and verbal or physical actions of a sexual nature. It is important to note that an offensive environment does not need to involve a request for sexual favors. An offensive environment also may be created by lewd jokes or comments, displaying explicit or sexually suggestive material, or hands-on behavior.

In order to handle such an issue in an appropriate manner, the management should take the following actions:

1. Establish a sexual harassment policy that defines clearly what will not be tolerated and states the penalties for violation.
2. React promptly to reports with even-handed, thorough investigation.
3. Keep all instances confidential.
4. Keep appropriate documentation and decide on the appropriate disciplinary action.

Culture

Culture is a learned behavior. Someone who lives in the United States learns from its culture a unique set of beliefs, values, attitudes, habits, customs, traditions, and other forms of behavior. Besides other cultures like African, Asian, Latino, European, and American, there are cultural variations, such as African-American, Asian-American, Hispanic-American, European-American, and French-Canadian, for example. These cultural variations are a blend of cultures.

Culture influences the way people behave, and there are many differences among the various cultures. For instance, American culture is more individualistic than the Asian or Latin cultures. Consider also the differences between the genders in these cultures. America's multicultural society gives us an opportunity to learn from one another instead of simply thinking "my way is best." It is best to be aware of and respect the culture of others and try to harmonize with it; otherwise, misunderstanding might occur.

Multicultural management is a recognition of cultural differences in the hospitality workplaces attributable to membership in a distinct ethnic group. Multicultural management is an approach to managing the workplace that allows for differences in values arising from gender, economic level, and age group, as well as ethnic group. In today's hospitality industry, it is necessary for managers—and, indeed, all employees—to have a knowledge of cross-cultural awareness and an understanding of ethnic identity. Cultural barriers in hospitality workplaces do exist; it is important to understand ethnic diversity, minorities, and how to train ethnic groups in order to understand the various cultural aspects in our hospitality workplace.

Cultural Barriers

Culture can be manifested in many ways, such the style of dress, language, food, gestures, manners, and so on. Although many individuals have difficulties dealing with foreign customs and language, these are relatively easy components, because they are visible and comprehensible. It is much harder to detect and to deal with values, assumptions, and perceptions.

Adjusting to another culture can be particularly frustrating if one comes from a low-context culture and has to operate in a high-context culture. A low-context culture is one in which the bulk of information, intentions, and meanings are conveyed in words and sentences; context, therefore, plays a smaller role. High-context cultures are those in which the context is of great importance and what is behind the words is as important as the words themselves.

The Anglo-Saxon culture is a low-context culture. Information and intentions are expressed in words and sentences in the clearest possible manner. The prevailing culture in Japan is a high-context culture; not only does what is said count, but how it is said, who said it, and when. What was not said is also significant, as are the pauses, the silences, and the tone. In high-context cultures, reading between the lines and interpreting the meaning behind the words is of utmost importance; the words themselves have different meanings and do not always convey true intentions to an outsider. For example, the Japanese rarely use the word *no*; instead, they use a host of substitutes that may not convey their true intention to the western ear. Similarly, when Japanese use affirmative statements, they do not assign the same meaning to them as we do.

Language

Language can be another barrier to cultural understanding. Even when people use the same language, misunderstandings and misinterpretations occur. The same word and symbol have different meanings to individuals from different cultural backgrounds.

Ethnic Diversity

Ethnic diversity refers to accepting all people regardless of appearances or mannerisms. Cultural diversity enriches the workplace. America's ethnic diversity is growing. By the year 2000, women will comprise 47 percent of the work force; Hispanics, 29 percent; African-Americans, 18 percent; and Asian-Americans, 11 percent.[5] These core groups will be the backbone of the hospitality industry. The growth projected for the Asian and Hispanic populations in the United States will, in the twenty-first century, mean that one quarter to one third of all workplaces will belong to racial or ethnic minority groups.[6]

Personal Cultural Barriers

We too often approach others from our own cultural perspective and expect them to be like us. We react when people respond or behave in a way that is "different." These behaviors may lead to stereotyping, when we always consider certain groups to behave in a certain way. A bad experience with one person does not mean that all experiences with others from that culture will be bad. Preconceived negative attitudes about certain groups are called *prejudice.*

Ideally, the managers of tomorrow will welcome the ethnic diversity that they are bound to encounter, and they will have a personal desire to learn more about cultures and environments different from their own. But even those employers who don't see cultural pluralism as an extension of the practices of American democracy realize that they must be prepared to function effectively as hospitality managers in a pluralistic environment. Culture has a profound impact on the attitudes, priorities, and behavior of individuals and groups. To be able to interact with people from different cultures is vital in order to understand their values, norms, and priorities.

Hospitality managers have a responsibility to develop and recognize the realities facing the hospitality industry in the next ten to fifteen years. Ethnic and cultural diversity is a large part of that reality.

Summary

1. Marketing and human resources are specialized departments that serve other departments of the hospitality industry.
2. The main purpose of marketing is to create customers. It includes environmental, social, political, technological, and competitive analysis. Place, product, price, promotion, packaging, programming, and people altogether make up the marketing mix of hospitality.
3. Efficient, guest-focused employees are an important aspect for the success of an industry. Applicants have to go through a recruitment and selection process, orientation, and careful training.
4. Employees are evaluated by performance appraisals. In order for an appraisal to be fair there has to be a close link among job analysis, job description, and the appraisal.
5. Every hospitality industry is required to comply with the Equal Employment Opportunity Commission, to make modifications to the workplace and practices for disabled, and keep the workplace free of all forms of harassment.
6. As America's ethnic diversity is growing, management needs to recognize cultural differences. In this sense it is essential to avoid stereotyping and consider differences such as language, values, and perceptions.

Key Words and Concepts

Age Discrimination Act
Americans with Disabilities Act
Civil Rights Act
Comparison matrix
Compensation
Competitive analysis
Corporate philosophy
Culture
Demographics
Economic analysis
Environmental analysis
Equal employment opportunity
Equal Employment Opportunity Commission
Equal Pay Act
Exempt and nonexempt employees
Expense accounts
Fair Labor Standards Act
Focus groups
Harassment
Job description
Life-styles
Market demand
Market share
Marketing action plan

Marketing goals and objectives
Marketing mix
Orientation
Performance appraisal

Performance evaluation
Place, product, price, and promotion
Political analysis
Positioning

Productivity standards
Product life cycle
Recruitment
Selection
Social analysis

Target markets
Task analysis
Technological analysis
Training

Review Exercises

1. What is meant by the term *market assessment*? In this context explain the purpose of environmental analysis.
2. Explain the purpose of competitive analysis and explain the terms *comparison matrix* and *positioning*.
3. Describe the importance of price and product and list two ways used to determine price.

4. What is the difference between marketing and sales?
5. Briefly explain the process of employee selection.
6. Name and describe positive and negative effects of performance evaluation, in consideration of the like-me syndrome and halo effect.
7. Define culture and its impact on the hospitality industry in today's pluralistic environment.

Notes

[1] Alastair M. Morrison, *Hospitality and Travel Marketing*, Albany, N. Y.: Delmar, 1989, p. 14.
[2] Timothy N. Troy, "Hospitality Associations Waging War in Minnesota," *Hotel and Motel Management, 208,* 15, September 6, 1993, p. 6.
[3] Ibid.
[4] Ibid.
[5] Dennis Law, "Making Diversity Work," *Restaurants and Institutions, 104,* 2, January 15, 1994, p. 84.
[6] Ibid.

Leadership

13

After reading and studying this chapter you should be able to do the following:

- ➤ Distinguish the characteristics and attributes of leaders
- ➤ Define leadership
- ➤ Contrast the approaches taken by leadership theorists
- ➤ Distinguish between transactional and transformational leadership
- ➤ Distinguish between leadership and management
- ➤ Define ethics and apply importance of ethical behaviors to the hospitality industry

*O*ne must always look ahead, but it is difficult to look further than one can see.

—*Winston Churchill*

*L*eadership transfers potential into reality.

—*Keith Davis*

Leadership

Fascination with leadership goes back many centuries. However, lately it has come into prominence as the hospitality, tourism, and other industries strive for perfection in the delivery of services and products in an increasingly competitive environment. Leaders can and do make a difference.

Few tasks or goals can be accomplished by one person working alone. For this reason, society has many organizations. Few groups, however, can accomplish much without an individual who acts as leader. The leader can and often does have a significant influence on the group and its direction.

Consider, for example, the effect on history of a leader like Hitler. He rose from the ranks of corporal to become a dictator who, for a short while, ruled most of Europe. This example shows that a leader can be negative as well as positive. Given the significance of the contribution that leaders can make, it is important to understand how leaders emerge and what makes them effective.[1]

Characteristics of Leaders

Leaders can be identified by certain characteristics. For example, the U.S. Guidebook for Marines lists the following traits:

- ➤ Bearing
- ➤ Courage
- ➤ Decisiveness
- ➤ Dependability
- ➤ Endurance
- ➤ Enthusiasm
- ➤ Initiative
- ➤ Integrity
- ➤ Judgment
- ➤ Justice
- ➤ Knowledge
- ➤ Loyalty
- ➤ Tact
- ➤ Unselfishness

A Marine officer will likely add that what is most important is integrity. Integrity has been described as doing something right even though no one may be aware of it.

In addition to the leadership traits, there are also identifiable practices common to leaders:[2]

1. Challenge the process: active, not passive; search for opportunities; experiment and take risks
2. Inspire a shared vision: create a vision; envision the future; enlist others
3. Enable others to act: not alone; foster collaboration; strengthen others
4. Model the way: plan; set examples; plan small wins
5. Encourage the heart: share the passion; recognize individual contribution; celebrate accomplishments

Definitions of Leadership

Because of the complexities of leadership, different types of leadership, and individual perceptions of leaders, leadership has several definitions. Many definitions share commonalities, but there are also differences. In terms of hospitality leadership, the following definition is appropriate:

Leading is the process by which a person with vision is able to influence the activities and outcomes of others in a desired way.

Leaders know what they want and why they want it—and they are able to communicate it to others and gain their cooperation and support.

The study of leadership can be divided into four different stages:

1. 1900–1945: Traits-of-a-great-person theory
2. 1930–1970: Behavioral leadership
3. 1970s 1980s: Contingency theory and situational leadership
4. 1990s: Leader-manager

Traits-of-a-Great-Person Theory

Studies on leadership go back through the ages to *The Prince,* written in 1517 by Machiavelli. In 1869, Sir Francis Galton's so-called great man or trait theories suggested that the qualities in leaders might be inherited. So, from 1900 to 1945 the study of great leaders emphasized the trait theories. It was considered necessary to have traits similar to great leaders in order to be successful. In addition to physical and mental abilities, personality characteristics such as dominance, need for achievement, need for power, self-esteem, and self-confidence were seen as essential for leadership. Examples of great leaders who possessed some or all of these traits include the following:

➤ Queen Elizabeth I
➤ Mahatma Gandhi
➤ Napoleon Bonaparte
➤ Franklin D. Roosevelt
➤ George Washington

➤ Mao Tse-Tung
➤ Abraham Lincoln
➤ Golda Meir
➤ Winston S. Churchill
➤ Martin Luther King, Jr.
➤ Adolf Hitler

Behavioral Leadership

The traits-of-a-great-person theory prevailed until Stogdill's analysis of studies done on traits uncovered no consistent patterns in successful leaders. Other research concluded that characteristics associated with leadership could be learned. Therefore, the study of leadership shifted to the study of the behavior of leaders.

From 1945 to the 1960s, the behavioral science approach to leadership emphasized the establishment of relationships with others. Abraham Maslow, a respected clinical psychologist and a pioneer in the development of need theories, described a hierarchy of human needs. Maslow's need theory proposed that behavior is driven by the urge to fulfill five fundamentals needs: physiological, social, love, esteem, and self-actualization (see Figure 13-1).

These needs generally coincide with a person's life cycle, with physiological needs being primary in the first few years of life, social during our teens and twenties, love during the late twenties to early fifties, esteem in the forties to sixties, and self-actualization, according to Maslow, later—if ever.

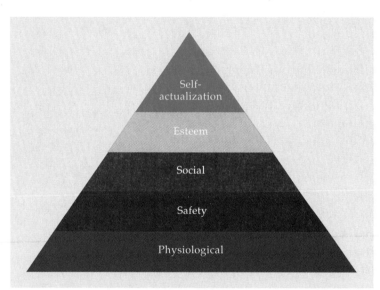

Figure 13-1   *Maslow's Hierarchy of Needs*

Theory X and Theory Y

Douglas McGregor contrasted the philosophy of the human relations approach with the efficiency orientation of the scientific management. McGregor's Theory X assumes the following:

1. The average human being has an inherent dislike for work and will avoid it if possible.
2. Most people, because they dislike work, must be coerced, controlled, directed, or threatened with punishment before they will put forth effort toward the achievement of organizational objectives.
3. The average human being prefers to be directed, wishes to avoid responsibility, has relatively little ambition, and wants security above all.

Theory Y assumes the following:

1. Expending physical and mental effort at work is as natural as play and rest. The average human being does not inherently dislike work.
2. External control and the threat of punishment are not the only means to direct effort toward organizational objectives. People will exercise self-direction and self-control in the service of objectives to which they feel committed.
3. Commitment to objectives is a function of the rewards associated with their achievement. The most significant rewards—the satisfaction of ego and self-actualization needs—can be direct products of effort directed toward organizational objectives.
4. Avoidance of responsibility, lack of ambition, and emphasis on security are not inherent human characteristics. Under proper conditions, the average human being learns not only to accept but also to seek responsibility.
5. Imagination, ingenuity, creativity, and the ability to use these qualities to solve organizational problems are widely distributed among people.

Individuals holding Theory Y assumptions view the task of management as follows:

1. Managers are responsible for organizing the elements of productive enterprise—money, materials, equipment, people—in the interest of economic ends.
2. Because people are motivated to perform, have potential for development, can assume responsibility, and are willing to work toward organizational goals, managers are responsible for enabling people to recognize and develop these basic capacities.
3. The essential task of management is to arrange organization conditions and methods of operation so that working toward organizational objectives is also the best way for people to achieve their own personal goals.

Thus, unlike Theory X managers, who try to control their employees, Theory Y managers help employees learn how to manage themselves.

Approaches to Leadership

Contingency Theory and Situational Leadership

Contingency theory links leadership style to the requirements of a particular situation, meaning that the leader's personal style must be appropriate to the situation. In some circumstances, such as a crisis moment, it may be appropriate for the leader to take command and issue direct orders to be obeyed precisely. Such situations usually require an immediate decision, as in the case of a fire, power outage, bomb scare, and so on. In these situations, the leader

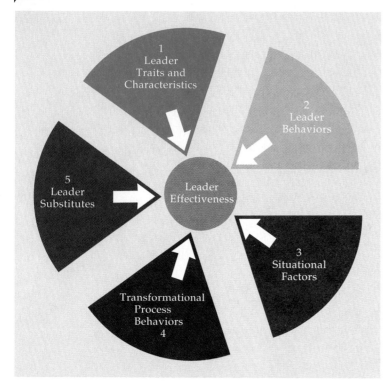

Figure 13-2   *Leadership Factors* (Donald D. White and David A. Bednar, *Organizational Behavior: Understanding and Managing People at Work,* 2d ed. Boston: Allyn and Bacon, 1991, p. 385.)

assumes a Theory X persona; however, she or he should quickly revert to the more participative Theory Y leadership style for maximum effectiveness. Success depends on the leader's ability to adapt his or her style to the situation. Many leaders fail to adapt sufficiently, causing problems for both the leader and the organization.

More detailed explanations of various behavior styles may be found in texts on leadership. However, effective leader behavior is influenced by several common factors. Figure 13-2 illustrates some of the factors acknowledged to contribute to organizational outcomes.[3]

Authoritarian, Democratic, and Laissez-Faire Leadership

Authoritarian leaders are those who make all or almost all the decisions regarding a group activity. This is considered a *task-oriented* approach.

Democratic leaders are those who delegate a great deal of decision-making responsibility to group members. This is considered a *relationship-oriented* approach. Some leaders abdicate the role entirely; in other words, neither the leader nor the group make any decisions. This kind of leadership behavior is classified as *laissez-faire.*

Theory Z Leadership

Theory Z was proposed by William Ouichi in 1981 and became part of the so-called Japanese management. This leadership-management style focuses attention on forming and maintaining manager-employee relationships. Ouichi contrasted the characteristics of American and Japanese organizations and recommended that the United States adopt some Japanese management practices that result in richer, long-term relationships with employees. Such relationships are achieved by involving employees in participative decision making by consensus.[4] Many U.S. corporations, including hospitality and tourism organizations, have moved toward this style of management.

Theory Z encompasses the best of the American and Japanese approaches. The Theory Z model includes the following:

Human Resources Treatment—Job security and opportunity for advancement within the organization to produce strong individual commitment to organizational purposes and goals

The Use of Group Dynamics—Intensive application of Kurt Lewin and Abraham Maslow's models of group problem solving, participation, involvement, particularly in the Japanese "quality circles" approach to high-quality products

Shrewd World Market Penetration—Product development and pricing and marketing in selected key areas, such as automobiles, electronics, and computers

Adaptation of Management Principles and Techniques to the Natural Culture—Techniques created in other countries adopted in consonance with Japanese culture and life-styles. Values, norms, and expectations, long strong in Japanese culture, interwoven with new technological and management practices

Transactional Leadership

Transactional leadership is viewed as a process by which a leader is able to bring about desired actions from others by using certain behaviors, rewards, or incentives. In essence, an exchange or transaction takes place between leader and follower.[5] Figure 13-3 shows the transactional model of leadership.

This concept illustrates the coming together of the leader, the situation, and the followers. A hotel general manager who pressures the food and beverage director to achieve certain goals in exchange for a bonus is an example of transactional leadership.

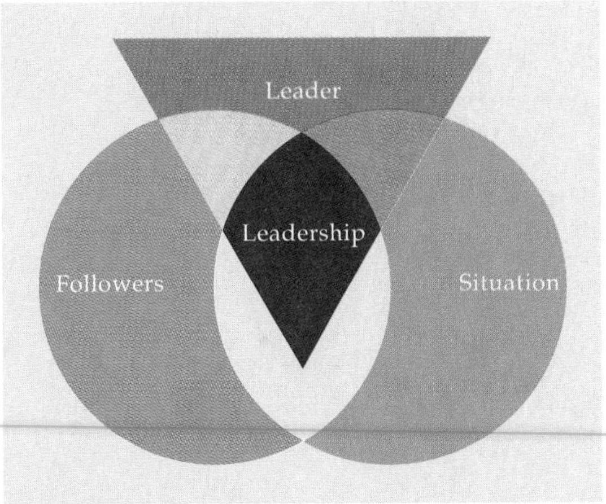

Figure 13-3 *Transactional Model of Leadership* (Warren Bennis, *On Becoming a Leader.* Reading, Mass.: Addison-Wesley, p. 45.)

Transformational Leadership

Leadership involves looking for ways to bring about longer-term, higher-order changes in follower behavior.[6] This brings us to transformational leadership. The term *transformational leadership* is used to describe the process of eliciting performance above and beyond normal expectations.[7] A transformational leader is one who inspires others to reach beyond themselves and do more than they originally thought possible; this is accomplished by raising their commitment to a shared vision of the future.[8]

Transformational leaders have a hands-on philosophy, not in terms of performing the day-to-day tasks of subordinates, but by developing and encouraging their followers individually.[9] Transformational leadership involves three important factors:

1. Charisma
2. Individual consideration
3. Intellectual stimulation

Personal Profile: Herb Kelleher

Herb Kelleher, CEO of Southwest Airlines, is the living embodiment of the words *one of a kind.* With his charismatic personality, he is a person who leaves a distinctive mark whatever he does.

Since the birth of Southwest Airlines in 1971 as a tiny Texas commuter airline with four airplanes, Herb Kelleher—simply Herb to even his least close acquaintances—has nurtured Southwest Airlines into the eighth largest airline, with revenues of $1.2 billion a year. The company has been profitable every year since 1973. When other carriers lost billions or were struggling in bankruptcy during the early nineties, Southwest was the only company that remained consistently profitable—a record unmatched in the U.S. airline industry—cheerfully pursuing its growth plans, by buying more planes, expanding into new cities, hiring personnel. Southwest is also a model of efficiency: it is an eleven-time winner of the U.S. Department of Transportation's Triple Crown, a monthly citation for the best on-time performance, fewest lost bags, and fewest overall complaints. Now that it is once again a time of prosperity, Kelleher's operation, based on flights covering relatively short distances for prices sometimes shockingly low, is likely to further advance in its rapid growth and become even more of a leading power.

Herb Kelleher and a Southwest Airplane

One of the keys to this success lies in the company's mission. Southwest Airlines aims at providing cheap, simple, and focused airline service. Kelleher devoted enormous attention to thousands of small decisions, all designed to achieve simplicity. Among these small but tremendously strategic decisions were the removal of closets at the front of the planes, to improve passengers' speed in boarding and departing; no onboard food, except snacks, which is justified by the short distances the flights cover on average (about 375 miles). Southwest also refused the computerized reservation system used by travel agents. Nearly half of all Southwest tickets are sold directly to customers, saving annually about $30 million. There is no assigned seating, no first-class seating, no baggage transfer. Planes have been standardized: Southwest only operates one type of aircraft, the 737, which simplifies flight crew training and maintenance personnel training.

These relatively minor privations have their positive counterpart in the fact that Southwest ground crew can turn around a plane at the gate in about fifteen minutes! The airline is especially appreciated by its customers for its low fares and on-time schedules.

Who is behind all this? The airline's success is credit-

Martin Luther King, Jr.

Dr. Martin Luther King, Jr., was one of the most charismatic transformational leaders in history. King dedicated his life to achieving rights for all citizens by nonviolent methods. His dream of how society could be was shared by millions of Americans. In 1964 Dr. King won the Nobel Peace Prize.

In the hospitality and tourism industry, one of the outstanding transformational leaders is Wayne Calloway, CEO of Pepsico. He had a vision that Pepsico could become the best consumer products company in the world. He envisioned a day when pizza, tacos, and chicken would be as convenient and easy to get as a bag of potato chips. With this vision, Calloway set about changing the way the company's Pizza Hut, Taco Bell, and KFC chains offer their services to the public. Now Pizza Hut's delivery and carry-out services earn twice what the eat-in restaurants do, and vendors at football stadiums, basketball arenas, school cafeterias, and airport shops sell Pizza Hut pizza.[10]

Another transformational leader is Herb Kelleher, president and CEO of Southwest Airlines. He is able to inspire his followers to pursue his corporate

ed to Kelleher's unorthodox personality and entrepreneurial management style. Born and raised in New Jersey, he was the son of the general manager of Campbell Soups Inc. He began to show leadership qualities as student body president both in high school and in college. From his original idea of becoming a journalist, Kelleher shifted his goal on the practice of the law. By the mid-1960s, he was successfully practicing in San Antonio, Texas, his wife's hometown. However, he was always seeking the possibility of starting a venture of his own. The big chance came in 1966, when a banker client, Rolling King, suggested that Texas needed a short-haul commuter airline. That was the trigger: Southwest was born in 1971.

Steve Lewing, a Gruntal & Co. analyst, describes Kelleher as "brilliant, charming, cunning and tough."[1] He is, indeed, a unique character. He is a man characterized by a strong sense of humor, who has appeared in public dressed as Elvis, or the Easter Bunny, who "has carved an antic public persona out of his affection for cigarettes, bourbon, and bawdy stories."[2]

The CEO, like all great leaders, never stepped into an ivory tower. He is directly supervising his business, personally approving expenses over $1,000. His outstanding hands-on efforts also lead to unusually good labor-management relations, on the basis of the motto "People are the most important of resources." In fact, he has managed to establish very strongly that old bond of loyalty between employees and their company that may have disappeared elsewhere in the American corporate environment.

He represents some sort of a father figure to his employees, as well as the jester, the "Lord of Ha-Ha." This personal feature is, and must be, reflected in his personnel: "What we are looking for, first and foremost, is a sense of humor," says Kelleher, "and then people who have to excel to satisfy themselves."[3] The effort that he gets out of his employees makes the real difference. Unlike workers at most other carriers, Southwest employees are willing to pitch in whenever needed. For example, a reservation clerk in Dallas took a call from an anxious customer who was putting his eighty-eight-year-old mother aboard a flight to St. Louis. The woman was quite frail, the fellow explained, and he wasn't quite sure she could handle the change of planes in Tulsa. "No sweat," replied the clerk, "I'll fly with her as far as Tulsa and make sure she gets safely on the St. Louis flight."

Kelleher's outstanding leadership ability is also shown in his long-term thinking. He has gathered a top-rank team of potential successors, which will guarantee the airline's future prosperity. However, Kelleher will be hard to replace. He is the leader who inspires, the amiable uncle to refer to, the cheerleader who motivates, the clown who makes it fun.

[1] Kenneth Labich, "Is Herb Kelleher America's Best CEO?", *Fortune, 129*, 9, May 2, 1994, p. 52.
[2] Ibid.
[3] Ibid.

vision and reach beyond themselves to give Southwest Airlines that something extra that sets it apart from its competitors.

Kelleher recognizes that the company does not exist merely for the gratification of its employees; he knows that Southwest Airlines must perform and be profitable. However, he believes strongly that exceptional performance can best be attained by valuing individuals for themselves. Passengers who fly Southwest may see Herb Kelleher; he travels frequently. But he will not be found in the first-class section. More likely he will be found serving drinks, fluffing pillows, or just wandering up and down the aisle talking to passengers. The success of Southwest and the enthusiasm of its employees indicate that Herb Kelleher has achieved his goal of weaving together individual and corporate interests so that all members of the Southwest family benefit. Kelleher proves that transformational behavior (visioning, valuing, articulating, inspiring, empowering, and ongoing communication) can be practiced by leaders in all types and at all levels of an organization.[11]

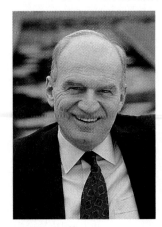

Wayne Calloway

Another great leader in the restaurant industry was Ray Kroc of McDonald's, whose actions tell the tale. Consider the following example of how Ray Kroc instilled his vision of cleanliness:

On his way back to the office from an important lunch at the best place in town, Ray Kroc asked his driver to pass through several McDonald's parking lots. In one parking lot, he spotted paper littering the parking area. He went to the nearest pay phone, called the office, got the name of the store manager, and called him to offer help in picking up the trash. Both Ray Kroc, the owner of the McDonald's chain in his expensive business suit, and the young manager of the store met in the parking lot and got on their hands and knees to pick up the paper.

This anecdote has been told thousands of times within the McDonald's system to emphasize the importance of the vision of cleanliness.

In their fascinating book entitled *Lessons in Leadership: Perspectives for Hospitality Industry Success,* Bill Fisher, executive vice president of the National Restaurant Association, and Charles Bernstein, editor of *Nation's Restaurant News,* interviewed more than one hundred industry leaders and asked each to respond in an up-close-and-personal manner to some excellent questions. Some of their answers follow.

Bill Fisher

"Experience is a hard teacher. It gives the test first, and then you learn the lesson." Richard P. Mayer, former chairman and CEO of Kentucky Fried Chicken and president of General Foods Corporation, says that the key traits and factors that he looks for in assessing talent include the following:

> ➤ Established personal goals
> ➤ The drive and ambition to attain those goals, tempered and strengthened with integrity
> ➤ Proven analytical and communications skills
> ➤ Superior interpersonal capabilities
> ➤ A sense of humor
> ➤ An awareness and appreciation of the world beyond her or his business specialty
> ➤ Receptivity to ideas (no matter the source)
> ➤ A genuine deep commitment to growth and profitability of the business.[12]

Ferdinand Metz, certified master chef and president of the Culinary Institute of America, believes the essence of success is to possess exemplary leadership qualities—"being a fair manager, an inspiring motivator, and most of all, a diplomat when dealing with people." These leadership qualities alone, however, do not ensure success. A good deal of expertise in the field is also needed. This knowledge, combined with personal qualities, will allow you to make a significant contribution to your chosen profession.[13]

Joseph A. McInerney, President and CEO, Forte Hotels, North America

Joseph McInerney, President and CEO of Forte Hotels, North America, who was recently voted Economy Lodging Person of the Year, suggests that leaders cannot be transient citizens; rather, they should give back to society. McInerney, who is described by his associates as an outstanding leader, has a democratic style that empowers associates. He urges motivation through education and community service. As chairperson of the American Hotel and Motel Association's Educational Institute and as a community leader involved in several organizations, the example he sets is a model for us to follow.

James Irwin is president and CEO of Emco Foodservice Systems, a major food service distribution firm headquartered in Pittsburgh, Pennsylvania, and a member of the Food Service Distribution Hall of Fame. He commented that "many people are not willing to pay the price for success, yet do not realize the rewards far outweigh the costs. Many people follow a path of 'least resistance' that limits their ability to exercise their full potential." He suggested that "success is exceptional performance and achievement on a consistent basis over a period of time," and "a successful person will lead with an authority earned by integrity and not compromise ethics or morals for financial gain or position."[14]

The essence of success has as many meanings as there are people to ponder it. One concept of success is to couple one's personal and family interests, dreams, and aspirations with a business or professional career that complement and fortify each other.

Another aspect of leadership is the ability to motivate others in a hospitality working environment; decision making is also essential. These are discussed in Chapter 14.

Examples of Leadership Excellence

Isadore Sharp is the founder, president, and chief executive officer of the Four Seasons Hotels and Resorts. Sharp was named Canada's outstanding CEO of the year in 1992. He was chosen from a blue-chip list of Canadian executives as the business leader who best exemplifies excellence in corporate achievement, leadership, vision, innovation, and global competitiveness. In just thirty years, Sharp advanced his business from a single hotel on Jarvis Street in downtown Toronto to become the world's largest luxury hotel and resort operation, with forty-three hotels in seventeen countries.

Isadore Sharp

Issy Sharp, as he is known, has the ability to conceive a vision of what is possible, the business acumen to plan for success, and the unique gift to inspire others to help carry the dream through to reality. Sharp was an architect working with his father in a two-man construction company when he chose to develop a property in Toronto into an elegant, hospitable home-away-from-home for business or leisure travelers.

Since opening that first hotel, Four Seasons has grown into a top international luxury hotel chain. Sharp credits his staff as the reason for Four Seasons' success. Isadore Sharp also plays a key role in the community; not only is he a director of several corporations, but he also has a special affinity for activities that support cancer research because he lost a young son to the disease. He initiated the corporate sponsorship for the Terry Fox Marathon of Hope and continues to direct the annual run, which has been tagged as the

John E. Martin, President and CEO of Taco Bell

largest fund-raising event in the world, having raised some $35 million by the spring of 1993.[15]

John E. Martin, president and CEO of Taco Bell Corporations, took over in 1983, when Taco Bell was a regional chain suffering from an identity crisis. However, since 1989, its total system sales have quadrupled to $2.6 billion and total units have tripled to roughly 3,300. Taco Bell has built a commanding 70-percent share in the Mexican-style quick service restaurant category. In recent years, sales and profits have risen dramatically; by 2001, the goal is to reach ten thousand points of distribution and $30 billion in sales. Martin sees the Taco Bell brand being sold not only in restaurants, but also in such nontraditional venues as carts, kiosks, hospitals, schools, airports, and even supermarkets.

Martin intends to improve the image of the industry by putting more dignity into it and making real careers for people. He has already simplified the restaurants, making the manager more self-sufficient, and increased incentives. Unit general managers have the authority to hire their own assistants, schedule labor, authorize many purchases, and make many other decisions that previously needed an area supervisor's sign-off.

The TACO system—total automation of company operations—saves managers up to fifteen hours per week, allowing them more time to interact with customers and to train employees. The system even provides the manager with a daily profit-and-loss statement to keep track of targets.

Martin has other innovative ideas, such as using a machine that can make twelve hundred tacos per hour, and preparing and distributing high-quality food products made outside the restaurants to reduce kitchen space and labor.

"It's ridiculous to think that a restaurant system must be thousands of little factories across the country all doing the same repetitive process," he says.[16]

Van E. Eure's food service career began as a teenager, waiting tables at The Angus Barn, known to loyal patrons as North Carolina's "Beefeater's Haven." The Angus Barn was established in 1960 by her father, Thad Eure, Jr., and his partner, Charlie Winston. After college, Eure taught high school English and elementary school in Kenya, Africa, for five years; in 1982, she returned to the United States to join her father in the restaurant business. In 1984, she was promoted to senior dining room manager and, following the death of her father in 1988, she took over the operation of the restaurant with her mother, Alice Eure. Today, the restaurant has a seating capacity of six hundred and employs 180 people.

Eure's professional and civic activities include the following: member, Knights of the Vine; member, La Chaine des Rotisseurs; board member, North Carolina Citizens of Business and Industry; board member, Public Service Company of North Carolina; board member, Theatre in the Park; member, The Fifty Group (a local networking organization of top executives); and member, The Foundation of Hope (for research and treatment of mental illness, founded by Thad Eure, Jr.). In 1991, Eure was named Master Lady by the Raleigh chapter of Knights of the Vine and was awarded the Mondail Medal of Honor by the National Chaine des Rotisseurs.

Van E. Eure

Student Glimpse: Michael R. Thorpe:

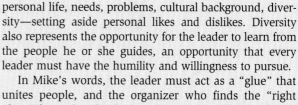

The leader of the future will be a holistic one.

Michael, who has just successfully completed his studies, earning a Bachelor of Science Degree in Hotel and Restaurant Management at the United States International University, is the outstanding example of the leadership skills that can be acquired throughout the school and college career.

Mike's leadership abilities developed from an early age, with his involvement in The Boy Scouts of America. Looking back at that memorable time, Mike recognizes how important it is for a leader to be a good role model. He emphasizes the fact that it is necessary to make a sharp distinction between "good" leaders and "bad" leaders, thus establishing a learning process that is based on the identification of both "shoulds" (positive examples, experiences, activities, skills) and "should-nots" (mistakes, negative attitudes). Michael's experience with The Boy Scouts was one that provided him with fundamental values and skills, which were immediately acknowledged when he achieved the rank of Eagle Scout.

In high school as well as in college, Mike's leadership skills were progressively developed and utilized. He believes that the key to learning is involvement. In fact, he always took part in school activities,

Michael Thorpe

also emphasizing the importance of maintaining a broad horizon of interests. In particular, Michael chose to actively participate in a variety of extracurricular activities, including academic, service-oriented, and sports organizations. He stresses the belief that there is a strict correlation among such fields that shapes the overall personality of the leader. "The leader of the future will be a holistic one," Mike says.

Michael's involvement in academic organizations—such as the student body government council, in sports (he was the captain of the football team and vice president of the football club), and in service-oriented enterprises, such as the Hosteur's Society HRTM Club, for which he was elected president—helped him develop the necessary skills for a high-quality interaction with people. He learned that a good leader is someone who is able to gather a group of individuals and coordinate each single talent, skill, propensity, and personality in a successful teamwork, joining forces in the pursuit of one common goal. Each member of the team must be fulfilled in his or her need for belonging, personal satisfaction, recognition, and so on. In order to accomplish this task, Mike understood that a leader must also be extremely respectful of each individual's personal life, needs, problems, cultural background, diversity—setting aside personal likes and dislikes. Diversity also represents the opportunity for the leader to learn from the people he or she guides, an opportunity that every leader must have the humility and willingness to pursue.

In Mike's words, the leader must act as a "glue" that unites people, and the organizer who finds the "right place" for each individual, a place in which he or she will be able to excel, and perform at his or her full potential.

Work experience throughout his college career has also taught Mike that workers will function at their best in a work environment that is appealing, challenging, and that provides them with the right tools—in terms of knowledge, motivation, rewards, climate—to produce the optimal outcome.

In order to achieve such results, Michael excludes, as much as possible, the carrot-on-a-stick approach. He feels that such a method is a superficial remedy that doesn't get to the root of the problem—thus not solving it—and doesn't consider the fact that a leader deals with human beings intrinsically characterized by a distinct intelligence and personality. Furthermore, when dealing with subordinates' failures or mistakes, Michael prefers to approach the person(s) in question from his or her point of view, trying to understand what the cause of the inefficiency might be, and at the same time performing a thorough self-analysis in order to establish whether that person's poor performance is determined by his own possible leadership mistake.

Mike greatly respects a leader who creates a sense of cooperation, community, and teamwork. Just like in a family, the leader should step down from an intolerable ivory tower, and be open to each member of the team, to listen and be willing to help with possible personal problems, emphasizing the importance of open communication. And, just like in a family, the leader must be the caring parent who can also progressively impose discipline and obtain the results expected depending on the memebers' potential.

The role of a father Mike sure knows about. In fact, he has a splendid child of three, who represents, among other factors, the ultimate challenge for leadership. "While workers' livelihood does depend on the employer/leader, nothing more than a little infant depends on his dad, who will represent, for the first and most delicate stage of a child's life, the one and only role model, the hero."

The Distinction Between Leadership and Management

Leadership is an ageless topic; it has been described as a social influence process that can occur in nearly any interaction among people. Leadership has a broader scope than management, which came in vogue about one hundred years ago with its more narrow focus on accomplishing organizational goals. Modern management was invented, in a sense, to help the new railroads, steel mills, and auto companies achieve what legendary entrepreneurs envisioned. Without such management, these complex enterprises tended to become chaotic in ways that threatened their very existence.[17]

Managing is the formal process in which organizational objectives are achieved through efforts of subordinates. *Leading* is the process by which a person with vision is able to influence the behavior of others in some desired way. Although managers have power by virtue of the positions they hold, organizations seek managers who are leaders by virtue of their personalities, their experience, and so on.

The differences between management and leadership can be illustrated as follows:[18]

Manager	*Leader*
administers	innovates
is a copy	is an original
maintains	develops
focuses on systems and structure	focuses on people
relies on control	inspires trust
has a short-range view	has a long-range perspective
asks how and when	asks what and why
has an eye on the bottom line	has an eye on the horizon
initiates	originates
accepts the status quo	challenges it
does things right	does the right thing

Leadership focuses on style and ideals, whereas management focuses on the method and process. Leadership does not produce consistency and order, as the word itself implies; it produces movement.[19]

The leadership challenge is about leading people, not merely managing them. Leadership begins where management ends, where the systems of rewards and punishments, control and scrutiny, give way to innovation, individual character, and the courage of convictions.[20]

Markets, customers, technology, and competitors continually change. The active leader anticipates these changes and strategically adapts the organization to continue to prosper in the following ways:

1. Repositioning products/services to build a competitive advantage
2. Recruiting talented people to execute the new strategies

Corporate Profile: Carlson Companies

One of America's recent corporate hospitality success stories is Carlson Companies, Inc. Beginning in 1938, entrepreneur Curtis Carlson had the vision to realize potential and popularity. With an idea, a mail drop, $50 borrowed capital, and trading stamps, he founded the Gold Bond Trading Stamp Company, in Minneapolis. Carlson marketed the trading stamp concept from local to regional and finally to national markets in Super Value food stores.

Carlson and several other partners collectively bought a 50-percent interest in the Radisson Hotel in downtown Minneapolis; within two years, he bought out all the other partners. Carlson took the hotel chain to twenty-two hotels in twenty-three years, but freely admits that he was not smart enough to expand by franchising. But Carlson was smart enough to hire Juergen Bartels as president of Carlson Hospitality Group. Bartels explained to Carlson that it was not necessary to put down your own money in order to expand a successful hotel company; it could be done by franchising. There are now 336 Radisson hotels and they are growing, especially in eastern Europe.

Curtis Carlson describes Juergen Bartels as one of the only people he knows who works harder than he does. Juergen Bartels says his boss is "intense, absolutely goal-driven. His work is his life. He is a task master."[1] He adds that he agrees with that and it does not intimidate him.

The Carlson Hospitality Group also includes TGI Friday's restaurants in 238 locations in eight countries; Country Lodging, a limited-service hotel with country-

Curtis Carlson and Juergen Bartels

style charm at thirty-five locations in the United States and Canada; and Country Kitchen, a family-style restaurant chain with 245 locations in three countries.

Before Carlson ever heard of TGI Friday's, Carlson ran Haberdashery restaurants in the Minneapolis area. Although moderately successful, this restaurant never took off. Later came Country Kitchen. Carlson was initially approached when the company operated fewer than ten restaurants; he liked the name but felt that the profit potential was small. Ironically, a few years later, he bought the chain, which by then was much larger. Carlson explained that the sales were there, but they were not making money. He said, "I thought it was a case of poor accounting or management. So I thought I was smart enough to take those restaurants, but then we bought it and never made any money either!" Today, however, the chain, which is all franchised, is doing well.

The 1990s are providing an interesting challenge for Carlson: how to transform from owner-operator to a management company and maintain quality standards with rapid growth. President and CEO Juergen Bartels has a management team with a "Yes, I can" mentality. With Bartels' philosophy that "No one should be last," aggressive goals and guidelines are set annually and underperforming managers and franchisees are regularly weeded out.[2] Bartels adds that "the basics here are growth and providing quality, and those that can't provide both are gone."

Carlson Hospitality now lends its lodging and food-service expertise via management contracts, joint ventures, or "O.P.M."—other people's money.

[1] This section draws on Bill Carlino, "Carlson Cos," *Nation's Restaurant News, 27,* 13, March 29, 1993, pp. 43–84.

[2] Ibid.

---

3. Establishing organizational resources that tightly focus on new strategies[21]

The most effective leaders share a number of skills, and these skills are always related to dealing with employees. The following suggestions outline an approach to becoming a hotel leader rather than just a manager:

➤ Be decisive—Hotel managers are confronted with dozens of decisions every day. Obviously, you should use your best judgment to resolve those decisions that come to roost at your doorstep. As a boss, make the decisions that best meet both your objectives and your ethics, and then make your decision known.

➤ Follow through—Never promise what you can't deliver, and never build false hopes among your employees. Once expectations are dashed, respect for and the reputation of the boss are shot.

➤ Select the best—A boss, good or bad, is carried forward by the work of his subordinates. One key to being a good boss is to hire the people who have the best potential to do what you need them to do. Take the time and effort to screen, interview, and assess the people who have not only the skills that you require, but also the needed values.

➤ Empower employees—Give people the authority to interact with the customer. The more people feel important, the better they work.

➤ Enhance career development—Good bosses recognize that most of their people want to improve themselves. However, career development is a two-edged sword: If we take the initiative to train and develop our people properly, then the competition is likely to hire them. The only way a boss can prevent the loss of productive workers looking for career development is to provide opportunities for growth within the organization.

➤ Seek support—Our industry is changing daily, from the type of services we offer to the ways we offer them. Depending on how we integrate change into the work place, people can either resist it or support it. As a boss, involve people in any change that affects them.

➤ Don't have all the answers—Bosses who don't admit a lack of knowledge or expertise, who don't find good people and rely on them, and who feel they have all the answers will not go too far up the ladder.

➤ Don't be tough-minded, hard-nosed and abrasive—These characteristics scare people into performing for the short run, but after a while the adrenalin is replaced with subtle resistance. If you want to manage for the long term, you have to motivate people on their terms, not yours, which means you have to be receptive to dealing with employees as people.

➤ Don't play politics—Some managers mortgage the future to look good now. Knowing the right people and earning favors is one way to promote your future, but at the point at which your reliance on politics becomes obvious and excessive, you become a liability to your company.

➤ Don't shoot the messenger—If you get bad news once, just shooting the messenger will give you bad news again. And you really don't have to shoot the messenger: Just accuse him or her in front of others of being negative, standing in the way of progress, and not being a team member.

There is no big secret to being a good boss. It all comes back to the relationship between you and the people who work for you. In other words, treat others as you would want to be treated.[22]

Management

Managers forecast, plan, organize, communicate, motivate, and control the efforts of a group to accomplish predetermined goals. Management establishes the direction that the organization will take. Sometimes this may be done with help of employees or outside consultants, such as marketing research specialists. Managers obtain the necessary resources for the tasks to be accomplished and they supervise and monitor group and individual progress towards goal accomplishment.

Top managers, such as presidents and chief executive officers who are responsible for the entire company, tend to focus most of their time on strategic planning and the organization mission. They also spend time on organizing and controlling the activities of the corporation. Most top managers do not get involved in the day-to-day aspects of the operation. These duties and responsibilities fall to middle and supervisory management. In hospitality lingo, one would not expect Bill Marriott to pull a shift behind the bar at the local Marriott hotel. Although capable, his time and expertise are used in shaping the company's future. Thus, although the head bartender and Bill Marriott may be considered management, they require slightly different skills to be effective and efficient managers.

Managerial Skills

In addition to the management functions of forecasting, planning, organizing, communicating, motivating, and controlling, there are other major skill areas: conceptual, human, and technical.

Conceptual skills enable top managers to view the corporation as a complete entity and yet understand how it is split into departments to achieve specific goals. Conceptual skills allow a top manager to view the entire corporation, especially the interdependence of the various departments.

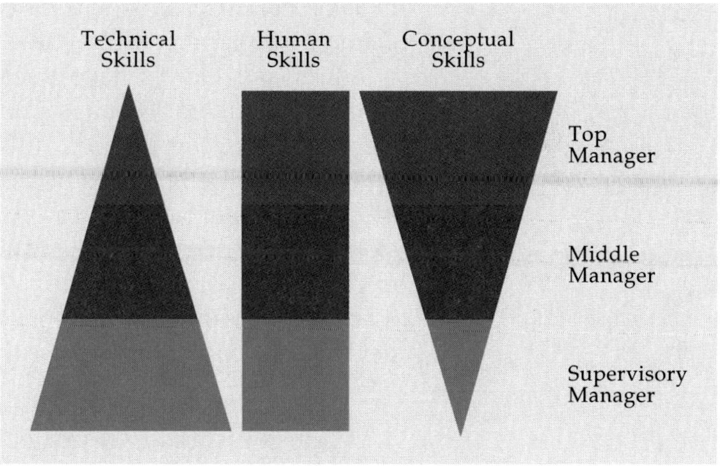

Managers need to lead, influence, communicate, supervise, coach, and evaluate employees' performances. This necessitates a high level of interpersonal human skills. The ability to build teams and work with others is a human skill that successful managers need to cultivate.

Figure 13-4 *Management Skill Areas*

Managers are required to have the technical skills to understand and use techniques, methods, equipment, and procedures. These skills are more important for use in lower levels of management. As a manager rises up, the need for technical skills decreases and the need for conceptual skills increases (see Figure 13-4).

Ethics

Ethics is a set of moral principles and values that people use to answer questions of right and wrong. Ethics can also be defined as the study of the general nature of morals and the specific moral choices to be made by the individual in his or her relationship with others.[23]

Much individual interpretation of ethics is based on one's own value system. Where did this value system originate? What happens if one value system is different to another? Fortunately, certain universal guiding principles are agreed on by virtually all religions, cultures, and societies.[24] At the very root of all principles is that all people's rights are important and should not be violated. This belief is central to civilized societies; without it, chaos would reign.

The foreword of *Ethics in Hospitality Management,* edited by Stephen S. J. Hall, the Robert A. Beck Professor Emeritus at Cornell University, poses the age-old question: "Is overbooking rooms ethical? How does one compare the legal responsibilities of the innkeeper to the moral obligations?" He adds that to compound the situation further, what is a "fair" or "reasonable" wage? A "fair" or "reasonable" return on investment? Is it "fair" or ethical to underpay employees for the benefit of the investors?

"English Common Law left such decisions to the 'reasonable man.' A judge would ask the jury, 'Was this the act of a reasonable man?'"[25] Interestingly, what is considered ethical in one country may not be in another. For example, in some countries it is considered normal to bargain for rooms; in others, bargaining would be considered bad form.

Ethics and morals have become an integral part of hospitality decisions, from employment (equal opportunity and affirmative action) to truth in memos. Many corporations and businesses have developed a code of ethics with which all employees use to make decisions. The development of a code of ethics became necessary because too many managers were making decisions without regard to the implication of the impact of such decisions on others. Hall is one of the pioneers of ethics in hospitality; each year, he organizes a scholarship for an essay on a topic related to ethics in hospitality. Hall also developed a code of ethics for the hospitality service and tourism industry:

1. We acknowledge ethics and morality as inseparable elements of doing business and will test every decision against the highest standards of honesty, legality, fairness, impunity, and conscience.
2. We will conduct ourselves personally and collectively at all times so as to bring credit to the service and tourism industry at large.
3. We will concentrate our time, energy, and resources on the improvement of our own products and services and we will not denigrate our competition in the pursuit of our own success.
4. We will treat all guests equally regardless of race, religion, nationality, creed, or sex.
5. We will deliver all standards of service and product with total consistency to every guest.

6. We will provide a totally safe and sanitary environment at all times for every guest and employee.

7. We will strive constantly, in words, actions, and deeds, to develop and maintain the highest level of trust, honesty, and understanding among guests, clients, employees, employers, and the public at large.

8. We will provide every employee at every level all of the knowledge, training, equipment, and motivation required to perform his or her tasks according to our published standards.

9. We will guarantee that every employee at every level will have the same opportunity to perform, advance, and be evaluated against the same standard as all employees engaged in the same or similar tasks.

10. We will actively and consciously work to protect and preserve our natural environment and natural resources in all that we do.

11. We will seek a fair and honest profit, no more, no less.

The saying "Do unto others as you have them do unto you" goes back to the Greek and even Chinese cultures. This is a belief that most cultures would agree is a good one to guide decisions. Forte Hotels International for many years adopted the belief of Lord Forte that we should take care of our guests as we would like to be taken care of.

Robert Hass, CEO of Levi Strauss Co., has an interesting comment on corporate ethics and value: "Companies have to wake up to the fact that they are more than a product on a shelf. They're a behavior as well."[26]

Some corporations use an aspirations statement to define shared values that will guide both work force and corporate decisions. For example, at Levi Strauss, each employee is expected to take part in the so-called core curriculum—a series of training programs that deal with values, ethical practices, empowerment, and an appreciation of diversity.[27] The purpose is to release the enormous power of involved employees.

Ethical Dilemmas in Hospitality

In the old days, certain actions may not have been considered ethical but management often looked the other way. Following are a few scenarios that are not seen as ethical today and are against the company's ethical policies:

1. As catering manager of a large banquet operation, the flowers for the hotel are booked through your office. The account is worth $15,000 per month. The florist offers you a 10-percent discount. Do you accept this? If you accept this, with whom do you share it?

2. As purchasing agent, you are responsible for procurement of $5 million worth of perishable and nonperishable items for a major restaurant chain. In order to get your business, a supplier offers you a substantial bargain on a house. You can live in the house, which will be under another person's name, for as long as you continue to buy from this supplier. The quality of this supplier's products and services are equal to the others. What should you do with the offer?

3. An edict had recently come from the executive committee of the hotel that reservations from a certain part of the world were only to be taken through the embassy because the hotel had experienced severe problems with guests from this part of the world. On one occasion, one of the occupants of a suite had sent a servant to the park to collect wood, which they then used to make a fire in the room in order to prepare food. Now, a group of well-dressed men approach you and offer greetings and say that their boss, a very distinguished individual, would like to stay for an indefinite period. They produce a briefcase full of $100 bills as a deposit.

To be recognized as the world's best first-class hotel organization, to constantly strive to improve, allowing us to prosper as a business for the benefit of our guests, our employees, and our shareholders.

Fundamental to the success of our mission are the following:

PEOPLE:
Our most important asset. Involvement, teamwork, and commitment are the values that govern our work.

PRODUCT:
Our programs, services, and facilities. They must be designed and operated to consistently provide superior quality that satisfies the needs and desires of our guests.

PROFIT:
The ultimate measure of our success—the gauge for how well and how efficiently we serve our guests. Profits are required for us to survive and grow.

With this mission come certain guiding principles:

QUALITY COMES FIRST:
The quality of our product and service must create guest satisfaction; that's our number one priority.

VALUE:
Our guests deserve quality products at a fair price. That is how to build business.

CONTINUOUS IMPROVEMENT:
Never standing on past accomplishments, but always striving—through innovation—to improve our product and service, to increase our efficiency and profitability.

TEAMWORK:
At Hilton, we are a family, working together, to get things done.

INTEGRITY:
We will never compromise our code of conduct—we will be socially responsible—we are committed to Hilton's high standards of fairness and integrity.

Figure 13-5 *Hilton's Corporate Mission* (Courtesy of Hilton Hotels Corporation, Beverly Hills, California.)

You decline, stating that the hotel is full, which it was not. What should have happened?

These and other ethical dilemmas or competing claims are not always as simple as right or wrong.

There are three key categories of questions to be answered when making decisions:

1. Is it legal? Will I be violating either civil law or company policy?
2. Is it balanced? Is it fair to all concerned in the short term as well as the long term? Does it promote win-win relationships?
3. How will it make me feel about myself? Will it make me proud? Would I feel good if my decision were published in the newspaper? Would I feel good if my family knew about it?[28]

Social Responsibilities in Business

"Ethics is broadly concerned with how persons or organizations act, or should act, in relations with others."[29] The so-called breakdown of socially acceptable behavior appears to be a universal problem. Whatever the cause, this malaise has affected business, government, and society.

In recent years, society's interest and awareness of social responsibility has increased enormously. For example, the "greening" of North America has led to a decrease in the use of hazardous chemicals, including some pesticides. The protection and preservation of the environment has become a major issue for most of the population.

Social responsibility, however, goes beyond changing from nonbiodegradable fast food containers to becoming involved in the community in which the company or one of its hospitality-tourism operations is located. This is known as giving something back to the community.

For example, consider Hilton's corporate mission (see Figure 13-5).

Summary

1. Leadership is defined as the process by which a person is able to influence the activities and outcomes of others in a desired way.
2. Traditional theories of leadership include the traits-of-a-treat-person theory, behavioral leadership, and Theory X, Y, and Z.
3. Approaches to leadership include the contingency theory, situational theory, authoritarian, democratic, laissez-faire, transactional, and transformation leadership.
4. Managing is a process in which organizational goals are achieved through efforts of subordinates, whereas leading is the process of influencing the behavior of others.
5. Managers have to forecast, plan, organize, and control the efforts of a group in order to achieve goals. They need to be skilled in conceptual, human, and technical areas.
6. In questions of employment, realistic advertising, room overbooking, and aspirations, ethics and morals have become an integral part of hospitality decisions.
7. Society's interest in social responsibility has increased and influenced hospitality in forms of recyclable fast food containers and involvement in the community in which the hotel is located.

Review Exercises

1. Define leadership and name essential qualities of a good leader.
2. Explain situational leadership, Theories X and Y, and laissez-faire leadership.
3. Distinguish between transactional and transformational leadership. Why is Wayne Calloway an excellent example of transformational leadership?
4. Briefly describe why Taco Bell leadership is an example of excellence.
5. In what ways have ethics and social awareness influenced the hotel industry?

Key Words and Concepts

Authoritarian, democratic, and laissez-faire leadership
Behavioral leadership
Contingency theory
Hierarchy of human needs
Human skills, conceptual skills, and technical skills
Leadership
Management
Professionalism
Situational leadership
Theories X and Theory Y
Theory Z
Trait theories
Transactional leadership
Transformational leadership

Notes

[1] John A. Wagner III and John R. Hollenbeck, *Management of Organizational Behavior.* Englewood Cliffs, N.J.: Prentice Hall, 1992, p. 408.

[2] James M. Kouzes and Barry Z. Posner, *The Leadership Challenge: How to Get Extraordinary Things Done in Organizations.* San Francisco: Jossey-Bass, 1987. p. 8.

[3] Donald D. White and David A. Bednar, *Organizational Behavior: Understanding and Managing People at Work,* 2d ed. Boston: Allyn and Bacon, 1991, p. 385.

[4] White and Bednar, op. cit., pp. 407–412.

[5] Ibid.

[6] White and Bednar, op. cit., p. 408.

[7] H. M. Burns, *Leader.* New York: Harper and Row, 1978, p. 84.

[8] Ibid.

[9] Ibid.

[10] Patricia Sellers, "Pepsi Keeps on Going after No.1," *Fortune, 123,* 5, March 11, 1991, pp. 62–70.

[11] White and Bednar, op. cit., p. 413.

[12] W. P. Fisher and C. Bernstein, *Lessons in Leadership: Perspectives for Hospitality Industry Success.* New York: Van Nostrand Reinhold, 1991, p. 44.

[13] Ibid., p. 35.

[14] Ibid., p. 29

[15] This draws on Doug Caldwell, "Isadore Sharp: Outstanding CEO of the Year," *Canadian Manager,* Spring 1993, pp. 16–17.

[16] Based on James Scarpa, "Leadership Awards," *Restaurant Business, 90,* 8, May 20, 1991, p. 97.

[17] John P. Kotter, *A Force for Change: How Leadership Differs from Management.* New York: Free Press, 1990, pp. 3–4.

[18] Warren Bennis, *On Becoming a Leader.* Reading, Mass.: Addison-Wesley, p. 45.

[19] Ibid.

[20] Kouzes and Posner, op. cit., p. xvii.

[21] James A. Belasco, *Teaching the Elephant to Dance.* New York: Plume, 1991. p. 6.

[22] Charles Brewton, *Hotel and Motel Management, 207,* 6, April 6, 1992, p. 13; reprinted with permission courtesy of *Hotel and Motel Management.*

[23] Angelo M. Rocco and Andrew N. Vladimir, *Hospitality Today: An Introduction.* East Lansing, Mich.: The Educational Institute of the American Hotel and Motel Association, 1991, p. 390.

[24] Ibid.

[25] Stephen S. J. Hall (ed.), *Ethics in Hospitality Management: A Book of Readings.* East Lansing, Mich.: The Educational Institute of the American Hotel and Motel Association, 1992, p. 75.

[26] Jim Impoco, "Working for Mr. Clean Jeans," *U.S. News and World Report, 115,* 5, August, 2, 1993, p. 50.

[27] Ibid.

[28] Rocco and Vladimir, op cit., p. 27.

[29] William D. Hall, *Making the Right Decisions: Ethics for Managers.* New York: John Wiley and Sons, 1993, p. 3.

Management
Service
and
Professionalism

After reading and studying this chapter you should be able to do the following:

- ➤ Describe corporate philosophy and corporate culture
- ➤ Name and describe the functions of management
- ➤ Explain the importance of having a management philosophy
- ➤ Identify and describe the attributes of professionalism
- ➤ Describe your ideal career path and write a resumé
- ➤ Describe how to prepare for an interview

Before identifying the key management functions, we need to first realize the critical importance of the corporate philosophy, culture, values, and the corporation's mission, goals, and objectives.

Corporate Philosophy

The past definition of corporate philosophy is changing from managers planning, organizing, implementing, and measuring to counseling associates, giving them the resources, and helping them to think for themselves. The outcome is a more participative management style, which results in associate empowerment, increased productivity, and guest and employee satisfaction. Corporate philosophy has strong linkages with quality leadership and the total quality management (TQM) process.

Corporate philosophy embraces the values of the organization: these include ethics, morals, fairness, and equality. The new paradigm in corporate American hospitality is the shift in emphasis from the production aspect of our business to the focus on the guest-related services. The philosophy of "whatever it takes" is winning over "it's not my job." Innovation and creativity are winning over "that's the way we've always done it." Successful organizations are those who are able to impart their corporate philosophies to employees and guests alike—Disney Corporation is a good example of a corporation that has a permeating corporate philosophy.

There is no set formula for a corporate philosophy. However, to be truly effective, a corporate philosophy must be unique to the organization. Common denominators of a successful corporate philosophy include the following:

1. A clear statement of purpose
2. A definition of the responsibilities of the business
3. Adherence to principles ahead of profits

The most important element in maintaining an organization's image is the practice of making corporate philosophy part of the daily lives of the people involved. Keeping the philosophy alive begins at the top and is conveyed to every level, so that people at the bottom are committed and involved.

See Figure 14-1 for examples of management philosophies that are shared by the whole organization.

Corporate Culture

Corporate culture is the overall style or feel of a company. A company's culture governs how people relate to one another and their jobs. It can be

Hyatt Regency • San Francisco

"My purpose is to create and promote a dynamic, positive, and growing environment in which I am committed to consistently providing the quality of the product and service to our guests."

ABDUL SULEMAN
REGIONAL VICE PRESIDENT,
HYATT HOTELS, SAN FRANCISCO

Our philosophies of operating business at Hyatt Hotels, San Francisco:

1. Our health comes first, family second, and our job comes third. When the first two are taken care of well, then our performance at work will be excellent.

2. We have two rules in our hotel. Rule number one: The customer is *always* right. Rule number two: If you ever have any doubts in your mind, always go back to rule number one.

3. Attitude toward the guest must be pleasant, caring, attentive, thoughtful, courteous, service oriented, positive, helpful, and friendly with a smile.

4. Be knowledgeable of our product and believe in it.

5. No hotel meeting is so important that a guest cannot interrupt us. The guest always comes first.

6. Always recommend the hotel's food and beverage outlets before *any* outside facility.

7. Greet our guests with a warm welcome and smile. Use their names, whenever possible.

8. Give our guests a warm good-bye and invite them back.

9. Respond to guests' wishes within ten minutes of the request. Follow up with a phone call within twenty minutes to ensure their satisfaction.

10. Our customers deserve the most courteous attention we can give them. They are the life blood of this and every business. They pay our salary. Without them, we would have to close our doors. Don't ever forget it.

11. Always present a professional image. Wear an immaculate uniform, including footwear, name tag, and have good personal grooming standards.

12. Guard your habits—bad ones can destroy. You are what you do, not what you say.

13. Good management means good manners and common sense.

14. All guests complaints must be resolved before leaving the hotel. Find solutions, not excuses. Always listen to the guest and have an empathetic attitude. Understanding a guest's position goes a long way toward bringing them back.

15. Ensure that all employees know their role during emergency situations and are aware of procedure.

16. Top line produces bottom line.

17. Treat the hotel's money like it is your own. If you watch the pennies, the dollars will take care of themselves.

18. Make sure you are always on time for meetings and appointments. There is no excuse for being late.

19. Phones should be answered promptly and courteously within three rings. When transferring a call, identify the caller being transferred and the nature of the call. Phone calls should never be screened. Of course, it goes without saying, we don't put people on hold and never get back to them.

20. All work areas and back of the house should be neat, clean, and organized at all times.

21. It is very important that our guests receive all messages and packages on time.

22. We believe in management by walking around.

23. We believe in two-way communication and an open-door policy.

24. See the good in people and try to develop those qualities. A positive and productive mind-set results in positive and productive performance.

25. We have faith and trust in our employees. We believe our product is our people.

26. Never put off until tomorrow what you can do today.

27. There is absolutely no excuse for anyone to be rude to any customer.

28. Teamwork and respect for each other is important. Be a team player and be open and honest with each other.

29. Quality of the product and service with consistency is a must. Do not compromise when it comes to standards. Consistency is essential and provides our assurance of quality, which results in absolutely unshakable customer loyalty.

30. Stay away from gossip and rumors. Remember, anything you say about someone may (and usually does) get back to them. There are few secrets. Never talk behind people's backs.

31. Our job is our motivation.

32. Have confidence and believe in yourself but be humble.

33. Manage your time effectively—short conversations, to the point. Make every minute on the job count. Some of us waste half of our time.

34. Think objectively and keep a sense of humor. Make the business fun for you and others.

35. Service is not a luxury, but it is an essential ingredient for the success of our business. Business goes where it's asked and stays where it's appreciated.

36. Get involved in the community and be a part of the community. The community's success is our success.

37. People like to do business with the people they know and trust.

38. We are in business to make money but we want to give our customers their money's worth. We are honorable businesspersons.

39. We would rather lose revenue than business.

40. We don't want to think we are number one—we want to keep striving to be number one.

41. Pay attention to details. What makes us different from others is doing the little things right.

42. Be loyal to our guests, our job, fellow employees, our boss, our hotel, and the company we work for.

43. Be creative, keep learning and growing—change with the times. These changes not only help us professionally, but also in our total life. Never be afraid to take risks.

Figure 14-1 *Hyatt Regency San Francisco's Operating Philosophy* (Courtesy The Hyatt Regency San Francisco.)

summed up with the phrase, "This is how we do things around here." The casual image of the Chart House restaurant chain is a definite part of their corporate culture. However, don't be fooled—their managers may appear casual, but they are very professional. Each of the major corporations has a culture, some more pronounced than others. It is a good idea to align yourself with a corporation that blends with your culture, values, and style.

Mission Statement

A mission statement is a short statement of the central purposes, strategies, and values of a company. Essentially, a corporation's mission statement should answer the question, "What business are we in?" A good mission statement will go beyond the obvious and include the corporation's purpose, values, and strategies (see Figure 14-2).

Mission Statement

The Ritz-Carlton, Laguna Niguel, will be recognized internationally as the leading five-star, five-diamond resort hotel in North America. We will be unique in combining the genuine warmth and vitality of southern California with the traditional setting found in the finest hotels of Europe.

Every guest will feel that he or she is our most important guest. They will find us easy to do business with, and will be impressed by our uncompromising, consistent service and our ability to anticipate and fulfill even their unexpressed wishes. They will appreciate our creative, sophisticated, world-class cuisine and services. Our versatile entertainment will enhance our elegant, relaxing atmosphere. In addition, our guests will enjoy the unparalleled beauty of our location along with the museum-quality art collection.

Our employees will be proud of their association with the hotel and will be an integral part of our success. They will see the Ritz-Carlton as the best hotel to work in, a place where they can grow personally and professionally. Our staff will remain committed to continuously improving and refining our facilities and service.

The owners and the corporate office will be proud of the hotel, and will have confidence in us. They will see us as a source of qualified managers for new hotels. The owners and the corporate office will be committed to helping us refine the facility's quality and improve its profitability, in partnership with the executive committee.

The community will also be proud of the hotel, and will see it as a cooperative, involved business resident of the county.

Figure 14-2 *Mission Statement, Ritz-Carlton, Laguna Niguel* (Courtesy Ritz-Carlton, Laguna Niguel.)

Goal

A goal is a specific target to be met. In a hotel, for example, one of the goals might be to increase occupancy from 80 to 85 percent. Another might be to maintain the average daily rate (ADR) at $78. Goals may be written for each department on a variety of topics from alcohol awareness training to reducing employee turnover. Today, most corporations involve their employees in the goal setting. This not only ties in with total quality management, but also encourages employees to buy into the process and increases the likelihood that goals may even be exceeded.

Objectives

Objectives are the actions that are needed to accomplish the goal. Using the hotel occupancy example, the objective will state how the goal will be met. The objective then identifies the specific actions necessary to produce the desired result. In order for the hotel to increase the occupancy from 80 to 85 percent, specific actions might include the following:

- ➤ Conduct a travel agent sales blitz in key feeder cities
- ➤ Host ten travel agents familiarization (FAM) tours
- ➤ Direct mail a number of American Express, Visa, Master, Discover card holders, and so on

Once the corporate philosophy, culture, mission, goals, and objectives are finalized, the management functions will have guidance and direction to help steer the organization to success.

Key Management Functions

The key management functions are forecasting, planning, organizing, decision making, communicating, motivating, and controlling. These management functions are not conducted in isolation; rather they are interdependent and frequently happen simultaneously, or at least are overlapping.

Forecasting

This is the first of the management functions and involves a forecast of expected business volumes. In hotel terms, that means occupancy percentages and in restaurants, the number of covers. Similarly, in institutional food service, we will need as close an estimate as possible of guests to enable management to plan effectively in order to cater for everyone. Forecasting is important because problems may arise if we either over- or under-forecast because the subsequent functions of management will be planned on slightly inaccurate assumptions.

Restaurant managers forecast how many covers they will do on a given night by taking several variables into account, including the following:

The time of year—Summer, fall, winter, spring (to allow for seasonal fluctuations).

The day of week—Demand is different on each night of the week, with Friday generally being the busiest.

Expected weather—Fine weather may increase demand whereas foul weather may decrease it.

Advance reservations—Any reservations already made become the starting point of the count of the expected number of covers.

Forecasting takes various factors into account, evaluates them, and produces a calculated guess as to how much business will come our way. Because it is the first management function, it is important to do it accurately because those that follow are based on the forecast of business.

A sales director and the sales team going over the sales forecast (Courtesy the Pan Pacific Hotel, San Diego, CA.)

The majority of the products and services offered in the hospitality industry are perishable items. The value of hotel rooms or prepared food items perish if they are not sold within a certain period of time. A restaurant manager and chef will forecast how many guests to prepare for the next week, then order food and schedule employees. Hotels publish weekly and fourteen-day forecasts to enable all the departments to gauge the volume of business for their outlets and allocate resources accordingly. Restaurants, food-service management, and travel and tourism organizations all make similar projections to forecast the expected business volume.

Planning

There are two main types of planning: long-range or strategic, and short-range or tactical. Long-range, strategic planning is the process of determining the major objectives of an organization along with the policies and strategies that will govern the acquisition, use, and disposition of the resources that are necessary to achieve those objectives. Strategic plans are made for five years or more into the future. Tactical plans are made for up to one year.

An example of strategic hospitality planning for a restaurant chain would be as follows: Do we modify or change our concept? Kentucky Fried Chicken made a strategic move when they changed their name to KFC. This downplays the fact that the chicken is fried, a method of cooking that is not well perceived by the more health-conscious population of the 1990s. Strategic planning also assesses the opportunities and alternatives for expansion into international markets.

In tourism terms, a country or a destination would make a master plan of how they would reach the predetermined goals of increasing the number of tourists, encouraging them to stay longer, spend more, and exceeding tourists' expectations of a quality visit.

Hospitality corporations make long-range plans, in areas ranging from human resources development to financial plans, and from hospitality renovation to the operation of their franchise division.

The more senior a manager, the longer the planning horizon is. A corporate manager at the top of an organization is primarily occupied with the company's vision, mission, organizational objectives, and major policy areas. Middle-level managers' planning responsibilities focus on translating the objectives of the organization into goals for the front-line managers and supervisors. Front-line managers are involved in scheduling employees and developing and executing plans to achieve the organizational goals.

Tactical plans have a shorter time frame and narrower scope than strategic plans. A tactical plan is concerned with what the lower levels of management and employees must do to achieve the strategic goals.

Operational plans provide managers with a step-by-step approach to accomplish her or his goals. The overall purpose of planning is to have the entire organization moving harmoniously towards the goals.

There are seven steps in organizational planning:

1. Setting objectives—This first step in planning decides the expected outcomes—goals/objectives. The goals should be specific, measurable, and achievable.

2. Analyzing and evaluating the environment—This involves analyzing the political, economic, social, and other trends that may affect the corporation. The level and intensity of turbulence is evaluated in relation to the organization's present position and the resources available to achieve goals.

3. Determining alternatives—This involves developing courses of action that are available to a manager to reach a goal. Input may be requested from all levels of the organization. Group work is normally better than individual input.

4. Evaluating alternatives—This calls for making a list of advantages and disadvantages of each alternative. Among the factors to be considered are resources and effects on the organization.

5. Selecting the best solution—This analysis of the various alternatives should result in determining one course of action that is better than the others. It may, however, involve combining two or more alternatives.

6. Implementing the plan—Once the optimum solution is decided on, the manager needs to decide the following:

   Who will do what?
   By when?
   What resources are required?
   At what benefit?
   At what cost?
   What reporting procedures will there be?
   What authority will be granted to achieve the goals?

7. Controlling and evaluating results—Once the plan is implemented, it is necessary to monitor progress toward goal accomplishment.

Organizing

Once the vision, mission, goals, objectives, and plans for the company have been agreed on, the work necessary to complete those tasks requires organization. Organizing is the process of arranging the resources of the corporation in such a way that activities systematically contribute to the corporation's goals. The purposes of organizing are to give each person a specific task and to ensure that these tasks are coordinated.[1]

Most corporations are made up of two organizations: a formal one and an informal one. The formal organization is the one depicted by the corporate organizational chart. It shows the authority, responsibility, and chains of command.

The informal organization is the "shadow organization" that emerges as people interact with one another on the job. It reflects the way "things really get done around here."[2]

In recent years corporations have been down-sizing or right-sizing their management and organizational structures. Most hospitality operations are organized according to the best way of serving the guest. Most of the segments that makes up the hospitality industry have similar organizational structures, whether it be in the kitchen, restaurant, hotel, airline, cruise line, or others.

Decision Making

Centralized decision making means that decision making takes place at the corporate level. In a centralized corporation, most decisions are channeled down the chain of command from the top managers. Lower-level employees simply follow policies and procedures. Marriott is an example of a centralized company. However, even centralized corporations have adopted initiatives such as TQM and empowerment, which have given more leeway to the front-line employees to do whatever it takes to satisfy the guest.

Decentralized decision making is the extent to which the decision making is spread throughout the organization. Managers at every level are empowered to make decisions. The more decisions made at lower levels, the more decentralized an organization is said to be.

Span of control or span of management refers to the number of people that one manager can effectively manage. There is no set limit to the number of people that a manager can supervise because it depends on the type of organization (centralized versus decentralized) and the degree of its sophistication in terms of efficiency and effectiveness. The trend today is for the span of control to increase to twelve or more. Previously, management theorists had suggested a comfortable maximum span of control of six to eight subordinates. The reasons for increasing the span of control are to remain competitive by reducing costs, increase efficiency by allowing a greater say in the operation by all levels of employees, and to increase the amount of available computerized information.

The success of all organizations, be they large multinational corporations or sole proprietorships, depends on the quality of decision making. Beginning with mission, goals, and objectives, the success of all organizations depends on decision making.

There are two main types of decisions: programmed decisions and nonprogrammed decisions. A programmed decision is a decision that recurs on a regular basis—for example, when the number of New York steaks goes below a specified number, an order for more is automatically placed. Programmed decisions generally become a standard operating procedure (SOP).

A nonprogrammed decision is nonrecurring and made necessary by unusual circumstances, such as which computer hardware and software a restaurant should install, or whether to expand by franchising or company-owned restaurants. These are unique decision situations that will not likely recur for several years.

The more sophisticated a company is the more programmed decisions are made. Many large corporations have policy and procedure manuals to guide managerial and supervisory decision making. Nonprogrammed decisions call for greater analysis, innovation, and problem-solving skills.

Decision makers follow a process of eight major steps:

1. Identification and definition of problem
2. Identification of decision criteria
3. Allocation of weights to criteria
4. Development of alternatives
5. Analysis of alternatives
6. Selection of alternative
7. Installation of alternative
8. Evaluation of decision effectiveness

Figure 14-3 illustrates the decision-making process.

Step 1: Identification and Definition of Problem
A problem exists when there is a discrepancy between current and desired results. The decision making process begins with identifying and defining the problem(s). It is not always easy to identify the problem because other issues may muddy the waters. To illustrate the point, there is an interesting story of a

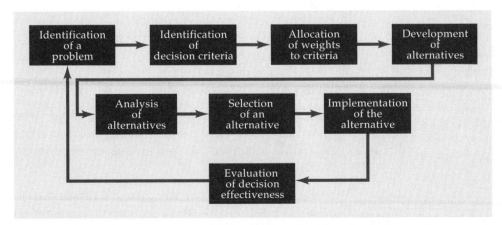

Figure 14-3 *Eight-Step Decision-Making Process* (Stephen P. Robbins, *Management,* 3d ed. Englewood Cliffs, N.J.: Prentice Hall, 1991, p. 153.)

maximum security prison warden who was about to retire after a distinguished career. One day, an associate reported to him that the pass key for the section in which the hard-core prisoners were housed was missing. This presented the warden with a dilemma: If he reported the missing keys to his supervisors, his exemplary career would be tarnished—indeed, disciplinary action against him might be taken. The real problem, however, is not the loss of the keys or how to find the keys; it is containing the hard-core prisoners who might escape.

In a hotel setting, problem situations can be identified with respect to guest check in. In some of the larger city-center, convention-oriented hotels, there are frequently long lines of guests waiting to check into the hotel. Defining this problem is best done by writing a problem statement, i.e., the problem is that it takes too long for guests to register, or guests do not like waiting to register. Once the problem has been accurately stated, it becomes easier to move to the next step in the decision-making process.

Herb Kelleher, president of Southwest Airlines, made the decision to remove the closets at the front of Southwest planes. This was in response to a problem: It took too long to turn around the planes. To be competitive and successful, it is necessary to reduce the turn-around time in order to squeeze more flights into each day. The situation that caused or contributed to the turn-around problem was that the first people on the plane typically went to the closets first and then grabbed the nearest seats. On landing, the departing passengers were held up while the people in the front rows rummaged through the closets for their bags. The airline now turns around about 85 percent of its flights in fifteen minutes or less, and is one of the most profitable airlines, with a remarkable 16 percent average return on equity over the past several years.[3]

Step 2: Identification of Decision Criteria

Once the problem has been identified and defined, it is necessary to determine the criteria relevant to the decision. Suppose the problem is that we are hungry; then the decision criteria might be the following:

1. What type of food would we prefer?
2. How much time do we have?
3. How much do we want to spend?
4. How convenient is parking?
5. What is the restaurant's reputation?
6. How is the food quality?
7. How is the service?
8. How is the atmosphere?

These criteria are developed by the group who would like to eat out at a restaurant. Criteria that are not identified are usually treated as unimportant.

Step 3: Allocation of Weights to Criteria

To the decision makers, the decision criteria all have differing levels of importance. For instance,

Table 14-1
Criteria and Weight
in Restaurant Selection

How much do we want to spend?	10
How is the food quality?	9
How much time do we have?	6
What type of food would we prefer?	8
How is the atmosphere?	6
How is the service?	7
How convenient is parking?	6
How is the restaurant's reputation?	6
How far do we want to go to a restaurant?	7

is the expected cost of the meal more important than the atmosphere? If so, a higher weight should be attached to that criterion.

One method used to weigh the criteria is to give the most important criterion a weight of ten and then score the others according to their relative importance. In the meal example, the cost of the meal might receive a weight of ten, whereas the atmosphere might be awarded a weight of six. Table 14-1 lists a sample of criteria and weights for the decision of restaurant selection.

Step 4: Development of Alternatives

In developing alternatives, decision makers list the viable alternatives that could resolve the problem. No attempt is made to evaluate these alternatives, only to list them. Using the restaurant scenario, the alternatives are shown in Figure 14-4.

Step 5: Analysis of Alternatives

The alternatives are analyzed using the criteria and weights established in steps two and three. Figure 14-5 shows the values placed on each of the alternatives by the group. (It does not show the weighted values.)

The weighted values of the group's decision on which restaurant to go to are shown in Figure 14-6.

KFC
Taco Bell
Pizza Hut
McDonald's
Applebee's
The Olive Garden
Wendy's

Figure 14-4 *Restaurant Alternatives*

	KFC	Taco Bell	Pizza Hut	McDonald's	Applebee's	Olive Garden	Wendy's
Price	9	10	10	10	7	7	9
Type of food	7	8	9	8	8	9	8
How much time	9	9	7	10	7	6	10
Quality of food	7	7	8	7	8	8	8
Atmosphere	7	7	8	7	9	9	7
Service	6	6	7	7	8	9	7
Convenient parking	10	10	10	10	10	10	10
Restaurant reputation	8	8	8	7	8	9	8
How far away	8	8	8	10	7	7	8
Total	71	73	75	76	72	74	75

Figure 14-5 *Analysis of Alternatives*

	KFC	Taco Bell	Pizza Hut	McDonald's	Applebee's	Olive Garden	Wendy's
Price	90	100	100	100	70	70	90
Type of food	56	64	72	64	64	72	64
How much time	54	54	42	60	42	36	60
Quality of food	63	63	72	63	72	72	72
Atmosphere	42	42	48	42	54	54	48
Service	42	42	49	49	56	63	49
Convenient parking	60	60	60	60	60	60	60
Restaurant reputation	48	48	48	42	54	54	48
How far away	56	56	56	60	49	49	56
Total	511	529	547	540	521	530	547

Figure 14-6 *Weighted Values Analysis*

Once the weighted values are totaled we can see that Pizza Hut and Wendy's are the restaurants with the highest scores. Notice how these are not the restaurants with the highest scores before the weighted values were included.

Step 6: Selection of Alternative

The sixth step involves the selection of the best alternative. Once the weighted scores for each alternative have been totaled, it will become obvious which is the best alternative.

Step 7: Installation of Alternative

Installing the alternative means to put the decision into action. Sometimes, good decisions fail because they are not put into action.

Step 8: Evaluation of Decision Effectiveness

The final step in the decision loop is to evaluate the effectiveness of the decision. As a result of the decision, did we achieve the goals we set? If the decision was not effective, then we must find out why the desired results were not attained. This would mean going back to step one. If the decision was effective then no action, other than recording the outcome, needs to be taken.

Communicating

Communication is the oil that lubricates all the other management functions of forecasting, planning, organizing, motivating, and controlling. Additionally, because managers spend a high percentage of their time communicating, this makes the communication function doubly important. Managers interact with others throughout the day by the following means:

➤ Telephone
➤ Mail/fax
➤ Memos and other internal/external written communication
➤ Personal face to face meetings

The simplest method of communication involves a sender, a message, and a receiver. However, merely sending a message cannot ensure that the message will be received and understood correctly.

Several factors can distort the communication process, ranging from noise interference to poor listening skills and inappropriate tuning. The middle of a busy lunch service is not the time to be asking the chef a question or bothering her or him with some communication on the policy of company sick-pay benefits.

Face-to-face tends to be the best means of communication. The instant feedback provides both sender and receiver with a better understanding of the communication. In contrast, one-way communication does not allow the receiver to respond or check the intended meaning and find out what action the receiver should take.

Some of the barriers to effective interpersonal communication are the following:[4]

➤ Hearing what we expect to hear
➤ Ignoring information that conflicts with what we think we know
➤ Evaluating the source
➤ Differing perceptions
➤ Words that mean different things to different people
➤ Inconsistent nonverbal signals
➤ Effects of emotions
➤ Noise

Effective communicators use techniques to improve the communication process, such as the following:

➤ Being sensitive to the receiver's world
➤ Being aware of symbolic meanings
➤ Using clear, direct, simple language
➤ Moving from defensive to supportive communication
➤ Understanding the relationship between two parties
➤ Being aware of the level of trust

Grapevine/Informal Communication

Most organizations have informal communication channels known as *grapevines*. Informal communication can both help and hinder effective communication.

Informal communication with staff can help develop trust and commitment. People who have the best understanding of the jobs are those employees who are doing the jobs. Therefore, by communicating with the staff informally, the following benefits may be gained:[5]

➤ Identify potential problems
➤ Gain staff commitment to organization
➤ Gather information to use in decision making and planning

Some ideas suggested for effective informal communication include the following:[6]

➤ Do not be a stranger—Walk around the department and make yourself accessible to your staff
➤ Use employees' names when talking with them so that they feel recognized and respected
➤ Keep your staff informed—If you keep them updated on what is going on in your department and at your property, they are more likely to keep you informed as well
➤ Maintain an open-door policy, and be sure that your employees know about it
➤ Be sure your employees know that you want, value, and need their ideas
➤ Listen noncritically and objectively to employees' concerns and contributions

➤ Do not react emotionally or critically when someone brings you bad news
➤ Use good listening skills—An employee won't talk if no one is listening
➤ Never miss an opportunity to compliment an employee for a quality contribution.

Informal communication is a powerful tool that sometimes is overlooked. If used properly, valuable information will be provided, relationships and commitment will be developed, and a positive working environment will be created, thereby strengthening the communication links throughout the entire organization.[7]

Motivating

Motivation is the art or process of initiating and sustaining behavior toward certain goals. Motivation is all about inspiring someone to do something because he or she wants to do it, not because someone says to do it. As the American and Canadian hospitality and tourism industries have right-sized the organizational structure by reducing the number of levels of management, there is an increasing need for motivation. One hotel general manager, Steve Pelzer, said that his biggest problem was how to motivate employees. This section will help you understand and influence your own motivation and that of those you will lead in the future.

The following motivational theories have been suggested by scholars and experts on motivation:

➤ Intrinsic and extrinsic theories
➤ Vicarious theories
➤ Content theories
➤ Process theories
➤ Goal-setting theories

Intrinsic and Extrinsic Motivation

Intrinsic and extrinsic motivation refer to the source of a person's motivation. Intrinsic motivation relates to the internal stimuli or need that occurs within us and causes us to be motivated. An example is the good feelings that occur when a task has been well done. Extrinsic motivation is caused by external stimuli. Being praised by a colleague is an example of extrinsic motivation.

Vicarious Motivation

Vicarious motivation relates to our seeing another person rewarded or punished; we perceive that we will receive similar treatment for similar actions. We naturally want to please so when we see another person receiving compliments for their actions the positive motivational effect is likely to rub off on us.

Content Theories

There is no single cause of motivation; instead, several factors may influence a person's desire to do things. Some suggest that motivation is linked to need satisfaction. This is closely related to the need–drive goal cycle, in which motivation occurs when a need within us initiates a drive toward a certain goal. For example, if a food service manager who seeks recognition (a need) meets certain goals, she or he will receive a bonus (a goal). The individual may work long hours (a drive) in order to accomplish the goal. Once the goal has been achieved, the need will be temporarily satisfied, and the behavior will subside until the need is reactivated. One of the interesting aspects of motivation is that different people have different needs.

One of the significant content theories of motivation is Maslow's hierarchy of needs. Maslow's theory has influenced motivational techniques for many years. The theory suggests that there are five basic needs or motives common to adults:

1. Physiological needs: Necessities for life, including food, air, and fluids, all of which are essential to our physical existence
2. Safety needs: The security and assurance that our physiological needs will be met in the future
3. Love and belonging needs: Social needs such as the need for affection or the need for acceptance by others
4. Esteem needs: The needs of self-respect and respect from others
5. Self-actualization needs: The need for self-fulfillment; the need to reach one's potential[8]

Figure 14-7 shows Maslow's five needs together with examples of how each might be satisfied in an organizational setting.

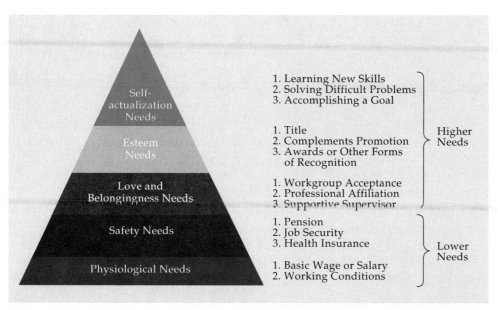

Figure 14-7 *Maslow's Needs Hierarchy in Organizational Settings* (Donald D. White and David A. Bednar, *Organizational Behavior: Understanding and Managing People at Work,* 2d ed. Boston: Allyn and Bacon, 1991, p. 149.)

Table 14-2
Herzberg's Motivators and Hygiene Factors

Motivators	Hygienes
Work itself	Company policies and administration
Recognition	Salary
Responsibility	Working conditions
Achievement	Relationships with supervisors
Growth	Relationships with peers
Advancement	Relationships with subordinates
	Security
	Status

Although Maslow's theory was first proposed in 1943, it is still widely and highly regarded as having a significant influence on management and employee motivation.

Another widely accepted and influential theory of motivation is Frederick Herzberg's explanation of motivator and hygiene factors. While studying managers in the work environment, psychologist Frederick Herzberg concluded that two separate and distinct sets of factors influenced individual motivation. Herzberg referred to these groups of factors as satisfiers and dissatisfiers, or motivators and hygienes. Table 14-2 shows both the motivators and hygiene factors.

The main premise of Herzberg's theory is that if the hygiene factors are not met, it is unlikely that much motivation will occur, no matter how many of the motivators are met. However, once the hygiene factors have been met, significant motivation will occur once the motivator factors are present.

Process Theories

Process theories are concerned with the decision to make an effort. We process information on a certain topic and then decide the amount of effort to be used to do a particular task. There are two main process theories: expectancy theory and equity theory.

The expectancy theory is based on the premise that people will put out effort equivalent to the perceived rewards. If people think they are definitely going to receive rewards, they are more likely to be motivated and give the extra effort required to achieve the goals. Bonuses utilize the expectancy theory of motivation. For example, if a food service manager meets or exceeds a predetermined level of profitability, she or he will receive a financial, and possibly other, bonus incentives. Figure 14-8 shows a simplified version of the Expectancy Model.

Equity theory relates to the exchange of individual contributions for organizational rewards. Equity theory suggests that an individual's motivation relies on three important variables:

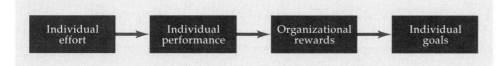

Figure 14-8 *Expectancy Model* (Stephen P. Robbins, *Management,* 3d ed. Englewood Cliffs, N.J.: Prentice Hall, 1991, p. 440.)

1. The inputs an individual perceives she or he is contributing
2. The outcomes (rewards) an individual perceives she or he is receiving
3. The way in which an individual's inputs and outcomes compare to the inputs and outcomes of another person[9]

Many of us tend to evaluate our own efforts in comparison to outcomes/rewards and then compare them to the outcomes/rewards of others doing similar activities. Our motivation will likely be affected positively or negatively by the level of satisfaction based on the comparison.

Goal-Setting Theories

Both companies and individuals are better off when they set goals; even if they are not all reached, the results will be better than if no goals were set. As a result, many companies have included some form of goal setting as part of the reward and recognition programs.

Goal setting is a key element in management by objectives (MBO). With MBO, goals are generally set by employees, not managers. Once the employee has set the individual and group/department goals, management approves the goals. Employees are far more likely to achieve and even exceed goals that they have been a part of setting rather having them prescribed from above. Quality assurance programs and, more recently, total quality management and empowerment have contributed greatly to employee motivation.

Controlling

The purpose of control is to provide information to management for decision-making purposes. Control closes the cycle of management function by determining whether or not the corporation reached its goals. Remember that at the outset, criteria are set, and the quality levels are established. The last management function is to determine how well we have done what we said we would do.

The control function provides management with the necessary information to make informed decisions on the organization's progress toward meeting the predetermined goals. Control has three main elements:

1. Establishing standards of performance
2. Measuring current performance against expected performance
3. Acting on significant variance from expected performance

Corporate Profile: The Ritz Carlton Hotel Company

A Commitment to Excellence and Quality Service Worldwide

The Ritz Carlton Hotel Company was officially organized in the summer of 1983, although the Ritz-Carlton's history and tradition long precede that date. With the purchase of The Ritz-Carlton, Boston, and the acquisition of the exclusive rights to use the name came a rich heritage. Built in 1927, The Ritz-Carlton, Boston, has nurtured a tradition of excellence rooted in the philosophy of the celebrated hotelier, Cesar Ritz. The landmark property is the only Ritz-Carlton of that era to continuously operate since opening.

Beginning with one hotel in 1983, the company now operates thirty-one hotels worldwide (twenty-one city hotels and ten resorts) in the United States, Hong Kong, Australia, Mexico, South Korea, and Spain. Expansion in Asia continues with the opening of hotels in Singapore (late 1995) and Osaka, Japan, (Spring 1997).

Horst Schulze

The Ritz-Carlton Hotel Company, with headquarters in Atlanta, Georgia, has built its reputation on reliable service and commitment to quality. The Ritz-Carlton mission is to provide the finest personal service and facilities, instill well-being, and fulfill even the unexpressed wishes and needs of guests. Under the charismatic leadership and insistence on high standards of Mr. Horst Schulze, president and chief operating officer of Ritz-Carlton, the company was awarded the prestigious 1992 Malcolm Baldrige National Quality Award. The Ritz-Carlton is the first and only hospitality organization to have ever won this coveted honor, given by the United States Department of Commerce for quality management.

Quality planning begins with president Schulze, whose commitment to excellence is apparent in the many innovations and changes he has initiated over the years. Perhaps the most significant is the launching of a comprehensive quality management program. Hallmarks of the program include participatory executive leadership, thorough information gathering, coordinated planning and execution, and a trained workforce that is empowered "to move heaven and earth" to satisfy customers. Committed employees rank as the most essential element. All are schooled in the Company's Gold Standards, which include a credo, motto, three steps of service, and twenty Ritz-Carlton basics. Each employee is expected to understand and adhere to these standards, which describe processes for solving problems guests may have as well as detailed grooming, housekeeping, and safety and efficiency stan-

---

Unfortunately, reality is not as simple as these three elements. Many variables—some controllable, some uncontrollable—distort the picture. All three of these main elements are all interrelated with other management functions, such as planning and decision making. Both practicing executives and management theorists agree that control is a vital and necessary part of management.

Service and Total Quality Management (TQM)

The increasingly open and fiercely competitive marketplace exerts an enormous pressure on service industries to deliver superior service.

dards. "We are ladies and gentlemen serving ladies and gentlemen" is the motto of all Ritz-Carlton hotels, exemplifying anticipatory service provided by all staff members.

To provide such service, the employees training process is the finest in the industry. To underscore the importance of maintaining quality service as the organization grows, Mr. Schulze himself conducts the employee orientation at each new hotel. The two-day orientation, however, is just the beginning. Employee indoctrination at The Ritz-Carlton Hotel Company includes one hundred additional hours of on-the-job training, daily inspections for appearance, periodic performance reviews, and, again, an unrelenting emphasis on quality. The Ritz-Carlton aims to convince employees that they are important members of an elite team always looking for ways to improve. The company also rewards exceptional performance with things like fully paid vacations. Much of the responsibility for ensuring high-quality guest services and accommodations rests with the staff. A significant example of the responsibility given to employees is the fact that each Ritz-Carlton staff member is empowered to make a decision that could cost the hotel up to $2,000. Mr. Schulze insists that it is not the amount of money that is important, but, rather, the emphasis on the corporate environment that encourages employees to make decisions and speak up. "They need to feel part of the organization and really work for the organization," Schulze says.

The company's philosophy ultimately results in high-standard properties. All Ritz-Carlton Hotels offer twenty-four-hour room service, twice-daily maid service, complimentary shoeshine, terrycloth robes in all guest rooms, a floor reserved for nonsmokers, and in-house fitness facilities. Other special features include The Ritz-Carlton Club, a private lounge with complimentary food and beverage presentations throughout the day and the services of a special concierge, as well as dining rooms that represent culinary excellence and top value. A highly trained concierge staff stands by to respond to additional guest needs.

The Ritz-Carlton Hotel Company also maintains a sophisticated guest recognition program designed to determine and fulfill the needs of repeat visitors by tracking their individual requests and preferences. A guest who visits The Ritz-Carlton, Atlanta, can expect the same individualized service at any Ritz-Carlton, from New York to Sidney, Australia.

Each property is designed to be a comfortable haven for travelers and a social center for the community. The architecture and art work are carefully selected to complement the hotel's environment. "We go to great lengths to capture the spirit of a hotel and its locale," says Mr. Schulze. "This creates a subtle balance and celebrates a gracious, relaxed lifestyle. The Ritz-Carlton Directory of Hotels and Resorts welcomes the guest in a promising way: "We trust you'll find The Ritz-Carlton warm, relaxed yet refined; a most comfortable home away from home."

RITZ-CARLTON is a federally registered trademark of The Ritz-Carlton Hotel Company.

Inspired by rising guest expectations and competitive necessity, many hospitality companies have jumped on the service quality bandwagon.

The Ritz-Carlton Hotel Company, winner of the 1993 Malcolm Baldrige National Quality Award, has a credo that is printed on a small laminated card that all employees must memorize or carry on their person at all times, when on duty. The reverse side of the card has the Ritz-Carlton Basics (see Figure 14-9), which are twenty steps to successful service.

The quality movement began at the turn of the century as a means of ensuring consistency among the parts produced in the different plants of a single company so that they could be used interchangeably. TQM is a participative process that empowers all levels of employees to work in groups to establish guest service expectations and determine the best way of meeting or exceeding those expectations. Notice that *guest* is the term preferred over *customer*. The inference here is that if we treat customers like guests, we are more likely to

1. The credo will be known, owned, and energized by all employees.
2. Our motto is: "We are ladies and gentlemen serving ladies and gentlemen." Practice teamwork and lateral service to create a positive work environment.
3. The three steps of service shall be practiced by all employees.
4. All employees will successfully complete training certification to ensure they understand how to perform to the Ritz-Carlton standards in their positions.
5. Each employee will understand their work areas and hotel goals as established in each strategic plan.
6. All employees will know the needs of their internal and external customers (guests and employees) so that we may deliver the products and services they expect. Use guest preference pads to record specific needs.
7. Each employee will continuously identify defects throughout the hotel.
8. Any employee who receives a customer complaint owns the complaint.
9. Instant guest pacification will be ensured by all. React quickly to correct the problem immediately. Follow up with a telephone call within twenty minutes to verify the problem has been resolved to the customer's satisfaction. Do everything you possibly can to never lose a guest.
10. Guest incident action forms are used to record and communicate every incident of guest dissatisfaction. Every employee is empowered to resolve the problem and to prevent a repeat occurrence.
11. Uncompromising levels of cleanliness are the responsibility of every employee.
12. Smile—We are on stage. Always maintain positive eye contact. Use the proper vocabulary with our guests. (Use words like *good morning, certainly, I'll be happy to,* and *my pleasure.*)
13. Be an ambassador of your hotel in and outside of the work place. Always talk positively. No negative comments.
14. Escort guests rather than pointing out directions to another area of the hotel.
15. Be knowledgeable of hotel information (hours of operation, etc.) to answer guest inquiries. Always recommend the hotel's retail and food and beverage outlets prior to outside facilities.
16. Use proper telephone etiquette. Answer within three rings and with a smile. When necessary, ask the caller, "May I place you on hold?" Do not screen calls. Eliminate call transfers when possible.
17. Uniforms are to be immaculate; wear proper and safe footwear (clean and polished), and your correct name tag. Take pride and care in your personal appearance (adhering to all grooming standards).
18. Ensure all employees know their roles during emergency situations and are aware of fire and life safety response processes.
19. Notify your supervisor immediately of hazards, injuries, equipment, or assistance that you need. Practice energy conservation and proper maintenance and repair of hotel property and equipment.
20. Protecting the assets of a Ritz-Carlton hotel is the responsibility of every employee.

Figure 14-9   *The Ritz-Carlton Basics* (Courtesy The Ritz-Carlton Hotel Company)

exceed their expectations. One successful hotelier has insisted for a long time that all employees treat guests as they would like to be treated themselves.[10]

TQM is a continuous process that works best when managers are also good leaders. A successful company will employ leader–managers who create a stimulating work environment in which guests and employees (sometimes called *internal guests* when one employee serves another, who in turn serves a guest) become an integral part of the mission by participating in goal and objective setting.

Installing TQM is exciting because once everyone becomes involved there is no way of stopping the creative ways employees will solve guest-related prob-

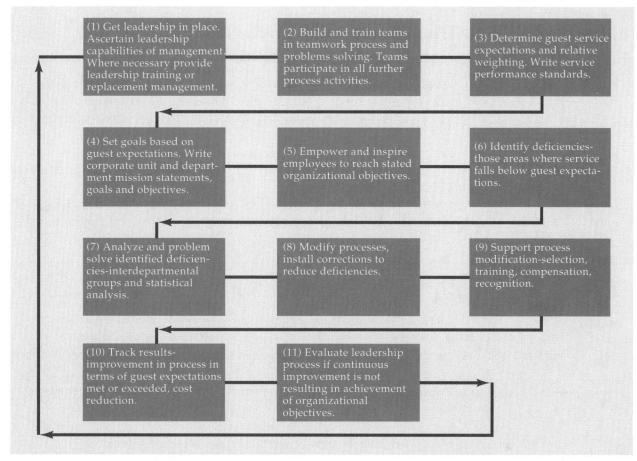

Figure 14-10   *Eleven Steps in Quality Management*

lems and improve service. Other benefits include cost reductions, increased guest and employee satisfaction, and, ultimately, profit. The quality leadership process has eleven key steps which are shown in Figure 14-10.

Top executives and line managers are responsible for the success of the TQM process; when they commit to ownership of the process, it will be successful. Focused commitment is the foundation of a quality service initiative, and leadership is the critical component in promoting commitment. Achieving TQM is a top down–bottom up process that must have the active commitment and participation of all employees, from the top executives down to the bottom of the corporate ladder. The expression, "If you are not serving the guest, then you had better be serving someone who is" still holds true today.

The difference between TQM and quality control (QC) is that QC focuses on error detection, whereas TQM focuses on error prevention. Quality control is generally based on industrial systems and, because of this, tends to be product oriented rather than service oriented. To the guest, services are experiential; they are felt, lived through, and sensed. The moment of truth is the actual guest contact.

Professionalism

Being professional means having absolute confidence in your ability to deliver superb product and service. Professionalism begins with one's appearance. This includes grooming, personal hygiene, appropriateness of dress, hair length and style, makeup, jewelry, and so on.

In his book *Front Office Psychology*, H. V. Heldenbrand suggests certain pointers for clerks (see Figure 14-11); although the book was written in 1944, these pointers still hold true today.

A number of attributes contribute to professionalism. The examples given below concern food service professionals, but they transcend the boundaries

---

1. I would not "run down" the management or the hotel, or both, by whom I was previously employed.

2. I would accept instructions concerning my new job attentively and responsively, even though I was already familiar with some of the procedures.

3. I would not waste the time of the manager, my fellow employees, nor myself telling about "how we did it at the last place."

4. I would strive for a manner of impersonal courtesy toward all my employee associates.

5. I wouldn't bring any personal interests to work with me, nor have friends drop in to visit while on duty or wait around for me to be relieved.

6. I wouldn't have my wife or women or men friends telephone me while on duty unless the house were afire.

7. I wouldn't come in before it was time to go on duty and loiter, and I wouldn't loiter after I was off duty.

8. If the hotel has a bar, I would never patronize it—I would do my drinking, if any, elsewhere.

9. I would never put an I.O.U. in the cash drawer for one cent for one minute. In fact, I wouldn't put any in at all!

10. If I ate my meals in the hotel dining rooms, I would eat at the quietest hours, because the waitresses as little work as possible, not kid them any more than I really thought I had to, and get in and out of the dining room as quickly as possible.

11. If I had to take any of the women employees out (I would be a lot smarter if I didn't), I would not make the hotel the place of meeting or delivery.

12. I would be very conservative regarding "extracurricular" friendships with guests—both men and women, particularly women. Large quantities of TNT lie concealed in unwise personal friendships with people with whom we are doing business.

Figure 14-11 *Heldenbrand's Pointers on Professionalism* (H. V. Heldenbrand, *Front Office Psychology*. Chicago: American Hotel Register Company, 1944, pp. 4–5.)

of food service to other parts of hospitality management. Professionalism can be summed up with these ten points:

1. Attitude: Willing to take instruction and criticism
2. Dependable: On the job everyday, without fail
3. Cooperation with others: Working at close quarters in most cases, it is essential that one gets along with his or her fellow workers.
4. Willingness to work: When directed to do a task, do it willingly without prodding. Work hard
5. Initiative: Doing a task without being told
6. Cleanliness: The key to good health—germs spread rapidly
7. Interest: One must have some interest in food production in order to be successful.
8. Artistic ability: A very desirable trait, but not necessarily needed
9. Health: Good physical health is necessary because of the long hours on your feet and, in some cases, heavy lifting.
10. Stick-to-it-ism: This word, brought forth from one of Walt Disney's cartoons, is a must; to accomplish any task requires these qualities.[11]

Career Paths and Resumé Writing

Creating your own career path can be both an exciting and a daunting task. Often, we do not know exactly where we want to be in five or ten years. The best advice is to follow your interests. Do what you love to do and success will soon come. Often we assess our own character and personality to determine a suitable path. Some opt for the accounting and financial and control side of the business; others, perhaps with more outgoing personalities, vie for sales and marketing; others prefer operations, which could be either in back or in front of the house.

It is a good idea to build your resume with work experience. The experience will also help to relate to the academic course work. Most colleges have a system of faculty advisors—many have industry contacts that may be helpful in taking the first step along your career path.

Corporate recruiters have to distinguish you from hundreds of resumes they receive. Here are some tips from a selection of recruiters that hopefully will enable you to succeed in you career:[12]

Where are you going?

Are you conscientious? Make sure your resume is letter perfect. Have your resumé proofread by several industry practitioners as well as professors and friends.

How to Write a Resumé

A good resumé includes the following information:

➤ Heading
➤ Career objective

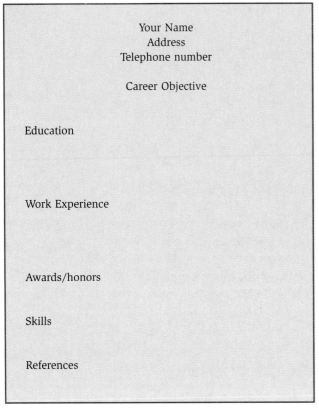

Your Name
Address
Telephone number

Career Objective

Education

Work Experience

Awards/honors

Skills

References

Figure 14–12   *Sample Resumé Format*

➤ Education
➤ Career experience
➤ Other accomplishments such as scholarships, awards, honors, teams, volunteer work, and so on
➤ References, including telephone numbers

A suggested format for a resume is shown in Figure 14–12.

Perfecting a resumé can take more than a few hours. It is a good idea to show it to several people who know you and some who are used to reviewing resumés. It is natural to be slightly unsure of the right words to use. One suggestion is to consider your accomplishments. You may have worked on the school prom committee or as a volunteer for a worthy organization. Everyone has done something that can embellish the resumé—remember that you have to stand out from your peers or competition.

Consider a young woman who was a star on the track team in high school. She was not going to put that on her resume because she did not think it was important. But, when asked what she did to become an accomplished athlete, she replied that she had to train (long hours of practice require dedication); when asked what it took to win, she said determination. These same qualities are the same as what it takes to be successful in business.

Cover Letter

Every time you mail a resumé, it is important to send a cover letter to introduce yourself and explain why you are sending your resumé. Because this is your first contact with the company you are approaching, you need to make a good impression. A businesslike letter has your name, address, and telephone number at the top right-hand corner of the page. The letter should begin with "Dear Ms. or Mr. ____:" and might begin, "I am pleased to apply for the position of ____ at the XYZ company. I will be available for summer work experience on May 28, 19xx. Your company was recommended to me by ____ who worked with you last year. Enclosed is a copy of my resume in which you will notice" (here is where you mention some skills or relevant experience that qualify you for the position).

The final paragraph should restate your keen interest in the position and end by requesting an interview. The appropriate close is "Yours sincerely," followed by your name, leaving room for your signature.

Are you qualified? Recruiters typically look to three things to judge a student's job qualifications: academic record, work experience, and extracurricular activities.

Academic Record

A recruiter can easily discard resumés of students with a cumulative GPA below a B. Jeff Speck suggests that omitting a mediocre GPA from your resumé is not the best solution, simply because most students willingly include their averages. If you have a low overall GPA, one solution might be to list your GPA in the major if that is significantly higher.

If you have good grades, were on the dean's list, graduated with honors, and so on, then put this on your resume. Academic distinction is one sure way of gaining the attention of the recruiter.

Work Experience

Your record should prove that you have accomplished something every summer and possibly while going to school. Obviously, experience in the same or a similar capacity is desirable. An internship or co-op work experience is an additional asset. Include other work experiences that you have had because they all add up—even jobs such as hostessing may suggest that you have obtained some good interpersonal experience. Being a busperson or a quick service food employee may not sound very exciting, but it is where most of us began. Each of the beginning-level positions give us exposure to a work-place environment and allow us to gain experience.

Extracurricular Activities

Achieving recognition as an eagle scout or in activities like student leadership always improves your chances for employment. If you ever excelled in sports or club activities, use this information in your resumé to show commitment and dedication. Volunteer work is an excellent way to look good on a resumé, especially if you organize an event that contributes to an organization. A resumé, in itself, will not secure you employment, but it will likely open the doors to an interview.

Preparing for the Interview

No matter how many interviews we try, most people still have butterflies in the stomach. These feelings are natural, because we are on edge about a face-to-face meeting that could have a major impact on our career and lives. An interview is like sitting next to someone on an airplane flight—it takes us about twenty seconds to determine if we really want to talk to the person sitting next to us or read a magazine.

Questions for an Interview

Mona Melanson, a staffing consultant with Bank of America has wisely suggested a ten-step approach to polish your interviewing skills.

1. Ask yourself how well you fit the jobs for which you're interviewing. You are going to be grilled about your skills, education, motivation, accomplishments, strengths, and weaknesses. The interviewer is asking himself or herself, "Why should I hire you for this job?"

2. A good way to begin is to match your skills and qualifications to those required for that position. You could gather data from a variety of sources, in categories such as education and training, extracurricular activities, summer/part time jobs, and volunteer/community service. In these categories, jot down feedback from your professors, employers, and other people with whom you have interacted. Remember that in management training interviews, recruiters want to see leadership and initiative capabilities.

3. Once you have completed your list, you will probably be surprised at how many items there are. Next, highlight five or six items that correspond to some of the job qualifications specified. Then prepare a brief talk about those so you can use them during an interview.

4. Do your homework on the company. Do research in the library, call the company's public relations office, and ask your career office for the names of former students now working for the corporation in which you are interested. Find out about the corporation's philosophy, mission, goals, objectives, and culture. Become knowledgeable about the size, organization structure, and future plans of the corporation.

5. Be ready to ask questions of the interviewer. Ideally, these should be work-related questions; wait until later to discuss salary (have patience; nothing disturbs an interviewer more than someone who wants to discuss money up front). The appropriate time to inquire about the compensation and benefit package is generally toward the end of the interview—if the interviewer has not already mentioned it.

6. Stage a number of dress rehearsals with someone else—a roommate, a friend, a career counselor, or a professor. Give your interviewer a list of questions that you think you might be asked. Record, or—even better—video your interviews. Remember, some taboos include the following:

   ➤ Shaking hands like a wet fish
   ➤ Mumbling, fidgeting
   ➤ Going off on tangents
   ➤ Appearing unnecessarily tense
   ➤ Using slang or malapropisms

Personal Profile: Cindy Rainey

In 1989, while I was a "fresher" in the Hotel, Restaurant, Management Program at the United States International University in San Diego, California, I decided to gain experience in the hotel industry. I took the initiative and followed up on a talk given to our introductory class by the director of human resources at the Sheraton Grande Torrey Pines.

I began as a part-time cocktail server and restaurant hostess. After full-time summer employment, I was promoted to floor supervisor, which oversaw the restaurant, bars, and pool snack bar. The next summer, I worked as a cook in the kitchen and then was promoted to room

Cindy Rainey

service manager. As room service manager, I was directly responsible for hospitality suites, in-room dining, minibars, payroll forecasting, budgeting, hiring, and training. It was exciting to have so much responsibility.

I am currently assistant food and beverage manager—restaurants and bars. I graduated in 1993 and will soon be moving within the Sheraton Corporation to a property in San Francisco. *Advice to current hospitality students:* Definitely get as much work experience as you can. The experience will complement your academic studies and you will benefit both ways. Be prepared to start at the bottom and work your way up.

> ➤ Speaking too softly or too loudly
> ➤ Avoiding eye contact

Body language is important during interviews. Some experts suggest adopting a similar posture to the interviewer. Remain composed, relaxed, and confident, and demonstrate visible interest.

7. Dress in a businesslike manner. A man should wear a business suit, dress shoes, a pressed white shirt, or a reasonably conservative shirt—and no earrings. A woman should wear a business suit, blouse, hose, and shoes, with conservative jewelry and makeup. For both men and women, the first impression is extremely important. Image is everything!

8. Arrive early; if possible, go to the location once before the interview to be certain you know where it is. Remember that a smile and a firm handshake make a good impression. Once the interview has begun, listen to the questions carefully, because interviewers often complain that students do not answer questions correctly. One tip is to rephrase part of each question you are asked at the beginning of your answer. This technique also gives you more time to formulate your responses. Remember to stress your strengths. For example, offer statements such as "I have been told by one of my professors that I express myself well both in writing and orally," or "I work well under pressure" or "I have a positive attitude."

9. At the close of the interview, thank the interviewer for the opportunity to discuss your qualifications. Before shaking hands, it is fully acceptable to ask the interviewer about when you might expect to hear about a decision.

10. Write a thank-you note to the interviewer, reinforcing the reasons why you feel you could perform well on that job.[13]

Skills   Communication skills
Knowledge   Research corporations
Experience   Attending professional meetings
Eagerness   Seeking out opportunities
Perseverance   Preparation for the interview
Send resumés

Congratulations
to the next hospitality
and tourism superstar

Figure 14-13   *Elements of a Career Search* (Adapted from Nona Star and Karen Silva, *Travel Career Development,* 4th ed. Boston: Houghton Mifflin, 1990, p. 264.)

Figure 14-13 shows elements of a career search.

Following are suggestions for questions to ask the interviewer:

➤ What are the duties and responsibilities of this position?
➤ Please describe the training program.
➤ How would you characterize the management philosophy at your company?
➤ If I join your company, what will my career path likely be?
➤ Given my education and background, how would you estimate my chances for advancement?
➤ Does your company offer promotional opportunities by region, nationally, or internationally?

Do not ask how much salary the position offers until either you have been offered a position or until you are well into the final stages of the interview.

Following are some questions that an interviewer might ask:

➤ When are you available, and what are your available hours?
➤ What is your (hotel, restaurant, or tourism) work experience?
➤ What are/were your duties and responsibilities?
➤ How well do you think you succeeded in meeting your duties and responsibilities?
➤ What are your goals and ambitions?
➤ Where do you see yourself three/five years from now?
➤ What did you like most and least about your job?
➤ Describe how you would prepare an item of the menu.
➤ Why should I hire you?
➤ What qualifications do you have that make you think you will be successful in the hospitality industry?

Overall, remember that good judgment comes from experience, and experience comes from bad judgment, and success is not what you are, it is what you have overcome to be what you are.

Summary

1. Every company operates according to its corporate philosophy and culture; creates a mission statement that outlines the central purposes, strategies, and values of the corporation; and strives to achieve certain goals and follow objectives in order to achieve these goals.
2. The key management functions are forecasting, organizing, decision making, planning, communicating, motivating, and controlling.
3. Forecasting considers and evaluates various factors and produces an estimate of how much business is expected.
4. Most organizations are made up of a formal and an informal organization, which plan either for long- or short-term purposes. Both types have to make programmed and nonprogrammed decisions.
5. Communications links all management functions together. Managers interact via phone, fax, memos, face-to-face, and grapevine information.
6. A manager has to be able to motivate the people he or she works with in order to achieve goals. Numerous theories of motivation exist, including intrinsic and extrinsic theories, content theories, process theories, goal-setting, and reinforcement theories.
7. An important element of excellent management is professionalism. Professionalism requires attributes such as good attitude, reliability, cooperation, initiative, interest, cleanliness, artistic ability, and health.
8. A good resumé should be grammatically correct and include academic record, work experience, and extracurricular activities.

Review Exercises

1. Explain the difference in long- and short-term planning and list the seven steps in organizational planning.
2. Distinguish between formal and informal organization.
3. Identify the eight major steps in decision making. Why is a company more sophisticated when it makes more programmed decisions?
4. Define motivation and explain vicarious motivation and expectancy theory.
5. Describe the relationship among corporate philosophy, quality leadership and service, and total quality management.
6. What ten steps should be considered to gain the most from a job interview?

Key Words and Concepts

Centralization
Communicating
Controlling
Corporate culture
Corporate philosophy
Decentralization
Decision making

Equity theory
Expectancy theory
Forecasting
Goal-setting theory
Herzberg's motivation
    and hygiene factors

Maslow's hierarchy
    of needs
Mission, goals, and
    objectives
Motivating
Organizing

Planning
Professionalism
Service
Span of control
Total quality management

Notes

[1] Norman M. Scarborough, *Business: Gaining the Competitive Edge.* Boston: Allyn and Bacon, 1992, p. 138.

[2] Ibid, p. 158.

[3] Stephen P. Robbins, *Management,* 3d ed. Englewood Cliffs, N.J.: Prentice Hall, 1991. p. 153.

[4] Leonard R. Sayles and George Strauss, *Human Behavior in Organizations.* Englewood Cliffs, N.J.: Prentice Hall, 1966, pp. 238–246.

[5] Karen L. Seelkoff, "Nine Steps to Better Communication," *Hotels, 27,* 11, November 1993, p. 24.

[6] Ibid.

[7] Ibid.

[8] Adapted from Donald D. White and David A. Bednar, *Organizational Behavior: Understanding and Managing People at Work,* 2d ed. Boston: Allyn and Bacon, 1991, pp. 148—149.

[9] White and Bednar, op. cit., p. 178.

[10] Personal conversation with Lord Forte, chairman of the board, Forte Hotels International, May 1971.

[11] Robert Haines, *Food Preparation for Hotels, Restaurants and Cafeterias.* Alsip, Ill.: American Technical Publishers, 1973, p. 4.

[12] Jeff B. Speck, "The Inside Scoop: What Corporate Recruiters Really Look for When Reviewing Hundreds of Student Resumés," *National Business Employment Weekly, 6,* 3, Fall 1989, p. 28.

[13] This section draws on Mona Melanson, "Beat the Butterflies: A Ten-Step Approach to Polish Your Interview Skills," *The College Edition of the National Employment Weekly, 6,* 3, Fall 1989, p. 31.

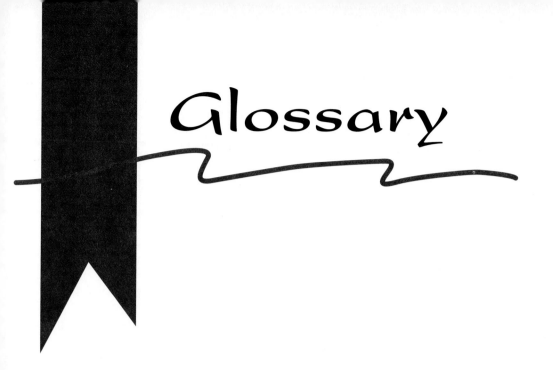

Glossary

A

Actual market share The market share that a business actually receives compared with the fair market share, which is an equal share of the market.

ADA American with Disabilities Act.

ADR See Average daily rate.

AHMA American Hotel and Motel Association.

A la carte 1. A menu on which food and beverages are listed and priced individually. 2. Foods cooked to order compared with foods cooked in advance and held for later service.

Alcohol Naturally occurring and easily synthesized compound that induces intoxication when consumed.

Allocentric Psychological term referring to someone who enjoys varied and unfamiliar activities.

Ambiance The combined atmosphere created by the decor, lighting, service, possible entertainment (such as background music), and so on, that enhances the dining or lodging experience.

Amenities Features that add material comfort, convenience, or smoothness to a guest's stay. Examples include hair shampoo, an iron and ironing board in each room, in-room coffee maker, and so on.

Aperitif A fortified wine flavored with one or more herbs and spices, usually consumed before a meal.

Apollo Name of a commonly used airline reservation system.

Authoritarian leadership A type of leader who delegates very little authority and tends to make the bulk of the decisions affecting a group.

Average daily rate (ADR) One of the key operating ratios that indicate the level of a hotel's performance. The ADR is calculated by dividing the amount of dollar sales by the number of rooms sold.

Average guest check The average amount each group spends. Mostly used in a restaurant setting.

B

Baby boomers Anyone born in the twenty-year period from 1946 through 1965. Baby boomers represent the largest segment of the population—about eighty-one million United States residents in 1990. Baby boomers travel more frequently than their parents, and regard travel as a necessity rather than a luxury.

Back of the house Refers to the support areas behind the scenes in a hotel or motel, including housekeeping, laundry, engineering, and food service. Also refers to individuals who operate behind the scenes to make a guest's stay pleasant and safe.

Bar mitzvah A Jewish religious ritual and family celebration commemorating the religious adulthood of a boy on his thirteenth birthday.

Batch cooking   The cooking of food in quantities for consumption throughout a meal period. Used in noncommercial food service to avoid putting out all the food at 11:30 and having it spoil. Batches are cooked for readiness at 11:30, 12, 12:30, etc.

Bat mitzvah   A Jewish religious ritual and family celebration commemorating the religious adulthood of a girl on her thirteenth birthday.

Bed and breakfast   A rate that combines a night's accommodation with a breakfast the following day. The breakfast can be either a full or continental breakfast.

Behavioral leadership   A leadership style that considers needs, drives, motivation, personality, behavior, work groups, and the management of change.

Benchmarking   A process by which an organization reassesses its traditional business practices by comparing them with the best practices of other organizations.

Beverage cost percentage   Similar to food cost percentage, except it relates to beverages.

Boardroom-style meetings   A type of meeting setup designed for a small number of participants who will sit around a rectangular table.

Bonding   A recreational process by which people form relationships built on the experiences they have enjoyed together.

Budgeting   The process of forecasting sales and costs.

C

Call package   In bar operations, it is the group of spirits that the bar offers to guests who ask for a specific name brands.

Capture rate   A term used in hotel food and beverage to describe the number of hotel guests who use the food and beverage outlets.

Catchment area   The geographical area that falls within a specific radius established to determine the size of a restaurant's market (usually 1 to 5 miles).

Catering   Part of the food and beverage division of a hotel that is responsible for arranging and planning food and beverage functions for conventions and smaller hotel groups and local banquets booked by the sales department.

Central reservations system   Allows guests to call one phone number to reserve a room at any of the specific chain's properties.

CFA   Culinary Federation of America.

Champagne   Sparkling wine made in the Champagne district of France.

Chef de partie (shef-de-par-tée)   Also known as station chef. Produces the menu items for a station under the direct supervision of the chef or sous chef.

CHRIE   Stands for Council on Hotel, Restaurant, and Institutional Education.

City ledger   A client whose company has established credit with a certain hotel. Charges are posted to the city ledger and accounts are sent once or twice monthly.

Classroom-style meetings   A type of meeting setup generally used in instructional meetings, such as workshops.

Clinic   A form of meeting whose attenders learn by doing.

Club   Association of persons with a common objective, usually jointly supported and meeting periodically.

Cold calling   A type of prospecting whereby sales representatives call on individuals or organizations and have no idea if these people will turn out to be true sales prospects.

Commercial food service   Operations that compete for customers in the open market.

Compensation   Remuneration including salary, wages, and benefits.

Competitor analysis   An analysis of competitors' strengths and weaknesses.

Concept   The elements in a food-service operation that contribute to its function as a complete and organized system serving the needs and expectations of its guests.

Concierge   A uniformed employee of the hotel who has a separate desk in the lobby or on special concierge floors and answers questions, solves problems, and performs the services of a private secretary for the hotel's guests.

Contingency theory   According to this theory, every management situation is different and every manager is different; therefore, there are few universal management principles.

Contractors   Companies that operate food service for the client on a contractual basis.

Contribution margin   Key operating figure in menu engineering, determined by subtracting food cost from selling price as a measure of profitability.

Controller   Head accountant who manages the accounting department and all financial dealings of the hotel.

Convention Generic term referring to any size of business or professional meeting held in one specific location, which usually also includes some form of trade show or exposition. Also refers to a group of delegates or members who assemble to accomplish a specific goal.

Conventions and visitors bureaus 1. Organizations responsible for promoting tourism at the regional and local level. 2. A not-for-profit umbrella organization that represents a city or urban area in soliciting and servicing all types of travelers to that city or area, whether for business, pleasure, or both.

Corporate travel agencies Also known as outplants, corporate travel agencies specialize, either partly or wholly, in handling corporate or government accounts.

Corporate travel manager Individuals employed by corporations, associations, government agencies, and other types of organizations to coordinate the organization's travel arrangements.

Covers The guest count of a restaurant.

Cuisine Food cooked and served in styles from around the world.

D

Database Organized collection of information, such as names, addresses, prices, and dates.

Democratic leadership Democratic leaders delegate a great deal of authority and allow group members to make many of their own decisions.

Demographics Statistical study of the characteristics of human populations.

Decision making The process of choosing a course of action among alternatives to solve a specific problem.

Destination Location where travelers choose to visit and spend time.

Destination-management companies Organizations in charge of developing and implementing tourism programs.

Diversity An increase in the heterogeneity of an organization through the inclusion of different ethnic groups.

DOC Director of Catering.

Dram shop legislation Includes laws and procedures that govern the legal operation of establishments that sell measured alcoholic beverages.

Du jour French expression used in menus, meaning "of the day."

#

Economics The science relating to the production, distribution, and use of goods and services.

Ecotourism Balance between tourism development and the preservation of natural and cultural heritages; new segment of the industry in which travelers learn about or advance the environment and its causes.

EEO Equal employment opportunity.

EEOC Equal Employment Opportunity Commission.

Elastic Demand changes with economic conditions.

Employee training For many organizations, it is an ongoing activity that is conducted by a training department, a training manager, or by line management or specially selected individuals within each department.

Entremetier (awn-truh-mit-tee-háy) Vegetable chef.

Entrepreneur Individual who creates, organizes, manages, and assumes the risk of an enterprise or business.

Environmental analysis An analysis of how the uncontrollable and controllable factors will affect a hospitality and travel organization's direction and success. It is an element of situation, market, and feasibility analyses, and provides a foundation for long- and short-term marketing plans.

Equal Pay Act An act that prohibits discrimination in which employers pay men more than women for jobs requiring substantially equal skills, effort, and responsibility.

Equity theory A theory of job motivation that emphasizes the role played by an individual's belief in the equity or fairness of rewards and punishments in determining his or her performance and satisfaction.

Ethics A set of moral principles and values that determine what is good and what is bad. The study of the general nature of morals and the specific moral choices to be made by the individual in his or her relationship with others.

Ethnic restaurants A restaurant featuring a particular cuisine such as Chinese, Mexican, or Italian.

European plan An accommodation-only rate that includes no meals.

Executive committee A committee of hotel executives from each of the major departments within the hotel generally made up of the general manager, director of rooms division, food and beverage director, marketing and sales director, human resources director, accounting and/or finance director, and engineering director.

Exempt employees   Those employees who under Section 13(a)(1) of the Federal Minimum Wage Law are not required to be paid overtime. This is because they are primarily engaged in managerial or administrative functions.

Expectancy theory   A theory that suggests employees will produce in accordance with the expected return or compensation.

Expense accounts   Accounts primarily used for entertaining purposes.

Exposition   Event held mainly for informational exchanges among trade people. Large exhibition in which the presentation is the main attraction as well as being a source of revenue for an exhibitor.

F

Fair Labor Standards Act of 1938   Established a policy for minimum wage and a maximum length of the work week.

Fair market share   A market share based on each business receiving an equal share of the market.

Familiarization (fam) trips   Free or reduced-price trip given to travel agents, travel writers, or other intermediaries to promote destinations.

Fermentation   The chemical process in which yeast acts on sugar or sugar-containing substances, such as grain or fruit, to produce alcohol and carbon dioxide.

FIFO   See First-in, first-out.

Finger foods   Appetizers and bits of foods that can be eaten without the aid of utensils.

Fining   Process by which wine that has matured is filtered to help stabilize it and remove any solid particles still in the wine.

First-in, first-out (FIFO)   The supplies that are ordered first are used first.

Fixed costs   A cost or expense for a fixed period and range of activity that does not change in total but becomes progressively smaller per unit as volume increases.

Floor supervisor   Supervises day-to-day work of room attendants at larger motels. Also called assistant housekeepers.

Focus groups   A gathering of eight to twelve people who are interviewed as a group by a facilitator.

FOM   See Front office manager.

Food cost percentage   A ratio comparing the cost of food sold to food sales, which is calculated by dividing the cost of food sold during a given period by food sales during the same period.

Forecasting   Process of estimating future events in the food service industry.

Fortified wines   Wine to which brandy or other spirits have been added to stop any further fermentation and/or to raise its alcoholic strength.

Forum   A public assembly or lecture involving audience discussion.

Franchise   Refers to 1. the authorization given by one company to another to sell its unique products and services, or 2. the name of the business format or product that is being franchised.

Franchisee   Person who purchases the right to use and/or sell the products and services of the franchiser.

Franchiser   An individual or company that licenses others to sell its products or services.

French service   Restaurant service in which one waiter (a captain) takes the order, does the tableside cooking, and brings the drinks and food and the secondary or back waiter serves bread and water, clears each course, crumbs the table, and serves the coffee.

Front office manager (FOM)   Person who manages the front office department.

Front of the house   Comprises all the areas the guests will contact, including the lobby, corridors, elevators, guest rooms, restaurants and bars, meeting rooms, and restrooms. Also refers to employees who staff these areas.

Full-service restaurants   A restaurant that 1. has more than a dozen or so main-course items on the menu, and 2. cooks to order.

G

Gaming   Wagering of money or other valuables on the outcome of a game or other event.

Garde manger (gar-mawn-zháy)   Pantry chef who prepares all cold appetizers, desserts, and salads.

GDP   See Gross domestic product.

General manager   Head manager in an organization. Ultimately responsible for the operation of the hospitality establishment and the supervision of its employees. Held directly accountable by the corporation or owners for the operation's level of profitability.

Grievance   A complaint filed by an employee against the employer or employer's representative.

Gross domestic product (GDP)   Total value of goods and services produced within a country, minus the net payments on foreign investments.

Gross operating profit   Revenues minus operating costs before taxes.

Gross operating revenue   Total payments received for goods and services.

H

Hops   The dried, conical fruit of a special vine that imparts a special bitterness to beer.

Horizontal integration   Having representation in the multiple sectors of the market place. May be achieved by purchasing or developing a mid-scale hotel chain or an all-suite or economy chain, so the corporation has representation in each price range.

Hospice   An old French word meaning "to provide care/shelter for travelers." The word hospitality is derived from this word.

Hospitality   1. The cordial and generous reception of guests. 2. Wide range of businesses, each of which is dedicated to the service of people away from home.

Hotelier   Keeper, owner, or manager of the property.

Human resources manager or director   Manages the hotel's employee benefits program and monitors compliance with laws that relate to equal opportunity in hiring and promotion.

I

Illegal aliens   Individuals who move to another country illegally, without permission to enter as either immigrants or refugees. Also called undocumented workers.

Incentive travel   Marketing and management tool currently used to motivate people by offering travel rewards for achieving a specific goal.

Institutional food service   Operations that serve people who are members of particular societal institutions, such as hospitals, colleges, schools, nursing homes, the military, and industry.

J

Job description   A description of the duties and responsibilities involved with a particular job.

Joint venture   A commercial undertaking by two or more people.

K

Kitchen brigade   System of kitchen organization in which the staff is divided into specialized departments, all contributing collectively to the preparation of a meal.

L

Labor cost percentage   Similar to food cost percentage, except it relates to labor.

Labor intensive   Relying on a large work force to meet the needs of guests.

Lager beer   The beverage that is normally referred to as beer; it is clear, light-bodied, and refreshing.

Laissez-faire leadership   A leadership style of minimal involvement.

Leadership   The process by which a person with vision is able to influence the activities and outcome of others in a desired way.

Leads   In the convention and visitors bureaus' lingo, leads are prospective clients.

Leisure   Freedom resulting from the cessation of activities, especially time free from work or duties.

Leveraged money   Where loans are used to finance most of the purchase price.

Liaison personnel   Workers who are responsible for translating corporate philosophy to the contractor and for overseeing the contractor to make sure he or she abides by the terms of the contract.

M

Malt   Germinated barley.

Management   The functions of forecasting, planning, decision making, communicating, organizing, motivating.

Management contracts   A written agreement between an owner and an operator of a hotel or motor inn by which the owner employs the operator as an agent (employee) to assume full responsibility for operating and managing the property.

Marketing mix   The term used to focus on the pertinent Ps: place, product, price, promotion, partnership, packaging, programming, and people.

Market niche   A specific share or slot of a certain market.

Market segment   Smaller, identifiable groups that can be defined using any set of characteristics, such as those found in geographic, demographic, or psychographic information. Subgroups of customers who share a specific set of needs and expectations.

Mashing   In the making of beer, it is the process of grinding the malt and screening out any bits of dirt.

Mash tub   In the making of beer, it is a large stainless steel or copper container used to mix and heat water and grains.

Meeting   Gathering of people for a common purpose.

Meeting planner   Coordinates every detail of meetings and conventions.

Menu engineering   Tool in menu planning that uses the menu as a whole, not individual items that make up the menu, as a measure of profitability.

Mise en place (miss-en-plás)   French phrase meaning "everything in its place"; state of overall preparedness; having all the necessary ingredients and cooking utensils at hand and ready to use at the moment work on a dish begins.

Multiplier effect   Concept that refers to new money that is brought into a community to pay for hotel rooms, restaurant meals, and so on. To some extent, it then passes into the community when the hotel or restaurant orders supplies and services, pays employees, and so on.

Must   A mixture of grape pulp, skins, seeds, and stems.

N

National tourism organizations (NTOs)   Organizations national governments use to promote their countries.

Networking   The process of meeting with and gathering information from an ever-expanding channel of acquaintances.

Night auditing   The process of verifying and balancing the guests' accounts.

NRA   National Restaurant Association.

NTOs   See National tourism organizations.

O

Occupancy forecast   Forecast of hotels occupancy for a given period.

On-line   Access to a computer via a terminal.

Operating ratios   Ratios that indicate an operation's performance.

Overbooking   Lodging practice of booking 10 to 15 percent more reservations than available to combat the loss of revenue resulting from guests who make reservations but who do not arrive.

P

PABS   See Profit analysis by segment.

Par stock   Level of stock that must be kept on hand at all times. If the stock on hand falls below this point, a computerized reorder system will automatically reorder a predetermined quantity of the item.

Performance evaluation or appraisal   A meeting between a manager and one of his or her employees to 1. let the employee know how well he or she has learned to meet company standards, and 2. let managers know how well they are doing in hiring and training employees.

PMS   See Property management systems.

POS   See Point of sale.

Point of sale (POS)   Computerized system that allows bars to set drink prices according to the specific ingredients served.

Poissionier (pwa-saw-nee-héy)   Fish station chef.

Political analysis   An analysis of the impact that current and pending legislation may have on the organization.

Portfolio financing   The grouping of several investments with a portfolio that spreads the investment risk.

Positioning   Process of establishing a distinctive place in the market (and in the minds of potential guests).

Pour-cost percentage   Similar to food cost percentage, except used in beverage control.

Prime cost   The cost of food sold plus payroll costs (including employee benefits). These are a restaurant's largest costs.

Product life cycle   The stages of market acceptance of products and services.

Product specification   The establishment of standards for each product, determined by the purchaser. (For example, when ordering meat, product specification will include the cut, weight, size, percentage of fat content, etc.)

Productivity standards   Standards of measurement established to gauge employee productivity.

Professionalism   The body of qualities or features such as competency, skill, and so on characteristic of a profession or professional.

Profit analysis by segment (PABS) Using a combination of marketing information and cost analysis, this process identifies average revenues generated by different market segments and then examines the contribution margin for each of the segments considering the cost of making those sales.

Proof Figure representing liquor's alcohol content.

Property management systems (PMS) A system of storing and retrieving information on reservations, room availability, and room rates. The system may also interface with outlets (bars, restaurants, etc.) for recording guest charges.

Psychocentric Psychological term referring to a self-inhibited, nonadventuresome person.

Psychographic research Attempts to classify people's internal motives and behavior.

Q

Quick-service restaurants Restaurants that offer quick service.

R

Recreation Refreshment of strength and spirits after work; a means of diversion.

Resort Place providing recreation and entertainment, especially to vacationers.

Resumé Short, written account of a job applicant's work experience, education, and other qualifications.

Rollover To roll a booking over from one occasion to the next.

Room occupancy percentage A key operating ratio for hotels that is calculated by finding the number of rooms occupied and dividing by rooms available.

Rules of order Procedural guidelines regarding the correct way to conduct a meeting.

Russian service Restaurant service in which the entree, vegetables, and starches are served from a platter onto the diner's plate by a waiter.

S

SABRE Name of a commonly used airline reservation system.

Saucier (sauce-see-háy) Saute cook.

Segmenting Splitting the market with user groups that have common characteristics.

Self-operators Companies that operate their own food service operations.

Seminar A type of meeting that involves a lecture and a dialogue that allow participants to share experiences in a particular field.

Service encounter Period of time in which a customer directly interacts with either personnel or the physical facilities and other visible elements of a hospitality business.

Sexual harassment Occurs whenever any unwanted sexually oriented behavior changes an employee's working conditions and/or creates a hostile or abusive work environment.

Shoppers People who are paid to use a bar like regular guests, except they closely watch the operation.

Situational leadership The leader alters leadership style depending on the situation.

Social analysis An analysis of social trends and customs used in compiling an upscale marketing plan.

Sommelier (so-mal-ee-yáy) In a restaurant, the person with considerable wine knowledge who orders and serves wines.

Sous chef (soo-shef) A cook who supervises food production and who reports to the executive chef; he or she is second in command of a kitchen.

Sous-vide (sou-veed) Air-tight pouches of prepared food that can be quickly reheated.

Sparkling wine Wine containing carbon dioxide, which provides effervescence when the wine in poured.

Spirits Another name for distilled drinks.

Spreadsheet Computerized version of an accountant's ledger book that not only records numeric information but also performs calculations with that information as well.

Stewarding The department in a hotel or food-service operation responsible for the back of the house cleanliness in the food and beverage areas; the cleanliness of the china, cutlery, glassware; and the custody of related food and beverage equipment.

Symposium A formal meeting at which several specialists deliver short addresses on a specific topic or related topics.

Suites Combined living space with kitchen facilities, or a bedroom section with an attached parlor.

Suggestive selling Employees suggestively sell products and services of the operation.

T

Table d'hote   French for "table of the host." During medieval times, poorer travelers had to eat with the landlord and his family in the kitchen, and they were served the "ordinary" fare at a nominal cost.

Target market   The market that the operation wants to focus on.

Taverns   Establishments that serve some food but specialize in alcoholic beverages.

Technological analysis   An analysis of the technological changes that may impact the company.

Technology   All the uses derived from discoveries and innovations to satisfy needs; generally refers to industrial technology.

Texture   Referring to food and wine, texture is the combination of the qualities in food or wine that correspond to sensations of touch and temperature, such as softness, smoothness, roundness, richness, thickness, creaminess, chewiness, oiliness, harshness, silkiness, coarseness, and so on.

Theater-style meeting setup   A meeting setup usually intended for a large audience that is not likely to need to take notes or refer to documents. It generally consists of a raised platform and a lectern from which the presenter addresses the audience.

Theme parks   Based on a particular setting or artistic interpretation and operate with hundreds or thousands of acres of parkland and hundreds or thousands of employees running the operation.

Theme restaurants   A restaurant distinguished by its combination of decor, atmosphere, and menu.

Theory X   A traditional set of assumptions some managers make about human nature that governs their management style. According to Theory X, the average employee 1. dislikes work and must be directed and threatened with punishment in order to put forth adequate effort, and 2. avoids responsibility and values security above anything else.

Theory Y   A set of assumptions some managers make about human nature that governs their management style. According to Theory Y, 1. the average employee does not inherently dislike work, 2. external control is not necessary if employees are committed to the organization's objectives, and 3. commitment to objectives is achieved by associating rewards to the attainment of those objectives.

Theory Z   Author William Ouchi's term for the Japanese management style, which is characterized by employing people for a lifetime, promoting managers slowly, and making decisions on a collective or consensus basis.

TIPS   Stands for training for intervention procedures by servers. Sponsored by the NRA, TIPS is a certification program that informs participants about alcohol and the effects of alcohol on people, the common signs of intoxication, and how to help customers avoid drinking too much.

TOs   See Tourism offices.

Total Quality Management (TQM)   A process of total organizational involvement in improving all aspects of the quality of product or service.

Tourism   Travel for recreation or the promotion and arrangement of such travel.

Tourism offices (TOs)   Organizations in charge of developing and implementing tourism programs for individual states. Also referred to as destination marketing organizations.

Tourists   People who take trips of 100 miles or more and who stay at least one night away from home.

Tour operators   Agencies that sell tour packages to groups of tourists and usually include an escort or guide with the tour.

TQM   See Total quality management.

Trade show   Event held for informational exchanges among trade people. Also called exposition.

Transactional leadership   Determines what subordinates need to do to achieve objectives, classify those requirements, and help subordinates become confident they can reach their objectives.

Transformational leadership   Leadership through personal vision and energy, inspiring followers, and having a major impact on the organization.

Travel and tour wholesaler   Company or an individual who designs and packages tours.

Trends   Prevailing tendencies or general movements.

Triple net lease   A lease in which the lessee must pay for all alterations, insurance, utilities, and possible commercial fees (e.g., landscaping or parking upkeep, security, etc.).

Truth-in-menu laws   Provisions that prohibit misrepresentation of items being sold. They require that the descriptions on the menu must be accurate.

Turnover rate   Calculated by dividing the number of workers replaced in a given time period by the average number of employees needed to run the business.

U

Undocumented workers Individuals who move from another country illegally, without permission to enter as either immigrants or refugees. Also called illegal aliens.

Uniform system of accounts A system of accounts used in the hospitality industry whereby all accounts have the same codes and all accounting procedures are done the same way.

V

Variable costs Costs that will vary according to the volume of business.

Vertical integration The ownership of or linkage with suppliers of raw materials or airlines owning hotels.

Vintage Year in which a wine's grapes were harvested.

W

Well package In bar operations, it is the least expensive pouring brand of drinks that the bar uses when the customers do not ask for a specific name brand.

Whiskey A liquor distilled from a fermented mash of grain to which malt, in the form of barley, is added.

White spirits Denomination that classifies spirits such as gin, rum, vodka and tequila.

Wines Fermented juice of grapes or other fruits.

Word processors Computerized replacement for typewriters as the writing tool of choice.

Workshop A usually brief intensive educational program, conducted by a facilitator or a trainer, designed for a relatively small group of people, that focuses especially on techniques and skills in a particular field.

Wort In the making of beer, it is the liquid obtained after the mashing process.

Y

Yacht club A private club located near a large body of water, whose main purpose is to provide facilities such as marinas to boat owners.

Yield management Practice of analyzing past reservation patterns, room rates, cancellations, and no shows in an attempt to maximize profits and occupancy rates and to set the most competitive room rates.

Index